Where Caciques and Mapmakers Met

JEFFREY ALAN ERBIG JR.

Where Caciques and Mapmakers Met

Border Making in Eighteenth-Century
South America

The University of North Carolina Press *Chapel Hill*

© 2020 The University of North Carolina Press
All rights reserved
Set in Arno Pro by Westchester Publishing Services
Manufactured in the United States of America

The University of North Carolina Press has been a member of the
Green Press Initiative since 2003.

Library of Congress Cataloging-in-Publication Data
Names: Erbig, Jeffrey Alan, Jr., author.
Title: Where caciques and mapmakers met : border making in eighteenth-century
    South America / Jeffrey Alan Erbig Jr.
Other titles: David J. Weber series in the new borderlands history.
Description: Chapel Hill : The University of North Carolina Press, 2020. |
    Series: The David J. Weber series in the new borderlands history |
    Includes bibliographical references and index.
Identifiers: LCCN 2019037841 | ISBN 9781469655031 (cloth) |
    ISBN 9781469655048 (paperback) | ISBN 9781469655055 (ebook)
Subjects: LCSH: Cartography—History—18th century—Political aspects—
    South America. | Charrua Indians—Land tenure. | Güenoa Indians—
    Land tenure. | Charrua Indians—Government relations. | Güenoa Indians—
    Government relations. | South America—Boundaries—History. | South America—
    Colonization—History. | South America—Ethnic relations—History. | Spain—
    Foreign relations—Portugal—History. | Portugal—Foreign relations—Spain—History.
Classification: LCC GA641 .E73 2020 | DDC 320.1/2—dc23
    LC record available at https://lccn.loc.gov/2019037841

Cover illustration: Francisco Requena y Herrera, *Cascadas del rio Cuñaré. Pequeño bote en que
los dos comisarios fueron à reconocer estas cascadas. B. Comisario español informandose de los
ynfieles por medio del Negro ynterprete.* Courtesy of the Oliveira Lima Library at the Catholic
University of America.

For Sari and Uma

Contents

Figures, Maps, and Tables

MAPS

TABLES

Acknowledgments

This book is about geographies of knowledge production, and my own geography of research and writing is no exception. For more than a decade now, I have drawn on the expertise, support, and overall goodness of countless people in each of the seven countries in which I have researched and worked. The final product has only come to fruition because of the generosity of colleagues, friends, and family, each of whom has enriched my life along the way.

It has been a privilege to be supported by a cadre of wonderful mentors, who have inspired me intellectually and opened countless doors. Kathryn Burns's enthusiastic support for this project in all its twists and turns, and her patient reading and rereading of its chapters, has made her its principal interlocutor. Her wisdom regarding archives and the power inherent in knowledge production undergirds this book's conceptual frame. Bernardo Michael first opened my eyes to connections between colonialism, space, and mapping and set me on the intellectual journey that would culminate in this book. John Chasteen has been a model for how to write and first introduced me to histories of the Río de la Plata, while Cynthia Radding has been a tireless champion who taught me to think globally and comparatively. Fabrício Prado has become the center of an international network of scholars studying the Río de la Plata, and I have been one of the principal beneficiaries of his generosity and friendship. Judy Bieber was my closest conversant and supporter at the University of New Mexico, reading this work cover to cover on multiple occasions. From the time that I arrived at the University of California, Santa Cruz, Gabriela Arredondo has been a persistent advocate, and her teaching me to talk across disciplines as a "historian inside-out" has greatly benefited the writing of this text.

I have personally benefited from generative intellectual support at each of my home institutions in the United States. At the University of North Carolina (UNC) at Chapel Hill and at Duke University, John Pickles and John French pushed me to make connections across disciplines and to take methodological risks, all of which proved worthwhile. John Sweet spent numerous hours helping me convey my ideas succinctly, while Becky Dobbs, Amanda Henley, and Philip McDaniel patiently guided me as I sought to bend digital mapping tools to my particular research questions. Jocelyn Olcott and Rebecca

Stein each helped me develop theoretical perspectives that inform this work, while Miguel La Serna, Lisa Lindsay, Donald Reid, Jay Smith, and Heather Williams helped me polish my thoughts and prose. Santiago Anria, Justin Blanton, Randy Browne, Angélica Castillo, Anne DeCecco, Elizabeth Ellis, Katharine French-Fuller, Jason Kauffman, Joshua Lynn, Joshua Nadel, Bryan Pitts, Ben Reed, Jeff Richey, and Elizabeth Shesko were all brilliant colleagues and unwavering friends. Mike Huner deserves special acknowledgment for reading numerous chapters of this work and for his invaluable support in interpreting and translating Guaraní-language terms.

At the University of New Mexico, I had the privilege of working with Karl Benedict, Chris Duvall, Tiffany Florvil, David Prior, Michael Ryan, Samuel Truett, Shannon Withycombe, and many other fabulous colleagues whose insights stretched my thought process spatially, temporally, and thematically. I am especially grateful to Fred Gibbs and Maria Lane, as our spatial humanities working group provided a setting for me to work through the promises and limitations of digital mapping for this project.

My colleagues at the University of California, Santa Cruz, have provided endless energy, support, and points for reflection. Within the Latin American and Latino Studies Department, I have been pushed to consider connections between historical events and present-day knowledge production, power relations, and struggles for social justice. Each member of the department has provided critical insights or much-needed encouragement, and Cecilia Rivas and Jessica Taft have been especially supportive in helping me think through the exact language of my translations and the exact form of this book's maps. I have also had the good fortune of being part of a brilliant writing group with Lily Balloffet, Matt O'Hara, Megan Thomas, and Zac Zimmer, all of whom provided incisive and creative comments on this book's conclusion and its maps.

This project also carries the fingerprints of an international network of scholars who took the time to read portions of the text or to help me work through ideas. Shawn Austin, Jordana Dym, Barbara Ganson, Patricia Marks, Dana Velasco Murillo, Adam Warren, and Yanna Yannakakis all served as outside readers of portions of this work, as did Brian Bockelman, Alex Borucki, Erika Edwards, Erick Langer, Allyson Poska, Denise Soares de Moura, Susan Socolow, Carolina Zumaglini, and other participants in the Río de la Plata working group. Lyman Johnson was a benevolent guide for me at the beginning of my field research, while Vera Candiani provided much-needed wisdom at the end. Nancy Appelbaum, Arne Bialuschewski, Sophie Brockmann, Lina del Castillo, Paul Conrad, Geraldine Davies Lenoble, Rebecca Earle, Júnia Ferreira Furtado, Marcelo Figueroa, Susan Gagliardi, Carla Lois, Mark

Meuwese, Barbara Mundy, Mauricio Nieto, Aleksandra Pudliszak, Sarah Radcliffe, Heather Roller, Heidi Scott, Lean Sweeney, Neil Whitehead, and Jesse Zarley all provided crucial feedback during conference panels, seminars, and workshops. At the John Carter Brown Library, I had the good fortune of working through the introduction and several chapters with Kenneth Banks, Leo Garafolo, Soledad González Díaz, Nicole Hughes, Nathaniel Millett, James Muldoon, Anne Ruderman, Jessica Stair, Amy Turner Bushnell, Bertrand van Ruymbeke, Shuichi Wanibuchi, and many other brilliant scholars. Julia Sarreal demonstrated exceeding patience in helping me consider connections to mission histories, while Gustavo Verdesio was an encouraging reader who helped me to connect this work to the present-day concerns of Charrúas in Uruguay.

Scholars in Latin America have had an equal hand in influencing and supporting this project. In Argentina, Gabriel Di Meglio, Norberto Levinton, Sergio Serulnikov, and Guillermo Wilde all inspired and supported this project, as did Lidia Nacuzzi, Aylén Enrique, and other members of the Sección Etnohistoria of the Universidad de Buenos Aires and the Periplos de las Fronteras research team at Argentina's Instituto de Desarrollo Económico y Social. Carina Lucaioli has been an astute colleague and provided fundamental insights as I worked to connect regional scholarship to hemispheric debates. Sergio Latini and I met by chance in Argentina's national archive, and he quickly became one of my closest colleagues and friends. In Uruguay, Diego Bracco, Ana Frega, José López Mazz, and Julio Trechera provided encouragement, insights, and support, while María Inés Moraes, Florencia Thul, and other members of the Pueblos y Números del Río de la Plata collaborative provided a forum in which to discuss my work. Adriana Clavijo has been an especially enthusiastic colleague and a great friend, while Martín Delgado Cultelli, Mónica Michelena, and other members of the Comunidad Charrúa Basquadé Inchalá have been exceedingly gracious in their assessment of this work. In Brazil, I offer my deepest appreciation to Elisa Frühauf Garcia and Tiago Gil for their invitations and ideas, and most of all to Iris Kantor for her thoughtful suggestions and logistical support. In Portugal, I owe special thanks to Paulo Sousa and Antonio for their energy and friendship as we worked together at the national library.

The stellar staffs at several dozen archival institutions worked tirelessly, professionally, and with great enthusiasm to help me identify and gain access to manuscripts, published sources, and cartographic materials. At the Newberry Library, Jim Akerman and Scott Stevens guided me through collections and helped me think through the possibilities and limitations of my project, while the library's staff patiently pulled hundreds of maps for me to consult. At the John Carter Brown Library, Kimberly Nusco, Neil Safier, and Kenneth Ward helped me comb through the library's map collection and also pointed me to numerous sources that I had not anticipated finding. Without similar support from the staffs of UNC's Wilson Library; Argentina's Museo Mitre, Academia Nacional, Museo Etnográfico, and Instituto Ravignani; Uruguay's Archivo General de la Nación and Biblioteca Nacional; Brazil's Arquivo Histórico do Rio Grande do Sul, Arquivo Nacional, Arquivo Público do Estado do Rio Grande do Sul, Biblioteca Nacional, Instituto de Estudos Brasileiros, Instituto Histórico e Geográfico Brasileiro, and Instituto Histórico e Geográfico do Rio Grande do Sul; Paraguay's Archivo Nacional de Asunción; Portugal's Arquivo Histórico Ultramarino, Biblioteca da Ajuda, Biblioteca Nacional, and Biblioteca da Universidade de Coimbra; and Spain's Archivo General de Indias, Archivo General de Simancas, Archivo General Militar, Biblioteca Nacional, Museo Naval, and Real Academia de la Historia, this project would not have materialized. The Oliveira Lima Library at the Catholic University of America was generous in sharing this book's cover image. The staff at Argentina's Archivo General de la Nación deserves additional praise for their benevolence and professionalism, which allowed me to develop a firm documentary foundation for this project before moving elsewhere.

This multiarchival and multicountry research project would have remained a dream had it not been for the generous financial support I received from myriad institutions. UNC History Department's Clein and Mowry Fellowships gave me the opportunity to explore archives when this project was in its early stages, while funding from the Tinker Foundation, the Mellon Foundation, and UNC's Institute for the Study of the Americas allowed me to begin my work in South America. A Foreign Language and Area Studies (FLAS) Fellowship provided me the support necessary to expand my work into Brazil. The Mellon Foundation and the Institute for International Education offered a lifeline to myself and others in response to the temporary cancellation of the Fulbright-Hays Program in 2010. Without this intervention, I would have lost a year of research. The Newberry Consortium in American Indian Studies and the Jeannette D. Black Memorial Fellowship provided access to vast corpuses of cartographic materials and time to sift through hundreds of maps. Funding from UNC's Program in Medieval and Early Modern Studies allowed me to carry my research across the Atlantic, to Portugal and Spain, and then to write my early chapters from Buenos Aires. With financial support from the American Council of Learned Societies, I was able to complete my manuscript from Albuquerque and build a geographic information system (GIS) database.

Bringing together such a wide array of historical evidence into a cogent analysis would have been an insurmountable task without the diligent work of numerous research assistants and editors. Victoria Bussmann, Pamela Gaviño, Renan Lacerda, Luisa Plastino, and Celina Rivera contributed to the creation of the database that undergirds this project's GIS maps, while Rachel Hynson proved to be a keen copyeditor as I prepared the manuscript to submit to press. At UNC Press, Chuck Grench and Dylan White shepherded the manuscript through each round of review, while Andrew Graybill and Benjamin Johnson were enthusiastic advocates who helped me find ways to make tangible connections across the Americas. Cate Hodorowicz coordinated this work's many moving parts as it moved to production, and Madge Duffey worked tirelessly on adjusting and readjusting its many GIS-based maps. Tamar Herzog and Alida Metcalf, who reviewed this manuscript, deserve special thanks for their thorough readings, critical comments, and practical solutions, all of which pushed me to precision and to deepening connections across the hemisphere.

At each stop of this journey, I have benefited from the hospitality and companionship of dear friends and family. I would like to thank in particular Carlos Lanzaponte, Natalia Ovide, Adriana de Napoli, Pablo Ansolabehere, Nicolás Gazzano, Juan Bogliaccini, Lucía Genta, and Juan Carlos and Humberto Battioni for always being available, for offering lively debates, and for providing me a place to stay. My parents, Karen and Jeff Erbig, have been uniformly encouraging despite my long absences and frenetic pace of work. They, along with my sister, Kerri Erbig, and my brother-in-law, Tony Espinoza, have provided listening ears and have kept me grounded. My Argentine family, Cristina Martínez and Pablo and Fede Niedzwiecki, have allowed me to fully partake in their lives, and our quotidian moments have made Buenos Aires my second home.

No one deserves more appreciation than my partner, Sara Niedzwiecki. She has been with this project from the beginning and has been the one constant throughout. She has somehow found a way to be a sounding board, a thoughtful reader, a wise confidant, a patient partner, the sustainer of our family, and an escape from work all at once. That her support never wavered, even in our most challenging moments of research, teaching, and job searching, is a remarkable feat, and I am forever grateful for her commitment. Along the way, our daughter, Uma, was born. I thank her for the endless joy she has brought to our lives but mostly for her not caring at all about this project and for her commitment to sleeping through the night whenever possible. Amid all transience, Sari and Uma are my home, and it is to them that I dedicate this book.

Abbreviations in the Text

AGI	Archivo General de Indias
AGMM	Archivo General Militar de Madrid
AGNA	Archivo General de la Nación, Argentina
AGNU	Archivo General de la Nación, Uruguay
AGPSF	Archivo General de la Provincia de Santa Fe
AHRS	Arquivo Histórico do Rio Grande do Sul
AHU	Arquivo Histórico Ultramarino
ANA	Archivo Nacional de Asunción
ANB	Arquivo Nacional do Brasil
ANHA	Academia Nacional de la Historia de la República Argentina
BA	Biblioteca da Ajuda
BNB	Biblioteca Nacional do Brasil
BNE	Biblioteca Nacional de España
BNP	Biblioteca Nacional de Portugal
BUC	Biblioteca da Universidade de Coimbra
IEB	Instituto de Estudos Brasileiros
IHGB	Instituto Histórico e Geográfico Brasileiro
IHGRGS	Instituto Histórico e Geográfico do Rio Grande do Sul
MM	Museo Mitre
MNM	Museo Naval de Madrid
NL	Newberry Library
RAH	Real Academia de la Historia
UFRGS	Universidade Federal do Rio Grande do Sul

Where Caciques and Mapmakers Met

Introduction

On New Year's Day in 1787, several Minuán Indians approached the encampment of a Portuguese mapping team along Brazil's southern border. According to the mapmakers' diaries, the Minuanes claimed possession of local lands and declared it their right to "tax all travelers" who passed through. They demanded aguardiente, wine, sugar, salt, tobacco, yerba maté, knives, textiles, and hats in exchange for safe passage. Five Minuán caciques remained in the Portuguese encampment the entire day and evening before allowing the mapmakers to continue on their way the following morning. Hoping to avoid further incident, the Portuguese travelers set up subsequent campsites in ranches belonging to nearby missions of Guaraní Indians, who were subjects of the Spanish crown. This strategy initially proved successful, but less than two weeks later, another Minuán cacique and his kin confronted the mapping team. This time, the Portuguese mapmakers immediately offered payment, and the Minuanes permitted them to continue their journey. The mapmakers did not make it far before yet another group of Minuanes halted their lumbering convoy the very next day. Having exhausted their resources during the previous two encounters, the Portuguese had no choice but to surrender horses and oxen that were carrying their cargo. The mapmakers eventually completed their journey, but with great difficulty.[1]

These encounters occurred during the boundary demarcations of the Treaty of San Ildefonso, signed by Portugal and Spain in 1777. This accord, following the model of the 1750 Treaty of Madrid, stipulated that the two Iberian crowns commission collaborative mapping expeditions to determine a definitive border between Brazil and Spanish South America. In both instances, parallel Portuguese and Spanish teams fanned out along the approximately ten-thousand-mile boundary—from near the Caribbean coast in the north through the Amazon and the Pantanal to the Atlantic coast in the southeast—with the aim of creating and cosigning maps that would serve as the preeminent legal base for future administration and land claims (map 1).[2] The boundary commissions were massive endeavors, employing between two and three thousand people apiece, who were divided into over a dozen contingents that each mapped a section of the border. Trained cosmographers, astronomers, geographers, and engineers were supported by hundreds of

Río de la Plata

LEGEND
······ Madrid Line
- - - San Ildefonso Line
——— Both

MAP 1 Approximate locations of the Madrid and San Ildefonso lines. This map is based on the original treaties' language, their subsequent instructions, and two contemporary maps: *Mapa dos confins do Brazil*; Requena, *Mapa geográfico*. Neither treaty line reached the Caribbean coast, given Dutch and French claims over adjacent lands. Article 9 of the Treaty of Madrid and Article 12 of the Treaty of San Ildefonso specified that the border would extend to "the end of [Spanish and Portuguese] dominions." "Tratado firmado en Madrid," 6; "Tratado preliminar," 8–9.

guides, laborers, and armed escorts as they modified and added precision to the general line agreed on by the Iberian royal courts. The Portuguese travelers waylaid in 1787 were therefore one of numerous mapmaking teams working along Brazil's southern border, all of whom the Minuanes intercepted and taxed.

The Iberians' desire to establish a borderline between their overseas possessions was part of a broader eighteenth-century trend that would continue through the following century. Although borders as geopolitical phenomena had existed for centuries, borderlines as precise cartographic divisions that superimposed exclusive imperial sovereignty on contiguous territories were a new phenomenon.[3] Sometimes royal courts drew on natural limits to devise their borders. Spain and France used the Pyrenees Mountains to separate their claims in Europe and the Mississippi River to divide them in North America, while Russia and China used the Amur River basin to partition their claims in Manchuria. Occasionally they relied on lines of latitude. In mainland North America, the forty-ninth parallel separated Britain's northern possessions from the French, while the thirty-first parallel separated its southern possessions from the Spanish. At times they referenced published maps to arbitrate a border, as occurred with Great Britain and France regarding Nova Scotia and Acadia, and with Great Britain, Russia, and China regarding Central Asia.[4] Most often, they drew on a combination of geographic features, settlement patterns, and historical sources to divide their territorial claims. The Luso-Hispanic agreements for South America, though built on the same premise as other accords, were unique in sending collaborative boundary commissions to walk and survey the borderlines from the ground.[5]

The treaties of Madrid and San Ildefonso, while ostensibly bilateral endeavors, were nonetheless intertwined with the activities of autonomous Indigenous communities throughout South America. Spain and Portugal's perpetual conflict over land claims was due to each empire's inability to establish footholds beyond continental coastlines or fragile corridors that ran through the interior.[6] Since the sixteenth century, Iberian officials had drawn on Native peoples' geographical locations to question their humanity, claim their lands, or appropriate their labor, yet while these ethnogeographic debates played out in administrative enclaves, metropolitan courthouses, and European print houses, Indigenous authority undermined imperial law in borderland spaces.[7] The Madrid and San Ildefonso boundary commissions sought to remedy this dissonance via the precision of on-the-ground mapmaking, but they too depended on Indigenous agents for geographic information, safe passage, guidance, and sustenance. Some Native people obliged. Payaguá canoers offered to guide one mapping team up the Río Paraguay, while Mbayá caciques displayed knotted recording devices to recount regional histories to another team. Two hundred residents of the Atures mission helped one Spanish team cross the Orinoco River's torrents; Waikerí, Sáliba, and Yaruro couriers relayed messages for others; Caripuna men and women shared a meal with a Portuguese team; and Taboca traders sold captives to both Portuguese and Spanish teams.[8] Other encounters were conflictive. Guaikurú archers besieged a Spanish mapping team in Mato Grosso, Tupi lancers attacked another team in Rio Grande de São Pedro, and Mura spies trailed Portuguese teams in the Amazon. Perhaps most famously, Guaraní mission dwellers garnered the support of Charrúas, Bohanes, Guenoas, and Minuanes to thwart the southern Madrid expeditions for half a decade.[9]

Native agents were not simply informants or antagonists; their actions derived from their own geographic visions or claims to authority. Rather than seeing themselves within the frames of European legal geographies, they incorporated imperial newcomers into their own sovereign spaces.[10] Their interactions with mapmakers, who represented the vanguard of Iberian claims to possession, constituted some of the most vivid examples of competing territorialities.[11] These concurrent encounters occupied few pages of the expeditions' itinerant diaries, which depict Native communities as part of a passing landscape, yet close analysis demonstrates that mapping teams entered into longer local histories and often challenged the local order. When Tupi lancers assailed Spanish mapmakers, they likely associated the imperial travelers with the expanding Guaraní mission complex and other encroaching settlers with whom the Tupi were embroiled in armed conflict. When Guaraní militias refused to cede their lands to Portugal, they drew on ancestral claims and historical enmity with Luso-Brazilians. When Minuán caciques halted the Portuguese team at the southernmost portion of the border, they were exerting their own claims over the grasslands the travelers were attempting to cross. The Portuguese efforts to avoid the Minuanes reflected a common strategy of the demarcation teams, and the brevity of their diary accounts was more indicative of imperial haste than of Indigenous absence.[12]

It has been less clear whether mapmaking and subsequent attempts to impose mapped lines on physical lands had any tangible impact on interethnic relations. Did the declaration and performance of an imaginary interimperial border engender meaningful changes for autonomous Native peoples? How could a border come into being in lands controlled by people who did not share that spatial vision? The answers to such questions are important not only to how we conceptualize mapmaking but to the very nature of interethnic relations in borderland spaces. The mapping of Luso-Hispanic borderlines dramatically restructured interethnic relations in southeastern South America. Recognizing Native sovereignty over partitioned lands reveals that the actions of Indigenous agents are what gave material life to imperial cartographic lines. While Indigenous societies probably did not imagine borderlines from the bird's-eye perspective of royal mapmakers, they were certainly able to conceive of borders as such and interpret imperial visions via their own epistemologies.[13] At the very least, they recognized the changing spatial practices—settlement patterns, trade routes, resource extraction, policing, assertions of lordship—of their imperial counterparts and sought to use them to their advantage. As a result, Indigenous and imperial territorialities came to coexist in ways that simultaneously resembled a borderline and, at least temporarily, reinforced the authority of certain Native polities.

Imperial Lines, Indigenous Lands

This assessment of the interplay between mapped lines and interethnic relations builds on two pillars of interdisciplinary research: the history of cartography and borderlands studies. In recent decades, historical studies of cartography have demonstrated how imperial mapmakers discursively appropriated space via selective and subjective representations of New World landscapes.[14] Some scholars have sought to articulate Indigenous spatial perspectives and practices via analyzing Native-authored maps or, more frequently, by identifying Native signs, names, and locations on imperial maps. Others have analyzed the process of mapmaking, from the collection of information to a map's final form, to show the active participation of Indigenous agents in the production of imperial or hybridized geographical imaginings.[15] The underlying premise of the power of maps nonetheless warrants further interrogation. Accounts of Native mapmaking often emphasize the colonization of Indigenous literacies, while narratives of imperial mapmaking tend to presume the subsequent realization of colonial territorial forms; yet few works demonstrate the mechanisms whereby mapping engendered material change. Informed by theories of hegemonic power relations, histories of cartography tend to position Indigenous peoples as subaltern imperial subjects and identify particular cartographic conventions, such as fixed borderlines, as patently European.[16] But such power dynamics were not omnipresent, as the limited and negotiated nature of imperial authority in borderland spaces—the precise areas where borderlines were drawn—made mapmaking less straightforward than commonly imagined.[17]

Skepticism about the material impact of imperial mapmaking is perhaps most evident in studies of interethnic borderlands between imperial agents and autonomous Native peoples in the Americas. Reacting against teleological national narratives that treated imperial limits (borderlines) and intercultural frontiers (borderlands) as synonymous, ethnohistorians have tended to dismiss mapped lines as fictitious expressions of imperial desire that were readily subverted or altogether ignored.[18] Scholarship on North American borderlands has tended to situate itself along a paradigmatic spectrum from "middle ground" to "Native ground," the former emphasizing multipolarity, exchange, and mutual dependence among imperial and Indigenous agents, and the latter underscoring the preexistence, persistence, and power of sovereign Native societies amid European colonialism.[19] Scholarship on Latin American borderlands has emphasized the permeability of socio-geographical borderlands via analyses of social ecology, human movement, interethnic diplomacy, intercultural exchange, and mestizaje.[20] Across the hemisphere, recent works have also tethered continental borderlands to transimperial maritime spaces, further eroding the significance of imperial or national divisions.[21] In each instance, scholars have demonstrated the limits of European imperial reach and illuminated Native territorialities, contributing to the visibility of present-day Indigenous communities. At the same time, reluctance to grant historical efficacy to cartographic lines overlooks the centrality of border making—drawing lines on a map and then attempting to replicate them on the ground—to eighteenth-century European territorial strategies in the Americas. Inattention to the construction of borders also conceals the participation of Native peoples in the production of these ostensibly European territorial arrangements, thus discarding a valuable lens of comparison between sites where borders were drawn and those where they were not.

The present study proposes a third way of imagining mapped borderlines in the contested spaces of early American borderlands. Imperial mapping did alter regional territorialities in some instances, but these transformations necessarily depended on the participation of autonomous Indigenous communities. In the case of the Madrid and San Ildefonso lines, the boundary commissions' presentation of borderland spaces changed how imperial administrators imagined and engaged those spaces. The mapping efforts created a new legal apparatus that made possible the issuance of land titles in previously disputed lands, incentivized the founding of forts and strategic settlements, transformed commerce into contraband, and led administrators to engage autonomous Native peoples as if they were imperial subjects. Meanwhile, the continued dominance of Indigenous polities over borderland spaces required that imperial agents solicit Native support to make the borderline operative or, alternatively, to access the other side. The invention of the border heightened imperial need—to stop contraband, to apprehend unauthorized travelers, to populate the countryside, or to prevent enemy incursions—and generated new risks for traders and settlers. Although these territorial reconfigurations resulted in dispossession, dislocation, or death for many Native people, some caciques and their communities leveraged imperial border making to expand their kinship, tributary, and trading networks. Whether these mapmaking expeditions succeeded or failed matters less than how they transformed territorial and interethnic engagement. By analyzing the dynamic production of space and the interplay between territorial imaginings and spatial practices, the significance of imperial legal geographies in Native lands comes into sharper relief.

To imagine borderland spaces in this way requires alternatives to the categories of resistance and accommodation. Native peoples did not simply foil or adapt to Iberian efforts; they altered the very structure of imperial governance, making borders necessary and transforming the meaning and form of mapped lines.[22] The boundary commissions were a response to the short territorial reach of imperial power, and they alone did not produce borderlines. The drawing of lines was instead a performative declaration to which local actors responded, and their aggregate responses, both for and against the border, transformed the imaginary line into meaningful spatial practices.[23] Furthermore, the eventual realization of borders as operative, albeit limited or temporary, territorial arrangements did not imply the vanquishing of Native sovereignty, as multiple means of imagining territory, possession, and authority coexisted. The flood of migrants to the newly drawn border simultaneously signified the materialization of cartographic lines (for imperial officials) and the arrival of potential kin, tributaries, and economic partners (for caciques). These seemingly contradictory territorialities operated concurrently, defining interethnic engagements and the divergent interpretations of their meaning.[24] In fact, it was not the production of borderlines but instead their subsequent dissolution that undermined Native authority in some instances. After many Native communities bound their livelihood to borderline territorialities, the rupture of such arrangements produced hostile, unpredictable, and ultimately uninhabitable worlds.

Beyond transforming eighteenth-century borderlands, the Madrid and San Ildefonso mapping expeditions created discursive precedents that continue to shape the ethnogeographic imaginings of regional historiographies. As the border thinking that emerged via these expeditions corresponded with projections of Native disappearance, the persistence of such territorial frames perpetuates present-day Indigenous invisibility.[25] Through compiling and ordering earlier accounts, and by producing voluminous natural histories and ethnographies, the boundary commissions generated a vast and frequently cited documentary foundation for historical accounts. In reading against the ethnographic grains of these sources, scholars often accept the geographic perspectives that the sources promulgate, particularly the conflation of borders with contiguous imperial control over the entirety of the countryside. The principal result has been to naturalize the historical processes whereby such a territorial order emerged in the historical records, as both the acceptance of borders as irresistible imperial impositions and the rejection of borders as meaningless discourse present space as a neutral stage of historical action. *Where Caciques and Mapmakers Met* instead explores intersections between geographic and ethnographic imaginings, particularly the disregard for Indigenous territorialities that has rendered mobile Native communities invisible, to show the centrality of border making to the structuring of historical memory and to posit alternative frameworks.

A Regional Approach

To assess the relationship between imperial mapmaking and interethnic relations, this book focuses on the southernmost portion of the Madrid and San Ildefonso demarcation efforts, which occurred in the Río de la Plata region (map 1).[26] Through the mid-seventeenth century, this Atlantic borderland was a backwater for Iberian endeavors; and with the exception of several ephemeral missions, colonial settlements were restricted to a tight riverine corridor between the Spanish port city of Buenos Aires and the Jesuit-Guaraní missions of Paraguay farther inland. Colonial settlement patterns changed in 1680, when a Portuguese expedition from Rio de Janeiro founded a small outpost named Colônia do Sacramento on the northern coast of the Río de la Plata estuary, thrusting the region into the center of global juridical debates regarding territorial possession and sovereignty. Over the next seventy years, the two Iberian courts signed four treaties to arbitrate access to the area while racing to establish settlements to fortify their claims. This corner of South America dominated deliberations in both Madrid and San Ildefonso, and half of the treaties' articles defining possession of specific lands referred to the region: six of thirteen for the former and six of eleven for the latter.[27] It was here, too, that the demarcation line varied most widely from treaty to treaty.

Interimperial disputes over territorial possession in the Río de la Plata were superimposed on a complex interethnic landscape. While Portuguese, Spanish, and Jesuit-Guaraní authorities made juridical claims to regional lands, autonomous Indigenous polities dominated the countryside. Organized into local and itinerant encampments (*tolderías*) of several dozen to over a hundred inhabitants, autonomous Native peoples limited imperial and missionary access to the regional interior. Imperial and ecclesiastical writers employed a number of ethnonyms to name their Indigenous counterparts—most notably, Charrúas and Minuanes—yet ethnic labeling varied according to locality, changed over time, and likely did not correspond to Indigenous self-identification.[28] Given the ambiguity of ethnic categories and the locality of Indigenous social organization, this book uses the term *toldería* as the principal means of identification; and where possible, it employs the names of individual caciques, treating ethnonyms as imperial modifiers rather than Native identifiers. It is nonetheless important to recognize the far-reaching networks of kinship, tribute, and commerce that certain caciques established and the collective authority that tolderías exercised over the region, whatever their local distinctions.[29]

Ethnohistorical studies of the eighteenth-century Río de la Plata have followed broader hemispheric trends, as scholars have deconstructed traditional conceptual divisions between colonial settlers and neighboring tolderías. Some have zoomed in on a single settlement and neighboring tolderías to show that interethnic exchange was just as common as interethnic conflict.[30] Others have recast tolderías' roles in long-standing regional narratives, highlighting their ties to the informal economies of rural contrabandists or their capacity to play one Iberian empire off the other. Still others have examined the emergence of ethnographic writings about tolderías in the eighteenth century, connecting knowledge production to changing imperial policies.[31] But the spatial paradigms of earlier scholarship have proven more difficult to upend, and even ethnohistorical studies continue to frame the region as a tripartite borderland between Portuguese, Spanish, and Jesuit-Guaraní settlers, thereby rendering tolderías' territorialities marginal or invisible.[32] By considering these local studies collectively, however, it becomes clear that at the time of the boundary commissions, the Río de la Plata countryside was Native ground. If local settlements dotted the perimeter of the region, and if each of these sites was circumscribed by an inward, local frontier with neighboring tolderías, it follows that the region's vast interior was dominated by autonomous Indigenous polities.[33] This reformulation forces us to reconsider the meaning of interethnic encounters and the significance of border making in tolderías' lands.

In order to develop a new geographical perspective that centers on Native ground, this book draws on approximately seven hundred manuscripts that mention tolderías or individuals associated with them, and reads them along-side other sources relating to Ibero-American territorialities. These include town council minutes, Jesuit missionaries' annual reports, journals from military campaigns, logbooks from forts, baptismal and marriage records from missions and towns, diaries from the boundary commissions, correspondence, newspapers, maps, chorographic reports, treaties, diplomatic treatises, and natural histories. Despite this diverse paper trail, source materials on tolderías are fragmented and geographically dispersed. Inhabitants of the tolderías left no written records; they entered historical sources only through ephemeral interactions with colonial agents, and the majority of their activities escaped written accounts. Records that do exist span at least seven countries and two dozen archival repositories, each containing a limited portion of available documentation from a restricted geographical vantage point.[34] I use geographic information systems (GIS) to read across the territorial limits of each archive, tracing the movements of individual tolderías between isolated imperial settlements and identifying aggregate patterns of geographic positioning among tolderías over time. Since Native authorship and voices remain elusive, I instead seek meaning in Native actions.[35] This focus on tolderías' territorialities serves as a foundation on which to reinterpret the meanings of interethnic encounters and to read past the imperial or ecclesiastical tendency to project control over toldería lands. Attention to both archives of geographical knowledge and geographies of archival knowledge provides a more precise view of regional territorialities, distinguishing colonial settlements from the adjacent countryside and underscoring tolderías' integral role in the production of a borderline.

WHERE CACIQUES AND MAPMAKERS MET traces spatial practices in the Río de la Plata region over the course of the eighteenth century, marking the mid-century mapping expeditions as a key turning point. It combines top-down analyses of legal and diplomatic discourse with a bottom-up assessment of on-the-ground events. The first two chapters, which span from the 1680 founding of Colônia do Sacramento to the eve of the Madrid mapping expeditions in 1752, address the spatial practices of regional inhabitants prior to the demarcation of an interimperial borderline. Chapter 1 examines the colonial and Indigenous territorialities that defined the region and demonstrates that tolderías were the principal arbiters of access to and travel across it. Local relations often superseded imperial or Indigenous identities, and in the absence of any singular authority, territorial order tilted power relations in tolderías' favor. Chapter 2 examines the juridical battles that arose between Spain (and, by extension, the Jesuit-Guaraní missions) and Portugal prior to the Treaty of Madrid, as each sought to claim legal possession of regional lands. It inserts local interethnic relations into broader juridical debates to show how Iberian diplomats eventually turned to collaborative mapping expeditions to rectify their disputes and circumvent Native claims.

The next three chapters explore the impact of border-making initiatives on interethnic relations, beginning with the first boundary demarcations in 1752 and concluding in the early nineteenth century. Chapter 3 follows the Madrid and San Ildefonso mapping expeditions, contrasting the detailed diaries of demarcation officers with the geographical and ethnographic knowledge they produced. Whereas the events of the mapping expeditions reveal the continued dominance of tolderías over regional lands, demarcation officers presented stable landscapes and positioned tolderías as antiquated inhabitants in decline. Chapter 4 assesses how the knowledge produced by the boundary commissions transformed spatial practices in the region. Both Iberian empires sought to materialize the recently drawn borders, but while Spanish administrators sought to remove tolderías from their lands, Portuguese administrators pursued renewed pact making with caciques. Tolderías' divergent responses derived more from their geographic positioning than from purported ethnic identities. Chapter 5 examines the absence of Charrúas and Minuanes from written records by the 1830s, drawing connections to the boundary commissions while distinguishing the disuse of ethnic labels from Native absence altogether. It follows Indigenous captives and emigrants from tolderías who lived in colonial settlements, and it considers tolderías' participation in regional wars of independence. The book concludes by addressing historical memory— professional, political, and popular—of the boundary commissions in the Río de la Plata, connecting entrenched narratives of Native disappearance to colonial geographic imaginings that emerged in the eighteenth century.

CHAPTER ONE

An Archipelago of Settlements and Tolderías

In July 1731, a Jesuit priest named Miguel Ximénez and a Guenoa Indian named Francisco de Borja set out from the San Borja mission. They traveled for nearly a month, waylaid by floods and freezing rain, before arriving at Guenoa encampments (*tolderías*) near the headwaters of the Río Piraí, where they met Borja's kin and several prominent chiefs (*caciques*). Their aim was to broker peace between the Spanish settlement of Montevideo and neighboring Minuán tolderías. If they failed, the fighting that had erupted in the south would engulf the entire region, including their mission and the Guenoa tolderías (map 2).[1] The conflict had begun a year earlier, when one of Montevideo's inhabitants had killed a Minuán man and fled to the Portuguese settlement of Colônia do Sacramento (hereafter Colônia). When a commission of Minuanes went to collect the body of their fallen kin, Montevideo's city council (*cabildo*) offered condolences and gifts but not the perpetrator. The Minuanes were dissatisfied and attacked the city's ranches, killing nearly two dozen farmhands and cutting off Montevideo's food supply. Montevideo sought to break the blockade with the force of its militia, but this strategy proved futile. Half of the conscripted fighters deserted to Colônia, and the Minuanes confiscated the militia's five hundred horses.[2] By April 1731, the arrival of the rainy season suspended the fighting; Minuanes maintained possession of the countryside, while Montevideo's residents found themselves trapped within the city's walls, and their city council contemplated rationing food for the winter. Meanwhile, each side sought to garner allies, as the principal cacique, Yapelman, called on Guenoa tolderías in the north, and Spanish authorities solicited aid from the Jesuit-Guaraní missions.[3]

Jesuit authorities were wary of involving themselves in a conflict with the tolderías and sent Ximénez and Borja as envoys in a last-ditch effort to avert war. Along with generating bloodshed, war would likely impede the missions' access to livestock in the countryside. The peacemaking endeavor brought its own risks, however, as a trip by Ximénez to the tolderías the previous year had precipitated infighting and combat among the caciques, while Borja's decision to abandon the tolderías for Ximénez's mission had purportedly upset his family. The two men's return carried the potential of reigniting animosities and undermining the peace efforts. Indeed, both were cudgeled in a surprise attack

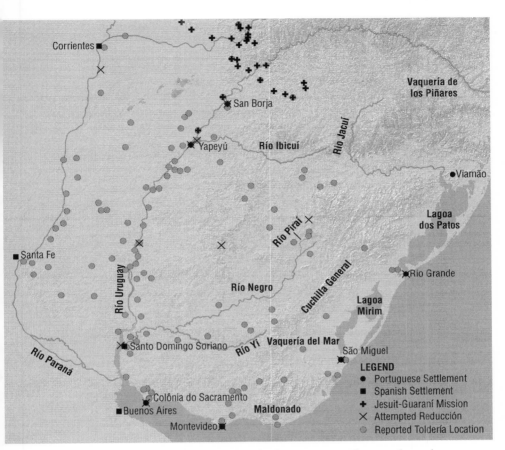

MAP 2 Settlements and tolderías of the Río de la Plata, 1675–1750. This map shows the sites of Portuguese, Spanish, and Jesuit-Guaraní settlements and over three hundred locations of tolderías, as reported in manuscript records during these years. Colonial settlements were limited to coastlines and riverine corridors around the region's perimeter, whereas tolderías collectively controlled the interior. Religious officials attempted to establish small mission hamlets (*reducciones*) with tolderías, yet these settlements generally did not come to fruition and rarely lasted longer than several months. The data set used to mark tolderías' reported locations here and in subsequent maps was originally cited in Erbig, "Borderline Offerings," and has since been updated to include newly identified records. Basemap copyright: 2014 Esri.

by a man sent by Borja's family.[4] Deliberations between Ximénez, Borja, and the caciques nonetheless proved successful. According to Ximénez's account, the caciques shared his reticence toward a war that would bring missionary militias to their tolderías and responded magnanimously when the priest bestowed gifts on them.[5] Once the waters subsided, the caciques sought out other

Native leaders from the south, including Yapelman, to whom they owed their allegiance. They returned with Yapelman himself, who received more gifts from Ximénez and accepted the priest's pleas for peace, promising to instruct other tolderías throughout the region to respect the pact they had made.[6]

The conflict between the Minuán tolderías and Montevideo demonstrates how territorial dynamics structured interethnic relations in the Río de la Plata. Imperial and ecclesiastical settlements—including Montevideo, Colônia, and San Borja—dotted the region's perimeter, and they depended on peaceful relations with tolderías to obtain natural resources in the interior and sustain their local populations. Since tolderías arbitrated access to the countryside, both Ximénez and Montevideo's city council approached neighboring caciques with remunerative gifts before considering armed combat. The missions' militias certainly wielded the collective strength to engage Minuanes and Guenoas, but experience had taught them that the results would be mutually disastrous. For their part, Montevideo's ragtag militia was entirely ill equipped, and their desertion to Colônia indicates that they were aware of the futility of their campaign. The spatial limits of colonial agents were also evident in their lack of familiarity with the geography of the interior. Ximénez relied on a Guenoa guide, while Montevideo's militia lost track of the tolderías once they distanced themselves from the walls of the city. Yet despite tolderías' collective dominance over rural space, the Minuanes and Guenoas in conflict with Montevideo were unable to monopolize access and were keenly aware of their own limitations. Procuring peace would enable them to avoid the costs of war, to protect trade partnerships, and to maintain potential allies in a multipolar world.

The eighteenth-century Río de la Plata was an archipelago of settlements and tolderías. Imperial and ecclesiastical population centers were strung along riverine corridors or coastal enclaves and surrounded by mobile encampments of autonomous Native peoples. Both colonial settlements and Native tolderías constituted local centers of economic, social, and cultural activity. Each exhibited limited territorial control, yet tolderías tended to control much larger stretches of land as their strategic mobility enabled them to arbitrate access to the countryside. In this context, local ties often superseded imperial or ethnic affiliation. Writings and drawings from the region's settlements often depicted the region as a series of consolidated territories—a tripartite borderland between Portuguese, Spanish, and Jesuit-Guaraní establishments—but neither empire nor the missions possessed contiguous territorial control. Imperial and ecclesiastical spatial visions were simultaneously myopic and ambitious; they projected local relations on the entire region and conflated disparate tolderías via uniform ethnonyms. Placing the spatial imaginations and practices of settlements and tolderías on even ground reveals the local motivations driving broader regional patterns and the interplay between imperial claims and Indigenous actions.[7]

Dotting the Landscape

The Río de la Plata was a region composed of flatlands and fluctuating rivers, divided by several stretches of highlands. Stretching from its eponymous estuary in the south to the Ibicuí and Jacuí river systems in the north, the region was bounded on the west by the Río Paraná and on the east by the Atlantic Ocean (map 2). During the first half of the eighteenth century, its inhabitants developed a multipolar, nodal world organized around settlements and tolderías. Competing imperial and ecclesiastical settlements dotted the region's perimeter: the Spanish cities of Corrientes and Santa Fe lay to the west; Jesuit-Guaraní missions (subject to the Spanish crown) lined the north; the Portuguese settlements of Rio Grande and São Miguel appeared in the east; and Colônia (Portuguese) was situated between Santo Domingo Soriano and Montevideo (Spanish) in the south. These fixed settlements were superimposed on existing Indigenous geographies. Charrúas, Minuanes, Bohanes, Guenoas, Yaros, and other autonomous Native peoples moved their tolderías throughout the region's interior, incorporating new settlers into existing networks of tribute, kinship, and trade and arbitrating settlements' access to the feral livestock that proliferated in the countryside. Geographical positioning was paramount, and local affinities and interests often superseded imperial, ecclesiastical, or ethnic allegiances.

Local Settlements

Unlike modern territorial states, early modern governments relied on contingent, reciprocal relationships to define sovereignty. Viceroyalties were not groups of consolidated provinces but series of horizontally unaligned localities connected by their shared vertical allegiances to a common authority.[8] The principal territorial designations of the Río de la Plata region—Spanish governorships and Portuguese captaincies—did not exercise complete territorial possession or control but instead constituted collections of discrete settlements tethered to a shared governor and in frequent competition with one another.[9] Given their location on the fringes of competing empires, each settlement was of strategic importance for its respective governor and therefore wielded significant amounts of leverage in negotiations with him. They also served as important centers for the social, economic, and political lives of colonial settlers, with city or town councils as their principal governing bodies. Simply put, settlements functioned as a series of relatively autonomous points on the map, each with its own interests and needs.

Colonial settlements in the Río de la Plata came in myriad forms, yet all shared similar population sizes, hybrid purposes, and spatial significance. Jesuit-Guaraní missions averaged 2,500 to 4,700 residents apiece, with some peaking at over 7,000, while the Spanish cities of Buenos Aires (in the year 1744), Corrientes (1753), and Montevideo (1757) counted 10,056, 1,800, and 1,991 inhabitants, respectively; Portuguese Colônia had 3,000 residents in 1732.[10] Missions, cities, and forts alike maintained military defenses, supported commerce, promoted religious-civic life, and anchored imperial claims of territorial possession. Given these hybrid functions, eighteenth-century writers often used the term *plaza* (*praça* in Portuguese) to classify such diverse sites as Santa Fe, Colônia, Montevideo, São Miguel, and Rio Grande. Most often associated with urban squares, *plaza* also referred to "any fortified place" or "a settlement where considerable commercial operations are undertaken."[11] Plazas were sites of civil governance, sometimes with their own governor. Although the term did not apply to missions, Jesuit-Guaraní settlements had important military and commercial roles as well. Beginning in the 1640s, the missions' several-thousand-member militias became the Spanish crown's premier military force against autonomous Native neighbors, the Portuguese, and rebellious Spanish subjects, while livestock and yerba maté provided the basis for lucrative mission economies. Most importantly, each type of settlement served the purpose of exerting imperial claims of territorial possession, and their distinctions bore little weight when engaging tolderías in the countryside.[12]

These competing settlements jockeyed for access rights over broad swaths of land, but in practice, each was largely confined to its immediate countryside. Ranches did not extend far beyond a city's, town's, or mission's population center, and most livestock roamed far beyond the reach of any single settlement. For this reason, colonial writers often distinguished their adjacent countryside, where livestock could be corralled and maintained, from lands beyond their control (*tierra adentro/campanha/sertão*), where wild cows, sheep, and horses proliferated.[13] To sustain a settlement, it was necessary to send expeditionary parties to garner livestock, which clustered in distant ranges (*vaquerías/vacarias*), and either slaughter them or herd them back to local ranches. At the turn of the eighteenth century, the two most important vaquerías were the Vaquería de los Piñares and the Vaquería del Mar; the former was located far to the north, near the headwaters of the Río Uruguay, and the latter was southwest of the Lagoa Mirim (map 2). While Guaraní and Portuguese agents competed over the Vaquería de los Piñares, residents of the missions, Santa Fe, and Buenos Aires clashed over access to the Vaquería del Mar. Even the missions did not act as unified agents, as journeys to the vaquerías spurred conflicts between actors from San Borja, San Miguel, Apóstoles, Concepción, and other Jesuit-Guaraní settlements.[14]

It was not only distance and competition that limited a settlement's ability to garner livestock but also the dominating presence tolderías exerted over the countryside. Mobile peoples stood between settlements and the resources they coveted, monitoring and controlling the region's vast plains. Assuming that herders from a settlement were able to locate and reach feral livestock and avoid detection, they then faced the onerous task of transporting herds back to their ranches. Furthermore, given that wire fencing did not yet exist, ranchers struggled to maintain their ruminant resources in the immediate environs of their population centers. In moments of peace, cows or horses were liable to wander away, and in moments of conflict, tolderías were able to extract them with ease.[15] Thus, in order to gain access to livestock, settlers had to either maintain positive relations with tolderías or find a way to overpower them. Peace was generally preferable to conflict, as no individual settlement had the capacity to engage a collectivity of tolderías with force. Even the missions generally sought to avoid belligerent encounters, given that their populous militias found themselves overstretched, exposed, and outmatched when venturing into the countryside.

The settlements that dotted the region's perimeter did not constitute points along seamless frontiers but rather isolated populations situated along riverine corridors and surrounded by tolderías. Santa Fe was wedged between Charrúas on the east and Abipones on the west, while Charrúas, Yaros, Guenoas, and Minuanes surrounded the Yapeyú mission and divided it from its ranches. The same was true for other population centers, such as the La Cruz mission, which reportedly erected a perimeter wall in defense against neighboring Charrúas.[16] By extension, tolderías' territorial limits did not derive from imperial control but from relations with other tolderías. It was not Santa Fe and Corrientes that formed a western limit for Charrúas, Yaros, and Bohanes but rather the presence of Abipones, Mocovíes, and other Native peoples across the Río Paraná.[17] In the same way, to the north of the Ibicuí and Jacuí rivers, one would have found Guaraní and Tupi-speaking peoples.

These territorially based power relations belie traditional notions of imperial authority in the region. The 1702 Battle of the Yí provides a clear example. Colonial chroniclers and postcolonial writers alike have pointed to this event, in which Guaraní militias from the missions massacred hundreds of Charrúas, Yaros, and Bohanes, taking hundreds more captive, as evidence of Guaraní military superiority.[18] Yet Guaraní militias did not act alone. In this case and in others, Guenoa allies were key participants in the defeat of enemy tolderías, making the victory less a story of imperial dominance than one of strategic alliances.[19] Moreover, rather than a battle pitting missionary forces and Guenoas against Charrúas and their allies, this incident involved only a handful of settlements and tolderías. Neither Guenoas nor Charrúas were centralized or homogeneous groups, and the vanquishing of several tolderías did not imply the defeat of an entire perceived ethnicity. Indeed, in the same year as this incident, Guenoa tolderías attacked the Yapeyú mission; and just two years later, Guenoas, Yaros, and Bohanes defeated mission forces near Colônia and along the region's southeastern coast. Finally, the scale of fighting along the Río Yí was more the exception than the rule, as most other military expeditions commissioned by settlements resulted in abbreviated skirmishes or no conflict at all.[20]

The years following the Battle of the Yí provide a more representative picture of relations between settlements and tolderías, as they demonstrate each side's territorial jockeying amid a military stalemate. During these years, Jesuit-Guaraní missions collaborated with one another in an attempt to extract cattle from the Vaquería del Mar and to establish ranches south of the Río Ibicuí, closer to home. With this maneuver, they aimed to circumvent jurisdictional disputes with Santa Fe, Buenos Aires, and the Portuguese and to obviate travel through tolderia-controlled lands. While few records exist to detail excursions from the missions to the Vaquería del Mar, the 1705 diary of Jesuit Silvestre González conveys the trepidation that travelers felt after the Battle of the Yí. During their two-month journey, González and others from the San Borja mission remained vigilant to detect and evade Yaros "and other nations that have joined together to seek vengeance for our having killed their [kin] four years ago."[21] They relied on Guenoa guides to help them evade Yaros and enemy Guenoa tolderías. This dependency reveals the missions' lack of knowledge of the countryside, as well as the diversity of Guenoas at the time, as each tolderia had distinct relations with nearby missions. By 1743, Guenoas represented approximately one-third of San Borja's residents, yet conflicts between the mission and other Guenoa tolderías never ceased.[22]

Tolderías maintained control over the countryside, and as mission dwellers entered into Guenoa-controlled lands to extract livestock, conflicts abounded. Journeys from the missions to the Vaquería del Mar in 1704 and 1706 proved disastrous, and attacks against tolderías in 1700, 1701, 1704, 1707,

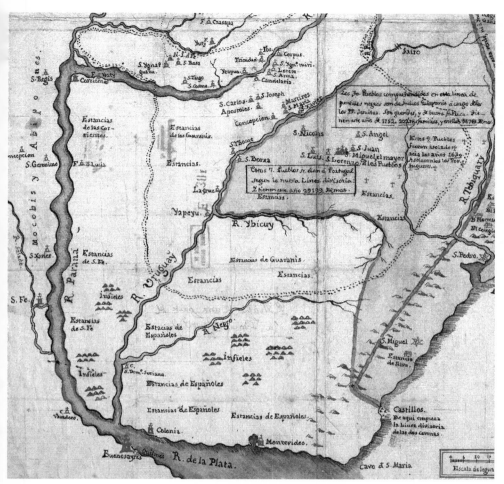

FIGURE 1 José Cardiel, *Mapa de la Governacion del Paraguay y de la de Buenos Ayres*, 1752. Cardiel drew this map in an effort to protect the Jesuit-Guaraní missions' land claims amid a pending Luso-Hispanic partition. Tolderías appear as infidels (*infieles*), a common identifier used to distinguish them from mission Indians, and entirely outside a bounded realm of mission ranches (*estancias*). This geographic rendering contradicts the corpus of manuscripts regarding tolderías' locations at the time. España. Ministerio de Cultura. Archivo General de Simancas, MPD, 06, 032.

and 1708 led to retribution by Guenoas.[23] Following the 1708 attacks, Guenoas and Bohanes blockaded the missions from the vaquerías. Armed agents from the missions retaliated by killing forty-one people from a Guenoa toldería and taking numerous captives. Meanwhile, Guenoas and Bohanes killed thirty-eight people from the Yapeyú and La Cruz missions and took twenty-six captives. Neither side could gain the upper hand, and despite an intervention by the Spanish governor in 1707, the missions were unable to procure safe passage to the vaquerías. While Jesuits complained that a blockade of the vaquerías would result in the starvation of the missions, Guenoas had their own claims on regional resources. Charrúas enacted a blockade on the other side of the Río Uruguay around 1715, presenting a similar crisis in the missions.[24] Maps drawn from the perspective of the missions demonstrate that Jesuit-Guaraní territorial claims reached as far south as the Río Negro (figure 1); however, tolderías controlled most of those lands throughout the eighteenth century.

Tolderías' territorial dominance became especially clear when Spanish and Portuguese agents attempted to connect their disparate settlements. Since the sixteenth century, Santa Fe had served as a key point on the Spanish royal roads that connected the viceregal capital in Lima to Buenos Aires and the missions, while Corrientes was an intermediate point between Santa Fe and the Paraguayan capital of Asunción. Movement between these far-flung locales required that travelers cross lands and waterways controlled by tolderías; thus, in moments of conflict, they found themselves exposed to attacks, as occurred numerous times between 1707 and 1714.[25] Most colonial accounts pointed to Indigenous bellicosity; however, proceedings from a viceregal investigation revealed a different story. In them, residents of Corrientes and Asunción argued that attacks along the Paraná and Uruguay rivers and in the countryside were a direct response to earlier raids on tolderías, in which agents from the missions had taken numerous captives.[26] River travel had always been a negotiated enterprise, as tolderías positioned themselves alternatively as traders, blockaders, and toll takers. In 1691, for example, Jesuit Antonio Sepp recounted a trip along the Río Uruguay in which he bought horses from several Yaro tolderías; he later found his boats under siege by the other Yaro tolderías, who were under the leadership of the cacique Moreira. Decades earlier, a cacique named Guayramâ reportedly claimed several islands in the Río Uruguay and obliged "all who navigated [the river] to pay tribute."[27] Ultimately, settlements depended on peaceful relations with tolderías in order for their inhabitants to transit Native lands and waterways without incident.

The Portuguese tended to be more successful in this regard. Much like Santa Fe and Corrientes, the Portuguese establishments in Rio Grande and San Miguel existed as a means to access cattle ranges and to connect Colônia to Laguna, which was farther north along the Atlantic Coast. By 1703, Portuguese explorers had opened the "Coastal Route" (*Caminho da Costa*), a pathway that began in Colônia and continued along the coast to Maldonado, Rio Grande, and eventually Laguna; within three decades, livestock traders added a line of access northward from Rio Grande all the way to the markets of Sorocaba, near São Paulo.[28] The perpetual presence of Spanish and mission militias, combined with the Spanish foundation of Montevideo in 1725, made the first leg of this journey fraught with obstacles for Portuguese traders. For this reason, authorities from Laguna made numerous attempts to develop positive relations with the Minuán tolderías that dominated the territories between Rio Grande and Colônia. Rather than trying to engage the tolderías with military force, Portuguese administrators chose to provide frequent payments, generally in the form of tobacco, yerba maté, and aguardiente. In exchange, Minuán tolderías provided guides for the travelers and defense against Spanish and missionary hostilities.[29] The survival of this expansive network of trails, which simultaneously sustained Colônia and fed the Sorocaba markets, depended on Minuán collaboration. Even the Portuguese Overseas Council (*Conselho Ultramarino*) in Lisbon recognized this need as an imperial imperative, and the Portuguese acquiesced each time Minuanes demanded greater payments.[30]

Portuguese settlements generally did not exhibit the same tensions with each other as their Spanish and mission counterparts. This may have been due to their smaller number, the perpetual threat of incursions from Buenos Aires and the missions, or their reliance on trade relationships with Minuanes and other tolderías. As advance posts in the extreme south of Brazil, these settlements relied heavily on imperial support from distant administrative and economic poles, such as Rio de Janeiro, São Paulo, and Salvador da Bahia; therefore, their conflicts were vertical in nature. For example, English travelers who arrived in Rio Grande in 1742 recounted that the soldiers stationed there had dismissed many of the city's ranking officers and appointed locals in their place. The soldiers then detained the brigadier governor from Laguna and would not let him leave until he promised to dispatch the clothes, provisions, and money that had been promised to them and resolved their grievances.[31] Local interests, while not generating conflict with other Portuguese settlements, could still supersede imperial fealty.

Given the short territorial reach of colonial settlements and the vast plains that separated them, individuals desiring to break free from administrative control were able to establish informal living arrangements in the countryside. Military deserters, criminals, traders, and others often found life in the countryside more welcoming than that in a particular settlement. Few documents exist about these people, but this is more a result of the limited purview of colonial writers than the emptiness of rural spaces. Nonetheless, a close look at records pertaining to the countryside offers glimpses of this world, in which informal relations did not lend themselves to official regulation or recording. In these spaces, settlers who had abandoned Portuguese, Spanish, and mission population centers lived together unencumbered by the restrictions of imperial allegiances. They developed informal economies based on trade and short-term or seasonal labor stints, at times working on the ranches of a given settlement or participating in cattle roundups. Most importantly, these settlers maintained close relationships with local tolderías, whether as inhabitants, neighbors, or tributaries, and they occasionally functioned as arbitrators between tolderías and individual settlements.

Both Portuguese and Spanish authorities disapproved of this lifestyle and made efforts to bring unsanctioned living arrangements under official control. When Portuguese officials sent an expedition to scout potential sites for a settlement in Rio Grande in 1728, they stumbled on one such arrangement. In a letter to the Portuguese king, the governor of Rio de Janeiro recounted that the explorers found thirty Portuguese and sixty Spaniards, who were presumed to be "criminals from Buenos Aires, and bandits, which will be motive for Castile to allege that those lands belong to it on account of being inhabited by its vassals."[32] The cohabitation of Spanish and Portuguese settlers indicates that imperial rivalries carried little weight beyond the geographical purview of either crown. Officials nonetheless evaluated these nascent population centers through the lens of interimperial rivalry. Both the governor and his informant assumed that the Spaniards were criminals from Buenos Aires, demonstrating their association of informal living arrangements with extralegal behavior. More importantly, the governor feared that Spain would use the presence of its vassals as a means to claim regional lands. This concern points to the limited range of Portuguese and Spanish imperial projects, as well as their dependence on informal relationships to access the countryside. Indeed, after receiving news of these settlers, the governor sought to establish an even larger colony composed of individuals who frequented the area.[33]

These unsanctioned communities frequently depended on tolderías or included individuals from them. In 1718, for example, the governor of Buenos Aires complained of two populations established far away from Colônia, each composed of Portuguese vassals and independent Native peoples. Frustrated by their consumption of feral livestock, the governor denounced the prevalence of such communities: "These sorts of men, both from Portuguese and Spanish settlements[,] often join together, and seized by the liberty that they desire, attempt to accompany the barbarians [tolderías]."[34] Similarly, in 1734, a Portuguese writer noted that a number of Spanish settlers had "formed ties with the Indians that inhabit [lands near Maldonado and north of Montevideo, hunting] with the Indians and establishing themselves in the country-side that [the tolderías] currently possess." The text then pointed out the vast number of mestizo children that these relationships had come to produce.[35] Given their position beyond the scope of local points of authority, other groups like these likely existed—and, from the few recorded cases, it is clear that trade and, at times, kinship with tolderías were core attributes of such communities' survival.

Despite official complaints about unsanctioned actors in the countryside, administrators often depended on them to circumvent regulations and develop trans-imperial trade relations. In fact, one reason the governor of Rio de Janeiro wanted to found a settlement in Rio Grande was to establish trade with the Jesuit-Guaraní missions.[36] A 1723 agreement between Portuguese officials from Laguna and Spanish vassals near Rio Grande provides an even more illustrative example. According to a series of reports from Laguna officials, the Spaniards had come from Santa Fe and Colônia with the intention of selling livestock to Laguna's residents and brokering a trade relationship between Santa Fe and Laguna. They explained that Santa Fe's merchants were upset with Spanish forces stationed near Colônia because they were impinging on Santa Fe's cattle supply. Laguna's ranking official agreed that a commercial relationship would be of mutual interest, and the Spanish traders set out for Santa Fe to close the deal.[37] This trans-imperial arrangement likely depended on pre-existing relationships between the Spanish go-betweens and the Minuán tolderías, who controlled lands between Rio Grande and Colônia. The previous year, this same group of traders had acted as intermediaries between Laguna and Minuán tolderías near Rio Grande, delivering payments from the Portuguese to the principal caciques and returning to Laguna to express the caciques' demands for more. The traders advised the Portuguese officials that to maintain positive relations with the Minuanes, they would have to provide regular payments. They also reported that whenever payments are lacking, the Minuanes "become rebellious," implying that they had had similar experiences in the past.[38]

Mobile Tolderías

As imperial and ecclesiastical settlements dotted the perimeter of the region, its interior was Native ground. Archaeological records suggest that human settlements first appeared in the region twelve thousand years ago, and Guaraní migrants from the Amazon basin likely arrived around the fourteenth century, occupying the islands and coastlines of the Paraná and Uruguay rivers. While archaeological evidence reveals little about relationships between Guaraní and autochthonous societies, it was around that same time that numerous mounds (*cerritos/montículos*) in the region fell into disuse.[39] European travelers arrived in the sixteenth century and, often with Guaraní guides, began traveling along the region's western and northern limits. Despite limited archaeological and written records regarding Native societies farther inland, seventeenth-century slave trades, disease outbreaks, and mission activities appear to have generated significant human displacement, and parts of the region resembled the "shatter zone" of southeastern North America, where polycentric confederations and "petite nations" emerged.[40] By the end of the seventeenth century, as colonial settlements multiplied on the region's edges, locally organized tolderías maintained control over the interior, alternatively collaborating and competing with one another and incorporating new settlers into nodal networks of kinship, trade, and authority.

The term *toldería* (*toldaria* in Portuguese) was broadly used by colonial writers in the Río de la Plata to refer to the portable encampments of autonomous Native communities. It derived from the tentlike buildings (*toldos*), made of rods and hides, that constituted such encampments, and it carried both social and spatial connotations. A toldería was simultaneously a kin-based community and a mobile center of authority.[41] Estimates regarding tolderías' total populations varied widely, as most lived beyond the myopic vantage points of imperial eyes, and observers generally applied their calculations to one of several imagined ethnic polities rather than to tolderías collectively. Nonetheless, when considering the population estimates from numerous locales, tolderías likely accounted for between five and ten thousand people at any given time.[42] Individual tolderías were generally composed of about thirty to one hundred people, although they frequently joined with others to form encampments of several hundred occupants. The few imperial observers who entered tolderías noted that they included cemeteries, grazing grounds, and gathering places; observers also witnessed a wide range of economic activities, including hunting, fishing, herding feral livestock, cultivating honey, and domesticating horses.[43] A scarcity of sources prohibits a detailed discussion of social organization, but it appears that tolderías generally had at least one cacique as well as healers and spiritual leaders, and sometimes one person occupied several of these roles. The periodic union of distinct tolderías also indicated broad networks of kinship ties or political allegiance. Indeed, despite the local movements of most tolderías, certain principal caciques were able to garner support, broker agreements, and offer protection for multiple tolderías, each of which had its own cacique.

This diversity and locality belie the broad ethnic categories ascribed to tolderías by imperial authors. Little evidence exists to suggest that such "imposed identities"—Bohanes, Charrúas, Guenoas, Minuanes, Yaros, and others—were meaningful to the Native peoples to whom they referred; rather, they reflected imperial observers' attempts to catalog inhabitants on a regional scale and define political relationships that would apply to broad populations.[44] These large and homogeneous ethnic categories enabled imperial writers to assume uniformity of action by members of the same group, yet contradictions in their use abounded. Jesuit writers, for example, debated whether "Minuanes" was simply a mispronunciation of "Guenoas" or whether "Yaro" was a phonetic transcription of "Charrúa," while others contended that they were all separate nations.[45] More importantly, the intermittent and contradictory uses of such terms in imperial writings occluded the local, material factors that shaped Native interests, power dynamics, social organization, and actions. Indigenous communities that shared an ethnonym in imperial records frequently fought one another, pacts made with individual caciques rarely included all peoples identified by the same ethnonym, and multiple ethnonyms were often ascribed to single communities.[46] To understand tolderías' dominance over the countryside amid relatively small populations and localized social organization requires looking past supposed ethnic uniformity and focusing on material concerns and logics of mobility.

The mobile lifestyles of tolderías were strategic choices that maximized territorial control and access to resources and trade. Movement between distant locales enabled tolderías to gather different resources at different times of the year, and thus they frequently relocated according to the season, returning to the same stopping points (*paraderos*) along their itineraries.[47] One observer noted that Minuán tolderías "ordinarily go to the hills of Maldonado during the summer, and in winter retire to the part of the Río Negro that drains in the Uruguay, where they make drinks from honey," while another explained that the highlands near Maldonado were "common habitation for the Minuanes during certain seasons because of the many deer that they can hunt there."[48] As the hills of Maldonado were near the Vaquería del Mar, and bee colonies existed near the Río Negro, these tolderías were able to maximize both resources. This movement from lowlands in the winter to highlands in the summer indicates transhumance as well, particularly given the proliferation of livestock in the region. Occupying both locales at the same time would not have been a realistic possibility, as seasonal variance in precipitation often restricted movement. Flat as the region may have been, a vast network of rivers and creeks cut across it. Moments of heavy rainfall, most frequent in the autumn and winter months of April through September, caused sudden rises in the water table and transformed shallow streams into fast-moving currents that could not be traversed on foot. It was for this reason that Francisco de Borja and Miguel Ximénez struggled to arrive at the Minuán tolderías in the winter of 1731 and why the caciques were forced to wait before they could contact Yapelman.[49] Knowledge of river crossings and changing currents was therefore essential for regional inhabitants, as it allowed them to herd livestock to particular locales and then maintain them there until the waters subsided.

Awareness of the vacillations of river depth also provided mobile peoples with a strategic advantage over their sedentary counterparts. By positioning their tolderías relatively close to a particular settlement, they could time their raids on ranches to coincide with heavy rainfalls. Records from the area of Santo Domingo Soriano, which was located near the delta of the Río Negro and prone to inundations, demonstrate this strategy. On multiple occasions in 1746, outsiders entered Soriano's ranches, extracted livestock, and then quickly absconded to their tolderías. Each time, the town reacted by putting together an armed force to recover the losses and enact punitive measures, only to find itself restricted by the rising water table.[50] The fact that Indigenous raiders were able to transport livestock across the same lands points to the calculated timing of such actions. Otherwise, the raids would have resulted in either the death of those responsible or armed incursions into the tolderías. A similar situation arose during the 1731 conflict in Montevideo, as the city's inhabitants found themselves blockaded simultaneously by Minuanes and the rising tides of local waterways.[51]

By knowing the region's fluvial systems, tolderías could better protect themselves and arbitrate access to the countryside. Rivers provided sustenance and safety, as their lush surroundings offered wood, shelter, animals, and places to hide. More importantly, they funneled the movement of travelers; thus, by establishing themselves next to a ford or at the headwaters of a river, tolderías could control vast expanses of land. Despite the region's relatively flat terrain, travelers and herds were unable to cross it in a straight line; instead, they followed coastlines until they found areas shallow enough to ford. Tolderías' use of fords was not lost on travelers, who often named them for the people who controlled them, as occurred with Minuanes' Ford (Paso dos Minuanos) and Young Chief's Ford (Paso del Caciquey), both occupied by Minuanes. Similarly, rafts traveling the Río Uruguay between Santo Domingo Soriano and the Jesuit-Guaraní missions frequently encountered Charrúas or Yaros encamped at the river's main crossings.[52] Headwaters and highland passes could be used in the same manner. It is likely for this reason that the Guenoa tolderías were encamped along the Río Piraí during the 1731 conflict with Montevideo, as this river was near the headwaters of the Río Uruguay, the Rio Grande, and the Rio

Jacuí watersheds, making it a key conduit for rural travelers. Minuán tolderías' seasonal migration to the hills of Maldonado followed this pattern as well, as the highlands divided rivers emptying into the Río Negro from those that flowed eastward. This hilly area, known as the Cuchilla General, became a sort of regional highway between Colônia and Rio Grande.

The strategic location of tolderías also explains the permanent imperial settlements that eventually came to occupy the same spaces. Long before the Spanish established plazas in Montevideo and Maldonado, Minuanes used those areas as stopping points where they could access large cattle reserves and trade with foreign ships. By occupying such sites, they could also position themselves as intermediaries between foreign traders and other tolderías farther inland.[53] Over the course of the eighteenth century, Spanish, Portuguese, and missionary forces strived to station troops along river crossings or headwaters previously occupied by tolderías. At midcentury, the Spanish sought to establish a settlement in Minas, near Maldonado, "to prevent enemy Indians from invading Montevideo's farms and ranches, [and so that the Portuguese and other nations could not] enter by land and invade Montevideo."[54] By closing this highland pass, the city would dramatically reduce its exposure to land-based attacks. Decades later, as Spanish and Portuguese militaries fought over Batoví between the headwaters of the Ibicuí and Bacacaí rivers, they discovered that Minuanes had a long-standing claim of their own: as Spanish settlers began to occupy the area, they came upon Native cemeteries atop a nearby hill. Due in part to Minuán attacks, they soon abandoned the site.[55]

By positioning themselves in strategic locales, certain caciques could control corridors and extend their influence throughout the region (map 3). After procuring peace with Miguel Ximénez in 1731, for example, Yapelman left the tolderías near the Río Piraí to "give the news to his vassals that were near the [Río Cebollatí, southwest of the Lagoa Mirim], and also to two other caciques that lived in the ranches of San Miguel [the mission]."[56] Assuming that these were the farthest tolderías under his control, Yapelman's reach extended from the Atlantic coast southeast of the Lagoa Mirim all the way to the mission ranches. Others demonstrated a similar range of influence. Yaguareté, one of the first caciques who met with Miguel Ximénez that year, moved his tolderías between the Río Piraí and Colônia.[57] Likewise, a cacique named Tacú, who was a key player in the peace negotiations between Minuanes and Montevideo, appeared in Rio Grande several times in the following years, making pacts and developing kinship ties to Portuguese leaders. Charrúa caciques demonstrated similar patterns, bringing together numerous tolderías under their aegis. For example, a cacique named Campusano appeared between Corrientes

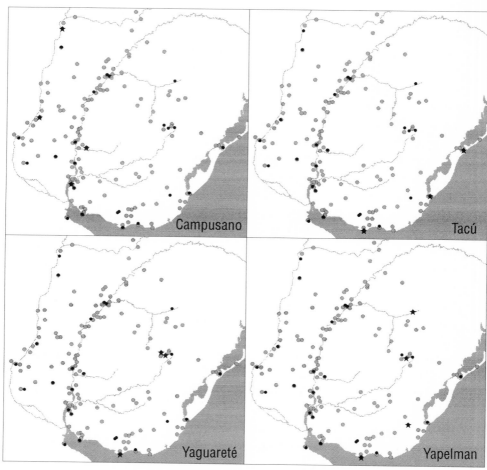

MAP 3 Caciques' range of movement before 1750. This map shows the locations of caciques as recorded in extant manuscript records. Each gray dot represents an instance in which a toldería was reported to have been at a particular place, and black dots represent caciques who appeared in multiple locales. Black stars indicate specific caciques mentioned in the chapter.

and Santo Domingo Soriano, from the Río Paraná to east of the Río Uruguay.[58] Extant sources do not recount the exact routes of travel these caciques undertook, but caciques appeared to follow dominant physical features. Minuán caciques developed spatial networks largely along the Cuchilla General and coastal routes, while Charrúas traveled between the Paraná and Uruguay rivers and their tributaries, occasionally crossing the Río Uruguay at its main ford: the Salto Grande.

The broad territorial reach of particular caciques implies a certain level of hierarchy among tolderías. Knowledge of regional geography alone would not have been enough to exercise such broad control, since such knowledge was not exclusive to any particular cacique or tolderia; and while the use of force was certainly an option in expanding one's control, no single tolderia had a monopoly on violence. Therefore, for a given cacique or tolderia to develop an expansive range of influence, it had to meet the localized demands of other tolderías. This was often achieved by providing protection or resources and trade items. In the 1731 conflict between Minuanes and Montevideo, the four caciques who met with Ximénez had no direct involvement in the conflict.[59] Nonetheless, the principal cacique, Yapelman, had the authority to call on these caciques and others throughout the region to join in the defense of tolderías near Montevideo. In spite of this clear hierarchy in Ximénez's account, sources from Montevideo never mention Yapelman's name. Instead, they identify Tacú as their primary foe, a cacique who never appears in the priest's account. Furthermore, after meeting in Montevideo to hear the town council's petition for peace, Tacú then returned to the tolderías to consult with other caciques.[60] Thus, while Tacú and several unnamed caciques were those whose tolderías were in direct conflict with Montevideo, Yapelman was able to garner support for them through his authority over tolderías throughout the region. Presumably, if there had been conflict between the northern tolderías and missions, Yapelman would have had to provide support for their cause as well.

Principal caciques and their tolderías were also able to expand their influence through the provision of trade goods to both settlements and other tolderías. Throughout the region, as tolderías guided settlers to cattle ranges and aided in the slaughter of cows and other animals, they received payment for their services. Likewise, when they sold horses, bulls, and leather within a settlement, they were paid in kind. Instances of such relationships exist in the records from nearly every settlement in the region, including Rio Grande, Colônia, Yapeyú, La Cruz, Santo Domingo Soriano, and Santa Fe; at times, authorities even institutionalized annual payments.[61] Moreover, when French and British traders approached the coast in the late seventeenth and early eighteenth centuries, Minuanes in particular were often present to exchange cattle and leather for other goods. When taken collectively, these transactions demonstrate a frequent, if not steady, supply of external goods acquired by individual tolderías.

Payments to tolderías varied and almost never appeared itemized in account books, making it impossible to trace any specific flow of goods. Still, administrative correspondence and reports reveal that yerba maté, tobacco, aguardiente, fabrics, hats, staffs, swords, knives, firearms, and sugar were common gifts from imperial and ecclesiastical agents to tolderías. Without knowing the quantity of goods procured by tolderías, it is difficult to surmise their intention in any specific transaction. Indeed, many payments by colonial officials appear to have been symbolic, especially when given in exchange for safe passage or protection. These payments were generally in smaller amounts and directed at caciques themselves. For the caciques, they likely signified recognition by a settlement of the caciques' authority. Thus, when representatives from Laguna offered payment to Minuán caciques in exchange for the ability to settle near Rio Grande, the caciques had the freedom to reject their offer.[62] They had no physical need for the items that Portuguese settlers possessed, but the caciques wanted a level of payment that acknowledged their authority. Still, certain nonsymbolic trade goods flowed from settlements on the perimeter toward the interior. In their attack on Yapeyú's ranches in 1701, Guenoas used firearms acquired from the Portuguese in Colônia. Three years later, in an attack on Santo Domingo Soriano, they used guns acquired from both Colônia and the missions.[63]

The flow of external trade goods to the region's interior shaped relations among tolderías. As competing tolderías jockeyed for regional control and allegiances, the capacity to proffer demanded goods was a strategic advantage. This was evident in a conversation recorded in 1693 by Spanish captain Gabriel de Toledo. While making a journey from Corrientes to Colônia, Toledo came upon a Charrúa toldería, where he was received by a Spanish-speaking cacique named Francisco. Toledo asked Francisco for news on an ongoing conflict between his tolderías and their Guenoa enemies.[64] According to Toledo, Francisco lamented that his tolderías were "very concerned that [Guenoa Indians] will defeat and destroy us, now that they have become friends with the Portuguese settled in the Islands of San Gabriel [Colônia do Sacramento]." Given that the Charrúas and Guenoas were in a state of war and therefore not communicating with each other, Toledo asked how Francisco could possibly know of the Guenoas' alliance with the Portuguese settlers. The cacique replied that he had news from "other Indians on the frontier" between Charrúas and Guenoas: "Having seen them with several knives, beads, and other trade items, I asked them where they had acquired the said goods. They said to me that the Guenoas had provided them in abundance, along with rolled tobacco and several types of cloth."[65] Francisco explained that Guenoas acquired these items from the Portuguese in exchange for horses and meat, and he worried that this privileged trade position would enable the Guenoas to inflict damage on Charrúa tolderías.

In the competition between Charrúa and Guenoa caciques for the allegiance of tolderías wedged between them, territorial positioning was paramount. Despite internal conflicts and diversity, tolderías identified as Charrúa appeared more frequently along the west of the Río Uruguay, while those identified as Guenoa and Minuán tended to be to the east.[66] As each sought to expand its range of influence and control, Charrúa caciques and those farther east jockeyed to garner the support of tolderías situated between them (map 4). From Francisco's account, it appears that the two principal means of building such connections were military might and the provision of desired goods. For tolderías located between Charrúa, Guenoa, and Minuán geographic strongholds, this meant negotiating their position between the rival groups rather than competing directly against them. Guenoa tolderías had gained the upper hand over Charrúas in the provision of trade goods, and the linchpin of their success was their trade relationship with the Portuguese in Colônia. Positioned more toward the coast, Guenoas were able to integrate themselves into the Atlantic economy and thus provided goods that Charrúa tolderías could not. In the same investigation that produced Gabriel de Toledo's account, other deponents testified that Guenoa tolderías were trading cows and horses in Colônia for tobacco, knives, sugar, and cloth.[67] While Charrúa tolderías had access to tobacco and knives through their relationships with Santa Fe, Corrientes, or the missions, they likely could not provide the same range of goods as their Guenoa rivals. Recognizing the utilitarian and symbolic value of such items, Francisco and other Charrúa caciques found themselves outmatched in the competition over intermediate tolderías.

Given the advantage that Guenoas held because of their relationship with Colônia, it is unsurprising that over the next few decades other tolderías sought to establish direct partnerships with Portuguese officials there. By 1703, Colônia's governor, Sebastião Xavier da Veiga Cabral, reported positive relations with Yaros, Guaraní, Serranos, Chanás, Bohanes, and Charrúas, in addition to those already established with Guenoas.[68] By circumventing Guenoa intermediaries, other tolderías could access valuable trade goods and strengthen their position. These tolderías sought similar partnerships throughout the region. Charrúa tolderías already possessed long-standing commercial relations with Santa Fe and Corrientes, but those wedged between

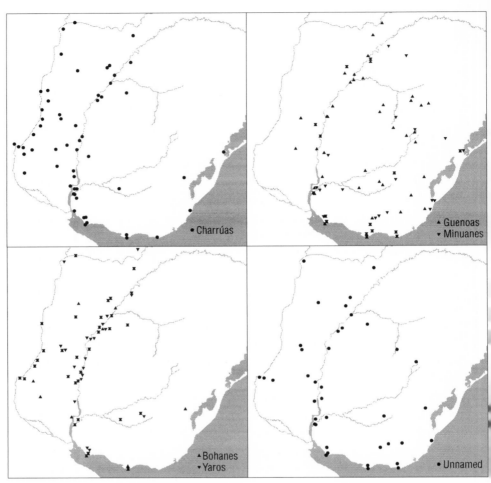

MAP 4 Reported toldería locations by ethnonym, 1675–1750. This map uses the same data as Map 2, filtering and stylizing it according to the ethnonyms used in historical records. Colonial writers tended to identify tolderías west of the Río Uruguay as Charrúa, those east of the river as Guenoa or Minuán, and those in between as Yaro or Bohan. Outliers, such as Charrúas along the Atlantic coast, likely derive from the ambiguous spatial knowledge of colonial writers rather than the presence of tolderías identified as such.

Charrúas and Guenoas did not have the same territorial advantage. They instead pursued trade with travelers up and down the Río Uruguay, acquiring such items as tobacco, bread, yerba maté, knives, pins, and metal fishhooks in exchange for horses.[69] These commercial ties allowed individual tolderías to maintain their livelihoods without submitting to the hierarchical relations that others sought to establish.

Mutual Interests in a Multipolar World

The perpetual competition among tolderías and settlements generated a multipolar world in which no single group was able to assert unilateral dominance. In this context, local arrangements frequently outweighed imperial or ethnic allegiances. Individual settlements and tolderías continually sought to establish bonds with others that shared similar interests. These pacts tended to be short lived, as the plurality of local aims and constant changes in territorial conditions simultaneously produced new opportunities and points of conflict. While scholars have traditionally sought to explain these trends in terms of allegiances between ethnicities and empires, they are better understood as the negotiation of shared or competing interests between individual settlements and tolderías.[70] Whether for access to resources and trade goods or for defense, settlements and tolderías developed fragile relations of mutual dependency in the face of a profusion of competitors.

Relations between Santa Fe and neighboring tolderías led by the Yasú family demonstrate how interests could align. Juan, Miguel, and Pedro Yasú were well-known Charrúa caciques who positioned their tolderías across the Río Paraná from Santa Fe during the seventeenth and early eighteenth centuries, forging commercial ties with the city. In exchange for weapons, horses, and foodstuffs, the caciques supplied captives, many of whom were also Charrúas. Santa Fe's participation in this trade also underscored the primacy of local relations, as their purchase of Indigenous captives defied imperial prohibitions.[71] This relationship extended beyond trade; both sides came to each other's aid in times of strife. In 1710, amid conflict with Abipones and Mocovíes from the west, Santa Fe found itself reduced to the limits of its city walls and depended on peace with Charrúas for survival. Five years later, its city council attempted to thwart an expedition ordered from Buenos Aires against Charrúa tolderías in the area and offered refuge to the Yasús and their kin. In fact, when the expedition finally came upon several tolderías, the tolderías were on ranches operated by residents of Santa Fe. Maintaining these local bonds also entailed enacting justice against one's own kin. In 1713, when a Charrúa attacked and injured a boy from Santa Fe, Juan Yasú wrote to the city council and promised that if the boy died, he would take the life of the attacker.[72]

Farther north, residents of Corrientes and other Charrúa tolderías demonstrated similar bonds. This tendency toward local allegiance also manifested itself in other settlements in the region. During investigations of a rebellion in Paraguay in the late 1720s, deponents from Corrientes accused Jesuits and Guaraní of abducting Charrúa women and children while Charrúa men were working in some of the city's ranches. The declarants also complained that the missions' aggression came at a moment in which Corrientes was at peace with local Charrúas, relying on them for livestock, river crossings, and cattle-based products.[73] Corrientes was eventually able to restore relations with the tolderías, and thereafter, their relationship contrasted sharply to that between the tolderías and the missions, whom the Charrúas prevented from slaughtering cattle.[74]

These bonds of local interdependency were perhaps most evident in Colônia. From its founding in 1680, Colônia served as the farthest Portuguese settlement in the extreme south of Brazil. Across the river from Buenos Aires and separated from the rest of Brazil by Jesuit missions, Colônia's inhabitants relied heavily on local tolderías for their survival. From the beginning, they offered payments to tolderías in an effort to win their support before Spain had the chance to do the same. These pacts consistently proved beneficial to Colônia, whether to gain advance warning of Spanish and Jesuit-Guaraní military movements or for access to the countryside and its resources.[75] As the years passed and the Spanish attempted to blockade Colônia, the plaza's relationship with tolderías became essential for the sustenance of its residents. Accordingly, in a letter written in 1715, Spanish officials in Buenos Aires lamented the impossibility of permanently unseating the Portuguese from Colônia, given their relationship with Charrúa, Minuán, and other tolderías. If these ties were not somehow broken, Buenos Aires feared that Colônia would be able to gain access to the river's entire northern shoreline and all its major ports.[76]

Consequently, one of Buenos Aires's principal strategies for breaking the Portuguese hold on Colônia was to curry the favor of Minuán tolderías. From the first years of Colônia's foundation, Spanish troops reached out to tolderías in order to convince them not to trade with the plaza or guide its inhabitants to local cattle ranges.[77] By 1705, Spain was able to take control of Colônia, but the Treaty of Utrecht returned it to the Portuguese in 1715. During the following decade, Buenos Aires sent no less than six commissions to garner support from Minuán caciques. In each instance, representatives of the Spanish governor offered payments of yerba maté, tobacco, and other goods in the hope that the Minuanes would cease to provide a lifeline to Colônia.[78] This strategy was often unsuccessful, given that the Portuguese opened their coffers as well; but in the race to secure Minuán favor, Spanish authorities occasionally gained the upper hand. In 1737, a Portuguese military officer reported that the countryside was full of Minuanes, who "communicate with the Portuguese and with the Spanish, whichever provides a better coexistence. . . . At present, they are found to be friends of the Spanish because the countryside is full of them impeding the Portuguese from taking cattle to Colônia."[79] With Colônia, and later Montevideo, hanging in the balance, both empires recognized that without Minuanes on their side, they would never be able to establish a foothold on the Río de la Plata's northern shore. This conflict frequently gave Minuanes the upper hand in pact making, and savvy caciques continually played one side off the other in order to extract greater payments.[80]

While the Portuguese and the Spanish jockeyed for control of Colônia, Charrúa, Minuán, Guenoa, Bohan, and Yaro tolderías sought to use the plaza as a means to gain an upper hand on their Native competitors and as a counterbalance to the settlements of their various locales. After the Battle of the Yí, for example, numerous tolderías sought refuge in Colônia while they recovered and regrouped. Although the plaza's residents were wary of taking on refugees, its leadership was cognizant that developing ties with tolderías was in its best interest and offered the tolderías 3,000 cruzados worth of goods.[81] Tolderías sought similar refuge in settlements throughout the region, generally remaining in the proximity of a particular locale for a number of months. While official records do not always provide a clear picture of the motivations that tolderías had for their brief stays, it is most likely that these respites related to wars with other mobile peoples or a seasonal lack of resources. Municipal governments were generally able to provide security over their locale, and settlements at times had cattle reserves that they could offer. This occurred in 1748 and 1749, as numerous tolderías simultaneously sought refuge in settlements throughout the region. During those years, a conflict between Charrúa and Minuán tolderías seems to have spilled over to the entirety of the region's countryside. Charrúas appeared in Yapeyú and the Spanish blockades of Colônia, while Minuanes sought refuge in Rio Grande. Each group cited the aggression of the other as its primary motive for seeking shelter, and they requested clothing and sustenance for the upcoming season. Each settlement acquiesced.[82]

This strategy of using settlements as temporary refuges also explains why tolderías established small hamlets, known as *reducciones*, with missionaries from time to time (map 2).[83] Such arrangements provided missions the opportunity to pursue spiritual goals and strategic alliances, and at the same time offered tolderías relief from their external conflicts. During the latter part of the seventeenth century and into the eighteenth, a number of reducciones appeared, only to dissolve within several months or years. These included San Andrés (Guenoas/Yaros, 1657), Jesús María (Guenoas, 1682), San Joaquín

(Charrúas/Yaros, 1690–93), and San Joseph (Charrúas, 1743). Each of these reducciones operated as a distinct settlement; however, they were all near either San Borja or Yapeyú. Few records exist of these sites, but since provisions would have been necessary to sustain them, close proximity to established missions made logical sense. Furthermore, if these arrangements came about in moments of duress for the tolderías, they would likely have needed to tap into existing missions' reserves.

In some instances, the urgency of a given tolderías's need caused it to latch onto an already existing mission rather than found one separately. This occurred in the Franciscan mission of Santo Domingo Soriano, which Bohan tolderías used during the summer of 1702 to 1703 as a refuge. Arriving in November 1702, the Bohanes sought protection from Minuán tolderías, which the mission's administrators willingly provided in the hope that their guests would eventually form a reducción of their own. By April 1703, however, local officials learned that the Bohanes had not only reconciled with their Minuán counterparts but made plans to leave the mission and take a number of its women with them. In response, the mission's authorities proposed founding a new settlement nearby for the Bohanes, in order to separate them from Soriano's inhabitants. Eventually, the Bohanes absconded, leaving Soriano's bewildered administrators to complain that the Bohanes had done so "for their own motives, without cause, reason, or pretext."[84] Despite this accusation of irrationality, the Bohanes' reconciliation with the Minuanes would have made settlement at Soriano unnecessary, and Minuán tolderías were a stronger ally than were Franciscan friars.

Other reducciones appear to have existed as well, though the scarcity of source materials and the ephemerality of such sites make a precise estimate elusive. In a map drawn in 1749, Jesuit Joseph Quiroga marked a reducción that had been established with Minuán tolderías near the headwaters of the Río Negro. Due to the newness of the establishment, however, Quiroga noted that he was unable to locate it with precision, and the reducción is absent from maps produced in subsequent years.[85] Two years before Quiroga drew his map, Jesuit José Cardiel had lamented the failure of a Guenoa reducción along the Río Uruguay, suggesting that despite their best efforts, the priests had been unable to overcome the Guenoas' purported barbarism. In the end, the Guenoa tolderías left the reducción and returned to their kin in the countryside.[86] Considering these brief references alongside an awareness of the tangible benefits that temporary settlements provided to mobile peoples, it is possible that more reducciones appeared than have been accounted for. The brevity of their existence produced a scant paper trail yet was indicative of tolderías' broader patterns of mobility. Some may have already been paraderos along the tolderías' seasonal itineraries, which would explain both the tolderías' openness to remaining for several months and their eventual abandonment of the locale.

Conclusion

In April 1731, the governor of Buenos Aires, Bruno de Zavala, penned a letter to the Council of the Indies (*Consejo de Indias*) in Spain in which he contrasted Montevideo's situation with that of Colônia. The Minuanes' blockade on Montevideo had confronted the city with the need to ration food among its residents; it had also prevented the Spanish from producing the fifty thousand leather hides it had arranged to sell under the *real asiento* of Great Britain. Meanwhile, the Portuguese in Colônia not only had access to the riches of the countryside but were able to travel freely between their plaza and other parts of Brazil to the north.[87] Time was short and the stakes were high, so Zavala reached out to Jesuit authorities for aid, which resulted in Miguel Ximénez's and Francisco de Borja's journey in August of that year. He also turned to a less expected ally. While Ximénez was pleading his case to Guenoa caciques in the north, Zavala began providing regular payments to Charrúa tolderías in exchange for their aid if peace negotiations broke down. If the Minuanes and Guenoas refused to negotiate, three hundred Charrúas would join soldiers from Buenos Aires to break the blockade.[88] In the end, peace prevailed. Following their meeting with Ximénez, nine Guenoa caciques traveled to the tolderías near Montevideo; soon after, the Minuanes parleyed with their Spanish counterparts. In March 1732, the Spanish provided 600 pesos' worth of gifts to the caciques, and the Minuanes agreed to allow Montevideo's inhabitants to return to their ranches. The caciques refused to return the five hundred horses that they had confiscated, and Montevideo accepted the loss.[89]

The resolution of the conflict between Minuán tolderías and the Spanish in Montevideo was not the triumph of Spanish diplomacy or military might but rather a typical episode that reinforced broader territorial dynamics.[90] In accepting a peace agreement in which they offered unilateral payment to Minuanes for access to the countryside, Montevideo's city council acknowledged the tolderías' territorial control. In seeking aid from the missions and from Charrúa tolderías, the Spanish governor sought to build alliances across imperial and ethnic divisions. For their part, Minuán and Guenoa caciques found a solution that recognized their authority in the countryside without forcing them to engage in further combat. Montevideo posed little threat alone, but united forces from Buenos Aires, the missions, and Charrúa tolderías would have been a formidable foe. Both sides also recognized the benefits of mutual exchange, and the pact included promises to reopen commerce between Minuanes and Montevideo and to allow the Minuanes to enter the plaza to sell goods.

Cognizant of the control that tolderías exerted over the Río de la Plata's countryside, Portuguese and Spanish administrators were unsatisfied with their own positions. Positive relations with tolderías allowed them access to the resources that they needed, yet neither side could gain the upper hand on their imperial rival. Furthermore, the interposing settlements of Colônia and Montevideo prevented either empire from acquiring legal possession of the region, as they undermined the possibility of contiguous territorial claims. This structural issue grew increasingly apparent as decades passed, and both empires deemed it unsustainable. As a result, the Spanish and Portuguese developed competing discourses of regional possession that belied the territorial practices in which they engaged on a daily basis. This dissonance between territorial discourse and territorial practice would be the motor behind the radical changes that occurred during the eighteenth century's middle decades.

CHAPTER TWO

Projecting Possession

In October 1703, the Portuguese governor of Colônia and the Spanish governor of Buenos Aires launched dueling investigations. One month earlier, Colônia's chaplain, Manuel González, had been run through with lances on a ranch outside the Portuguese plaza. Portuguese investigators determined that the perpetrators were one of three groups that had been in the area at the time of the priest's death: a Spanish troop from Santa Fe, Charrúas, or Bohanes. Spanish investigators were able to account for the whereabouts of the first two, but they could not exonerate the Bohanes.[1] Both governors therefore turned to discussing whether or not Bohanes were vassals of the Spanish crown. Colônia's governor, Sebastião Xavier da Veiga Cabral, argued that they were, since several Bohán tolderías had previously established themselves next to Santo Domingo Soriano (hereafter Soriano), a Franciscan mission sponsored by the Spanish crown, where they were baptized. He therefore demanded reparations from Buenos Aires's governor, Alonso Juan de Valdez y Inclán.

Inclán dismissed Cabral's demands for reparations, yet he was careful in his response. He could have denied Bohanes' subjecthood to the Spanish crown. Indeed, deponents questioned by Spanish investigators had pointed out that the tolderías had only gone to Soriano to seek refuge from Minuanes and had left by the time Soriano's officials went to propose they settle there. Another option would have been to blame other tolderías instead, as numerous depositions claimed that Minuanes, Yaros, or other Indigenous nations (*naciones*) were responsible. In their estimation, none of these tolderías were subject to the Spanish crown, the Catholic faith, or laws of reason, since they had no fixed settlements.[2] In an internal report, Inclán agreed that no Spanish subject was among the guilty, but he chose a different line of argumentation in his response to Cabral. There, he affirmed that Bohanes were Spanish subjects but added the caveat that they were "not obedient because they go about the countryside untamed and idle." Since Bohanes were "vassals of the King that go about untamed, and not having a fixed location," the Spanish were under no obligation to remunerate the Portuguese for their losses.[3] Inclán then accused Cabral of selectively defining tolderías' vassalage according to Portugal's immediate needs. He claimed that when seeking reparations for González's death, Cabral deemed tolderías to be Spanish subjects, but when it fit Colônia's needs he had been quick to claim them as Portuguese vassals instead.

Inclán's discursive gymnastics are unsurprising, given that Portugal and Spain were embroiled in a decades-long dispute over legal possession of the Río de la Plata, and tolderías were at the center. Both Iberian empires advanced land claims beyond their settlements in the region by declaring sovereignty over tolderías, who controlled the countryside, and González's death had occurred beyond Colônia's immediate jurisdiction. For Inclán to suggest that Bohanes were not vassals would be to acknowledge a lack of Spanish territorial possession, but to claim their vassalage would require him to accept responsibility for their actions. In admonishing Cabral, he demonstrated that the same was true for Portugal. Inclán therefore labeled the Bohanes "disobedient vassals," a designation he extended to all tolderías in the region due to their mobile lifestyles. He stated that these "barbarian bandits" were "subjects that have not been able to be subjected to obedience," thereby denying any accountability for their actions.[4] To bolster his claim of Spanish territorial authority, he sent a troop to surveil the coastline from Colônia eastward to Maldonado. This gesture was strictly performative, however, as the Bohanes had been last seen traveling northwestward toward Corrientes, and the troop maintained its distance at each sign of tolderías.[5]

Portugal and Spain's perpetual conflict over legal possession of the Río de la Plata was inextricably tied to tolderías in the region. In a context in which effective imperial authority was limited to settlements, Iberian diplomats and Ibero-American administrators projected dominion over the countryside via an array of juridical arguments. Most notably, they proclaimed lordship over tolderías in order to make claims to their lands via proxy and sought to exhibit tolderías' subjecthood via baptism and the formation of reducciones. Such claims to sovereignty expressed in bilateral debates between the two Iberian empires were incongruous with the materiality of local territorial relations. Tolderías controlled rural spaces, exhibited decentralized political authority, maintained mobile lifestyles, developed bonds with multiple settlements across empires, and even traded with foreign ships. Events like González's death revealed this dissonance because they forced imperial authorities to selectively ascribe ethnic identities to tolderías and adopt elaborate explanations of their relationships with them. During the early eighteenth century, however, Portuguese and Spanish agents began to make two discursive shifts: they advanced claims to territorial exclusivity, and they replaced relational claims of territorial possession with the valorization of mapping. This transformation ushered in new patterns of interimperial and interethnic engagement by midcentury and would be entrenched thereafter.

Strategic Settlements and Juridical Jockeying

Beginning in 1680 with the Portuguese founding of Colônia, the two Iberian crowns began to jockey for access to and possession of the Río de la Plata's countryside.[6] They deployed armies of soldiers and jurists, equipped with firearms and quills, in an attempt to solidify their claims and eventually gain exclusivity. These individuals produced myriad diplomatic treatises and war reports that made the case for their respective crown's legitimate possession of the region, yet both sides ultimately depended on positive relations with tolderías in order to sustain their coastal or riverine footholds and access the countryside they claimed on paper. This incongruity between juridical aims and material relations engendered a perpetual struggle to claim possession through discursive acrobatics and strategic settlement. Iberian diplomats justified their territorial claims through a range of logics, but over time, they tended toward projecting possession from coastal settlements to the vast countryside. By occupying key entry points to the continental interior and then demonstrating that independent tolderías were imperial subjects, the dueling monarchies could construct broader claims to the region as a whole.[7]

Colônia's founding was a watershed moment that linked the Río de la Plata to global debates over legitimate territorial possession. It ushered in dueling logics of possession between Spain and Portugal and a constant feedback loop between juridical claims and physical settlements. In particular, it represented the first direct challenge in the region to the 1494 Treaty of Tordesillas, in favor of possession through settlement. From Colônia's founding to the 1750 Treaty of Madrid, both Iberian crowns established strategic settlements in the region in order to advance territorial claims. They chose sites not only for their sustainability and material benefits but also as a means to fortify their particular juridical arguments. Colônia enabled the Portuguese to reinvigorate maritime trading links to the Río de la Plata that had been established during the Iberian Union (1580–1640) and disrupted by its dissolution.[8] In particular, traders from Rio de Janeiro sought to use Colônia as a hub to smuggle African captives into Buenos Aires and to access silver transported from Spanish silver mines in Upper Peru. But Colônia was also part of a Portuguese effort at territorial occupation that included the extension of the bishopric of Rio de Janeiro to the Río de la Plata in 1667.[9] The new plaza permitted Portugal to claim joint navigation rights to the Río de la

Plata and access to the terrestrial resources between it and the rest of Brazil. New international standards for possession and new geographical knowledge would guide the locations of subsequent settlements, which in turn would shape the historical narratives jurists and negotiators would use to fortify their territorial assertions.

Situating Colônia's founding in a longer history of settlement and juridical jockeying helps bring this dynamic into focus. Upon Christopher Columbus's return from his first voyage to the Americas, Spain and Portugal sought rules to govern which crown could claim overseas possessions. The earliest iterations of this effort included the 1493 papal bull Inter Caetera and the Treaty of Tordesillas the following year. Each established an imaginary meridian dividing the Atlantic Ocean to provide Spain and Portugal monopolies of access to separate spheres of influence, while the 1529 Treaty of Zaragoza extended the Tordesillas meridian around the globe into the Pacific Ocean. From the beginning, however, shifting geographical knowledge and settlement patterns muddled the situation. The Tordesillas accord established its dividing line via a nautical measurement—370 leagues west of the Cabo Verde islands—that ignored the earth's curvature, thus impeding cosmographers' ability to demarcate it as a geographical meridian. The ambiguity of the meridian was exacerbated by Portugal's and Spain's unique standards for calculating leagues, their distinct starting points for the zero meridian, and the treaty's failure to specify from which island in the Cabo Verde archipelago the measurement should be made. Despite the treaty's original stipulations, no collaborative Luso-Hispanic demarcation ever occurred to resolve this uncertainty, and the more that navigators charted coastlines and cosmographers improved global measurements, the more conflicts arose.[10]

Meanwhile, as Iberian vassals traveled abroad, they developed corridors and enclaves of jurisdictional authority for their crown, and imperial jurisdictions occasionally overlapped one another. The constant flow of soldiers, settlers, and priests, each of whom served as the physical embodiment of Iberian sovereignty, coupled with persistent efforts to claim Indigenous vassalage and lands via conversion, raiding, and pact making, resulted in complex human geographies that could not be easily untangled.[11] This phenomenon did not come to a head in the Río de la Plata until Colônia's founding, but its articulation in the region was influenced by earlier conflicts farther north and across the Atlantic. In the early seventeenth century, Spanish settlers and Spanish-sponsored Jesuits from Asunción and Córdoba competed with Portuguese-sponsored slave-raiding frontierspeople (*bandeirantes*) from São Paulo for the souls and labor of Guaraní living in regions known as Itatín, Guayrá, and Tape.[12]

Bandeirante raids led Jesuits and Guaraní mission dwellers to evacuate all three regions, but the eventual arming of the missions' inhabitants in 1641 prohibited further Portuguese advances. A de facto division emerged along the Río Uruguay, with missions to the west and bandeirantes to the east, and the river would become a significant baseline for each side as they articulated future claims of possession in the Río de la Plata.[13]

In the wake of this conflict, European affairs produced direct challenges to the Treaty of Tordesillas and generated new means of claiming possession. Whereas the Iberian Union had blurred the lines between Spanish and Portuguese overseas dominions and brought agents from each empire into the same spaces, its schism required a new articulation of territorial difference. Spain continued to rely on the Tordesillas meridian to justify its claims, while Portugal developed two counterarguments. First, Portuguese diplomats used the ambiguity of the 1494 accord to suggest that the line should be drawn farther west than Spain had imagined it.[14] Second, mapmakers and jurists suggested that Brazil represented a continental entity different from the rest of South America. This geographical concept, known as the Brazil Island (*Ilha Brasil*), purported that a vast waterway divided the two realms; it began in a large lagoon known as the *Laguna de los Xarayes*, draining northward to the Amazon River and southward to the Río de la Plata (figures 2 and 3).[15] These arguments dovetailed with the end of Europe's Thirty Years' War, as the 1648 Treaty of Westphalia challenged the legitimacy of the papal bulls upon which the Treaty of Tordesillas was based. The Protestant Reformation led northern Europe to reject the authority of the Pope; accordingly, the Catholic arguments of proselytization employed by Spain to justify its dominions also came under attack.[16]

Given persistent challenges to the Treaty of Tordesillas, the notion of territorial possession through papal donation carried less weight over time, and by the early eighteenth century, even Spanish jurists turned to new arguments to support their claims. Iberian crowns and their competitors began to rely on the occupation or utilization of particular lands in order to gain international recognition of their claims. The founding of Colônia thus represented a Portuguese effort to solidify its claim to lands north and east of the Río de la Plata estuary. Although Portuguese diplomats drew on the natural limits of a Brazil Island and the ambiguity of the Tordesillas meridian to justify founding the plaza, its establishment prompted them to advance claims of possession through settlement (*uti possidetis*) as well.[17] Missionaries and Spanish administrators responded with a flurry of strategic settlements of their own. Jesuits ventured back across the Río Uruguay and founded seven

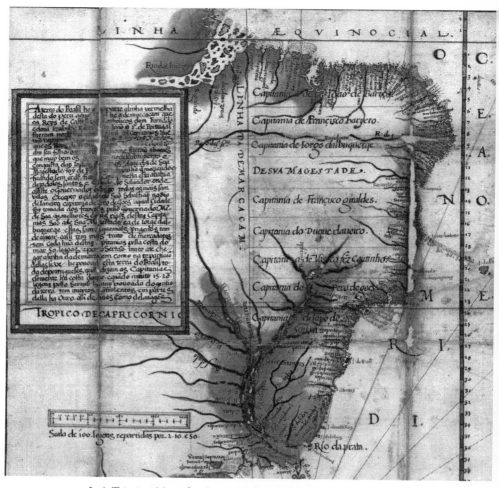

FIGURE 2 Luís Teixeira, *Mapa das Capitanias hereditárias*, c. 1574. Teixeira, a Portuguese cosmographer, aligned the Tordesillas meridian with the mouths of the Amazon River and the Río de la Plata, a gesture repeated by sixteenth- and seventeenth-century mapmakers. The captaincies drawn from the Atlantic coast to the Tordesillas meridian represent projections of access rights on an unconquered continental interior. Biblioteca da Ajuda.

new missions, the Siete Pueblos Orientales (hereafter Siete Pueblos), and the Franciscan mission of Soriano (under the Spanish crown) was moved to the river's eastern bank. In subsequent decades, Spain and Portugal brought settlers from the Canary Islands and the Azores, respectively, to establish new coastal settlements.[18]

Settlements alone were nevertheless insufficient for claiming possession. Rather, they served as one of many kinds of evidence that jurists could draw

FIGURE 3 Willem Blaeu, *Americae nova tabula*, 1665. Blaeu's map, which included the entire Western Hemisphere, demonstrates the concept of a Brazil Island. Blaeu, a Dutch cartographer, discarded the Tordesillas meridian but connected the Río de la Plata with the Amazon and Maranhão rivers to divide Brazil from the rest of South America. Wikimedia Commons.

on to develop arguments of natural or historical rights. Eighteenth-century advocates for Spanish or Portuguese possession of the Río de la Plata thus harked back to early expeditions to the region that carried the banner of their crown, pointing to vestiges of short-lived settlements and the erection of crosses or stone markers by travelers as proof of territorial possession. Diplomats scoured earlier treaties and maps for words or images that would justify their current territorial claims.[19] Their arguments differed in evidence and conclusions yet shared the common trope of stringing together instances of travel or settlement to argue that the other side had impinged on their rightful lands. Spanish advocates pointed to the foundation of Colônia as an egregious

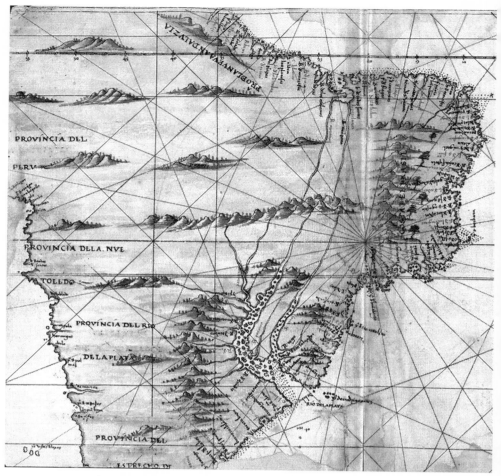

FIGURE 4 Alonso de Santa Cruz, *Islario general de todas las islas del mundo*, [1500s]. Santa Cruz, a Sevillian cosmographer at Spain's Casa de Contratación, labeled five provinces in his map: Nueva Andalucia, Peru, Nueva Toledo, Río de la Plata, and the Estrecho de Magallanes. Each was divided by lines of latitude and extended eastward to the Atlantic Ocean or Brazil. These provinces deviated from the territorial units issued in Spain's original South American charters. Biblioteca Nacional de España.

infraction by the Portuguese, while writers sympathetic to Portuguese interests made the same point with regard to the Siete Pueblos.[20] These contradictory claims highlight the ambiguity of what constituted an act of possession or evidence of first arrival.

To understand the parallel juridical narratives promulgated by Lisbon and Madrid, it is necessary to consider not only what constituted an act of posses-

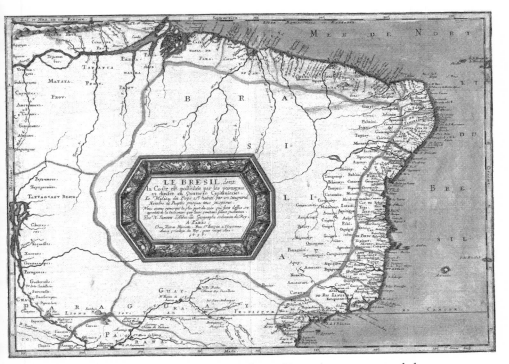

FIGURE 5 Nicolas Sanson, *Le Bresil*, 1656. Whereas Teixeira's 1574 map extended Portuguese captaincies in Brazil to the center of the South American continent, Sanson's map acknowledged their limited reach by restricting them to the Atlantic and Caribbean coastlines. Courtesy of the John Carter Brown Library at Brown University.

sion but also how far territorial possession actually reached. It was not until the mid-eighteenth century that Enlightenment ideas of bordered provinces began to supplant notions of enclaves and corridors. Previously, the establishment of a settlement did not necessarily imply possession of the adjacent countryside or all of the lands bounded by a geographical feature or a line on a map. Sixteenth- and seventeenth-century charters from Patagonia to the Massachusetts Bay Colony used lines of latitude to incentivize colonial expansion, but these crown-issued rights transformed as new ones were forged and were predicated on imperial possession acquired from other means.[21] In the case of South America, both Portuguese donatary captaincies (*capitanias donatarias*) (figure 2) and Spanish charters (*capitulaciones*) (figure 4) extended to the Tordesillas meridian but were effectively restricted to the coastlines.[22] In 1656, French royal geographer Nicolás Sanson identified fourteen Portuguese captaincies along the South American coast, presenting the rest of Brazil as "inhabited by a great number of [Indigenous] people, almost all unknown [to Europeans]" (figure 5). Similarly, one Jesuit writer remarked, "The Spaniards pretend that all of South America, Brazil excepted, is subject to the King of Spain . . . but strictly speaking, the Sea-coasts [and isolated inland towns] are the most they possess," while "Portuguese dominions reach nowhere above 100 leagues within land. The rest of [Brazil] is still in possession of the ancient owners."[23] Furthermore, since sovereignty flowed through interpersonal relationships rather than through rigid territorial jurisdictions, the idea of contiguous territories divided by precise borderlines was not yet an operative legal concept. In borderland spaces, subjects of a particular crown could establish settlements that interposed those of another, as occurred in the Río de la Plata.

The case of Colônia illustrates how these logics changed. Prior to the 1750 Treaty of Madrid, diplomats and administrators did not imagine the Río de la Plata as a territorial state in the modern sense. Spanish settlements competed with one another for access to the countryside and even erected stone markers to distinguish their jurisdictional limits.[24] It was also unclear whether Colônia represented the terrestrial extension of Brazil or an isolated enclave. The 1681 Provisional Treaty of Lisbon sought to resolve this ambiguity by limiting the reach of Colônia's territorial exclusivity to the range of a cannon shot fired from the plaza. This measure, much like a foot, league, or musket shot, was an estimate, since the distance of cannon fire depended on the size of the ball and the angle of its trajectory, and its imprecision was discussed regularly during jurisdictional disputes.[25] More importantly, the concept of a cannon shot signified that Colônia was an enclave and that its establishment along the Río de la Plata's northern coast, known as the Banda Norte, did not give Portugal exclusive access to the countryside. To formalize this point, the treaty's seventh article stated that subjects of the two crowns would share access to the countryside surrounding Colônia and would share in its resources. Diplomats and administrators continually referred to this idea over the course of the following decades, marking a clear distinction between the jurisdiction of the plaza and the shared right to access resources in the countryside (figure 6).[26]

During the early decades of the eighteenth century, coexistence in the Río de la Plata became increasingly problematic for Spanish and Portuguese administrators. The ambiguities of their territorial possession and the limits of their territorial control enabled third parties to establish themselves along the coast, particularly after the 1715 Treaty of Utrecht, which solidified the standard of uti possidetis. While the Portuguese occupied Colônia, French traders formed direct relationships with Minuanes and Guenoas near the coastline's other natural harbors—Mondevideo, Maldonado, and Castillos Grande—

FIGURE 6 Rodrigo Annes de Sá Almeida e Menezes, *Demonstración Convincente de la Extensión del Territorio,* [1725]. This map, which was part of a compendium of documents that Sá Almeida e Menezes compiled regarding Colônia, captured the competing Iberian interpretations of the Tordesillas meridian. Portugal located the meridian west of Colônia, reinforcing the notion of the Brazil Island, while Spain marked it east of Rio Grande, challenging the nascent Portuguese settlement there. The map also represented the logic of the 1681 Treaty of Lisbon by distinguishing the plaza of Colônia from the adjacent countryside and contouring the limits of shared territorial access. Biblioteca Nacional de Portugal.

seeking known resources (cattle) and suspected resources (mines).[27] The first reference to this trade occurred in 1683, and over the next forty years, at least thirteen reported incidents emerged of French traders slaughtering cattle or trading for leather with Minuanes, Guenoas, and other tolderías (table 1). One Portuguese official even reported in 1722 that Maldonado had previously operated as a French port.[28] In response to the French presence, officials from Colônia and Buenos Aires planned new settlements at the Banda

TABLE 1 Reported trade between tolderías and French ships

Year	Places	Ship, Captain	Partner
1683	Montevideo	El Señalado Armas de Francia, La Visconte	Guenoas, "other allies"
1706	Maldonado	Nantes, D'Escaseau	[-]
1706*	Islas de Flores (Montevideo)	Falmouth of St. Malo	[-]
1707*	Montevideo	[-]	Guenoas
1708	Maldonado	Atlas	[-]
1717	Montevideo, Maldonado, Rio Grande, Santa Catarina	Petit Danican	Minuanes
1717	Maldonado, Isla de Flores (Montevideo)	2 ships	Minuanes
1720	Maldonado, Castillos Grande	4 ships, Étienne Moreau	Guenoas
1720	Maldonado	[-]	Minuanes
1721	Castillos Grande, Maldonado, Montevideo	2 ships	"gentio livre"
1721	Montevideo, Maldonado	[-]	Charrúas, Bohanes, Yaros, others
1721	Montevideo, Maldonado	[-]	Minuanes
1722	Banda Norte	[-]	Minuanes

*The 1706 and 1707 exchanges in Montevideo may have been one and the same. Sources: AGI, Escribanía, 884 (Buenos Aires, 1683-11-08), cited in López Mazz and Bracco, Minuanos, 38–39; Betagh, Voyage Round the World, 329–30, 336–38; Mémoire pour servir d'addition, 24; Vianna, Jesuítas e Bandeirantes no Uruguai, 237–39; AGI, Escribanía, 877A, fs. 10v–59; RAH, Mata Linares, t. 102, fs. 168–69, 355–56; Coni, Historia de las vaquerías, 68; IHGB, Conselho Ultramarino, Arq. 1.1.25, fs. 43–52, 59v–62, 280–90; Lozano, Historia de la conquista, 3:472–76; IHGB, Conselho Ultramarino, Arq. 1.2.21, fs. 180–81v; AGI, Charcas, 264 (Buenos Aires, 1721-08-31); AGI, Charcas, 221 (Buenos Aires, 1721-09-12); Ponce de León, "Minuanes o Guenoas," 29.

Norte's principal harbors, but more often they sought to broker deals with tolderías. Occasionally these pacts proved successful, with individual caciques agreeing not only to avoid new trading partnerships but also to patrol the coast and report the presence of foreign ships.[29] Most often, the plurality of tolderías and their unique interests made agreements elusive. If French traders could provide more attractive payments than their Portuguese or Spanish competitors, a toldería would have little incentive to forgo trade. A direct link to the Atlantic economy afforded caciques access to better returns on their hides and opportunities to obtain objects of material and symbolic value.

British ships also anchored along the coastline, using the ambiguity of possession as an avenue to access. While both Portugal and Spain considered unsanctioned foreign ships to be pirates, sailors could claim that they believed they were on the lands of the other crown and therefore beyond the offended party's jurisdiction, as John Bulkeley and John Cummins did in 1741.[30] Interlopers from other empires increased the Iberian crowns' desire for exclusivity over the countryside of the Banda Norte, as they feared that unsanctioned access would eventually produce foreign settlements.[31] Without legal exclusivity, neither side could issue secure land titles and thus advance regulated settlements far beyond the reach of their extant population centers. Nor could they restrict access to outsiders through juridical means. Ibero-American officials began to see territorial possession as less a question of legal access to resources and more a question of legal ownership of resources as property. Access permitted sharing, but ownership implied exclusivity.

Spanish authorities made the first efforts to gain exclusivity over the Banda Norte, employing both military and juridical tactics. They undertook numerous invasions to dislodge Portuguese settlers from Colônia, and between 1705 and 1715, they occupied the plaza. More often, however, the Spanish sought to blockade Colônia and contain Portuguese settlers within its stipulated limits. To this end, they established the guard post of San Juan and coordinated between settlements to extract livestock from Colônia's vicinity. While generally a wartime measure, the blockade became a mainstay by 1737.[32] The success of this effort required collaboration between various Spanish and missionary settlements, but it was also contingent on the continued favor of local tolderías. For that reason, Spanish-American administrators pursued deals with nearby caciques under which their tolderías would lend support to the Spanish or refuse aid to the Portuguese in Colônia. Such favor proved elusive, however, as it required continual gifting to caciques or forging kinship ties, and blockading forces occasionally skirmished with nearby tolderías. Portuguese administrators in Colônia offered payments and attempted to foster close ties to Minuán and Guenoa tolderías themselves, thereby maintaining a lifeline that the Spanish and Jesuit-Guaraní blockade could not prevent. Only on the few occasions when tolderías decided in favor of the Spanish did the Portuguese find themselves without recourse.[33]

If military might could not dislodge the Portuguese from Colônia, juridical measures could at least fix the limits of the plaza and contain settlers within it. Here, mapping was paramount. By the 1730s, the king of Spain had ordered the mapping of a clear division between the plaza and what lay beyond. All

Portuguese possessions outside the plaza's jurisdiction would be burned, its vassals would be sent back to the plaza, and Spanish sentinels would patrol the countryside to keep the population contained.[34] Divorcing Colônia from the countryside thus became a central strategy for Miguel Salcedo, the governor of Buenos Aires, and signified a clear rejection of the Treaty of Lisbon's logic of shared space in favor of Spanish exclusivity. This deviation from earlier policies incited a sharp rebuttal from Portuguese authorities in Colônia and culminated in war from 1735 to 1737.[35]

Possessing Maps

The eighteenth-century drive for territorial exclusivity in the Río de la Plata region and other overseas borderlands brought mapmaking to the forefront of territorial disputes. Professional engravers always held a role in interimperial debates over jurisdiction, but through the end of the seventeenth century, their principal aim was to compile travel accounts or navigation charts and project them onto the globe as a geographic whole. Wary of the circulation of detailed information regarding their foreign lands, Iberian diplomats often chose to withhold accounts of continental interiors from international debates.[36] However, as uti possidetis supplanted the Treaty of Tordesillas as the principal foundation for claiming territorial possession, on-the-ground mapping assumed new juridical value as a means to demonstrate one's own claims. Furthermore, advances in mapping technologies, such as gridded maps with accurate longitude or the ability to take measurements amid tree cover and uneven horizons, provided imperial authorities the opportunity to visualize continental interiors as never before. Rather than theorizing where dividing lines should run, mapmakers could directly observe, measure, and represent territorial features as a means to fortify their claims.

The competing arguments of territorial possession employed by Spain and Portugal generated parallel lineages of cartographic representation. Cartographers and engravers throughout Europe adopted one of two representations of Iberian claims to South America during the seven decades following Colônia's founding. London-based cartographer Herman Moll placed Brazil's southern limits as far north as São Paulo, harking back to earlier divisions between the Jesuit-Guaraní missions and Portuguese bandeirantes (figure 7). This placement of the border was also evident in the works of Dutch cartographers Joan Blaeu and Frederik de Wit, as well as in maps drawn by French royal geographers Nicolás and Guillaume Sanson. By contrast, French cartographer Guillaume de L'Isle depicted Brazilian territorial possession extending con-

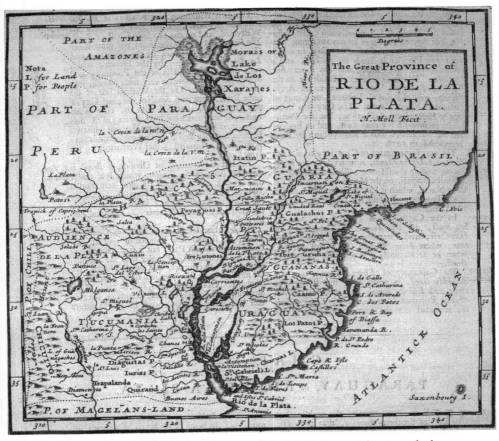

FIGURE 7 Herman Moll, *The Great Province of Rio de la Plata*, 1701. This map, which appeared within Moll's multivolume *A System of Geography*, followed seventeenth-century Dutch engravers in placing the interimperial division north of the Jesuit-Guaraní mission complex. Newberry Library.

tiguously to Colônia along a strip of land called the "King's Captaincy" (*Capitania del Rey*) (figure 8), a gesture repeated in the works of Nicolas de Fer, Johann Baptiste Homann, and others.[37] Whether favoring Portuguese or Spanish logics of possession, eighteenth-century maps were nonetheless incongruent with regional territorial conditions, as contemporary cartographic conventions struggled to account for interspersed settlements or shared territorial access. As engravers published maps based on written travel accounts, they generally assumed the completeness of territorial possession and drew imaginary lines to encompass the aggregated settlements founded by one crown or the other. This tension was perhaps most apparent in the work of

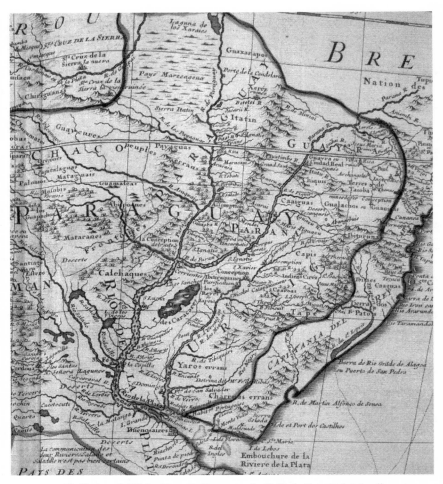

FIGURE 8 Guillaume de L'Isle, *Carte du Paraguay, du Chili, du Detroit de Magellan, etc.,* 1703. L'Isle's map, which included all of southern South America, was the first to include the Capitania del Rey. Newberry Library.

French geographer Jean Baptiste Bourguignon d'Anville. The 1737 version of his *Carte de L'Amérique Meridionale* (figure 9) represents Montevideo as an enclave amid contiguous Portuguese territories, while the 1748 version represents Colônia as an enclave within Spanish territories (figure 10).[38]

Amid this cartographic ambiguity, Spain and Portugal began in the 1730s to hire scientists to demarcate their remote borderlands. The Castilian crown concentrated its efforts in northern South America, supporting a French geodesic mission led by Charles Marie de la Condamine. The mission's principal aim was to measure the circumference of the globe along the equator, but La Conda-

FIGURE 9 Jean Baptiste Bourguignon D'Anville, *Carte de L'Amérique Meridionale*, 1737. This portion of D'Anville's continental-scale map separated Montevideo from the rest of Spain's South American claims, situating it instead within the same stretch of Portuguese lands that had appeared in L'Isle's 1703 map. Bibliothèque nationale de France.

mine's map of the Amazon River lent cartographic weight to Spain's land claims in that area. Meanwhile, Portuguese authorities hired Jesuit mathematicians to create the "New Atlas of Portuguese America" (*Novo atlas da América portuguesa*); in this joint effort, Domenico Capassi mapped northern Brazil, and Diogo Soares mapped the southern coastline.[39] These projects demonstrated that not all mapmaking was the same. Cosmographers and engravers had printed maps of overseas territories for centuries, but their works no longer carried the same weight as maps derived from on-the-ground measurements and direct observations. Indeed, the French and Jesuit expeditions used the precision of their geographic renderings to cast doubt on previous perceptions of disputed territories.[40] These expeditions also reveal the limits of each crown's knowledge of the South American interior, including the Río de la Plata's countryside. Soares's maps focused entirely on the region's coastline, highlighting access points to the countryside rather than the nuances of the rural landscape itself, while Spanish authorities in the region relied on Jesuit missionaries, whose geographic expertise related to lands farther north. Thus, as late as 1759, one Spanish commander complained that no reliable map existed of the lands of the Banda Norte.[41]

The short territorial range of these mapping endeavors was due to the limited geographical knowledge of their informants. Jesuit and Guaraní mapmakers

FIGURE 10   Jean Baptiste Bourguignon D'Anville, *Carte de L'Amerique Meridionale*, 1748. This later iteration of D'Anville's continental-scale map shifted the borderline eastward to the Atlantic coast, thereby connecting Montevideo to the rest of Spain's South American claims and marking Colônia as an enclave. Newberry Library.

charted the lands surrounding the missions and waterways between Buenos Aires and Paraguay rather than the Río de la Plata's countryside.[42] For his part, Soares consulted frontierspeople (*práticos do país*) with experience traveling in the region as a knowledge base for his maps, contracting them to answer questionnaires (*notícias práticas*) about local lands and to correct the errors of foreign maps. He acquired detailed descriptions of lands north of the Río de la Plata—the Jesuit missions, cattle markets in Santa Catarina and São Paulo, and cattle

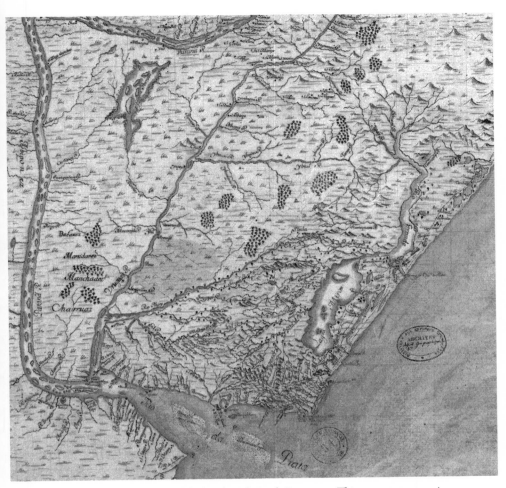

FIGURE 11 *Carte manuscrite de l'embouchure de Rio da Prata,* 1740. This anonymous map is possibly the one mentioned by Soares, as it includes details of the Brazilian coastline north of the Río de la Plata, Portuguese toponyms, and the livestock trade routes. Regardless of authorship, the map contrasts detailed knowledge of coastlines with limited information farther inland. It also indicates reliance on published maps of the region, as the ethnonym pattern of the western portion (Bohanes, Martidanes, Manchados, and Charrúas) and the competing notions of Portuguese territorial possession (a yellow line beginning in Colônia versus a red line beginning in the Atlantic Ocean) appeared in earlier atlases. Bibliothèque nationale de France.

ranges near what is now Porto Alegre—but information on lands between Rio Grande and Colônia was limited to trade with Native peoples and rumors of inland mines and cattle ranges. He lamented, "As my entire yearning was to see this countryside, I decided to also draw, with necessary caution, a small map of it, but it was not possible to complete it with the exactitude that I desire."[43] Whereas coastal calculations were reliable, the mathematician relied on guesswork to draw the countryside in the final versions of his maps (figure 11).

Paying Tribute While Soliciting Vassalage

The broad juridical debates about imperial possession and dominion, while discussed in royal courts and other European forums, ultimately depended on global conditions, particularly in the Americas. The claims exerted by Spain under the authority of papal bulls and the Treaty of Tordesillas were predicated on the advancement of Christianity, much like Portuguese claims in Africa and Asia. Likewise, the concept of uti possidetis was grounded in the idea that newly claimed lands must be vacant. In each of these debates, the status of Indigenous inhabitants of the Americas and elsewhere, specifically those who had not accepted Christianity, was a determining factor.

The Iberian crowns' exclusive presence in most of the Americas during the sixteenth century led Catholic theologians to establish terms of just appropriation of Native lands. These debates were predicated on the notion of papal donation and thus hinged on definitions of just war and natural law. Spanish theologian Francisco de Vitoria argued that Native peoples in the Americas naturally held dominion over their territories and rejected the idea that Native resistance to declarations of the Spanish king's lordship constituted just cause to seize their lands. For Vitoria, Bartolomé de las Casas, and others, legitimate land seizure could only occur in a context of humanitarian intervention, where the Native people in question had violated natural law (by practicing cannibalism or human sacrifice) or where they impeded the spread of the Catholic gospel and priests' rights to travel.[44] Contemporary travel accounts and cartographic iconography thus served to define Indigenous Americans' legal status and determine their relationships to the Spanish and Portuguese crowns. Most notably, the broad application of the ethnonym "Carib" to diverse Indigenous communities marked them as cannibalistic and therefore bereft of natural rights. These ethnogeographic imaginings were not limited to erudite scholars or print shops; they also permeated Iberian court cases over the legal status of Indigenous captives and subjects.[45]

During the seventeenth century, emergent Protestant empires challenged both pillars of earlier debates over possession: Iberian monopoly of access to overseas territories, and Native peoples' natural rights. Jurists posited that rights to land derived from use, rather than from papal donation or natural law, and that in the absence of exploitation, lands could be deemed vacant and claimed by the first taker. Some, like Hugo Grotius and Wolfgang Adam Lauterbach, considered agriculture to be the foundation of all territorial claims, while others, like Cornelius de Pauw, contended that hunting or fishing equally constituted territorial exploitation and dominion.[46] In this context, maps, settlements, military occupation, and trade served as evidence of productive imperial ownership, while varying juridical contexts emerged in the Americas with regard to Native rights.[47] Similar questions of sedentism undergirded Catholic missionary activity, as clergymen conflated sedentism and Christian civility, vassalage, and humanity. Missionaries often identified mobile peoples as "infidel Indians" (*indios infieles*), and the process of conversion involved settling on a new reducción or joining an extant mission. Therefore, to convert indios infieles was to "reduce them to the faith" (*reducirlos a nuestra santa fe / reduzi-los à fé*), "to our obedience" (*reducirlos a la obediencia / reduzi-los da nossa obediencia*), "to [Catholic] doctrine and village" (*reduzi-los á doutrina e aldeia*), "to settlements" (*reducirlos a poblaciones*), "to political and human life" (*reducirlos a la vida política y humana*), "to peace" (*reducirlos a la paz*), or "to the behavior of settled people" (*reducirse al trato popular*).[48] As sedentism was a necessary condition for order, reason, Catholicism, and natural rights, Native peoples who left missions for the countryside were deemed apostates.

By the eighteenth century, the issue of sedentism became paramount as jurists attempted to standardize acts of possession. Even if Catholic logics of papal donation were no longer authoritative, Indigenous acceptance of Catholicism implied that they were vassals of an Iberian crown.[49] When Native peoples exerted autonomy via mobility, land claims were less straightforward, as jurists demonstrated increased reticence toward acknowledging the rights of people who were not firmly established in a single location and who did not practice cultivation. The English employed such arguments to justify territorial dispossession in North America and Australia, and over time, Ibero-American officials in the Río de la Plata merged them with earlier logics.[50] Conversely, the Paraguayan Jesuit Domingo Muriel contended that although mobile peoples' claims to lands were weaker than those exercised by sedentary peoples, their occupation of a given place, coupled with herding or trading, served as a legitimate determinant of their property and dominion. For Muriel, as mobile peoples did not necessarily seek territorial exclusivity, imperial occupation did not supersede their dominion but could coexist with it when new imperial settlements went unopposed.[51]

These juridical debates directly affected the thinking of Ibero-American administrators in their dealings with tolderías. Knowing that tolderías effectively controlled the majority of regional space, administrators sought to demonstrate that their crown could still claim possession of it, either by undermining Native land claims or by claiming tolderías as imperial subjects. Efforts to dismiss tolderías' territorial claims generally involved emphasizing their mobility, as occurred with the governor of Buenos Aires in 1721: "[Tolderías] have no right [over the land], because they are like gypsies, vagabond wanderers, that have no fixed lands, house, or home, and only inhabit the countryside because of the cows [that are there]."[52] For him, tolderías' mobility meant that they were mere "inhabitants" of the land, rather than legitimate possessors, a refrain that city officials repeated frequently.[53] There were two problems with this logic. First, it implied that if tolderías had no territorial claim, Spain was the region's legitimate possessor. This notion was likely rooted in the 1681 and 1715 treaties, which had limited Portugal's jurisdictional exclusivity to a cannon shot from the plaza of Colônia. But by denouncing the rights of tolderías because of their lack of settlements, the governor of Buenos Aires affirmed implicitly that settlements should serve as a standard for determining territorial possession. By this logic, since Spain had not yet founded settlements in the Banda Norte, it had no foundation for its own claim. Second, in seeking royal support for the expulsion of tolderías from the area, the governor assumed that Spain had the right and capacity to police it. In doing so, he ignored field officers' reports that the tolderías collectively had as many as three thousand archers, a force too strong to topple.[54]

Other Ibero-American administrators sought to claim Native lands via proxy, demonstrating tolderías' vassalage to their crown via pacts or the establishment of reducciones. A 1732 agreement between Montevideo and Minuán tolderías is instructive. The centerpiece of the peace accord was payment from the former to the latter in exchange for the lifting of their blockade on the plaza, yet the written agreement contained clauses declaring that tolderías were subjects of the Spanish crown. This nuanced language was likely of little importance to the Minuán caciques present at the parley and certainly had no direct impact on their relationship with Montevideo; however, it provided potential fodder for Spanish diplomats in their bilateral disputes with Portugal over the Banda Norte.[55] Whether as part of pacts or as independent endeavors, Spanish and Portuguese administrators most often sought to evince tolderías' vassalage by enticing them to settle on a reducción, but most of these efforts proved unsuccessful. Caciques likely understood the frequent payments given to them as an affirmation of their own authority rather than an incentive to subjugate themselves, and even when tolderías established a reducción, they treated it as a temporary arrangement.[56] A reducción could provide access to material goods or temporary shelter, but tolderías' seasonal movements almost always made such arrangements ephemeral.

Though few reducciones became permanent settlements, the possibility of establishing them was integral to the interimperial struggle over Colônia. In 1715, after ten years of Spanish occupation, the Treaty of Utrecht transferred the plaza back to the Portuguese. Frustrated over the loss, the governor of Buenos Aires considered retaking it, as it would give Spain "the advantage of dominating all of that countryside, and the reducción of the infidel Indians that inhabit it."[57] Wresting Colônia from the Portuguese would leave Spain as the lone imperial power with a foothold in the region, giving it leverage when dealing with tolderías. All that would remain would be to establish reducciones with tolderías, because "if they joined together with the Christians [Guaraní] and Spanish, [it] would be enough to oppose whatever insult our enemies might attempt."[58] Instead, with Colônia back in Portuguese hands, caciques were once again able to negotiate between the two crowns, and convincing tolderías to settle on reducciones was more difficult. The region was again exposed to foreign powers, as the Portuguese presence left juridical debates unresolved and mobile tolderías with multiple trading partners.

Portuguese officials attempted the same strategy upon their return to Colônia. For them, the tolderías represented both a lifeline to their plaza and Portugal's best chance at preventing future Spanish or French settlements in Montevideo and Maldonado. In 1718, Colônia's governor wrote to the Conselho Ultramarino in Lisbon: "What would help more than anything is if we were to have the Indians of [Montevideo] on our side because these are the ones that facilitate the Castilians in their undertakings there and the ones that obtain [cattle] for them." He argued that it was "necessary to take great care and industry in acquiring [the tolderías]" and that the Portuguese should attempt to form a reducción with them.[59] Days later, he made a pact with the Minuán caciques Chacadar, Francisco, and Loya. In exchange for the caciques' promise to guard the coastline against foreign ships, the Portuguese provided 200,000 reais worth of goods and help in locating a Minuán relative who had been sent to Rio de Janeiro. According to the governor's report, the agreement also included a Minuán promise to live under the protection of the Portuguese king and to be baptized.[60] This accord, like the 1732 pact between Montevideo and Minuanes, revealed the dissonance between imperial ambitions and material conditions. While the Portuguese governor sought to produce evidence of Minuán vassalage, Chadacar, Francisco, and Loya would more likely have interpreted baptism as a ceremonial consecration of ties and Portuguese payment as affirmation of Minuán authority. The plaza proffered 200,000 reais again in 1727, but no reducción was ever established.[61]

TABLE 2 Reducciones and attempted reducciones in the Río de la Plata, 1623–1750

From	To	Name	Ethnonym	Order	Location
1612	1612	[Never founded]	Charrúas	Jesuit	Buenos Aires
1623	1623	[Never founded]	Charrúas, Yaros	Jesuit	Mouth of Río Uruguay
1624	[1631]	San Francisco de Olivares	Charrúas	Franciscan	Mouth of Río Negro
1624	[1631]	San Juan de Céspedes [San Antonio de los Chanáes]	Chanás	Franciscan	Mouth of Río Negro
1653	[1653]	Concepción	Charrúas	Jesuits	Near Yapeyú
1655	1655	[Never founded]	Guenoas	Jesuit	Near Río Uruguay
1657	[1658]	San Andrés*	Yaros	Jesuitas	Arroyo Ibarapita-guazú
1660	[-]	Santo Domingo Soriano	Chanás, Charrúas	Franciscan	Mouth of Río Negro, west of Río Uruguay
1664	1666	Doctrina de Franciso de Rivas Gavilán**	Guaraní	Mercedarian	Itacurubí, near San Javier, Uruguay
1664	[-]	[n/a]**	Charrúas	Mercedarian	Sauce de Luna, near the arroyo Pay Ticú
1678	1678	[Never founded]	Guenoas	Jesuits	Near La Cruz and Yapeyú
1682	1708	Jesús/Santa María de Guenoas	Guenoas	Jesuit	Mouth of Río Ibicuy
1683	1683	[Never founded]	Guenoas	Jesuit	Between Santo Tomé, Yapeyú, and La Cruz
[1683]	[1683]	San Andrés*	Guenoas	Jesuit	Santa Tecla/Aceguá
1693	1693	San Joaquin	Charrúas, Yaros	Jesuit	Arecifes o Ytus del Río Uruguay
1702	1702	[Never founded]	Minuanes, Charrúas, Bohanes	Jesuit	Near Colónia

Year	Reducción	Group	Order	Location
1703	[Never founded]	Bohanes	Franciscan	Old site of Soriano
1706	[Never founded]	Charrúas	Jesuit	El Empedrado (near Corrientes)
1724	[Never founded]	Minuanes	Franciscan	Montevideo
1726	[Never founded]	Minuanes	[n/a]	Colônia
1736	[Never founded]	Minuanes	[n/a]	Rio Grande
1750	[Never founded]	Charrúas	Jesuit	Yapeyú
1750	[Never founded]	Minuanes	Jesuit	Montevideo
1750	Estancias del Bojurú	Minuanes	[n/a]	Rio Grande
1794	Nuestra Señora de la Concepción de Cayastá	Charrúas	Franciscan	North of Santa Fe

*San Andrés de Yaros and San Andrés de Guenoas may have been the same reducción or two separate attempts in the same site, as there is confusion among Jesuit sources. In a 1763 map by Jesuit José Cardiel, the reducción appears as "San Antonio de Guenoas y Yarros."

**The two 1664 Mercedarian reducciones might have been one and the same. Sources: *Cartas anuas*, 19:51, 92, 511; Techo, *Historia de la Provincia del Paraguay*, 135–37, 240; Latini, "Reducción de charrúas"; Cortesão, *Jesuítas e Bandeirantes no Itatim*, 248–50, 275–85; Acosta y Lara, *La guerra de los charrúas*, 1:18–19; Jarque, *Insignes misioneros*, 382–84; Cattáneo, "Relación del viaje," 184, 190; BNB, De Ángelis, MS 508 (22), doc. 526 (1-29;3;51); AGNA, IX, 6-9-7 (1743-04-30); Funes, *Ensayo*, 1:294–95; Furlong Cárdiff, *Cartografía jesuítica*, vol. 2, Láminas XX and XXXII; Sallaberry, *Los charrúas y Santa Fe*, 166; AGNA, VII, Biblioteca Nacional 289 (4390/1, no. 12; 4390/2; no. 5); López Mazz and Bracco, *Minuanos*, 19; Azara, *Descripción é historia*, 1:165; Hervás, *Catálogo de las lenguas*, 196–97; Sepp von Rechegg, *Viagem às Missões Jesuíticas*, 103–5; AGNA, IX, 41-3-8, exp. 4, fs. 14 18–46v, 48–53v; Trelles, "Vandalismo misionero," 22; AGI, Chile, 153 (Montevideo, 1724-08-29; Buenos Aires, 1726-09-15); AHU, Rio de Janeiro, Castro e Almeida (017-01), caixa 23, doc. 5305; "Carta de Cristovão Pereira"; "Copia da carta de Cristovão Pereira"; "Coleção de documentos" 4–6; "Brasil, Rio Grande do Sul, Registros da Igreja Católica, 1738–1952," images, FamilySearch; Cortesão, *Do Tratado de Madri*, 305; "Registro de atos oficiais," 235–36, 258; Leite, *História da Companhia de Jesús*, 6:528–30; AGNA, IX, 4-3-1 (Buenos Aires, 1750-10-12; Campo del Bloqueo, 1750-11-15; Las Vivoras, 1750-11-09); AGNA, IX, 2-1-4 (Montevideo, 1750-07-22, 1750-09-06, 1750-09-10); AGI, Charcas, 378 (Buenos Aires, 1751-04-26); Cortesão, *Antecedentes do Tratado de Madri*, 301-2; AGPSF, Acta de Cabildo de Santa Fe de 1750-09-25.

Missionaries most often undertook the labor of advancing reducciones, through which they hoped to subjugate and proselytize tolderías, gain access to the countryside, and stake a claim over regional lands. From the early seventeenth century, Jesuits, Mercedarians, and Franciscans pursued reducciones with Bohanes, Charrúas, Guenoas, Minuanes, and Yaros, much as they had with Guaraní-speaking peoples. At least twenty-one attempts were made between 1612 and 1736, and extant missions incorporated individuals from tolderías as well (table 2). Most efforts proved short lived or altogether fruitless, and religious leaders diagnosed tolderías' mobility as the problem. Jesuit José Cardiel argued that unlike sedentary Native peoples, those living in tolderías were "lazy vagabonds [who go] their entire lives without a fixed locale, always living on what they hunt or steal," adding that "because of their lack of rationality and order, their innate inertia, and the horror that they have of all kinds of work," previous proselytization efforts had come to no avail. As a remedy, Cardiel proposed founding colonies of settlers from the Guaraní missions in lands controlled by tolderías. He was convinced that if the tolderías could see the benefits of a sedentary lifestyle firsthand, they would choose to stay permanently on reducciones, but his plan never came to fruition.[62]

Despite the missionaries' minimal success, by the 1730s most settlements in the Río de la Plata were undertaking efforts to entice nearby tolderías to settle on reducciones.[63] In 1736, as Colônia was under siege, Portuguese officials aimed to strengthen their position farther north, in Rio Grande, by forming a reducción with Minuanes there. The reducción never materialized, however, as many Portuguese inhabitants of Rio Grande were fearful of the neighboring tolderías, who had raided for horses not long before. More importantly, the Minuán caciques were simultaneously negotiating with Spanish officials and had been seen entering and leaving Montevideo.[64] Montevideo's efforts had begun years before. In 1724, Franciscan friar Pedro Jerónimo de la Cruz proposed a reducción for what he calculated to be two thousand Minuanes who lived nearby, yet Minuán caciques rejected the offer.[65] Later, in 1743, Jesuits from Buenos Aires devised a plan to send Christian Guenoas from the San Borja mission to persuade the Minuanes living near Montevideo to settle. The Jesuits were careful to define the Minuanes' future legal status, proposing that "they will neither serve nor be entrusted to the Spanish (an idea that they extremely abhor) but rather attached to the Royal Crown, in order to protect them in a proper and gentle vassalage."[66] By providing material support and circumventing local authorities, the Jesuits calculated that they could gradually convince the tolderías to settle and thus accept vassalage. The Spanish crown authorized the installation of a Jesuit residency in Montevideo the following year, but the Minuanes again had little desire to enter into a relationship of dependency.[67] By the century's midpoint, the success of gradual incorporation through payment seemed improbable.

Interimperial Peace and Interethnic Violence

In 1749, a sharp change occurred in interimperial and interethnic relations in the region. Iberian diplomats for the first time articulated new standards for determining territorial possession—treaty maps and a precise continental borderline—as they negotiated what would become the Treaty of Madrid. As the competing arguments over the papal donation versus *uti possidetis* and natural limits had failed to resolve the perpetual territorial disputes, and nationally sponsored mapping expeditions were insufficient to garner international recognition, negotiators now put their faith in the union of diplomacy and on-the-ground mapmaking (table 3). While these deliberations were taking place far away in royal courts, the Río de la Plata once again became embroiled in interethnic violence. Spanish and Portuguese officials reported armed combat between tolderías; soon after, in both Montevideo and the western portion of the region, Spanish soldiers engaged the tolderías in fighting as well. As a result, the next three years saw both a dramatic reconfiguration of relations between tolderías and an increased number of caciques negotiating the possibility of reducciones.

The combined distrust for earlier accords and unilateral mapping endeavors led Portuguese and Spanish diplomats to enact new measures to determine legitimate territorial possession. Despite their disagreement about how to divide possession, they were unanimous in their diagnosis of the problem. Portuguese officials suggested that in the absence of mapping expeditions to clarify the Tordesillas meridian, interspersed and conflicting settlements had emerged: "The two crowns possess an undivided America, with neither being able to say with certainty what is theirs, beyond that which they have settled. In this way, Castile can say with much certainty that Cuyabá, Mato Grosso, and Pará are theirs, and Portugal that Buenos Aires, Tucumán, and Paraguay pertain to it."[68] Numerous maps had been produced over the years, but these works were considered untrustworthy. Jorge Juan and Antonio de Ulloa, Spanish interlocutors for the Madrid accords and participants in the La Condamine expedition to the Amazon, agreed: "[We should] not rely on the uncertainty and variety of those [maps] that are only made from diaries and nautical routes, nor on [those] that can be believed to be partial, for being national, to the interests of one of the two crowns."[69] Maps drawn from

TABLE 3   Treaties guiding territorial possession in the Río de la Plata up to 1750

Year	Treaty	Significance for Río de la Plata
1494	Tordesillas	Divided Spanish and Portuguese spheres of influence at 370 leagues west of Cabo Verde islands
1529	Zaragoza	Created an antimeridian of the Tordesillas meridian in the Pacific Ocean
1668	Lisbon	Spanish and Portuguese vassals could cross imperial frontiers (Article 3)
1681	Lisbon	(1) Colônia recognized as a Portuguese possession (Articles 2 and 3)
		(2) Vassals of both crowns gained common use of countryside (Article 7)
1701	Lisbon	Spain renounced rights over lands arbitrated in the 1681 treaty (Article 14)
1715	Utrecht	(1) Colônia returned to the Portuguese (Articles 5–8)
		(2) Uti possidetis supplanted papal donation as a measure of possession
1737	Paris	(1) Colônia affirmed as Portuguese
		(2) Reinforced principle of uti possidetis

engravers' tables in European cities relied on the geographically imprecise diaries of missionaries or travelers, while maps produced by direct observation and state-of-the-art measurement lacked the necessary transparency for them to be trustworthy.

The Treaty of Madrid, signed in January 1750, responded to these concerns by giving primacy to collaborative, on-the-ground mapping expeditions. The two crowns agreed to finance joint boundary commissions to determine a terrestrial borderline between their respective South American dominions, and this border would replace all previous standards of determining territorial possession. Teams of engineers, geographers, and cosmographers from both sides would meet periodically and travel the entire border in parallel contingents with the objective of cosigning jointly produced maps.[70] The diplomats who had congregated in Madrid provided general instructions for where to draw the borderline and developed a guide map that commissioned officials would carry as they traversed the continent, but the boundary commissions were responsible for negotiating details and transforming the theoretical parameters of the treaty's geographic vision into something compatible with local landscapes.[71] The maps they collectively underwrote would become the primary determinants of the extent of each crown's possessions, superseding earlier claims and accords in the arbitration of future disputes. The boundary commissions' work would become the baseline for imperial land policy throughout the rest of the colonial period.

The Treaty of Madrid represented a marked change not only in the way imperial negotiators determined possession but also in how they imagined it. Since at least Colônia's founding, interimperial accords had considered settlements to be the key markers of imperial possession, with dominion extending out from them according to juridical antecedents, natural limits, or relations with Native peoples. Each new settlement altered the physical and the juridical landscape of a given locale, shared access rights and interspersed settlements were conceivable, and maps served as representations of possession that had been determined through other means. The Treaty of Madrid employed the reverse logic—maps were not simply representations of territorial possession but rather the preeminent determinants of it. Although settlements and interethnic relations factored into the boundary commissions' determinations of the border's location, in instances where preserving the principle of uti possidetis would undermine their ability to draw a continuous borderline, officials chose to favor the line by relinquishing current holdings. The Madrid accord was thus otherwise known as the Treaty of Permuta, which literally meant to "exchange" or "transfer." In the Río de la Plata, Portugal ceded Colônia to Spain in exchange for the Siete Pueblos, while farther north along the Charcas–Mato Grosso border, Spain ceded the Santa Rosa mission so that a line could be drawn along the Río Guaporé. New settlements would be considered in future territorial disputes inasmuch as they were close to extant treaty lines.[72] The treaty also marked a shift in how Spain and Portugal discussed the territorial possessions of mobile peoples. By subordinating usufruct or ancestral rights to cartographic measurement, the Madrid accord undercut the notion that autonomous Native peoples could be considered legitimate possessors of land or independent agents. In the Río de la Plata, imperial officials began to envision tolderías as vassals regardless of whether they had accepted reducciones.

While negotiators deliberated in Madrid, officials in nearly all corners of the Río de la Plata suddenly gained traction in their efforts to establish reducciones. From 1749 to 1752, Charrúa or Minuán caciques met with colonial administrators throughout the region to discuss the possibility of establishing settlements. In 1749, as many as eighty Minuán families and four hundred people total approached Portuguese officials in São Miguel, who received them with food, clothing, and other items. Over the next four years, at least two hundred of these Minuanes were baptized in Rio Grande, and others remained nearby as salaried workers on a ranch belonging to the crown.[73] Meanwhile, another Minuán toldería discussed with Montevideo's authorities the possibility of a settlement outside the city. At least thirty-nine Minuanes spent the second half of 1750 waiting as Montevideo's authorities scrambled to find priests to administer the reducción and goods to provide the tolderías. Eventually, the Minuanes lost patience and absconded eastward toward São Miguel with other tolderías.[74] Lastly, in the north of the region, Guenoa and Minuán tolderías reportedly discussed forming reducciones with Jesuits near San Borja, while as many as 145 Charrúas approached the priests of Yapeyú with the same objective. None of these reducciones materialized, however, as Minuán, Charrúa, and Bohan tolderías began to join one another instead.[75]

Why would tolderías throughout the region suddenly see reducciones as a viable option? Spanish officials boasted that a series of military campaigns undertaken from 1749 to 1752 had vanquished their Indigenous counterparts, with some claiming that they had expelled all tolderías from lands west of the Río Uruguay. In 1749, after decades of attempting to promote tolderías' settlement via "gentle methods," Buenos Aires's governor, José de Andonaegui, ordered Montevideo's authorities to demand that neighboring Minuanes form a reducción. In the event that they refused, Montevideo's militia was to "go out to punish them and ruin them, ending them once and for all."[76] Several months later, the governor ordered authorities in Santa Fe to issue a similar ultimatum to neighboring Charrúas, "putting them to the knife in the event that they resist and making all who turn themselves in prisoners of war."[77] Though not the first Spanish military campaigns against the tolderías, this synchronized effort to kill or capture entire tolderías was unique.[78] By 1751, armed militias and mounted guards had killed 120 Minuanes near Maldonado and had taken 82 captives back to Montevideo. Expeditions near Santa Fe killed over 150 Charrúas and forced 339 more to form a reducción along the city's northwestern frontier, a clear divergence from earlier attempts at enticing tolderías to form reduccions via the proffering of material goods.[79]

Though deeply violent, these expeditions could not have been the cause of the tolderías' sudden amenability to reducciones. The campaigns did not vanquish the tolderías; rather, they escalated a broader back-and-forth in which the tolderías also claimed victories. Spanish casualties were fewer, but this was because the tolderías used raids to claim livestock or acquire captives, while imperial militias now sought submission or extermination.[80] Moreover, this flurry of Spanish raids was restricted to a handful of tolderías. While any population estimate is a matter of guesswork, there were likely between five thousand and six thousand individuals living in tolderías at this time. Killing or capturing close to five hundred people would have been devastating to the targeted tolderías; however, most tolderías remained untouched, including many that frequented Montevideo and Santa Fe. Following the expeditions, Spanish settlers near Santa Fe complained of continued exposure to attacks by Charrúas, and respondents to a 1756 questionnaire noted that Charrúas continued to live within Santa Fe's jurisdiction. Months after the expedition from Montevideo had concluded, Minuán attacks resumed to the point that the city proposed financing a permanent guard.[81]

A more plausible explanation to why tolderías suddenly viewed reducciones as viable can be found in the tolderías themselves. Tolderías throughout the region frequently competed with one another, and their interest in linking onto a settlement was usually the result of wartime duress. This was likely again the case at the eighteenth century's midpoint, as suggested by dialogue between the Minuán tolderías and Portuguese officials in São Miguel. The tolderías arrived in São Miguel at the beginning of June 1749, nearly two years before troops would leave from Montevideo to engage them, and approximately four months before the governor of Buenos Aires would authorize an expedition against Charrúas. One observer noted that, rather than fleeing the Spanish, the Minuanes had come to São Miguel "because the Indians called Tapes, and others called Charruas, in much greater numbers, are finishing them off and destroying them."[82] Seven months later, Spanish officials in Santo Domingo Soriano reported a similar situation for Charrúas, who were joining together with Minuanes, in part because the latter were greater in number.[83] Regardless of who ultimately possessed greater numbers, these tolderías' actions derived from relations with Indigenous neighbors rather than imperial interlopers. Duress from infighting between tolderías would also explain tolderías' theft of cattle and crops from settlements in the years preceding the Spanish expeditions.

Not all tolderías sought relationships with settlements during these years, as many joined other Indigenous communities instead. In particular, a large number of Charrúa, Bohan, and Minuán tolderías congregated somewhere around the Río Queguay. While a lack of details in the written records makes it difficult to surmise the exact nature of their relationship, officials in Montevideo, Yapeyú, and Santo Domingo Soriano all expressed concern. Despite their successes against a handful of tolderías, officials feared retribution by this new coalition.[84] This represented the first documented instance of Charrúa and Minuán tolderías joining in this way, and although it did not include all their tolderías, this coalition nonetheless constituted a change from earlier patterns of engagement. Thereafter, Charrúas and Minuanes appeared together with ever-increasing frequency, to the point that by the end of the century, some outside observers struggled to differentiate one from the other. This broader union was also significant for tolderías in the region not identified as Charrúa or Minuán, and other ethnonyms fell into disuse by the 1770s.[85]

Conclusion

The events of 1749 to 1752 were a turning point in interimperial and interethnic relations in the Río de la Plata. As Iberian negotiators reinvented the way that they would claim territorial possession, local administrators reimagined themselves vis-à-vis mobile Native peoples. The jurisdictional certainty and exclusivity that went hand in hand with clearly defined borders generated a new context for interethnic relations. Territorial possession in borderlands ceased to flow through Native peoples, imagined as vassals; instead, Ibero-American officials began to imagine vassalage as the product of living within certain territorial limits. These shifts coincided with transformations in relationships between colonial settlements and neighboring tolderías. Most notably, peaceful attempts to incorporate mobile Native peoples into imperial projects were no longer a necessary or feasible strategy, and imperial authorities directed their efforts to stamping out mobile lifestyles by any means possible. For many tolderías, these years brought crisis and reconfiguration. Broader conflicts between tolderías presented two logical possibilities for caciques: they could seek refuge with settlements, or they could forge new and more lasting ties with other tolderías. Increased aggression from Spanish settlements only exacerbated the problem and most likely impelled more tolderías to build bonds with one another than with the Spanish. Indeed, the only instance in which tolderías followed through on a proposed settlement was the case of the Minuanes in São Miguel with the Portuguese.

By the time the midcentury turmoil subsided, mapmakers from Spain and Portugal had disembarked in the region. Their presence would have a much more dramatic effect than the Spanish military campaigns on territorial relations in the region, both immediately and in the long run. For the first time, imperial agents would make the long journey and document their path from the Atlantic Coast near São Miguel to the mission strongholds deep inside the continent. Their activities at once revealed the key contradiction of Iberian territorial claims—Spain and Portugal sought to divide between themselves territories effectively controlled by tolderías—and set the stage for new territorial conditions in the region.

CHAPTER THREE

Mapping the Tolderías' Mansion

In early 1787, as summer turned to autumn, eleven Minuán tolderías were encamped along the Río Caciquey when they saw a rumbling caravan appear upon the horizon. The Minuanes had set up camp atop a hillock at the river's headwaters and its main ford and had likely seen the travelers coming for miles. The caravan was traveling along the principal route between the Spanish forts of Santa Tecla and San Martín and the Guaraní missions, and it was perhaps for this reason that Miguel Ayala Caraí and other caciques who governed these lands intercepted the travelers and extracted payments from them. Over the course of the next few days, the caciques—Caraí, Salteinho, Batú da Gama, Tajuy, and Maulín—halted the caravan several times, consumed its goods, and spent the night in its makeshift encampments. They reportedly explained to the newcomers that these lands belonged to their tolderías, and they taxed the travelers accordingly.[1]

The travelers in question formed part of the Portuguese and Spanish boundary commissions working under the Treaty of San Ildefonso. Weeks earlier, they had set out from Santa Tecla and were working their way northward to the Río Pepirí Guazú along a corridor that ran between the Guaraní missions and the Portuguese settlement of Rio Pardo. They had spent the previous three years mapping around the Lagoa Mirim, in lands controlled by the two crowns, but now they were traveling into Native ground. The first leg of their journey, between Santa Tecla and San Martín, cut through undulating grasslands controlled by Minuanes, while the second stretch would take them through forests belonging to Tupis. The demarcation teams traveled in several groups, separating supply convoys from trained mapmakers and dividing themselves according to empire. Each team kept a daily log of events, which revealed deep pasts and contested claims. Every diary followed a similar pattern: when close to the two forts, the mapmakers' activities were unobstructed; but when farther away, their tasks were interrupted by tolderías. In Caa Ibate, the Minuán caciques' "unbearable screaming noise [kept] us awake all night," wrote one demarcation official, while another griped of being "inconvenienced all day by [Tajuy's] visits" several days later.[2]

The mapmakers presented these encounters as mere perturbations, yet the Minuanes and their caciques likely experienced the events much differently.

While the mapmakers were encountering Native leaders for the first time, the Minuanes' attitudes and actions were part of a longer history with Spanish, Portuguese, and Guaraní neighbors. The "elderly" Salteinho's tolderías had been invaded by Montevideo's militias two decades earlier, while the "gruff, scowling" Batú da Gama had faced similar incursions just two years prior and had incorporated migrants from the missions into his tolderías. Miguel Ayala Caraí, whom the mapmakers lauded as "cheery," "more rational," a "lover of Spaniards," and "dear to the Portuguese," had worked on Portuguese ranches during his younger years and had both aided earlier demarcation teams in avoiding a flooded route and charged them a tax for their travels.[3] Caraí's tolderías possessed trade goods from Buenos Aires, Paraguay, the missions, and Rio Pardo, including Spanish saddles and Portuguese stirrups and bits.[4] They also controlled the lands through which the boundary commissions were passing, and one mapmaker wrote that they "charge not only contrabandists and travelers . . . with impertinent petitions, visits, and sometimes threats, but also go often to the missions' ranches and make them provide yerba maté, knives, tobacco, etc."[5] Just before the mapmakers arrived, the tolderías had evicted mission dwellers from one of their ranches, presumably for failure to make payment. The demarcation teams were aware of this, as those who had passed through the year before had "news of the Minuanes' bad predisposition." The new caravan therefore traveled "extremely lightly," recalled one traveler, "crossing much of the country by night and more to the west than normal," noting that "it was not possible to draw the route map as we had hoped."[6]

These incidents illuminate the central contradiction of the Madrid and San Ildefonso boundary commissions: Portuguese and Spanish officials partitioned borderland territories that neither empire effectively controlled. As geographers traversed the Río de la Plata to declare possession for their royal patrons, they encountered autonomous Native peoples who asserted their authority in myriad ways, including through knowledge sharing, the taxing of travelers, and violent engagement. These interactions constituted only a few pages in the boundary commissions' official reports, and tolderías were altogether absent from their maps. Nonetheless, this silence was more indicative of imperial ignorance than Indigenous absence. Close attention to the timelines and itineraries of the mapping expeditions reveals the spatial limits of imperial authority and the expansive spatial reach of Indigenous agents. Furthermore, comparing the events of these expeditions to the mapmakers' corpus of geographic and ethnographic knowledge illuminates how imperial officials sought to appropriate and resignify Indigenous territorialities to fortify imperial claims. The mapmakers sent to the Río de la Plata embodied a new territorial vision—one that assumed universal imperial possession instead of acknowledging Indigenous authority and overlapping claims—and their expeditions served as a watershed moment when this geographical imagination confronted on-the-ground realities.

This chapter explores both the limitations of the boundary commissions and the ideological changes they engendered. It begins by providing a logistical overview of the mapping expeditions to demonstrate that commissioned officers depended on local peoples for protection, sustenance, guidance, labor, and information. It then turns to an analysis of *mapping practices*, the "social and material processes" of the expeditions as they crisscrossed the region.[7] As demarcation teams attempted to reorder lands they knew little about, local agents mediated and sometimes frustrated the teams' efforts. Mapmaking did not occur in laboratories, and officials often found themselves embroiled in local conflicts. Reading against the mapmakers' tendency to treat Native peoples and other rural agents as a fixed part of a passing landscape, this chapter connects the interests and actions of these agents to the outcome of the expeditions. Finally, it assesses *mapping form*, or the visual and textual depictions of regional space that the expeditions produced. Despite persistently confronting spatial practices that belied imperial authority, the boundary commissions presented the region as Spanish and Portuguese dominions and, in turn, recast their relationships with autonomous Indigenous communities. From their makeshift campsites in the countryside, commissioned mapmakers penned some of the earliest and most frequently cited ethnographies of Native peoples in the region. The ethnogeographic logics evident in this corpus would structure imperial policy and historical memory regarding tolderías thereafter.

Imagining Borders

During the second half of the eighteenth century, Spain and Portugal signed two separate treaties to demarcate an interimperial borderline in South America. The first of these accords, negotiated in Madrid in 1750, represented a substantial shift in imperial logics of determining territorial possession. The two Iberian courts agreed to send joint mapping expeditions to walk and measure a border together, something that had never been done before in the Americas, much less on a continental scale. Although negotiators of earlier treaties had used maps and nautical charts to make their respective claims of territorial possession, none of these pacts resulted in joint boundary commissions. The Madrid agreement was therefore the first to link treaty making and on-the-ground mapmaking, a precedent that diplomats would follow for the

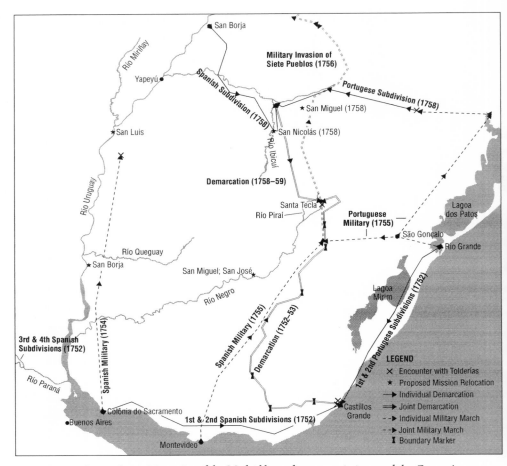

MAP 5   Approximate itineraries of the Madrid boundary commissions and the Guaraní
War. Sources: BA, 51-vii-48, f. 58; IEB, YAP-011, fs. 13–13v, 16, 20v, 22–23, 51v; AGNA, IX, 3-2-1
(Montevideo, 1761-08-25); Blasco, *Mappa remetido ao Sr. Marquez, q demonstra a parage*;
Blasco, *Mappa remetido do Sr. Marquez a sua Exª*; Blasco, *Traslado do Mappa; Plano del Rio
de la Plata*; Fúrlong Cárdiff, *Cartografía jesuítica*, vol. 2, Lámina XXIV.

next century and a half, as the in situ observing of the border became an essential performance that projected scientific objectivity. Ultimately, it took a
second accord, agreed on in San Ildefonso in 1777, for the logic of mapped borders to become a permanent cornerstone of American territorial organization. Local resistance and renewed Iberian tensions had undermined the
Treaty of Madrid's fragile peace, but the Treaty of San Ildefonso produced a
lasting territorial vision that would reshape and structure knowledge and policies thereafter.

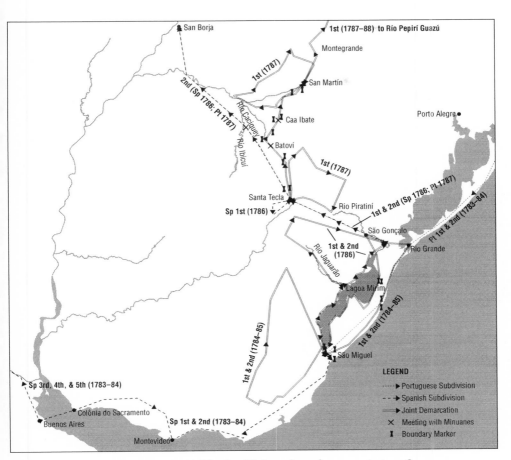

MAP 6 Approximate itineraries of the San Ildefonso boundary commissions. Sources: AGNA, VII, Lamas 32 [2635], f. 111; RAH, Mata Linares, t. 19, f. 105; Varela y Ulloa, *Plano topografico que comprende la parte septentrional*; Varela y Ulloa, *Plano topografico que comprende las vertientes*; Varela y Ulloa and Cabral da Câmara, *Plano topografico*.

The mapping expeditions for the Treaty of Madrid and the Treaty of San Ildefonso occurred in the 1750s and the 1780s respectively. In the Río de la Plata, several contingents of the broader Madrid boundary commission, known as subdivisions, first met along the Atlantic coast in Castillos Grande in 1752 and continued the following year to Santa Tecla—then a ranch belonging to the San Miguel mission. When Santa Tecla's occupants refused to offer support, the boundary commissions were forced to abandon their efforts (map 5). The occupants' resistance to the mapmakers derived from a centerpiece of the Madrid accord—the exchange of the seven Jesuit-Guaraní missions east of the Río Uruguay (the Siete Pueblos Orientales) for the Portuguese settlement of

Colônia do Sacramento—which would have forced the occupants of Santa Tecla to evacuate their mission. Three years of warfare ensued, with Iberian militias and Indigenous allies pitted against Guaraní mission dwellers and neighboring tolderías. It was only in 1758 that the demarcation resumed in the Río de la Plata; it was completed the following year.[8] But a 1761 accord signed in El Pardo annulled the Treaty of Madrid and left most of the region without an operative borderline. The San Ildefonso demarcation began in 1784 near São Miguel, and the mapping teams arrived at the Guaraní missions in 1786 and 1787 (map 6). Along the way, they emptied their coffers in payments to Minuán tolderías. The principal mapping efforts ended by 1791; however, the demarcation of several disputed areas remained incomplete into the nineteenth century, making the contested border a fixture of interimperial diplomacy and interethnic relations in the region.[9]

The method of these two treaties was simple. First, negotiators met in Europe with individuals knowledgeable about South American geography to design a general guide map of the continent. They drew on well-known and widely circulated maps to shape the guide map's final form. This was particularly important for disputed areas, such as the Amazon River basin and the Río de la Plata. The guide map for the Treaty of Madrid, officially titled *Mapa dos Confins do Brasil com as terras da Coroa de Espanha na América Meridional*, is commonly known as the "Map of the Courts" (*Mapa das Cortes*). Since the Treaty of San Ildefonso's negotiators produced no official map of their own, they too relied on the *Mapa das Cortes*, as well as Juan de la Cruz Cano de Olmedilla's *Mapa Geográfico de América Meridional*, to frame their debates (figures 12 and 13).[10] Second, Portuguese and Spanish diplomats drafted instructions for where the borderline should be drawn according to the dimensions and shape of the continent represented in the guide maps. Third, teams of trained mapmakers traveled to South America, walked the border, and drew a line, carrying the guide maps and instructions as guidelines for their efforts. Each mapping expedition began its travels with conferences to negotiate the nuances of the interimperial limit and to establish the itineraries for its respective teams. For the earlier treaty, these meetings occurred in 1752 in Castillos Grande; for the later treaty, officials met in 1783 in the Portuguese settlement of Rio Grande and again in 1784 at the southern tip of the Lagoa Mirim, from where they began their demarcation. Here, the rough edges of each general treaty began to emerge, and the first borderline disputes in the region occurred. In the case of the San Ildefonso expedition, the conferences set the stage for a protracted and antagonistic mapping effort. Both sides had taken advantage of the multiyear gaps between the signing of the treaty and its exe-

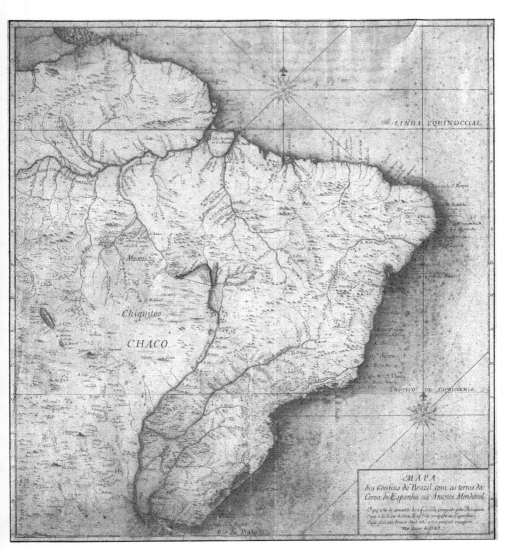

FIGURE 12 *Mapa dos Confins do Brazil com as terras da Coroa de Espanha na América Meridional*, 1749. Acervo da Fundação Biblioteca Nacional—Brasil.

cution to visit the countryside and to scour administrative archives for evidence that would support their territorial claims, and the conferences were their first opportunity to present their cases.[11]

This strategy for creating a legal border concentrated decision-making power in the hands of commissioned officers in the field. The *Mapa das Cortes* and the Cruz Cano map were small-scale renderings bereft of local nuance, and the boundary commissions often discovered inaccuracies and discrepancies in

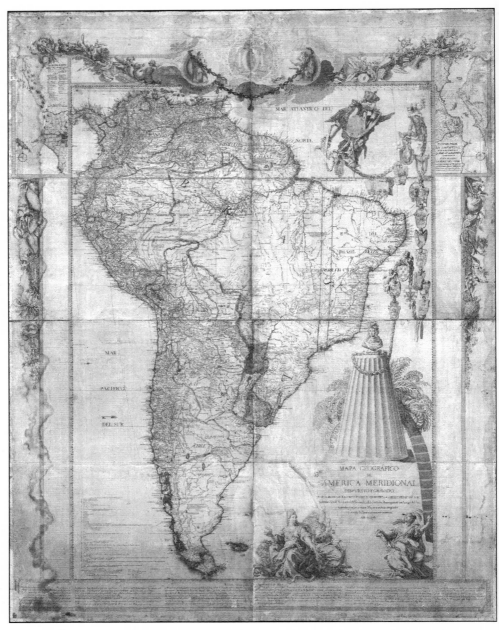

FIGURE 13 Juan de la Cruz Cano de Olmedilla, *Mapa Geográfico de América Meridional,*
1775. Acervo da Fundação Biblioteca Nacional—Brasil.

them. The Treaty of Madrid's third subdivision "found published maps [to be] full of errors" and "did not much follow the Court's map" because it contradicted the treaty. The first subdivision found similar flaws.[12] The two treaties also provided ambiguous geographic language, which was open to interpretation. Article 4 of the Treaty of Madrid stipulated that the borderline be drawn "in a straight line along the highest summits of the hills whose rivers run on one side to [the Lagoa Mirim] and on the other side to the Atlantic Coast [or] to the Río de la Plata." The mapmakers were then instructed to find "the principal origin [headwater] of the Río Negro, and [then] the principal origin of the Río Ibicuí."[13] Which peaks should serve as points along the division when ridges stood side by side rather than in a straight line? Which of the Río Negro's and the Río Ibicuí's many tributaries constituted their "principal origin"? Treaty makers sought to divide watersheds and navigation rights while preserving extant settlements for each crown, but these aims often came into conflict. The Treaty of San Ildefonso stipulated that the border run "along the southernmost stream that drains into the [Lagoa Mirim's northern] channel and that runs closest to the Portuguese fort of São Gonçalo," but no single river met both requirements.[14] As a result, Spanish and Portuguese mapmakers dedicated countless pages of correspondence to deciphering and debating their instructions, halting the demarcation for years at a time. The details mattered, as they were not simply executing a treaty but writing and drawing one into existence.

Portugal and Spain commissioned six subdivisions for the Treaty of Madrid and seven for the Treaty of San Ildefonso, each of which comprised several hundred laborers who worked with a parallel team representing the other crown. The subdivisions were grouped into northern and southern commissions that collectively employed between two and three thousand people per treaty.[15] The northern commissions worked along the Orinoco and Amazon basins, while the southern commissions mapped lands from Moxos and Chiquitos to the Atlantic Coast of the Río de la Plata. Despite the enormous geographical coverage of the southern commission, most of its subdivisions crossed the Río de la Plata: the first and second subdivisions focused on determining a border in the region, while the third and fourth Spanish subdivisions (and a fifth for the San Ildefonso demarcation) traveled along the Río Paraná on their way northward. Although the latter subdivisions would not meet with their Portuguese counterparts until they arrived at the borderlands between Paraguay and São Paulo, they nonetheless began their work of collection and observation as they navigated the Rio de la Plata's western corridor (maps 5 and 6).[16]

The chief administrators of these expeditions included military officers, diplomats, naval engineers, cosmographers, geographers, astronomers, mathematicians, watchmakers, priests, surgeons, accountants, notaries, and sometimes botanists. Authorities in Lisbon and Madrid appointed them for their expertise, for previous service to the crown, or for their noble standing. These individuals authored the principal sources that exist regarding the expeditions, and it is through their gaze that historians have come to understand these events. Their ultimate goal was to transform the theoretical guide maps into usable, large-scale maps and to negotiate the precise location of the borderline in a manner favorable to their crown. They mined local archives and consulted with informants as they scoured for bits of evidence to support their interpretation of the treaties' broad terms. These officials also kept a daily record of their itineraries to provide a description of the local landscape. Their diaries included geographical, hydrological, and cosmological measurements; coordinates for key rivers, fords, and peaks; and descriptions of local people and wildlife. This information, along with the guide maps, would serve not only as a way to stake a claim over the borderland but also as a tool for future administration and investment.

The handful of lettered elites who commanded the expeditions represented a tiny fraction of the overall labor force, as American actors occupied the vast majority of salaried posts and kept the commissions operative. While ranking officials debated the terms of the treaty and geographers surveyed the landscape, local guides (*baqueanos*) corrected errors in the *Mapa das Cortes* and other guide maps.[17] Legions of laborers carried chests of books and instruments, built and navigated rafts, blazed trails, set up campsites, collected specimens, and even prepared a masquerade ball. Some led the way through fields and forests, while others maintained lumbering oxcarts full of foodstuffs, tools, or the large marble obelisks they would later erect to signal the boundaries. Still others tended to the hundreds of livestock that traveled with each team, searching for pastures and rationing their meat while armed troops warily scoured their surroundings. One Spanish subdivision traveled with ninety-eight personal servants and slaves—the commanding officer alone had twenty-five—including cupbearers, cooks, musicians, and launderers. Occasionally, these subalterns even saved the lives of demarcation officials, as occurred in 1759 when a team of swimmers rescued the commanding Spanish officer after his canoe capsized; they pulled him out of the water with the treaty and instructions, while the *Mapa das Cortes* floated away. A similar series of events played out in 1785 and 1797, this time ending with the rescue of a drowning Portuguese engineer and the papers and maps held by the commanding officer of Portugal's second subdivision, respectively.[18]

Local guides were particularly important for their ability to translate Indigenous toponyms for the mapping teams. As the boundary commissions ventured inland, the landmarks that appeared on their maps were largely derived from Indigenous languages. The mapmakers camped in Caa Ibate (tall forest) and traveled through Caa Guazu (large forest). They charted the Ybira-yepiro (stripped-wood) River, the Apicasuro (dove hunting) highlands, and countless other sites with Guaraní names.[19] They thus took great care to procure Guaraní-speaking guides so that they could "make use of the true [names] in the maps of this campaign."[20] Indigenous toponyms often belied the demarcation teams' desire for fixed labels in their maps, however, as place names varied according to guide or shifted over time. Moreover, Native guides did not always recognize the toponyms noted in the mapmakers' instructions and reference maps, given that their dialect had changed over time.[21] This ambiguity, combined with the mapmakers' unfamiliarity with Native lands, led to heated debates over where to draw the border, as occurred with the Río Igurey. Despite both treaties explicitly declaring that the border should follow the river, neither the Madrid nor the San Ildefonso expeditions could find a waterway by that name. Earlier maps were inconclusive, and the mapmakers lacked Native guides. By the 1790s, both sides agreed that the Igurey was simply a misnomer for a different river, though they disagreed over which one. The Portuguese argued that it was the Río Garey, given "the similarity of the name," while the Spanish contested that Igurey was an "altered and corrupted" spelling of the Guaraní toponym Jaguare'y.[22] Beyond holding the border in abeyance, this case and others point to complex Indigenous territorialities that mapmakers struggled to codify.

Support for the demarcation efforts also came from settlers and Native communities along the way. Local administrators from both sides provided supplies, provisions, and laborers. In fact, operational oversight of the southernmost portion of the Madrid mapping expedition was one of the first responsibilities of the newly created governorship of Montevideo in the 1750s. In addition, local officials often shared historical and geographical records with demarcation officers, whether by identifying informants or by providing access to their archival repositories. Where administrators' knowledge ended, Native mission dwellers occasionally filled in the gaps. In some instances, caciques even presented information from their own record-keeping devices. In 1784, Spain's third subdivision consulted with three Mbayá caciques, who used "knots and signs" to calculate the number of casualties in a skirmish they had had with a Portuguese fort near the border.[23] Farther away from the purview of colonial settlements, rural ranchers served as the primary support of the mapping expeditions. It was frequently from these sites that the expeditions' geographers or mathematicians took their measurements of latitude and longitude.[24] When far beyond the ranches, the boundary commissions relied on the collaboration of autonomous Native communities. The San Ildefonso mapping teams sought out "Indians more knowledgeable of these lands" than the Guaraní-speaking guides that accompanied them, while one Madrid team offered gifts to "Guanana [Indians] extracted from the forests" to provide "information on their country and its rivers."[25]

Walking the Line

As the Madrid and San Ildefonso boundary commissions traveled through the Río de la Plata, they found themselves limited by the same social and territorial contexts that they hoped to order. In order to lengthen the gaze of imperial authorities, the mapmakers entered territories over which neither crown had effective control. They therefore depended on rural actors, who in turn recognized the expeditions' stakes and responded accordingly. Demarcation officers penned some of the first textual accounts of the region's rural landscape, and their encounters with local agents reveal spatial practices that had previously been recounted orally or had existed beyond administrators' purview. The mapmakers' were not trailblazers, however, and both the natural landscape and extant patterns of use forced them through particular geographical corridors. The third, fourth, and fifth subdivisions traveled along the royal roads that hugged the Río Paraná on their way to Paraguay. Meanwhile, the first and second subdivisions marched along more precarious pathways.

The accounts left by the boundary commissions indicate that at the time of the demarcations, tolderías continued to be the principal arbiters of borderland space. Mapmakers' itineraries and subsequent diaries dedicated a disproportionate amount of time to spaces of colonial authority; their haste and brevity elsewhere indicate areas where Native peoples ruled. For this reason, a timeline of events for the San Ildefonso demarcation is instructive. Whereas the first and second subdivisions worked for over two years around the Lagoa Mirim, they dedicated a mere five months to lands between Santa Tecla and Montegrande (map 6). Moreover, the content of these accounts contoured the spatial limits of Spanish and Portuguese territorial reach. When detailing lands close to the Lagoa Mirim, the mapmakers' diaries illuminated preexisting trade networks, which they attempted to police, often aggressively.[26] Yet as the expeditions moved inland into tolderías' lands, their accounts thinned and no longer included documentation of police actions or illicit settlements. In fact, the mapmakers often remarked at how ill-equipped their outposts were, as Batoví had only one overseer and six workers, and San Martín consisted of only thirty militiamen housed in a straw-roofed hut.[27] The stark juxtaposition—exerting imperial sovereignty over contrabandists versus rushing through the countryside to evade tolderías—coincided with the reach of Iberian territorial authority, which was restricted to the eastern corridor.

Despite the demarcation teams' best efforts to avoid tolderías, the corridors that directed their itineraries funneled them through river and highland crossings and made engagement with tolderías inevitable. As they traversed the countryside, mapmakers mentioned toponyms that referred to Native histories; they also discovered physical evidence of territorialities that existed beyond the purview of colonial settlements. They camped at Minuanes Crossing (Paso dos Minuanos), crossed the Minuanes Stream (Arroyo dos Minuanos), felt the Minuán Winds (Vento Minuano), and paid tribute to caciques near the Young Chief River (Río Caciquey). The travelers marked on their maps the Baumaxahate Stream (Arroyo Baumaxahate) and the Aceguá Hill (Cerro Aceguá), both of which may have meant "cold peak." Guenoas reportedly buried their dead atop the latter. The mapmakers noted other features that referred to known caciques and their kin: the Zapata Stream (Arroyo de Zapata), the Batú Stream (Arroyo de Batú), and the Jozé Minuano Crossing (Paso de Jozé Minuano). They came upon abandoned ranches where tolderías had evicted occupants; crossed a waterway where a Native woman had been mauled by a wild feline, the Dead Indian Stream (Arroyo de la India Muerta); and erected a stone obelisk along the Black Belly Stream (Arroyo Barriga Negra), where Minuanes had reportedly found a man's decaying corpse.[28]

Sometimes engagement was more direct. In October 1752, the Spanish and Portuguese teams commissioned under the Treaty of Madrid had their first contact with tolderías while encamped near Castillos Grande, along the Atlantic coast. A number of Minuanes slipped into the Spanish team's camp during the dark of night and absconded with two hundred horses. In response, soldiers stationed in the nearby Portuguese fort of São Miguel set out to recover the horses, but they were unable to apprehend the perpetrators. Instead, they raided and took twenty-eight captives from a nearby toldería that was suspected of having a relationship with the original thieves. One month later, Minuanes again entered the expedition's encampments and extracted horses. A familiar pattern of events transpired, as a subsequent imperial raid abducted thirty-two people from what appear to have been other tolderías.[29] But these encounters were overshadowed by events that occurred several months later at Santa Tecla, when Guaraní leaders from the San Miguel mission refused to provide aid or supplies to the demarcation teams. As previously described, this confrontation prompted the suspension of the southern mapping expeditions, as the Portuguese teams returned to Rio Grande, and the Spanish retreated to Montevideo and Colônia.[30] It also initiated three years of fighting, which lasted from 1753 to 1756 and is commonly referred to as the Guaraní War.

The Guaraní War, though ostensibly a bilateral battle between Jesuit-Guaraní missions and Luso-Hispanic armies, was shaped by tolderías' actions. The war began only after several of the Siete Pueblos attempted to comply with the Treaty of Madrid and relocate to the Spanish side of the interimperial border, in tolderías' lands.[31] Caravans from the San Luis and San Borja missions set out to establish new settlements along the Río Miriñay and the Río Queguay, respectively (map 5).[32] Their plans changed, however, when tolderías rejected their arrival. According to the Jesuit Bernardo Nusdorffer, San Luis's march to the Río Miriñay incited aggressive opposition from Charrúas living there. A Charrúa cacique named Gaspar Cossero declared that his people would "expel the Lusistas [San Luis's migrants], even though they knew they would have to go to war with all of the [missions]." Another Charrúa intimidated the migrants by "forcefully removing" one of their ponchos, while others "were upset and threating to kill all of [the Lusistas]." Nusdorffer met directly with the Charrúas, gifting them "a large amount of yerba maté and tobacco," but his offerings did not assuage tensions. Amid a second attempt at relocation, this time backed by militias from the Yapeyú and La Cruz missions, the migrants gave up their endeavor: "The Lusistas wanted to return to their mission because they did not want to have war with the Charrúas. . . . Some wanted to join other missions, others wanted to look for other lands in the Paraná in order not to meddle anymore in the Charrúas' lands." The Paraná and Paraguay rivers were briefly considered as alternative sites, but they were controlled by Abipones and Payaguás, so the Lusistas returned home once again.[33] San Borja's migrants also faced comparable protests from Charrúa, Minuán, and Bohan tolderías, and they too returned to their missions. A project to relocate the San Miguel and San Juan Bautista missions to the Río Negro was discarded for similar reasons. The futility of these moves was unsurprising, as several years earlier, Yapeyú had rejected a proposal to form a new mission in the same site allocated for San Borja on account of it being tolderías' territory.[34]

Guaraní resistance to the Treaty of Madrid was not simply because they would have to move their missions but because there were no empty lands where they could relocate. Despite falling within Spanish territorial claims, the lands designated for new missions were controlled by Charrúas, Minuanes, and Bohanes. Cognizant of this, the migrants returned to their missions and prepared to face imperial armies rather than neighboring tolderías. Guaraní caciques certainly pointed to their ancestral claims as a basis for protest, as community histories, religion, and epistemologies were rooted in the local landscape. They would also protest the logistical difficulties of moving to new sites and making them self-sustaining.[35] Nonetheless, in their official opposition, they again emphasized the lack of available lands: "The infidel Charrúas and Minuanes [said] to us 'there are no lands for you. . . . If you want to enter into these lands it will have to be with war.' With their spears pointed at us, we returned to our mission and there remained, as there were no more lands to be sought out."[36] Rather than suggesting that there were no grounds for their move, Guaraní caciques instead argued that there were no grounds for them to move to. Refusing to be on the front lines against tolderías, the only option that remained for the mission dwellers was to resist the relocation of their settlement.

In response to Guaraní refusal to support the mapping expeditions, Spanish and Portuguese officials abandoned the demarcation efforts and prepared for military assault. Portuguese forces would engage the missions from Rio Grande and Viamão in the east, while Spanish soldiers would approach from the south, along the Río Uruguay, and for the next three years, warfare engulfed the north of the Río de la Plata region. Imperial forces and their allies pitted themselves against fighters from the missions and whatever support the missions could garner. Here again, tolderías served as important actors. Despite previous conflicts over Guaraní efforts to move to their lands, by the end of 1753, Charrúas, Minuanes, Bohanes, and Guenoas had all begun to collaborate with Guaraní forces against the imperial armies. Whether spying, participating in battles, or commandeering horses and supplies, they proved invaluable allies to the resistance efforts.

Why did many tolderías eventually align with the Siete Pueblos in their uprising against imperial armies, particularly after mission forces had participated in armed campaigns against them from 1749 to 1752?[37] One possible explanation is kinship ties. Charrúas, Minuanes, and Guenoas all had kin living in Yapeyú, San Borja, and other missions, and it is possible that they sought to lend them aid out of affinity or obligation. Indeed, Minuán spies provided advance warning to family members in San Miguel when Portuguese forces planned to march on the mission, while a faction of Yapeyú's inhabitants sought Charrúa aid before nearly rising up against the mission's priests.[38] However, many Minuanes eventually abandoned the resistance efforts, while others shifted their support to the Portuguese. Kinship ties may have been strong, but the support of local tolderías did not necessarily extend to the entire population of a given mission. A second potential answer is that Charrúas, Bohanes, Guenoas, and Minuanes hired themselves out as mercenaries to the mission armies. Indeed, their involvement in the war came at the request of Guaraní leadership, and they received numerous payments over its duration.[39] Still, yerba maté, tobacco, and a handful of other items would likely not have been enough for members of these tolderías to risk themselves in armed combat. Given the territorial dynamics of settlements and tolderías that defined the region up to this point, these payments more likely served as a symbolic recognition of the authority such tolderías carried over the countryside. Offering goods was akin to a request for actions that Guaraní fighters could not undertake themselves, rather than payment to hired mercenaries.

Tolderías' decisions to participate in the war more likely derived from their position as arbiters of the countryside. Fighters from tolderías mostly took up arms in their own lands, rather than traveling deep into mission territories, and their skirmishes with imperial troops occurred as royal soldiers and militias attempted to traverse their lands. As Spanish forces from Buenos Aires marched north along the Río Uruguay toward Yapeyú in 1754, Charrúas, Minuanes, and Guenoas came at the request of the mission's residents, routing the imperial army handily and forcing it back to Buenos Aires and Montevideo (map 5). In the east, Minuanes, Guenoas, and Guaraní halted Portuguese forces near the fort of Jesús Maria José, along the Rio Pardo.[40] This broad territorial engagement was also evident in the rebels' strategizing. A priest from the La Cruz mission gave payment of yerba maté, tobacco, and other items to Charrúas, Bohanes, and Minuanes "so that they would survey the countryside, its entrances, and its exits, and that they would promptly report on whatever news they had, and that they would incorporate themselves into the Guaraní forces to help them in the defense of their missions."[41] These "entrances and exits" referred to the pathways south and east of the missions that led to tolderías' lands, as the rural landscape would force imperial armies along these routes. They included the headwaters of the Río Ibicuí and the Río Piraí, sites occupied by tolderías for decades.[42] To guard these key crossings was not simply to protect the missions but to enforce tolderías' claims over the countryside.

By the end of the war, numerous tolderías had begun to side with the imperial invaders, and eventually the Guaraní missions found themselves defeated. Spanish and Portuguese military officials recognized the need to garner safe passage across the countryside if they hoped to procure victory, and in early 1755, imperial forces near Santa Tecla invited Minuán and Guenoa caciques to parley. They lavished the caciques with gifts, including clothing and money, seeking to procure the caciques' support. Responses from the Minuanes and the Guenoas varied; most refused to lend aid, but others used the opportunity for the benefit of their own tolderías. In particular, the cacique Moreira agreed to abandon the resistance and return with his closest kin to the countryside southwest of the Lagoa Mirim, near São Miguel. While he offered to aid the imperial efforts personally, he also leveraged that moment to find an exit for his tolderías and to reestablish peace with his Portuguese counterparts. Moreira's tolderías were precisely those that had raided the Spanish commission's encampment in 1752. Following that incident, he and his kin had taken the horses to the Yapeyú mission and eventually agreed to aid the missions' resistance efforts, waylaying imperial armies in the following years. But hoping to avoid the tolls of the imminent battles between imperial and missionary forces, he and others absconded from the war and returned to their previous abode.[43]

Moreira's actions demonstrate how internal motivations and territorial dynamics also shaped many tolderías' decisions to avoid or exit the war. Moreira and his tolderías had not participated in the resistance because of kinship ties with the missions' inhabitants, nor had they done so for any sort of pan-Indigenous identity. Rather, they had common cause with the Siete Pueblos in the conflict that emerged when the demarcation teams came onto their lands. Once the tolderías restored peace with imperial forces, there was no longer any need to continue in the war. Other caciques made similar decisions, especially after receiving payments from imperial armies and watching them move on to mission territories. In one case, a Minuán named Molina convinced sixty of his kin to abandon the San Miguel mission before the fighting reached them.[44] Tolderías whose lands were affected neither by the mission relocation projects nor by the subsequent military marches tended to avoid the war from the beginning, and many maintained peaceful ties with neighboring settlements throughout the war. Charrúa tolderías near Corrientes retained ties with the city's residents, while other Charrúas negotiated a settlement in Santo Domingo Soriano. A number of tolderías fought alongside Guaraní militias through the end of the war, yet the rebels' cause was lost when more and more tolderías eventually chose indifference or aid to imperial forces.[45]

In 1758, two years after the war ended, the Treaty of Madrid's southern boundary commissions resumed their activities. Their earlier maps were incomplete and some of their written documentation had been incinerated in the fighting, so they returned to the treaty's fourth article and the issue of the Río Ibicuí's origins.[46] Drawing on published maps and manuscripts provided by Jesuit officials, Portuguese and Spanish mapmakers presented competing visions. Specifically, Spanish officials argued that the map drawn by the Portuguese commission had underestimated the size of the region and failed to include the presence of Native peoples in it. They based their claim on reports that emigrants from the missions had incorporated with Charrúas and Minuanes in the area, numbering around 2,500 people in total. The Portuguese commanding officer retorted that the tolderías must have arrived after the map was drawn, but his claim was dubious. Not only had tolderías occupied those lands for decades before the war and engaged imperial armies during it, the historical maps referenced by the demarcation teams acknowledged their presence. One map, provided by the Jesuit Lorenzo Ovado, was even drawn during a military expedition against Charrúas in the 1740s.[47] Thus, despite the official Portuguese map, neither empire had consolidated control over these lands. The Spanish and Portuguese had formed new settlements in the wake of the Guaraní War, namely Rio Pardo, São Nicolau, and São Gonçalo, yet many refugees abandoned the missions and incorporated into Charrúa and Minuán tolderías, thus expanding Native authority.[48] The Madrid demarcations undoubtedly altered territorial dynamics along the border, just not according to imperial designs.

In legal terms, the Madrid borderline was short lived. In 1761, the Portuguese and Spanish crowns signed the Treaty of El Pardo, which annulled all parts of the Treaty of Madrid and its demarcations "as if they had never existed nor been executed."[49] The Siete Pueblos were returned to Spain and Colônia to the Portuguese, and administrators ordered that the stone obelisks erected during the demarcations be demolished or thrown into the ocean. In lieu of a new treaty, local officials reached de facto agreements over small portions of the border, as occurred in 1763 along the Lagoa dos Patos and the Rio Piratiní. However, these pacts did not obviate the need for a broader accord, and within four years, officials complained that the lack of a demarcation had left the question of possession uncertain.[50] During these years, Iberian militaries again turned their guns on one another, with Spain occupying Colônia, Santa Teresa, São Miguel, and Rio Grande in 1762 and 1763; Portugal pushing south to reclaim Rio Grande and take the Spanish fort of Santa Tecla in 1776; and Spain retaliating by taking control of Colônia and the island of Santa Catarina, farther north along the Brazilian coast. Similar patterns emerged throughout the continent, as imperial armies clashed and each side raced to establish new settlements in the absence of an overarching treaty.[51] It would not be until the 1777 Treaty of San Ildefonso that a borderline again became the legal standard and not until the 1780s that demarcation teams reappeared in the region. In the Río de la Plata, this new border was farther north and was again given primacy over settlements: all settlements taken in the years between the two treaties were returned with the exception of Colônia, which remained a Spanish possession.[52] By this point, the Jesuit order had been expelled from both Portuguese (1759) and Spanish (1767) dominions, and the missions were under duress, making armed resistance unrealistic.

The San Ildefonso demarcation produced little armed backlash in the region. Instead, it revealed tolderías' consolidated control over lands adjacent to the borderline and Spanish and Portuguese administrators' continued lack of knowledge of lands beyond the isolated settlements. Establishing fortresses in Santa Tecla and Rio Pardo did not imply control over or knowledge of the borderlands. Accordingly, once the demarcation parties moved north from Santa Tecla toward the missions, they found themselves obliged to proffer payment in exchange for safe passage. All along the newly designed imperial limits, Native peoples enforced their own territorial claims, causing the mapping teams to purposefully avoid certain areas.[53] Ultimately, Native restriction of travel through these unmapped territorialities proved more of an impediment to the demarcation efforts than the call to arms that had occurred three decades before. As late as 1797, the commanding officer of Portugal's second subdivision, Francisco João Roscio, complained of a lack of knowledge of the lands between Porto Alegre and San Martín (map 6), as they were "occupied by savage Indians, and transited little to none by the Portuguese, making this terrain unknown for the object that I discuss." Three years later, the commander of the third Spanish subdivision, Félix de Azara, complained that his office "lacked an exact drawing of the countryside and its frontier [with Brazil]."[54] Here and elsewhere along the imaginary border, administrators lamented the perpetuity of spaces unknown and unseen by imperial powers.

Geographies of the Future and Ethnographies of the Past

Despite their operational limitations, the Madrid and San Ildefonso mapping expeditions were key moments in the production of geographic and ethnographic knowledge about the Río de la Plata. The discursive trend they exemplified and to which they contributed had two central components: the normalization of the idea of the border and the reification of the region's Indigenous communities within geographically defined taxonomical categories. These sensibilities were part of broader epistemological shifts in the eighteenth-century Americas and the Atlantic world, and as such, the mapmakers' writings discursively incorporated the Río de la Plata into Enlightenment-era ideological frameworks. By introducing new legal geographies and by cataloging Native peoples according to naturalist understandings of space and human society, the boundary commissions ushered in a new era of engagement

with the region for Portuguese and Spanish officials. As they ignored Indigenous territorialities and retrospectively recast regional histories, they enabled
and impelled administrators to envision contiguous and consolidated territorial units rather than enclaves and corridors, and to imagine tolderías not as
future allies or converts but as unruly subjects or incorrigible barbarians.

Prior to the demarcation efforts, writings on the Río de la Plata's countryside were limited in their geographical reach and anecdotal in their accounts
of tolderías. Sixteenth-century chronicles conceptualized the region principally
as a pathway to Paraguay. Their geographical perspective was restricted to the
riverine channels that ran between Buenos Aires and the Paraguayan capital
of Asunción—principally the Río de la Plata estuary and the Río Paraná, which
many mapmakers considered one and the same—or to the narrow terrestrial
corridor that cut across the north of the region, connecting Asunción eastward
to the Atlantic coast.[55] For this reason, early maps of the region and the South
American continent alike provided oversized and detailed renderings of the
two rivers while demonstrating little consistency in their depictions of the region's countryside (figure 14). Knowledge of regional lands remained limited
despite larger imperial efforts to systematize geographical information on the
Americas, such as Spain's *Relaciones Geográficas*, as administrators in the Río
de la Plata met such endeavors with indifference.[56] During these years, imperial narratives of engagement with Native peoples consisted of episodic accounts of trade or warfare. Rather than offering systematic ethnographies,
travelers limited themselves to ascribing ethnonyms to Indigenous agents according to the locations where they encountered them.[57]

When Jesuit missionaries began to engage the northern portion of the region in the seventeenth century, they developed their own corpus of written
and drawn accounts. Their maps and reports served (until the boundary commissions) as the most detailed renderings of local peoples and lands, and they
demonstrated key shifts from the writings of earlier explorers. Specifically, as
priests and friars attempted to garner support for new mission settlements, they
aimed to locate non-missionized peoples and new resources. Beyond the administrative records of individual missions, the Society of Jesus developed a
voluminous archive of maps and descriptions of engagement with local
tolderías. Their drawings of regional lands almost always included ethnonyms,
as priests sought to map the locations of non-Christian peoples whom they
could eventually bring into the fold of Christendom (figure 15).[58] In spite of
these more detailed accounts, however, missionaries did not attempt to cate-
gorize tolderías in the region according to any universal ethnographic frame-

FIGURE 14 Levinus Hulsius, *Nova et exacta delineatio Americae*, 1602. Hulsius's map, which included all of southern South America, appeared in a multivolume series of European voyages. This portion of the map corresponded with the travel accounts of Pero Lopes de Sousa and Ulrich Schmidl, given its toponyms, the shipwreck near the Cabo de Santa María, and the use of the ethnonym "Zecuruas," which may have indicated Charrúas. Courtesy of the John Carter Brown Library at Brown University.

work. Furthermore, their geographic knowledge was limited to the lands near their missions and the various networks of roadways that connected them.

During the late seventeenth and early eighteenth centuries, Iberian cartographic production regarding the Americas turned to claiming resources and defining pathways. As Jesuits and Spanish and Portuguese administrators debated regional possession and sought to identify the locations of resources, much of their mapmaking focused on coastal charts or regional roadways. Here again, both drawn and written sources revealed the limited territorial visions of their authors. Jesuits provided details on the mission complex to the north

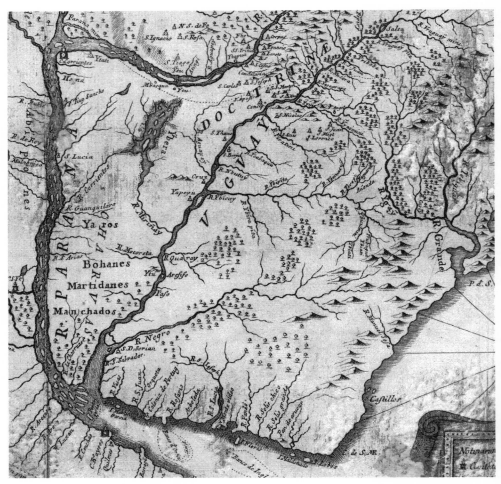

FIGURE 15 Giovanni Petroschi, *Paraquariae provinciae*, 1732. Petroschi's map of the Jesuit enterprise in southern South America, like many others drawn by the Society of Jesus, geolocates tolderías in the region. In this portion of the map, Petroschi lists Yaros, Bohanes, Martidanes, Manchados, and Charrúas between the Paraná and Uruguay rivers, an ethnonym pattern that would be replicated in maps throughout the century. Petroschi's map is a copy of a 1722 work produced by Jesuit Juan Francisco Dávila, which was consulted for the Mapa das Cortes. Fúrlong Cárdiff, *Cartografía jesuítica*, 1:44–49; Ferreira, "O Mapa das Cortes," 56. España. Ministerio de Cultura. Archivo General de Simancas, MPD, 04, 034.

of the region, while royal navigators drew coastlines and harbors. Despite competing claims for territorial possession, maps drawn in the region generally did not include borderlines, although they sometimes provided estimates of the Tordesillas meridian. Prior to the demarcations, the borderline was the product of European engravers' tables rather than American travelers' accounts. Jesuits continued to highlight Native peoples' purported locations, as proselytization remained a possibility, but imperial mapmakers were less consistent with their representations.

The lacuna of geographic and ethnographic information made the Madrid and San Ildefonso boundary commissions even more important for imperial administrators. Along with producing evidence of a legal border, mapmakers aimed to compile and organize information on the regional landscape in a format usable for future governance. Thus, they scoured local archives and interviewed countless informants along the way. The principal officers of the demarcation efforts were familiar with extant records, frequently citing earlier chronicles, route descriptions (*roteiros*), sketch maps (*croquis*), Jesuit histories, and oral testimonies as evidence of their claims. In framing this information, however, they presented an entirely new territorial vision that included fixed borders and provincial units. They also expressed new attitudes vis-à-vis tolderías in the region. Whereas earlier accounts depicted tolderías as active trading partners or potential converts, the writings of demarcation officials focused particularly on their nomadism, portraying them as obdurate, unchanging actors who impeded the realization of territorial order. This new territorial and ethnographic vision would orient imperial administration thereafter.

The mapping expeditions recorded geographical information in a variety of media, designed to be read in conjunction with one another. In addition to continual correspondence with their team members, counterparts, and imperial administrators, demarcation officials left day-by-day diaries of their activities. These voluminous tomes were meant to produce a level of detail that could not be captured by the treaty maps. José de Saldanha, the geographer for San Ildefonso's first Portuguese subdivision, explained in the introduction to his diary: "The painter, with a delicate brush, can represent nature but cannot express circumstances, news, and movements of events. This is the part reserved for the historian." Therefore, he concluded, "An extensive diary, which we compose in the countryside, is indispensable for the exact configuration of the drawings."[59] In their diaries, the mapmakers systematically identified rivers, highland peaks, and crossings, geolocating them with latitude and longitude coordinates. They then overlaid historical accounts on the physical landscape by using the occasion of crossing a particular geographical feature to recount events that had occurred there. Lastly, the mapmakers described local plants, animals, and terrain, sometimes collecting specimens or situating local flora and fauna in global taxonomies. The aim of this meticulous note-taking was not only to produce a border but to organize local knowledge and mobilize it as a tool for historical claims and future resource exploitation.

The thousands of pages that detailed the countryside would have been relatively useless if not combined with the visual representations presented in the treaty maps, which enabled readers to imagine the region as a unified whole. Saldanha conceded, "Nevertheless, this text [the mapmaker's diary] continues to be tiresome to read because of the multitude of additions of material." Accordingly, he and others took care in their diaries to refer to key points or sections of their maps, designing their textual and visual sources to be read side by side. Saldanha added that "a new map could also be of use, moreover, if several brief notes of the country's natural history are added to it."[60] The boundary commissions' maps included both medium-scale renderings of the region as a whole and large-scale drawings of specific points of contestation along the borderline. They located key settlements as well as the various obelisks that the expeditions erected. Collectively, the treaty maps presented the border as extant or achievable. Whereas the written accounts aimed to guide travelers, the maps were the bedrock of Spain's and Portugal's legal claims. Without these maps, the treaties would have carried little juridical or practical weight; thus, the chief officer of each side was required to sign off on the final versions.

Unlike earlier geographic renderings, the corpus of maps produced by the demarcation teams was legally binding and therefore established a new juridical precedent. Following the Treaty of Madrid, all subsequent peace agreements ordering territorial possession in the Río de la Plata included the concept of a fixed border. Despite the treaty's 1761 abrogation, diplomats and mapmakers involved in the Treaty of San Ildefonso used the Madrid expeditions' maps for their own negotiations. The materials produced by the San Ildefonso demarcation teams, in turn, served as the principal precedent for peace accords between Spain and Portugal in 1801 and for postcolonial border disputes in the region thereafter. Nonetheless, the realization of a legal border came not only through agreements but also through conflict. The Madrid and San Ildefonso demarcations transformed abstract disagreements over continental possession into localized border disputes, and subsequent disagreements among regional administrators over the borderline's precise location reinforced their agreement on its existence. The Spanish and Portuguese also presumed that they, rather than tolderías, were legitimate possessors, sometimes espousing retrospective histories by claiming to have possessed Native lands along the borderline since "time immemorial" or via the formation of short-lived reducciones decades prior.[61]

The acrimonious interactions between Portuguese and Spanish boundary commissions under the Treaty of San Ildefonso transformed the border from an imprecise idea to a discernible pattern of human settlement. The demarcation took nearly two decades to complete, with various delays and multiyear gaps, yet the persistent enmity ultimately contributed to the treaty's endurance. The case of the Rio Piratiní serves as a clear example. During the Treaty of Madrid's negotiations, this river was well within Portuguese dominions. But when the San Ildefonso accord designated the Lagoa Mirim as a neutral body of water, it required that the border extend westward along the first waterway north of the lagoon, which it assumed was also south of the Portuguese fort of São Gonçalo (map 6).[62] When the San Ildefonso demarcation teams arrived in the area in 1784, they disputed whether the Piratiní was the waterway in question. To further complicate matters, São Gonçalo was located on the river's southern coast, which would place it within Spanish dominion. Portuguese officers chastised their Spanish counterparts for "suddenly embarking" on demarcation activities, "despotically" commandeering goods from traders, and evicting settlers. Spanish officers retorted that the Portuguese were "lovers of formalities" who "unnecessarily delayed their tasks."[63] The two sides moved on to the Guaraní missions in 1786 only to revisit the issue a decade later. The dispute over the Rio Piratiní produced a vast array of arguments—historical, geographical, cartographic, and otherwise—to justify the competing claims, and it precipitated a rush to populate the area. The Spanish founded three forts along the nearby Rio Jaguarão to fortify their claims, while the Portuguese issued land titles (*sesmarias*) along the Piratiní's coast.[64] Similar disputes emerged farther north over the location of the Río Pepirí Guazú, the existence of the Río Igurey and the Río Corrientes, and whether the Portuguese forts of Coimbra and Albuquerque were on the Spanish side of the border, each one simultaneously holding the border in abeyance and hastening its materialization.[65]

As the expeditions' maps inscribed a legal border on the landscape, they left tolderías out entirely. Three factors likely explain this deviation from earlier maps of the region. First, the mapping teams were primarily concerned with visualizing the border and producing a general guide for administrators who read their textual accounts. This intention served as the principal filter for what they included in their maps—physical features, stone obelisks, pathways, settlements—and what they excluded. Second, the boundary commissions were reluctant to

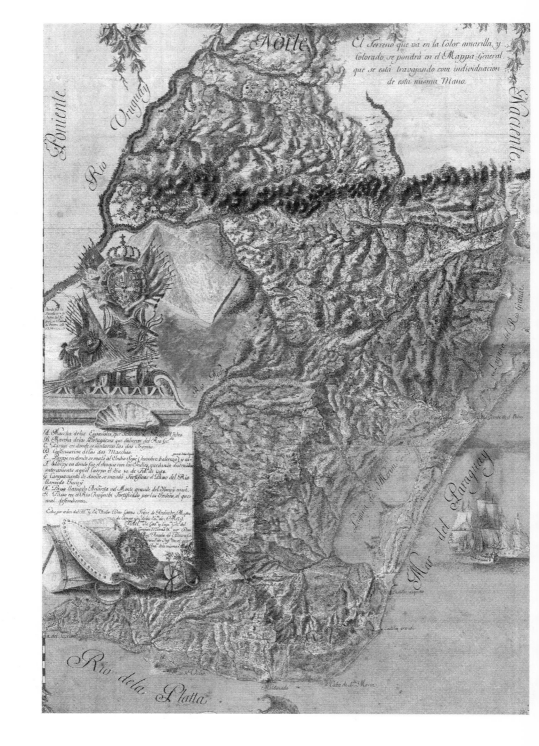

Norte

El Terreno que vá en la Color amarilla, y
colorado, se pondrá en el Mappa General
que se esta travajando con individuacion
de esta misma Mano.

Poniente

Rio Uruguay

Naciente.

Rio Grande

Laguna del Rio grande

Rio Negro

A. Marcha delos Españoles, que Salieron del Rio del Volvo.
B. Marcha delos Portuguezes que Salieron del Rio Gr.ᵈᵉ
C. Parage en donde se juntaron las dos Tropas.
D. Continuacion de las Marchas.
E. Parage en donde se mató al Indio Sepé (hombre baleroso) y al
F. Parage en donde fue el choque con los Indios, quedando destruidos
    enteramente aquel Cuerpo el dia 10 de Feb.ᵒ de 1756.
G. Campamento de donde se mandó Fortificar el Paso del Rio
    llamado Yacuy
H. Paso llamado Briarita del Monte grande del Ybicuy mui.
I. Paso en el Rio Chuynibi Fortificado por los Indios, el que
    mal defendieron.

Echo por orden del Ill.ᵐᵒ y Ex.ᵐᵒ Señor Don Gomes Freire de Andrade, M.ᵈᵉ
                    de Camara Gn.ˡ delos Ex.ᵗᵒˢ de S.M.F.
                    Fidel.ˢⁱᵐᵃ la Gen.ˡ y Cap.ⁿ Gn.ˡ del
                    Don Gervasio Yllanes & ᵃⁱⁱ Don
                    Angelo de Eluiaurg....
                    ...Coronel en Sar.ᵗᵒ mr. que
                    ... dela misma...

Laguna de la Merim

Mar del Paraguay

Rio de la Platta

Cabo de S.ᵗᵃ Maria

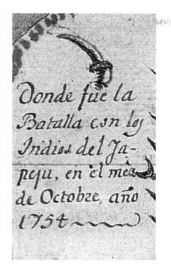

Donde fue la Batalla con los Indios del Japeju, en el mes de Octobre, año 1754

El Terreno que va en la Color amarilla, y Colorado, se pondrà en el Mappa General, que se està travajando com individuacion de esta misma Mano.

FIGURE 16 Miguel Angelo de Blasco, *Mapa Que Contiene las marchas*, 1756. Blasco's map provides a detailed rendering of the Madrid line, the adjacent landscape, and the itineraries of the demarcation teams and imperial armies. Lands between the Río Uruguay and the Río Negro are covered by a cartouche, and a small inscription to the left indicates where Spanish forces lost the 1754 battle. A caption in the upper right indicates that lands left unmarked would be included in a general map on which Blasco was working. España. Ministerio de Defensa. Archivo del Museo Naval.

draw lands they did not directly observe themselves, including vast areas between the Río Uruguay and the borderline. Given that these lands had received "scarce attention," the mapmakers left them as empty spaces or filled them with cartouches (figures 16 and 17).[66] Third, the expeditions' maps were prescriptive models of what the region could become. Tolderías had no place in these imperial designs, and their presence was considered temporary, a sentiment expressed by Andrés de Oyarvide, the geographer for Spain's second subdivision, who lamented the "class of people who for now populate [these lands, which] certainly

FIGURE 17 *Mapa Geographico del Terreno que demarcaron las Primeras Partidas*, 1759. Despite Blasco's promise to fill in vacant lands, the general map produced by the commissions the following year left those lands empty. España. Ministerio de Defensa. Archivo del Museo Naval.

FIGURE 18 Miguel Antonio Ciera, *Mappa geographicum*, 1758. Ciera's map was part of a broader work that followed his itinerary and included maps and drawings. Along with Charrúas, he marked Pampas, Abipones, and others in his maps. The Charrúas are notably south of the Río Negro, indicating that Ciera copied this ethnonym from other maps or that imperial claims of Indigenous absence in this area were unfounded. For details on Ciera's cartographic work, see Costa, "Miguel Ciera." Acervo da Fundação Biblioteca Nacional—Brasil.

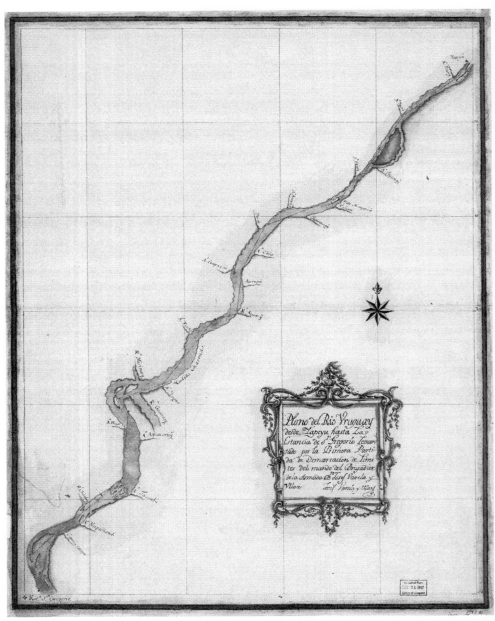

FIGURE 19 Josef Varela y Ulloa, *Plano del Rio Vruguay*, 1784. This map was presumably drawn before the boundary commissions began. Unlike the first subdivision's other maps, this one focuses on lands far from the border. Charrúas appear along the Río Uruguay's eastern coastline, across from the Río Miriñay, where they had resisted San Luis's relocation three decades earlier. Library of Congress, Geography and Map Division.

FIGURE 20 José de Saldanha, *Mapa Corográphico da Capitania de S. Pedro*, 1801. In this section of his map of the Portuguese captaincy of Rio Grande, Saldanha marked a "Povoação dos Minuanos" southwest of the borderline, yet none of the countryside's numerous tolderías appear. Acervo da Fundação Biblioteca Nacional—Brasil.

deserve a more enlightened and industrious nation."[67] Tolderías did appear in a 1758 map by Miguel Antonio Ciera, the cosmographer of Madrid's third Portuguese subdivision; a 1784 map by Josef Varela y Ulloa, the commanding officer of San Ildefono's southern Spanish commission; and an 1801 map by Saldanha. Ciera and Varela y Ulloa identified Charrúas along the eastern coast of the Río Uruguay, while Saldanha marked a "Minuán settlement" along the borderline (figures 18, 19, and 20). These were nonetheless exceptions to the rule. Ciera's marking may have been copied from earlier maps; Varela y Ulloa's contradicted his commission's other maps, in which tolderías' presence was drawn as empty space; and Saldanha's was likely due to the fixity of the site.

Despite the erasure of tolderías from nearly all treaty maps, demarcation officers frequently acknowledged them in their written accounts. While the military expeditions of the Guaraní War chronicled wartime engagement, members of the San Ildefonso demarcation teams penned taxonomic ethnographies. Via detailed descriptions of physical appearance, clothing, languages, customs, historical anecdotes, and geographical locations, they sought to classify Charrúas, Minuanes, and others according to rigid ethnic categories and situate them within the universal taxonomies of naturalist writers like Carl Linnaeus and Georges-Louis Leclerc.[68] They also adopted stadial theories of human development, situating tolderías alongside other mobile peoples of the Americas and assembling retrospective historical anecdotes to opine on the natural character of particular ethnic communities.

The San Ildefonso mapmakers described Minuanes, Charrúas, and others as antiquated actors who imperiled the realization of territorial states. Rather than understanding tolderías' mobility as a strategic response to environmental or social conditions, demarcation officials considered it evidence of barbarous character and a refusal to accept Christian civility. Unlike Guaraní on the missions, who had moved from the irrationality of mobility to the rationality of sedentism and become civilized Christian subjects, tolderías in the region were seen as unchanging.[69] Their mobility was no longer understood as a strategy but rather an attribute of their character, and "infidel Indians" (*indios infieles*) were no longer future Christians but rather irreformable savages. Thus, the mapmakers cataloged tolderías according to ethnonym and then compared them to mobile peoples of other areas, such as Abipones and Mocovíes of the Chaco and Tupis of southeastern Brazil. One writer even surmised that Minuanes had descended from Native peoples in North America, "whom they resembled in their features [and language]."[70] The more demarcation officials traveled and corresponded with one another, the more evidence they produced to support the paradigmatic division between sedentism and mobility.

The mapmakers also associated mobility with illicit behavior. This included laziness, drunkenness, violence, and theft, which writers understood as essential characteristics of particular ethnicities. Defined in this way, tolderías were not only unfit subjects but enemies of the empire. Varela y Ulloa argued that Charrúas and Yaros had worked with the Portuguese to "antagonize the Jesuit missions in the north [of the region]," while Diego de Alvear, the commanding officer of San Ildefonso's second Spanish subdivision, claimed that "several delinquents and criminals joined together with [the Minuanes], people of all castes and perversion, corrupting them and making them accustomed to thievery, violence, and other disorder. . . . They live today with little correction of those vices."[71] Other writers sought to understand mobility in conjunction with characteristics that they associated with tolderías. Francisco de Aguirre, the commanding officer of San Ildefonso's fourth Spanish subdivision, reasoned that "all Indian languages are poor . . . [because] a language cannot be abundant among people who lack furniture, houses, art, and animals."[72] Saldanha adopted a more conciliatory stance, suggesting that Minuanes' laziness derived from poor nutrition: "They are meager in their food, yet from this excessive laziness comes their austerity."[73] Whether derisive or paternalistic, each of these assessments added to a growing perspective that tolderías' mobility was their defining characteristic and that this characteristic was incompatible with proper vassalage.

Demarcation officials also employed historical accounts as a means to underscore what they saw as tolderías' incorrigible character. They derived much of their information from earlier Jesuit writings, yet they deployed historical evidence as a call to extirpation rather than proselytization.[74] In these retrospective retellings, as broad ethnonyms agglutinated contemporary tolderías and assigned them culpability for the travails of European adventurers, eighteenth-century tolderías appeared as direct descendants of sixteenth-century Indigenous antagonists. Charrúas received blame for the 1516 cannibalization of navigator Juan Díaz de Solís, while Minuanes purportedly killed Spanish governor Juan de Garay in 1583.[75] Such anecdotal remembrances ultimately presented tolderías as bellicose impediments to imperial prosperity. Aguirre claimed that Spanish merchants had long restricted themselves to waterways "because overland pathways would be populated by infidels," while Azara asserted that yerba maté forests had been underutilized because "the barbarians that live in them . . . try to hinder their [exploitation]."[76] The narrative arc of these historical accounts ultimately ended in expulsion or forceful subjugation. Aguirre explained: "Minuán Indians impeded [Montevideo's] settlers from traveling far for many years, until . . . [an expedition] annihilated them and the few that remained submitted to peace. . . . Nowadays there is a [Spanish] population eighty leagues or more inland from [Montevideo]."[77] For him and others, Minuanes were a waning relic of irrational lifestyles incompatible with the region's development, and therefore the midcentury military expeditions had liberated the countryside. This narrative both reinforced Spanish claims to possession and served as a precedent for future historical retellings.

Despite claims of objective observation, the mapmakers' accounts derived from each empire's experiences in the region. Tolderías had long restricted Spanish efforts to control the countryside, while the Portuguese competed with the Guaraní missions. Spanish officers thus tended to deride tolderías' mobility and question their ability to adopt agricultural lifestyles. Alvear wrote of Minuanes: "Their greatest glory is their free and wandering lifestyle, they are given to drunkenness and lust." He saw little difference among Charrúas, suggesting that their "wild, ferocious, and bellicose character has kept them from negotiation and communication."[78] Azara explained that despite missionaries' best efforts to missionize Minuanes, "they returned to their wandering and free lifestyle," and he recommended that Spanish governors "give up on their efforts to have them all form reducciones . . . [and] look for other ways to make use of them."[79] Portuguese officials agreed that tolderías lived "in a truly free state," yet refuted their Spanish counterparts' association of mobility with violent incivility. Saldanha argued, "[Minuanes] are not as cruel as the Tape Indians. It has never been reported that the Minuanes killed a Portuguese or Spaniard, even [when] they found them alone or lost in the countryside, as Guaraní have done numerous times." Sebastião Xavier da Veiga Cabral da Câmara, the commanding officer of San Ildefonso's southern Portuguese commission, concurred that Minuanes "ordinarily abstain from wrongdoing," yet he too conceded that they lived in a state of "sad liberty."[80]

The largely Spanish view of tolderías as unchanging and irrational wanderers not only represented a break with earlier discursive patterns but carried clear implications for future interethnic relations in the region. In particular, it ruled out the possibility that tolderías might become imperial Christian subjects. At the same time that Spanish officials sought to redefine the subjecthood of mission-dwelling Guaraní, incorporating them more closely as secular subjects, authorities contemplated the eradication of tolderías through the killing or capture of their inhabitants. These perspectives derived from most tolderías being placed within their crown's territorial jurisdiction through the imagined borderline; tolderías' autonomy belied Spanish claims of territorial sovereignty and was thus intolerable. Portuguese officials tended to adopt the opposite perspective and accept tolderías' mobility. These patterns were by no means universal, however, as Portuguese administrators in some parts of Brazil decried Indigenous mobility, while the attitudes of many Portuguese officials in the Río de la Plata resembled those of the Spanish in the northern part of the continent. In each instance, interethnic policies derived from whether officials were concerned more with accessing the opposite side of the border or with preventing foreign competitors from accessing their side. The positioning of the borderline conditioned that calculation.

Conclusion

In November 1787, after spending the winter encamped near San Martín, members of the San Ildefonso boundary commissions backtracked to erect ten obelisks south along the border to Santa Tecla (map 6). Half would be on the Spanish side of the border, and the other half would be on the Portuguese side, leaving neutral ground in between. Some members of the expedition were skeptical of this endeavor, given that the Minuanes "say that [those lands] belong to them" and "could topple [the obelisks] with ease." Their concerns were eventually eased after meeting with Miguel Ayala Caraí, who assured them that his people would leave the obelisks intact.[81] The boundary commissions then continued their work northward, toward the Río Pepirí Guazú and through forests controlled by Tupis, where they faced similar difficulties in marking the border. The mapmakers moved hastily through the forests, came across Native cemeteries, were intercepted by Indigenous agents, and sought aid from local settlements. Meanwhile, the empires maintained their bilateral debates about whether the Tupis were Portuguese subjects, whether Tupi lands belonged instead to Guaraní mission dwellers, or whether imperial settlers had been in the same area since time immemorial. Tupi responses, much like those of Minuanes and Charrúas, likely derived from their long history with Portuguese and mission settlers, with whom they were currently engaged in armed conflict.[82]

Accounts penned by boundary commissions' other subdivisions reveal similar engagements throughout the borderline, all the way to the Caribbean coast. The third and fourth Spanish subdivisions for the Treaty of San Ildefonso made payments to Abipones, who helped their teams make the journey from Corrientes to Paraguay. Once in Paraguay, the mapmakers sought to use Mbayás, who had recently battled against a Portuguese fort and who controlled borderland spaces, as a human border between imperial vassals. The second Portuguese subdivision for the Madrid demarcation drafted an ethnographic account of Native peoples along the Río Paraná. The Treaty of Madrid's northern Portuguese commission waited two years in the village of Mariuá for their Spanish counterparts, who were impeded by Indigenous people in the Orinoco; by 1756, a rebellion broke out among the village's Native inhabitants. Portugal and Spain sought the support of Indigenous agents and runaway slaves in the Amazon as both empires jockeyed for territorial control vis-à-vis each other and Dutch settlers.[83] All along the border, the contradictions between imperial lines and Indigenous lands were clear.

The demarcation efforts of the Treaties of Madrid and San Ildefonso were watershed moments for legal thought, geographic design, and interethnic relations. As such, they generated immediate responses from local actors through whose lands the commissioned mapmakers traveled, transforming customary relations between imperial administrators and Native neighbors. A close reading of the accounts and maps produced by the boundary commissions reveals the superimposition of an idealized territorial structure on extant territorialities. This change was first discursive, as textual accounts revealed the persistence of local, often Indigenous authority, while the expeditions' maps served as templates for future endeavors. Mapmakers envisioned complete territorial control, a stable borderline, and a sedentary population that could be easily administered. They cataloged the region's tolderías within timeless ethnic categories and ruled out the possibility of incorporating them as rational subjects. These discursive changes would have meant little had they not affected imperial policy and the tolderías themselves. They would have simply been the musings of lettered elites, filed in distant archives. Instead, the two demarcation efforts initiated a new way for imperial authors to experience their relationships with the tolderías and altered where the tolderías positioned themselves geographically. Border thinking engendered border practices and, as will be shown in chapter 4, the cumulative response to the proposed border transformed the region thereafter.

CHAPTER FOUR

Simultaneous Sovereignties

In 1785, a Minuán cacique named Bartolomeo was faced with a difficult choice: keep his kin in their homeland or move across the border into the Portuguese captaincy of Rio Grande. The Treaty of San Ildefonso had placed Bartolomeo's tolderías on the Spanish side of the Luso-Hispanic border, and Spanish authorities had launched an aggressive effort to remove the tolderías and make way for ranches. Early in the year, Spanish officials had offered Bartolomeo and his people "everything they wanted" if they would vacate their lands and form a reducción near Montevideo, while Spanish militias raided a nearby toldería formed by emigrants from the Guaraní missions, taking ninety-eight captives back to the missions. Faced with two undesirable options—reducción or raids—Bartolomeo sought instead to move his tolderías across the border.[1] The Portuguese viceroy in Rio de Janeiro opposed the move, however, deeming it "impractical" and fearing conflict with Spain. By the following year, Rio Grande's interim governor, Rafael Pinto Bandeira, reported that Bartolomeo and his people had been "destroyed" by the Spanish and that the cacique had sought refuge with other tolderías.[2]

Amid this turmoil, another Minuán cacique, Miguel Ayala Caraí, endeavored to organize a broader migration for one thousand Minuanes. Rather than moving across the border into Portuguese lands, they would relocate to the border itself, at a site called Batoví. Caraí met with Bartolomeo and other caciques, who reportedly saw no choice but to abandon the "lands which they inhabit, as their ancestors did for many centuries, and which are theirs by right of being the first settlers there."[3] To facilitate this relocation, Caraí attempted to broker a pact of mutual defense between the Minuanes and the Portuguese against the Spanish. He also sought a trade agreement whereby the Minuanes would sell livestock in the captaincy, sending representatives to procure a license of sale from the Portuguese. This case's paper trail does not reveal whether Bartolomeo and the other caciques ultimately moved to Batoví, but Minuán tolderías led by Caraí taxed the San Ildefonso boundary commissions moving through the area later that year.[4]

The contrasting trajectories of Bartolomeo and Miguel Ayala Caraí illustrate the changing territorial dynamics triggered by the mapping of a borderline in the Río de la Plata. As the logic of a border superimposed complete

Iberian territorial possession on a complex interethnic landscape, new networks of imperial and Indigenous authority emerged simultaneously. Tolderías experienced this process unevenly, as it presented existential threats to some and new opportunities to others. Bartolomeo's tolderías found themselves caught between a belligerent empire and an empire that privileged interimperial ties over interethnic agreements, while Guaraní migrants who had left the missions were brought back by force. Yet while these tolderías faced death and dispossession, Caraí and his kin saw their power increase. The cacique became one of the most important figures along the border during the 1770s and 1780s, developing kinship ties and political allegiances with other tolderías, with mission refugees, and with high-ranking imperial officials. Spanish and Portuguese administrators alike acknowledged his authority and frequently offered him payments in exchange for protection or for aid in enforcing or subverting the border.

The invention of an interimperial border transformed interethnic relations in the Río de la Plata, both at the border and beyond. The Madrid and San Ildefonso boundary commissions laid the legal and discursive groundwork for new imperial approaches to the countryside, as they impelled Ibero-American administrators to presume ownership of all resources and sovereignty over all people on their respective side of the border. The borderlines were not merely proofs of possession to be debated in metropolitan royal courts but embodied elements of emergent sociospatial ideals superimposed on divergent human landscapes. As imperial agents attempted to transform their nucleated settlements into contiguous and controllable jurisdictions, they confronted the persistent authority exercised by tolderías throughout the countryside. Yet border making did not simply reveal dissonance between imperial visions and the on-the-ground reality of Indigenous sovereignty; it reshaped regional territorialities altogether. Imperial efforts to materialize the border undermined the autonomy of tolderías distant from the border while enabling those closer to it to expand their authority, and tolderías' cumulative responses are ultimately what made the borderline a meaningful territorial arrangement.

Materializing Mapped Lines

Between 1750 and 1806, three different borderlines bisected the Río de la Plata: the Madrid line of the 1750s, the San Ildefonso line of the late 1770s through the 1790s, and a status quo line of the first several years of the 1800s (map 7). While the first two borderlines were established via interimperial treaties and boundary commissions, the status quo line was based on a regional agreement.

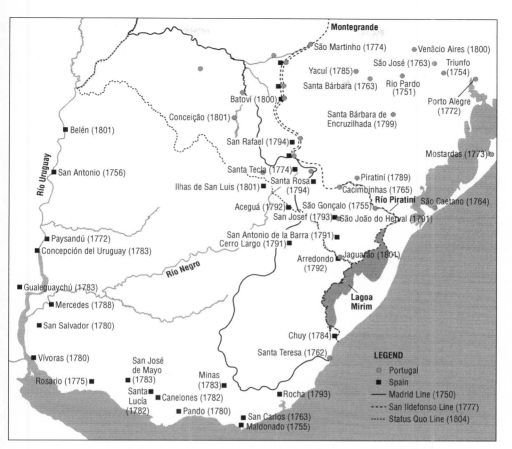

MAP 7 New borders and settlements, 1750–1806. This map shows the three borderlines that ran through the Río de la Plata, including the two stretches of neutral lands designated by the Treaty of San Ildefonso. Following the establishment of each line, Ibero-American officials founded new towns and forts on their respective side. Unlabeled settlements refer to Portuguese guard posts founded around 1801 and are derived from a map of Rio Grande drawn that same year: Saldanha, *Mappa Corographico da Capitania de S. Pedro*.

In 1801, as part of the War of the Oranges, Portuguese forces overtook the Siete Pueblos and adjacent lands. Although the Treaty of Badajoz, signed earlier that year, had already ended the war and reaffirmed earlier treaties between the two Iberian crowns, officials in the Río de la Plata agreed upon a new, status quo, borderline in 1804 and sought to deploy a boundary commission to modify the San Ildefonso line accordingly. But beginning two years later, British invasions of the Río de la Plata, the usurpation of the Spanish and Portuguese crowns by the French, and subsequent movements for political independence in Latin America undermined the demarcation of the adjusted line.[5]

TABLE 4 Officers of the southern commissions during and after the demarcations

Name (Crown)	During Expedition	After Expedition
Gomes Freire de Andrade (Portugal)	1st officer of demarcation	Governor of Rio de Janeiro and Minas Gerais
Francisco António Cardoso de Meneses e Sousa (Pt)	1st officer, 1st subdivision	Governor of Santa Catarina and Colônia do Sacramento
José Raimundo Chichorro (Pt)	2nd officer, 1st subdivision	Field marshal; participated in 1776 retaking of Rio Grande
José Custódio de Sá e Faria (Pt)	1st officer, 3rd subdivision	Governor of Rio Grande (Pt); explored in Patagonia (Sp)
Joseph Pinto Alpoim (Pt)	1st officer, 2nd subdivision	Provisional governor of Rio de Janeiro
Miguel Ciera (Pt)	Cosmographer	Edited treaty maps for Portuguese crown
Gaspar Tello y Espinosa (Spain)	1st officer of demarcation	Dean of Supreme Council of the Indies
Francisco Bruno de Zavala (Sp)	Captain of cavalry	Governor of the missions
Bernardo Lecocq (Sp)	Engineer	Engineer of borderland forts
Joaquín Gundín (Sp)	Geographer, pilot	Mapped coastline of Río de la Plata
Diego de Alvear (Sp)	1st officer, 2nd subdivision	Major general in Buenos Aires; adviser to viceroy
José María Cabrer (Sp)	2nd officer, 2nd subdivision	Published map of Río de la Plata
Andrés de Oyarvide (Sp)	Geographer, pilot	Published map of Río de la Plata
Félix de Azara (Sp)	1st officer, 3rd subdivision	Commander of the countryside; adviser to viceroy

MADRID

Name	Role	Description
Martín Boneo (Sp)	2nd officer, 3rd subdivision	Police intendant of Buenos Aires
Pedro Antonio Cerviño (Sp)	Engineer	Mapped province of Buenos Aires
Joseph Sourrière de Souillac (Sp)	Mathematician, astronomer	Mapped route between Buenos Aires and Chile across the Andes
Juan Francisco de Aguirre (Sp)	1st officer, 4th subdivision	Mapped countryside between Montevideo and Maldonado
Pablo Zizur (Sp)	Geographer, pilot	Part of expedition to salt flats on Buenos Aires's southern frontier
Lázaro Ribera (Sp)	2nd officer, 5th subdivision	Governor of Moxos
Sebastião da Veiga Cabral da Câmara (Pt)	1st officer of demarcation	Governor of Rio Grande
José Ignacio de Silva (Pt)	Secretary, 2nd lieutenant	Colonel in Rio Grande
José de Saldanha (Pt)	Astronomer, geographer	Governor of the missions
Francisco João Roscio (Pt)	2nd officer, 1st subdivision	Governor of Rio Grande
Alexandre Eloi Portelli (Pt)	Captain, engineer	Frontier commander in Rio Pardo
Francisco das Chagas Santos (Pt)	Engineer	Demarcation of status quo line
Joaquim de Fonseca Manso (Pt)	Astronomer, geographer	Sargent-major of the missions
Bento Sanches Horta (Pt)	Mathematician	Mapped captaincy of São Paulo
Francisco de Oliveira Barbosa (Pt)	Astronomer	Mapped captaincy of São Paulo

During this half-century span, the materialization of these cartographic lines was a centerpiece of Ibero-American governance and an integral component of broader administrative restructurings known as the Bourbon (Spain) and Pombaline (Portugal) reforms. Maps drawn by the Madrid and San Ildefonso boundary commissions were coveted tools that helped colonial officials imagine consolidated provinces and advance settlement initiatives. The demarcation teams took copious notes on natural resources, grazing grounds, watering holes, and river crossings, all of which would facilitate future settlements along the border. Likewise, they designed their maps as living templates on which new settlements could be drawn.[6] In a letter to Asunción's town council, the commanding officer of Spain's third subdivision for the San Ildefonso demarcations, Félix de Azara, wrote, "When some town or parish is founded or moved, the council can situate it upon [the map of Paraguay]. . . . It can continue adding what is new."[7] Likewise, José Custódio de Sá e Faria drew a map for the governor of São Paulo in which he "marked all of the places that according to our intelligence seem to be the most useful, which should be fortified or populated . . . for the establishment of the dominions of His Majesty in this part of the south of Brazil."[8] Demarcation officials were also important policymakers in the region. Some already occupied high administrative posts at the time of the expeditions, while others used the boundary commissions as a springboard into long careers in the new territorial units they had mapped (table 4).[9] They served as governors, advised viceroys, mapped new regions, designed borderland forts, certified land titles for settlers along the border, and founded new settlements.

Border drawing thus dovetailed with broader projects to restructure Spanish and Portuguese governance in the Americas. Portugal (1759) and Spain (1767) each expelled the Society of Jesus from its empire, expropriating former Jesuit landholdings and transferring missions to other Catholic orders or secular officials. In the Río de la Plata, both Spain and Portugal created a flurry of new administrative units designed to increase oversight of the countryside and border. Spain formed the Governorates of Montevideo (1751) and Misiones (1769), the Departments of San Miguel and Yapeyú (1769), the Viceroyalty of the Río de la Plata (1776), and the Intendencies of Paraguay and Buenos Aires (1782). Montevideo in particular gained newfound importance in administering the region's countryside, challenging Buenos Aires's jurisdictional reach. Portugal created the Captaincy of Rio Grande de São Pedro (1760); moved Brazil's capital from Salvador da Bahia to Rio de Janeiro (1763) and the captaincy's capital to Porto Alegre (1773); established parishes in Santa Ana (1770), Santo Amaro, Taquari, and Santo Antônio (1771), Porto Alegre and Viamão (1772), Mostardas (1773), Conceição do Arroio and Estreito (1774), and Caxoeira (1779); and divided Rio Grande into four judicial districts (1803).[10]

Within these new administrative units, Ibero-American officials deepened connections to Atlantic economies and imperial centers by promoting regulated trade and sedentary subjecthood. The liberalization of imperial trade in the Río de la Plata accelerated local commercial activity and the importation of enslaved Africans, while the growth of enslaved populations in mines and plantations in southeastern Brazil, the Caribbean, and elsewhere intensified demand for cattle and mules from the region. Brazilian livestock traders institutionalized a large cattle market in Sorocaba, near São Paulo, in 1750 and subsequently opened new roadways to connect it to Rio Grande.[11] Meanwhile, Spanish merchants transported jerky to the Caribbean to feed enslaved plantation workers, with one official calculating that cattle exports from the Río de la Plata could generate double the profits of all American mines combined.[12] Amid these growing commercial practices, imperial officials began to claim all feral livestock within their newly defined dominions as royal property, thereby transforming access rights into ownership rights. Spain issued a royal decree in 1764 to prohibit the transportation of animals into Brazil, and the viceroy of the Río de la Plata began a series of initiatives in 1784 to regulate the slaughter and sale of wild cattle and ranching on royal lands.[13] These efforts to recast long-standing livestock extraction as contraband were contingent on a precise borderline, as displayed by the Portuguese boundary commission's complaint in 1785 that their Spanish counterparts were intercepting traders and prosecuting them as smugglers: "[Land possession] has not yet been determined . . . therefore, what has been found does not appear to me to be contraband. . . . [The Spanish] responded that it indeed was because these lands expressly belonged to Spain."[14]

Administrators also used the border to control the movement of imperial subjects. Over the course of the eighteenth century, Spanish and Portuguese officials became ever more interested in monitoring and regulating their vassals' travels. Accordingly, they required licenses or passports of individuals who sought to enter the countryside and created increasingly long paper trails for travel and activities outside individual settlements.[15] The use of passports was a long-standing practice for movement between settlements; however, it was at this moment that administrators in the Río de la Plata aimed to control activities in the countryside as well. Military guard posts along the borderline were important to this endeavor because they allowed for surveillance of common travel routes, and the day-by-day records from such sites reveal the interception of individuals in the countryside. In the Río de la Plata, travelers along the "Wagon Way" (Camino de las Carretas) between the missions, Montevideo, and Maldonado would pass through the Spanish forts of Batoví, Santa Tecla, Cerro Largo, and Minas (map 7). Farther north, waterways such as the Río Paraná and the Río Paraguay both marked the border and served as pathways for people and goods. Officials in Buenos Aires, Montevideo, Rio Grande, and Porto Alegre all sought to control their subjects' movements in the countryside.[16]

The mutual desire to eliminate "contraband" (unsanctioned trade) and "disorder" (moving bodies) was inscribed in both border treaties and often led to collaboration between Portuguese and Spanish officials. The Treaty of Madrid's nineteenth article stated, "Along the entire frontier, commerce between the two nations will be prohibited and deemed to be contraband. . . . No person will pass from the territory of one nation to the other . . . without obtaining beforehand a license [passport]." The Treaty of San Ildefonso's seventeenth article repeated this sentiment, and its nineteenth required the return of runaway slaves.[17] In subsequent years, Ibero-American administrators worked with their counterparts to put the new rules into practice. Combing through manuscripts from borderland forts, one finds troves of correspondence regarding the return of fugitive slaves, military deserters, and individuals traveling without a passport.[18] Interimperial collaboration was no doubt limited, given that numerous studies have traced the growth of contraband networks at this time and it is unlikely that colonial officials would record their own noncompliance.[19] Nonetheless, imperial administrators knew that the apprehension and return of individuals and smuggled goods leaving their dominions required that they also keep track of those entering their territories. Good harmony (*boa correspondência/buena armonía*) between the two empires required at least an aura of mutuality in the joint policing of the border. In the Río de la Plata, Spanish officials often had more incentive to regulate settlement and commerce, as most feral livestock were situated on their side of the borderlines, but Portuguese officials were also invested in levying tariffs, centralizing authority, and restricting the flow of tobacco and other goods into Spanish territory.

Iberian diplomats envisioned borderlines as a means to end their decades-old dispute over territorial possession in South America, but their efforts instead concentrated imperial conflicts along the border itself. In the Río de la Plata, old arguments regarding possession of the Banda Norte gave way to new ones regarding the precise location of the interimperial boundary. These conflicts nonetheless fortified the border as a meaningful territorial arrangement. The most contentious portions of the borderline were the Rio Piratiní and

Montegrande, where the San Ildefonso demarcation efforts dragged on for decades (map 7). In each area, the demarcation team of one empire or the other sought to hold the border's certainty in abeyance while sending settlers and armed forces to occupy zones of jurisdictional ambiguity. Spanish officials decried recent Portuguese settlements south of the Piratiní, and Portuguese officials condemned new Spanish settlements in Montegrande.[20] Prior to the boundary commissions, these locales had not been prominent sites of contestation, and new jurisdictional conflicts created by the boundary commissions resulted in new settlement patterns that resembled a border.

This race to populate lands adjacent to the border dovetailed with the demarcation efforts. The boundary commissions provided imperial officials newfound legal authority to underwrite titles to lands beyond the reach of their settlements, and imperial officials strived in turn to create a human frontier along the cartographic line. Borderland settlements included forts and towns, while farmers and ranchers received titles to lands between settlements and adjacent to the border. Despite being much smaller in size than older settlements around the region's perimeter, these new establishments reinforced juridical claims and entrenched both empires along the border. Most borderland settlements appeared during the mapping expeditions (in the 1750s, 1780s, and 1790s), while the absence of an operative border in the 1760s and 1770s brought new settlements to a near standstill (map 7). Similar temporal patterns can also be observed for land grants (*sesmarias/mercedes*).[21] Spanish authorities began their efforts with a chain of forts along the borderline, while the Portuguese principally issued land titles to individuals. Each strategy had limitations— forts were necessary to protect and police local settlers, while agricultural production was necessary to sustain a fort—but both sides ultimately favored a continuous line of settlers over a string of forts, and the Spanish began to replicate Portuguese initiatives by the end of the century.[22]

The creation of new settlements and homesteads along the interimperial borderline was part of an explicit effort to establish imperial control far beyond the reach of existing population centers. At the time of the boundary commissions, Portuguese and Spanish territorial authority was limited to the various settlements that dotted the region's perimeter and portions of the fragile corridors that connected them. The interimperial borderlines did not supplant other local borderland dynamics, such as Montevideo's, Santo Domingo Soriano's, and Yapeyú's frontiers with Charrúas and Minuanes, or the "three frontiers" of Rio Grande: Vacaria, Rio Pardo, and Rio Grande.[23] Nor did they transform the vast territories that were beyond imperial control into consolidated, governable spaces. The desire to control the borderline instead engendered a jump in settlement patterns, from the vicinities of extant settlements to distant lands, thus creating a new borderland that had not previously existed, with Native-controlled lands in between. Administrators on both sides relied on new settlers—mission inhabitants interested in acquiring land titles or peasants from mainland Iberia, the Azores, and the Canary Islands—to populate both extant borderlands (Canelones, San José de Mayo, San Carlos, Pando, San Juan Bautista [Santa Lucía], Nossa Senhora dos Anjos, etc.) and the new interimperial borders (Minas, Rocha, Cerro Largo, Belén, Batoví, Rio Pardo, etc.).[24] Administrators offered land titles in exchange for a settler's promise to remain on the land, cultivate it, build houses, participate in local militias, support military officers, refuse harbor to contrabandists, and help sustain a local priest.[25] To their chagrin, these efforts to involve settlers in the policing of the borderline frequently failed, given the settlers' exposure and imperial authorities' inability to compete with other networks of regional authority.

Despite their ambitions, Iberian administrators struggled to materialize their designs on the ground. The sheer length of the borderline stretched their logistical capacities, and officials from each side frequently complained that they lacked the personnel and resources to monitor and control it.[26] As a result, contraband networks persisted and grew, and many individuals moved relatively freely through the countryside. Though the consequences for apprehension without a license or passport were severe, neither imperial government was able to achieve the omnipresence that it desired. Each effort to regulate commerce or limit movement was met with individuals and groups who persistently crossed the imaginary borderlines, occupied lands without titles, and slaughtered cattle they did not legally own. The border-making efforts also resulted in the growth of alternative networks of authority, as local administrators or strongmen moved goods and distributed land titles without their governor's or viceroy's consent.[27] Imperial officials complained about the very individuals to whom they had given land titles, accusing them of occupying lands beyond the limits of their titles, refusing to remain in one place, abandoning their properties, or harboring smugglers.[28]

The convention of neutral lands illustrates Iberian authorities' limited capacity to enforce the borderline. While the Treaty of Madrid projected a single line across South America, the Treaty of San Idefonso's fifth and sixth articles dictated that the boundary commissions draw parallel lines in areas where smuggling was particularly problematic. The purpose was to create complementary rows of military establishments—one on each side of the neutral lands—through which contrabandists would have to pass when transporting cattle and other commodities. Imperial officials also expected that these neutral lands would prevent future disputes between the two crowns regarding settlement and military activity; neither side could issue property titles for these lands, nor could they enter them with armed soldiers or guards (figure 21).[29] While the two crowns hoped these neutral lands would be a panacea for the problems of illegal trade and settlement, in the end they proved to be the opposite. Imperial subjects began to occupy what were supposed to be empty lands, and smugglers used these areas as a harbor from the mounted guards that the two empires placed along the edges. There was little that officers in borderline forts could do in response, as surveilling or pursuing individuals into neutral lands constituted a rupture of the treaty agreement and incited negative responses from the opposite side.[30] Designed to enhance the effectiveness of the borderline, neutral lands ultimately served to undermine its utility.

Engaging Tolderías

Despite imperial presumptions of authority, tolderías continued to control much of the borderline through the end of the eighteenth century, and imperial border making hinged on their support or indifference. Spanish and Portuguese settlements along the border were concentrated in the easternmost part of the region, near the Lagoa Mirim and the Rio Piratiní, while control over lands farther inland was more tenuous (map 7). Some inland forts, namely Santa Tecla and Rio Pardo, held upwards of fifty troops, but most others consisted of merely one or two dozen occupants.[31] Such a small number of troops could barely maintain a fort's existence, and military agents and settlers alike found themselves subject to the interests of Charrúa and Minuán caciques. Efforts to incentivize ranching and farming along inland portions of the border were likewise limited; tolderías' presence impeded the sale of land titles, depreciated their value, and undercut administrators' ability to collect payments on them, so administrators concentrated their settlement initiatives in other areas.[32] Tolderías also inhibited Spanish efforts to use the borderline as a roadway from the Siete Pueblos to Montevideo and Maldonado. Even with a chain of forts along this borderline pathway, one observer commented in 1801: "It is difficult to cross a country so extensive, rugged, and inhabited only by barbarous and ferocious Indians."[33] Imperial border making therefore prompted new strategies for engaging tolderías.

The invention of an interimperial border led Ibero-American officials to imagine spaces of interaction with tolderías as internal frontiers, thereby dismissing tolderías' claims over regional lands and resources. In the Río de la

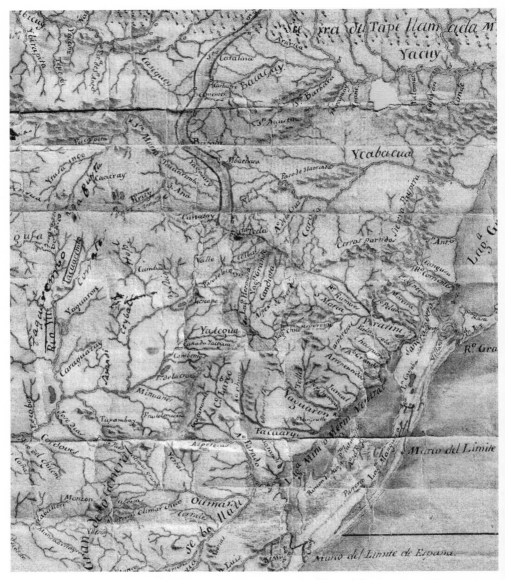

FIGURE 21 *Mapa Esferico de las Provincias Septentrionales del Rio de la Plata*, 1796. The San Ildefonso line included two stretches of neutral lands (marked with red lines), as shown in this section of a map of the work of the boundary commission's first and second subdivisions. The first began along the Atlantic Coast and encompassed the Lagoa Mirim (bottom right), and the second comprised lands between Santa Tecla and Montegrande (top middle). Together they covered approximately 3,000 square miles. Segarra, *Frontera y límites*, 18. España. Ministerio de Defensa. Archivo del Museo Naval.

Plata, colonial authorities continued to acknowledge tolderías' autonomy and natural rights in diplomatic discussions with their imperial counterpart; yet when developing internal policies, they often presumed Charrúas and Minuanes to be imperial subjects, subordinate clients, or lawless agents. This tendency manifested itself differently among Spanish and Portuguese administrators, and their respective strategies for engaging tolderías derived from the border's precise location. Since the Madrid and San Ildefonso lines situated most feral livestock within Spanish dominions, Buenos Aires's governors and viceroys asserted that all resources on those lands were their legal property and thus conceived tolderías' assertions of sovereignty and autonomy to be invalid. As settlers from the Guaraní missions in particular intensified efforts to establish new ranches and slaughter cattle far from their settlements, they did not imagine their expansion as an intrusion on tolderías' lands. Administrators celebrated such efforts at dispossessing tolderías and considered tolderías' responses, which included raiding or occupying these new ranches, as "invasions" of ranchers' rightful property.[34]

Spanish officials also demonstrated a declining interest in striking partnerships with or peaceably proselytizing tolderías. Despite tolderías' effective autonomy in the region, Spanish authorities imagined them to have a subordinate status by virtue of their living on imperial lands. With this territorialization of subjecthood came the expectation that tolderías abide by Buenos Aires's dicta or have imperial forces "punish" (*castigar*) or "exterminate" (*exterminar*) them.[35] Whether envisioning tolderías as imperial subjects or simply inhabitants of royal lands, Spanish agents interpreted Native refusal to respect imperial decrees as an affront to Spanish sovereignty. This new aversion to negotiation and pact making intensified over time, as settlement initiatives through evangelization, trade relations, and other partnerships gave way to campaigns for expulsion, extermination, or containment. Some administrators argued that settlement via evangelization was a futile pursuit, and even when tolderías proved amenable to reducciones, there was no guarantee that Spanish officials would be willing partners, as a group of Charrúas and Bohanes discovered in 1773.[36]

This tendency toward aggression was not part of a broader Spanish policy in the Americas. In fact, it contrasted markedly with concurrent peacemaking strategies vis-à-vis Native polities in other parts of the viceroyalty of the Río de la Plata, a divergence that likely derived from a heightened desire to solidify land claims near the border with Brazil.[37] Yet it did mirror the broader Iberian and Ibero-American disdain for mobile peoples that emerged during the eighteenth century amid hardening ideals of sedentary subjecthood and civility.[38]

The seasonal mobility of tolderías had always befuddled imperial and ecclesiastical writers, who understood sedentism to be integral to Christian subjecthood, but the eighteenth century saw intensified contempt for itinerant lifestyles. Writers frequently described tolderías as vagabonds, which contemporary dictionaries defined as "lazy people, who could work, and live with ambition, but do not do it" or "those who wander without residence or a clear dwelling place because they do not have a King, nor a homeland that they love."[39] Mobility signified vagrancy, landlessness, lawlessness, untrustworthiness, and irrationality, and tolderías' mobility prevented Spanish-American authorities in the Río de la Plata from recognizing the territorialities that undergirded tolderías' actions. For colonial officials, tolderías' resistance to Spanish incursions in their lands derived instead from a bad temperament or their corruption by the Portuguese or contrabandists. For example, in justifying several military expeditions against tolderías near the Río Uruguay, one official claimed that ranchers there had been exposed to "those people, who for no other reason than whim killed, robbed from their ranches, and set fire to their settlements and harvests."[40] Authorities opined that tolderías simply acted out of malevolence, making amicable relations impossible.

Frustrated by tolderías' mobility, Spanish officials adopted two principal strategies—military action and strategic settlement—that aimed to force tolderías to form reducciones. Beginning with the 1749 military expeditions near Santa Fe and Montevideo, Spanish-American authorities echoed a common refrain—"kill all of those who [refuse reducciones]"—and the subsequent campaigns to "clean the countryside" represented a stark shift from earlier policies.[41] Prior to 1749, military engagement between settlements and tolderías tended to be in response to acute conflicts rather than aimed at subjugation. Furthermore, when describing these earlier armed excursions, imperial writers tended to characterize them as military campaigns rather than police actions. These endeavors had often been in response to raids on ranches or attacks on imperial subjects traveling outside the settlements, and they frequently ended with pacts between a settlement and neighboring tolderías or with no engagement at all.[42] Most importantly, the objective had been neither settlement by force nor extermination. Although imperial and ecclesiastical agents had hoped that tolderías would ultimately accept a reducción and a relationship of vassalage, this had never been a precondition of ending military conflicts.

Preemptive military action to force settlement became a centerpiece of Spanish engagement with tolderías at the same time as the demarcation efforts. This occurred in three waves: military excursions near Santa Fe, Soriano, and

Montevideo in the 1750s; attacks from Soriano and Montevideo in the 1760s; and a sustained assault near the borderline from 1796 to 1806.[43] Commanding officers predicated their aggression on prior hostilities by the targeted tolderías, yet the objective of subsequent military campaigns was not simply to recover livestock or to dissuade tolderías from entering ranches. Their purpose was instead to purge the countryside of tolderías to make way for future settlements. This effort became systematized in 1797 with the formation of a corps of Montevideo-based mounted guards (*blandengues*), who along with local militias spent the next nine years in a perpetual state of warfare with Charrúas and Minuanes between the Río Negro, the Río Uruguay, and the interimperial border (map 7). They raided tolderías one by one, killing adult men and shipping hundreds of captive women and children to Buenos Aires.[44]

In some instances, imperial forces presented an ultimatum: form a reducción or face death. In 1801, a commission from Yapeyú invited the Minuán cacique Masalana "to establish a population in the vicinity of the San Marcos ranch [along the headwaters of the Río Queguay]. . . . I will mark for you a place large and comfortable enough to be populated." The commission's leader, Juan Ventura Ifrán, continued with a warning: "If you are ungracious and disregard this great charity . . . I will not desist until I have exterminated [your] malignant, inhuman, and harmful race."[45] Viceroy Gabriel de Avilés adopted a more conciliatory tone; he considered himself "obligated to punish [Masalana's tolderías] to make an example," yet desired to "forgive them for their crimes, and pardon them from the punishment that they deserve" in an act of "clemency and humanity." Both Ifrán and Avilés took for granted that Charrúas and Minuanes had impinged on the Spanish sovereign's territorial rights, and for them, "clemency and humanity" meant subjugation. Ifrán surmised that if Masalana accepted his offer, "we will be able to observe the conduct of these Indians and easily contain any excess or act of disorder. It will also lead to maintaining [their] respect and subjugation." Via the reducción of Masalana's tolderías and others, Avilés's government would be able to "take advantage of the incalculable benefits of those frontier lands."[46] Masalana's tolderías did not comply and instead absconded toward the interimperial border, while blandengues and Yapeyú's militias ambushed nearby Charrúa and Minuán tolderías over the next year. The violence was so severe that the blandengues' commanding officer, Jorge Pacheco, claimed to have extinguished all tolderías from the countryside. Such bombast did not match on-the-ground events, however, as the blandengues frequently found themselves hiding from tolderías or suffering defeat to, among others, Masalana.[47]

Given the limited success of the blandengues' extermination campaigns, officials in Buenos Aires also sought to eliminate tolderías through strategic settlements. By occupying key stopping points along tolderías' itinerant paths, settlers and militias would impede their access to necessary resources and force them to accept reducciones. The most ambitious of these projects occurred in Batoví, along the border with Brazil, where Spanish officials sent settlers in 1801 after abandoning a similar endeavor in Patagonia (map 7). Félix de Azara oversaw the Batoví project, which he envisaged as a solution to Pacheco's failed efforts to expunge tolderías by force: "My system is entirely the opposite, and it can be reduced to positioning the troop so that it covers advancing populations. I would manage things this way until the infidels have to abandon the countryside. . . . I will not take one step towards pursuing them even if I see them in front of me."[48] By creating lines of settlements strip by strip along the countryside, Azara conjectured that Minuanes' and Charrúas' lands would become so narrow that they would be forced to accept reducciones. He reasoned that Pacheco's campaigns were futile due to the vastness of the countryside, and he boasted that his plan would bring results in as little as a year and a half. But Azara's tactics were also ineffectual, as Charrúa and Minuán tolderías, together with Portuguese military forces, evicted the Spanish from Batoví and elsewhere later that year.[49]

Portuguese officials in the Río de la Plata adopted a much different approach to engaging tolderías, eschewing reducciones or extermination campaigns in favor of hierarchical collaboration and pact making. This regional tactic diverged from Portuguese policies in other parts of Brazil, as the Indian Directorate in Amazônia, Pará, and Maranhão sought to incorporate autonomous Native peoples as imperial subjects, while the termination of the Forbidden Lands policy in the eastern Sertão led to violent campaigns for territorial acquisition.[50] The borderline again explains the Río de la Plata's exceptionality. Since the San Ildefonso line in particular placed most feral livestock on the Spanish side of the border, Portuguese American agents sought partnerships with tolderías to gain access. Charrúas' and Minuanes' legal autonomy made them an important proxy for engaging the Spanish side of the border without inciting interimperial war, and tolderías' superior knowledge of the countryside allowed them to evade borderline forts as they transported livestock or guided smugglers.[51] Furthermore, the authority certain caciques and their tolderías exercised along the border made them an invaluable buffer against Spanish armed forces, as the governor of Rio Grande expressed in 1801: "Nothing is risked by letting [tolderías] work hostilely against our enemies, [or] at least perform the service that our explorers could do if we had them." He insisted that it was necessary to acquiesce to the caciques' "wild demands" and instructed the commander of Rio Pardo to "[be careful to not] offend them because beyond being grateful for their good will, we should avoid increasing our enemies."[52] Sustaining tolderías' support required frequent payments, but having them as enemies would have been even costlier.

Portuguese efforts at pact making proved beneficial in 1801, as collaboration with Charrúa and Minuán caciques enabled them to take control of the Siete Pueblos and borderland territories between the San Ildefonso line and the Río Uruguay. Tolderías expelled Spanish and Guaraní settlers and ranchers from lands as far south as the Río Queguay well before Portuguese troops arrived, resulting in a southward adjustment of the San Ildefonso line (map 7).[53] This partnership with tolderías was part of a longer pattern of cooperation during the eighteenth century's second half. In 1776, as Portuguese forces evicted the Spanish from Santa Tecla, Charrúas and Minuanes played an important role in Portuguese victory. Not only did Charrúas and Minuanes provide guidance and safe passage to the borderline fort, but they also maintained a protracted assault on the missions' ranches and cattle herds.[54] Their support was essential to Portuguese success, and Minuán and Charrúa caciques and Portuguese officials made similar pacts in 1786, 1805, and 1806.[55]

Relations between tolderías and administrators in Rio Grande ran deeper than wartime assistance. Charrúas and Minuanes were key trading partners, valuable informants regarding activities on the Spanish side of the border, and seasonal laborers on Portuguese ranches and hemp plantations.[56] Portuguese officials' need for tolderías' aid is perhaps best illustrated by Rafael Pinto Bandeira, who led the 1776 invasion of Santa Tecla before serving as the interim governor of Rio Grande during the 1780s. Pinto Bandeira developed an extensive smuggling network, making him both an agent of Portuguese expansion and a perpetual thorn in the side of his superiors. His success largely derived from his family's relationship with Minuanes; his father, Francisco Pinto Bandeira, had maintained ties with several Minuán tolderías, and Rafael married Barbara Victoria, the daughter of cacique Miguel Ayala Caraí. Following his campaign against the Spanish in 1776, Pinto Bandeira distributed approximately eight hundred heads of cattle, valued at over one million reais, to Minuanes for the aid they had provided.[57] The governor's dealings with Minuanes were so valued that the viceroy in Rio de Janeiro concluded that "perhaps all of his actions, as bad as they might be, should be overlooked and tolerated by whoever governs," and Pinto Bandeira maintained his post until his death in 1795.[58]

Performing Borders

Cartographic borders were undoubtedly European inventions designed to define territorial possession and produce governable states. Yet the need for an operative borderline, the determination of its location, and the line's material production in the Río de la Plata were inextricable from the activities of tolderías. The initial invention of a borderline had been a response to tolderías' control over regional lands, as it allowed Portugal and Spain to claim territorial possession without having to identify tolderías as imperial subjects; and when treaties begot mapping expeditions, tolderías had limited the activities of demarcation teams. Disputes over the borderline's precise location, and its movement over time, had derived from the fact that it cut through Native lands. Following the demarcations, as imperial administrators attempted to transform cartographic lines into operative territorial arrangements, their actions—declaring possession, occupying spaces, soliciting aid, offering payments, signing pacts, and undertaking raids—elicited responses from tolderías. Tolderías' replies ultimately determined the outcome of border-making projects, and while responses varied according to tolderías' locations in the region, when taken together, they tended to reproduce borderline territorialities.

The demarcation efforts ushered in a variety of changes for tolderías in the region, resulting in a general pattern of migration toward the borderline. Georeferencing the more than 280 recorded locations of Bohán, Charrúa, Guenoa, Minuán, and Yaro tolderías from 1750 through the dissolution of an operative borderline in 1806 reveals this trend (map 8). Over the course of slightly more than a half century, imperial records show both increased interactions with tolderías near the borderlines and decreased interactions with those in other parts of the region. During the 1750s, tolderías could be found as far west as Santa Fe and Corrientes; as far south as Colônia, Montevideo, and Maldonado; as far east as Rio Grande; and as far north as the Siete Pueblos. Conversely, by the 1790s and the 1800s, nearly all citations refer to tolderías in areas between the San Ildefonso line and lands immediately south of the 1804 status quo line. Anecdotal accounts recorded by members of the San Ildefonso boundary commission indicate a similar trend. According to the Spanish officer Diego de Alvear, "From the time of the conquest, [Minuanes] dominated the Campos de Vera, which is north of the Río de la Plata [estuary]. . . . Until recently, the residents of Montevi-

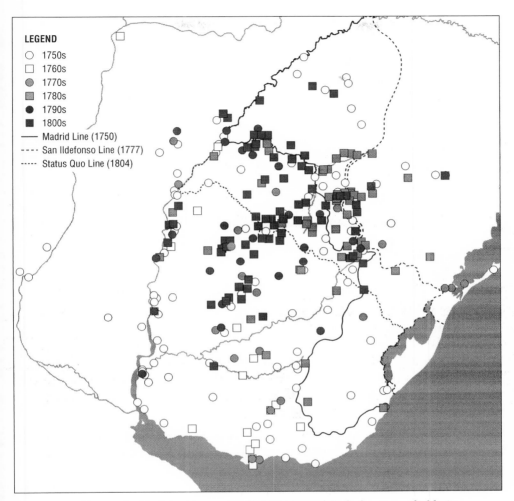

MAP 8 Reported toldería locations, 1750–1806. This map plots the locations of tolderías reported in over 280 manuscript records and stylizes them by decade. This plotting reveals increased records of activities near the border over time, coupled with decreased records in lands farther away.

deo and Maldonado tolerated their being nearby. . . . [The Minuanes then] took refuge in these lands [along the border], where they live today."[59] Portuguese geographer José de Saldanha noted that while Minuanes once populated lands south of the Lagoa Mirim, "they withdrew northward to where they are now [along the border] . . . sometimes going as far [west] as the Río Uruguay."[60]

To account for this broad geographical trend in the written records, it is necessary to distinguish colonial perceptions of tolderías' locations from their actual locations. The points plotted in map 8 represent tolderías that were mentioned in colonial texts, and given the limited spatial reach of colonial writers, more tolderías certainly existed than those represented in the map. The pattern of increased recorded activities near the borderlines also signifies a heightened presence of colonial agents, who in turn engaged with tolderías that were already living there. This is only a portion of the story, however, as the increased number of recorded interactions near the borderline was accompanied by a decreased number around the region's perimeter, where colonial settlers were more entrenched and therefore more likely to generate written documentation. Given the frequent references to tolderías in such areas in earlier decades, this discursive disappearance suggests tolderías' eventual absence from these lands. Indeed, some tolderías moved toward the borderline, while some individuals remained behind to work on local ranches and farms. The former moved beyond the purview of local record keepers, and imperial writers were unlikely to identify the latter according to ethnic identifiers if not clearly associated with tolderías.

Specific reactions to border-making initiatives nonetheless varied among tolderías, and they derived more from geographical positioning than from perceived ethnic affiliations. The myriad responses of tolderías identified by the same ethnonym belie any "Charrúa" or "Minuán" response to the border, but a distinction existed between those farthest from the border and those nearest to it. Broadly speaking, the former faced greater pressures and violence, while the latter found opportunities to exploit imperial initiatives and appropriate the boundaries for their own purposes. In the south and west of the region, far from the border, tolderías found themselves cut off from the Atlantic economy and threatened by new settlers. The Portuguese cession of Colônia to the Spanish dried up a once vibrant market for tolderías to trade livestock and other goods, and it eliminated the need for Minuán guides between the plaza and Rio Grande. It also resolved competing imperial claims to the northern coast of the Río de la Plata estuary, thus enabling Spanish administrators to distribute land titles south of the Río Yí.[61] The rapid establishment of settlements, guard posts, farms, and ranches between Soriano, Colônia, and Montevideo challenged tolderías' access to nearby livestock and impeded their itineraries, while violent militia campaigns threatened their lives.

In response to these changing conditions, some individuals from southerly and westerly tolderías sought partnerships with Spanish ranchers or moved to settlements, while some caciques agreed to form settlements. The lack of written records from ranches and the common use of generic terms, such as *indio* or *peón*, rather than ethnonyms to identify rural laborers hinder any assessment of scale, but extant records indicate this type of relocation. Imperial officials frequently commented on Minuanes' and Charrúas' dexterity in taming horses and herding cattle, Montevideo's cabildo recognized Minuanes as "useful men" on their ranches, and settlers near Maldonado relied on Minuanes for assistance in managing livestock.[62] Judicial and ecclesiastical records also reveal the presence of individuals identified as Charrúa or Minuán living in or immediately outside Santa Fe, Montevideo, and Maldonado through the end of the century.[63] Other tolderías turned to reducciones in moments of duress, though this was a risky proposition. Following the Guaraní War, several Charrúa families near Soriano agreed to settle nearby in exchange for Soriano's provision of one cow per day, but many of Soriano's residents balked and accused the newcomers of crimes against local women. The Charrúa families soon found themselves wedged between hostile hosts and nearby tolderías, and they ultimately returned to the countryside.[64] A similar instance involved Minuanes living near the Río Yí, where they faced a smallpox outbreak and an increasingly precarious environment. These tolderías, led by a cacique named Cumandat, attempted to negotiate a peace accord with Montevideo in 1762 and came to an agreement two years later whereby they settled about seventy-five miles north of the city, at the edge of its jurisdiction. These tolderías also found themselves exposed, and when a band of forty men raided their ranches six years later, the nearby Spanish guard proved ineffective in stopping the attack.[65]

More evidence exists of tolderías moving toward the border and integrating with those already there. For example, the Minuán cacique Moreira, whose tolderías were near the southern end of the Lagoa Mirim in 1759, stood alongside Miguel Ayala Caraí at Santa Tecla in 1775. Another Minuán cacique, Salteinho, was among those who accompanied Cumandat to Montevideo in 1762, and he then appeared with Caraí in 1787 as they taxed the demarcation teams. In the same way, the Charrúa cacique Ignacio "El Gordo" sought out a reducción in San Borja in 1794, only to return to the countryside and become a "supreme caudillo" six years later (map 9).[66] Joining with other tolderías was often a complicated enterprise, however, as evidenced by the stories of Miguel Salcedo and his two sons, Juan and Pedro Ignacio. All three had been baptized and raised in Cayastá, a Charrúa reducción in the southwest of the region, near Santa Fe; by the early 1790s, they had abandoned the reducción with some of their kin. Nonetheless, by 1794, Miguel appeared in Soriano, and Juan in one of San Borja's ranches, hoping to negotiate new reducciones. They had gone to the countryside but returned to seek refuge from contrabandists. Pedro Ignacio was apprehended in the blandengue expeditions of 1801, alongside other Charrúas and Minuanes.[67] Within a decade of leaving Cayastá, the Salcedos were all pulled back into the Spanish colonial apparatus.

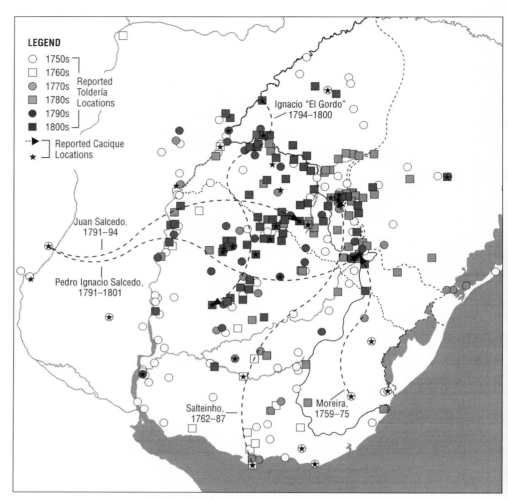

LEGEND

○ 1750s
□ 1760s
◐ 1770s Reported
◩ 1780s Tolderia
● 1790s Locations
■ 1800s

··▶⎤ Reported Cacique
★ ⎦ Locations

Ignacio "El Gordo"
1794–1800

Juan Salcedo,
1791–94

Pedro Ignacio Salcedo,
1791–1801

Salteinho,
1762–87

Moreira,
1759–75

MAP 9   Reported cacique locations, 1750–1806. This map shows the locations of caciques as recorded in extant manuscript records during these years. Each white or gray dot and square represents the same reported tolderia locations as in map 8, and each black star represents an instance in which a specific cacique was named. Dashed lines represent caciques who appeared closer to the border over time, though their precise itineraries are unclear.

For all the challenges faced by tolderias far from the various treaty lines, new opportunities arose for those who lived nearest to the border. In particular, imperial border-making initiatives provided tolderias with new chances to develop commercial ties, kinship relationships, and patronage networks. While the transfer of Colônia to Spanish control dried up numerous markets along the Banda Norte, it coincided with an expanding network of borderline commerce. Since imperial subjects were restricted from crossing the border, it created a demand for individuals with the know-how to transport livestock undetected across the line. Charrúas and Minuanes thus positioned themselves as commercial intermediaries, since their tolderías continued to exert some control over the regional interior. They guided Portuguese smugglers back and forth across the border undetected by Spanish cavalries, led them safely to cattle ranges, aided in the herding and slaughtering of cattle, and tamed wild horses. In other instances, they personally transported cattle and horses directly across the border, cutting out intermediaries and selling the animals to buyers on the other side.[68]

Although the growing number of outsiders entering the countryside threatened tolderías' autonomy, Charrúas and Minuanes retained their position as the principal arbiters of access to rural lands, particularly those between the Río Uruguay, Río Ibicuí, and the Río Negro. In some instances, they aided individual settlements in combating raids, as occurred in Soriano in 1757. But tolderías more often prevented imperial cavalries from pursuing contrabandists or fugitives into their lands. In 1795, when Spanish guards from Batoví attempted to apprehend contrabandists near the border, a number of Charrúas intercepted them and left at least two soldiers dead.[69] Ten years later, when a militiaman named Miguel Lenguasár found himself on the run from Spanish militias, Portuguese officials "recommended to the Infidel Indians that they let him pass to [Portuguese dominions], not only without experiencing poor treatment, but also with their guidance."[70] Individuals from Minuán, Charrúa, and Tape tolderías deposited Lenguasár on the Brazilian side of the 1804 status quo division soon after. Tolderías' control over the countryside was not lost on individual travelers either. In 1799, when a party of blandengues apprehended a Portuguese man named Juan Adolfo on the Spanish side of the border, he was unable to present a passport and claimed that he had lost it in an ambush by Charrúas as he transited the "unpopulated countryside."[71] Regardless of the veracity of this account, Adolfo's telling of it indicates that it was potentially believable, thus pointing to a broader acknowledgement of tolderías' presence and authority.

The control that certain caciques and their tolderías exhibited over borderland spaces was in many ways enhanced by Iberian efforts to enforce the borderline. As both empires' borderline institutions were notably weak, they frequently sought to establish partnerships with tolderías as a means to make the borderline operative. In October 1775, Spanish troops stationed at Santa Tecla invited a contingent of Charrúa and Minuán caciques to the fort, offering gifts and soliciting their aid in apprehending unauthorized travelers. The caciques agreed to monitor the countryside but demanded that the Spanish withdraw their troops into the fort and make specific personnel changes, to which the Spanish acquiesced. Despite this agreement, Minuán caciques guided Portuguese soldiers to Santa Tecla the following year, enabling the Portuguese to topple the fort. The Minuán caciques thus drew on the Spanish need to monitor the countryside in order to obtain payments from officers at Santa Tecla and regulate the activities of soldiers stationed there, and the caciques exploited the Portuguese desire to expel their imperial foe in order to obtain even higher payments from them.[72] Charrúas and Minuanes along the borderline were more than occasional allies of imperial agents; they also acted as the principal authorities in various locales. When the Portuguese forces abandoned Santa Tecla and retired northward later that year, Minuán caciques continued to control the area. They reported the Portuguese departure to scouts from the Guaraní missions but prevented the scouts from traveling to the area to see for themselves. Two years later, however, Minuán caciques again offered to apprehend contrabandists and deserters on behalf of the Spanish and to provide Spanish troops safe passage through the countryside.[73]

Miguel Ayala Caraí, the primary cacique involved in the events surrounding Santa Tecla, provides a clear example of how a savvy individual could use the influx of imperial actors to develop expansive networks of kinship and allegiance. Years before the Portuguese invasion, Caraí had married his daughter to its principal architect, Rafael Pinto Bandeira, and he was likely among the Minuanes who collected payments from Pinto Bandeira's personal account following the attack. At the same time, Caraí orchestrated the escape of Santa Tecla's ranking officer, Miguel Antonio de Ayala, with whom he likely shared familial bonds as well.[74] But Caraí had not always been a powerful cacique; he was born to an immigrant from Santiago del Estero and a Minuán woman, and he spent much of his youth as a ranch hand for Francisco Pinto Bandeira, Rafael's father. At some point, perhaps because of his ties to both Spanish and Portuguese leaders, Caraí rose to become cacique. In fact, "Caraí" was most likely an honorific rather than a surname.[75] By the 1770s, Don Miguel had become one of the most important figures in the borderland region, the "cacique of caciques." Whether managing the events at Santa Tecla, developing trade networks, brokering the settlement of his fellow Minuán cacique Bartolomeo, or collecting tribute payments from Spanish and Portuguese demarcation teams, Caraí positioned himself as a principal authority along the borderline.[76]

The influx of migrants to areas near the borderline also enabled some tolderías to expand their networks of kinship and power. Following the invasion of the Siete Pueblos in the 1750s, accelerating after the 1767 Jesuit expulsion, and continuing through the end of the century, many Guaraní abandoned the missions for other areas of the Río de la Plata region. While many of them settled in other missions, on ranches, or in nearby cities, others integrated into Charrúa or Minuán tolderías or formed tolderías of their own.[77] The level of desertions worried Spanish administrators, who tried to separate mission dwellers from neighboring tolderías. They believed that Charrúas and Minuanes had corrupted these "runaway Tapes [Guaraní]" (*tapes cimarrones*) and that their mobile lifestyles made deserters prone to steal cattle or take captives. Portuguese officials also sought to separate mission dwellers from tolderías after their taking of the Siete Pueblos in 1801.[78] For Minuanes and Charrúas, however, these migrants represented an opportunity to expand familial and tributary networks. By incorporating the newcomers into their tolderías or as clients, individual caciques could extend their range of influence. In 1785, refugees from the San Nicolás mission declared that they "recognized no other God or King than Batu of the Minuanes, to whose toldería they had sent all of their women and possessions in anticipation of the arrival of [Spanish forces]."[79] When Spanish troops attacked the former Nicolistas, killing seven people, the remaining refugees fled to Minuán tolderías for protection. Tolderías were likely destinations for runaway slaves as well, given the increased number of slave ships arriving to the region and fugitives' documented relations with other rural actors, but documentation of such relations remains thin.[80]

Distant tolderías who moved toward the border also developed ties with those already residing there, resulting in a significant sociopolitical realignment and a shift in ethnic labeling in colonial records. Whereas five ethnonyms regularly appeared in records written during the previous hundred years— Bohanes, Charrúas, Guenoas, Minuanes, and Yaros—by the 1770s only Charrúas and Minuanes remained. Furthermore, Charrúas and Minuanes, who for decades had been described in colonial records as antagonistic enemies, began to appear together on a regular basis to the point that imperial observers struggled to differentiate one from another. Some even suggested that Charrúas and Minuanes had killed or incorporated Bohanes, Guenoas, and Yaros.[81] This discursive shift resembled broader patterns in the Americas, whereby Native refugees or migrants drew on long-standing social and cultural ties to establish new polities, while European writers sought to identify Indigenous political partners via rigid ethnic labeling. The conflation of ethnic identities and Native political organization (tribalization) was commonplace in moments of colonial violence and crisis, yet the emergence and disappearance of ethnic identities (ethnogenesis and ethnocide) often belied

the categorization deployed in colonial writings (ethnification and ethniciza-
tion), masked territorially based social organization, and did not signify the
vanishing of people themselves.[82] A limited source base in the Río de la Plata
impedes the disentangling of Indigenous identities and colonial categories,
but this discursive shift nonetheless dovetailed with changing relationships
between tolderías and colonial settlements. No accounts exist after 1760 of
tolderías allying with Ibero-American settlers against other tolderías. Conflict undoubtedly existed between tolderías, and tolderías used agents from
one empire as partners against the other, but records suggest that local relationships between settlements and tolderías had become subordinated to Indigenous or imperial ties.[83]

The arrival of outsiders to the borderline also presented nearby tolderías
with challenges. New settlers brought pathogens, and when smallpox epidemics raged through the Siete Pueblos and other Guaraní missions, tolderías too
found themselves vulnerable, as occurred in 1762 and 1787. Andrés de Oyarvide, geographer for the second Spanish subdivision of the San Ildefonoso demarcations, observed, "All of these [Minuanes] are very fearful of contracting
smallpox, and if they know that there are sick individuals in some ranch, they
will not go there for a long time."[84] Ranches also brought physical violence,
and a general pattern emerged between Charrúas, Minuanes, and mission
ranchers. Guaraní mission dwellers would establish ranches deep inside
tolderías' lands, tolderías would raid those establishments, and Spanish authorities would deploy militias or blandengues in reprisal. Few ranches existed far
beyond settlements at midcentury, but the boundary commissions precipitated
the founding of many "advanced ranches" (*estancias avanzadas*), which were
located hundreds of miles from the missions and stretched southward through
Charrúas' and Minuanes' lands toward the Río Negro and the Río Yí (map 10).
This movement toward the center of the region engendered an unprecedented
slaughtering of wild cattle, particularly in the 1770s, and corresponded with a
spike in violent encounters between tolderías and mission actors. The presence of smugglers and cattle rustlers only exacerbated the situation.[85]

The founding of ranches would not necessarily have been a problem for caciques and their kin, as they likely did not hold the same concept of individual property rights as did their colonial counterparts. But if mission inhabitants
were to maintain ranches in Charrúa or Minuán lands, tolderías would have
expected them to recognize toldería authority and limit their levels of resource
extraction. Ranchers from San Borja seem to have acquiesced to such an arrangement, "[paying] in tribute all that [the tolderías] ask for, in particular
yerba maté and tobacco. . . . We give all of this continually." By 1784, however,

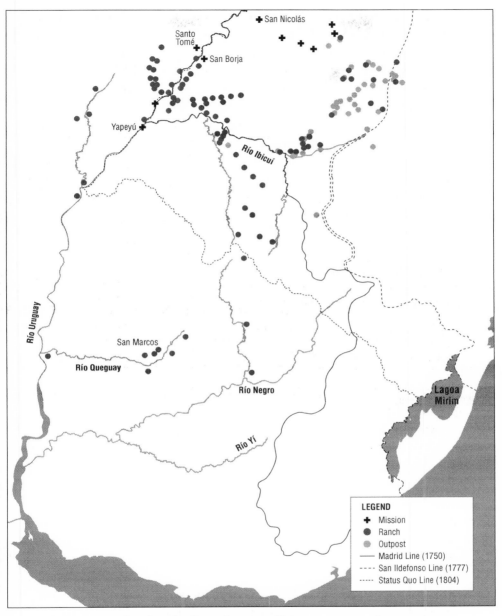

MAP 10 New ranches from the Guaraní missions. This map represents the approximate locations of mission ranches and outposts established during the second half of the eighteenth century, derived from four georeferenced maps. Though not an exhaustive rendering of ranch locations, it demonstrates their scattered nature between the Río Negro and the Río Ibicuí, lands controlled by tolderías. Sources: Fúrlong Cárdiff, *Cartografía jesuítica*, vol. 2, Lámina XXIV; AGNA, IX, 22-8-2 (map signed in La Cruz, 1784-09-14); Varela y Ulloa, *Plano topografico que comprende una parte*.

one administrator lamented that "the infidels are with their tolderías in our ranches consuming the cattle that we have herded. . . . Those that are outside of the ranches [commit] great insults, taking horses from cowboys or scattering the cattle that they have collected."[86] This aggression had resulted in the death of one mission resident and left another badly injured. Records of this event do not reveal the exact reason for the tolderías' change in behavior, but a consideration of the broader context provides important clues. The tolderías' occupation of ranches and raids against herders occurred during a moment of interimperial peace and was therefore not part of a broader war effort. It did coincide, however, with the peak of the missions' slaughtering of wild cattle. That tolderías targeted ranches and herders at this moment suggests that they had set limits on mission activities or required payments to reflect the scale of extraction, and when missions challenged these expectations, the tolderías responded with force. The ranch's administrators considered "the express and indispensable tribute to the infidels" a worthwhile expense given the revenue generated by hide exports, but their payments proved insufficient. By the time the boundary commissions passed through the area in 1787, the tolderías had forced the mission to abandon several of its ranches.[87]

Tolderías' eviction of ranchers often undermined Spanish efforts to fortify the borderline against Portuguese adversaries. The Portuguese toppling of Santa Tecla in 1776 coincided with Minuán and Charrúa attacks on new ranches founded by the Yapeyú, San Borja, Santo Tomé, and San Nicolás missions. One Spanish general argued that the tolderías' raids "[had] been promoted and encouraged by the Portuguese, [who offered them] shelter and protection and to buy from them whatever they steal from the missions." Yet these attacks had begun well before the Portuguese invasion and continued for months afterward, even after Portuguese authorities petitioned the tolderías to stop. A similar situation arose in 1801, as Portuguese armies followed Indigenous raiders to push the borderline southward, and Portuguese officials claimed possession of disputed lands on account of their being held by Charrúa and Minuán tolderías. Here again, the Portuguese found themselves unable to limit tolderías' actions when attempting to establish interimperial peace.[88]

The varied responses of tolderías do not fit neatly into the analytical categories of resistance or accommodation. For example, Charrúa and Minuán raids of mission ranches simultaneously undermined and reinforced the border. In taking livestock, charging tribute, or occupying ranches, tolderías rejected imperial claims to territorial possession and, by extension, individual claims to property, both of which were facets of the borderline's territorial logic. Yet by moving that livestock across the border to Portuguese buyers in Rio

Grande, these tolderías made new borderline economic networks possible. The same patterns were evident among caciques. Miguel Ayala Caraí and other Minuán leaders enabled borderline logic by permitting the establishment of the Spanish fort of Santa Tecla, agreeing to apprehend unauthorized travelers for the soldiers stationed there, and allowing the San Ildefonso mapping teams to erect stone boundary markers. But they also rejected imperial authority over borderland spaces by restricting Santa Tecla's soldiers to the confines of their fort, collaborating in their eventual eviction, and collecting tribute from boundary commissions. While these tolderías probably did not share the bird's-eye perspective of imperial officials, their experience of changing territorialities on a local level produced responses that simultaneously reinforced the borderline and limited its functionality. When taken together, however, this multiplicity of responses ultimately reinforced the borderline. Whether through migration or the incorporation of migrants, trade, or tribute, apprehending contrabandists or contrabanding themselves, tolderías made the borderline meaningful by their appropriation of it.

Conclusion

The invention of an interimperial border was a watershed moment for interethnic relations in the Río de la Plata. The Madrid and San Idlefonso mapping expeditions led Portuguese and Spanish officials alike to presume territorial possession of the entirety of their side of the border and, by extension, sovereignty over all inhabitants and ownership of all resources within their respective dominions. They pursued ideals of territorial order—sedentary subjecthood, regulated land titling, and controlled commerce—but rural subjects demonstrated proclivities toward mobility and informality while tolderías exercised territorial authority over the countryside. The precise location of the borderlines engendered divergent strategies between Spanish and Portuguese officials, but each confronted the conundrum of depending on settlers and tolderías to make the borderline operative while simultaneously attempting to increase control over these individuals. Location mattered to tolderías as well, as those farther away from the border found themselves well within the dominions of a hostile empire, while those closer to the division exploited imperial desires to enforce or, alternatively, subvert the border. Territorial conditions rather than imagined ethnic categories were thus the principal determinants of Indigenous action during the latter part of the eighteenth century, and despite myriad responses, tolderías' actions collectively made the borderline meaningful.

Over time, the opportunities that the borderline provided to tolderías gave way to challenges. As borderland institutions became more entrenched, settlers increased pressures on feral livestock, mounted guards persistently harried individual tolderías, and imperial authorities collaborated against mobile peoples. For these reasons, lands near the borderline became perilous spaces of conflict. The principal advantage of tolderías—their ability to control vast swaths of land with relatively small numbers of people and simultaneously engage distant locales—soon became a liability amid growing populations in the region. If border-making efforts transformed the countryside into a dangerous space for tolderías, the eventual dissolution of a legal border in the early nineteenth century would make it unpredictable and uncontrollable, thus presenting tolderías with difficult decisions about how to survive.

CHAPTER FIVE

Where the Lines End

On the morning of May 3, 1831, Montevideo's police force corralled seventy-nine Charrúa women and children into the city's military barracks. Once the captives were arranged in an orderly line, members of the city's noble families approached and selected one or two captives per family. The petitioners signed an agreement to "treat [their captives] well, to educate them, and to Christianize them," maintaining them in custody for a period of six years or, for the children, until their eighteenth birthday, whichever came last, and promising to never take them outside of Uruguay.[1] Those Charrúas not chosen during the distribution remained imprisoned until they were claimed by other families or died, usually of smallpox. A second convoy of captives who arrived in September filled the prison even further. Meanwhile, Montevideo's police withheld male captives over the age of fifteen from the distribution, considering them too dangerous to be entrusted to private citizens. Authorities instead imprisoned these Charrúa men, sent them to public works projects, banished them to the Malvinas (Falkland) Islands, or offered them to ship captains on the condition that the Charrúas never again set foot on shore. Lastly, four Charrúas, including the cacique Vaimaca Pirú, were turned over to a French schoolmaster and taken to Paris, where they were presented to the French Academy of Sciences and "offered permanently to public curiosity" via an ethnological exposition.[2]

These captives were from tolderías ambushed by the Uruguayan military near the country's northern border earlier that year. This event, known as the "Salsipuedes Massacre," is commonly remembered as one of the final military campaigns that definitively extirpated tolderías from the region. It occurred just one hundred years after Minuanes had blockaded Montevideo, forty-five years after tolderías had taxed the San Ildefonso demarcation teams, and thirty years after Charrúas and Minuanes had contributed to Spain's loss of the eastern Guaraní missions. How did tolderías, and the sociopolitical spaces they occupied, decline so quickly, particularly when some had expanded in power during the eighteenth century's final decades? What happened to the toldería residents who subsequently vanished from most written accounts? Whereas responses to these questions have focused on the threats tolderías faced to their survival or the actions of imperial agents, this chapter examines the spatial and discursive aspects of tolderías' disappearance, highlighting Indigenous agency in the process.[3] It argues that the making and unmaking of an interimperial border prompted tolderías' decline and, through analysis of civil and criminal cases, locates the activities of Charrúas and Minuanes beyond tolderías, distinguishing absence in historical records from absence altogether.

The displacement of Charrúas and Minuanes from written accounts was inextricably tied to the material and discursive processes initiated by the Madrid and San Ildefonso boundary commissions. This disappearance occurred in three ways. First, efforts to create an interimperial border coincided with the intensification of Spanish raiding of tolderías, as captive taking became a means to remove Charrúas and Minuanes from lands coveted by settlers. From the 1750s onward, unprecedented numbers of Minuán and Charrúa captives found themselves in coastal cities, distant frontiers, and other faraway places. Second, the changing territorialities brought about by the boundary commissions prompted numerous individuals to leave their tolderías for colonial settlements and ranches, while the ethnographic visions advanced by demarcation officials defined Charrúas and Minuanes strictly as people who lived outside the colonial system. When dissociated from tolderías, people once identified by ethnonyms appeared in the written records with generic markers such as "Indians," a discursive gesture that masked individuals' provenance or kinship ties. Third, as numerous tolderías near the border had hitched their livelihood to borderline territorialities, the early nineteenth-century dissolution of the border made the countryside uninhabitable. Coordinated transborder raids by Portuguese and Spanish forces left some tolderías without refuge, and the end of imperial rule placed tolderías at the center of rival armies' military campaigns. Whatever rewards border making had once offered to nearby tolderías suddenly vanished, and the short-lived benefits of alliances with military factions quickly gave way to the loss of autonomy.

Captivity and Territory

Captive taking had been an integral feature of interethnic relations in the Río de la Plata since at least the sixteenth century, but during the eighteenth century, Spanish raiders became the principal perpetrators. Abductions accelerated during the second half of the century, with well more than two times the number of Indigenous captives taken than in the preceding fifty years. Available evidence indicates that Spanish agents abducted far more people than their Native counterparts, while the Portuguese largely abstained from abductions (tables 5 and 6). These different approaches derived from the region's changing territorialities. Portuguese agents depended on tolderías' autonomy to maintain a lifeline to Colônia do Sacramento and, after the boundary demarcations, to access the Spanish side of the border. On the other hand, Spanish and missionary officials increasingly employed captive taking as a means of territorial appropriation and toldería depopulation. Spanish raids ebbed and flowed, peaking immediately before the Madrid expeditions and again after the San Ildefonso boundary commissions' conclusion.

Spanish efforts to acquire Indigenous captives in the Río de la Plata preceded Spain's territorial dispute with Portugal in 1680, yet captive taking was ultimately transformed by it. Beginning as early as 1598 and continuing throughout the seventeenth century, residents of Santa Fe traded with nearby Charrúas for captives whom the Charrúas had seized from other tolderías. This practice continued despite official prohibitions in 1542, 1612, 1618, and 1680 and numerous efforts from Buenos Aires to eliminate it, as Santa Fe's residents argued that they were rescuing captives from death: "Those who are captured or bought [by the Charrúas] are sentenced to death; they kill those captured from their enemies, executing this harshness with no exception for age or sex."[4] Captive acquisition through trade soon gave way to direct raids, which invariably brought Indigenous prisoners within a settlement's walls. Colonial officials envisioned captive acquisition as a byproduct of punitive raids and captive distributions as an avenue toward proselytization. Following these raids, officials would distribute captives to petitioners "for the purpose of indoctrinating and raising them in Christian education."[5] Territorial access influenced captive taking as well. In 1702, when armed militias from the Jesuit-Guaraní missions assaulted tolderías along the Río Yí, they justified their campaign on account of the tolderías having blockaded their access to cattle reserves and having disrupted Spain's fragile peace with Portugal. Mission fighters abducted five hundred captives and used them to populate the newly founded San Borja and Jesús missions. Similar campaigns by mission forces occurred in 1707, 1715, and around 1728, with captives being sent to Santo Angel, Loreto, and other missions.[6]

In 1750, a shift occurred in Spanish patterns of captive taking. Dovetailing with the Treaty of Madrid's cession of nearby lands to the Spanish crown, military expeditions from Santa Fe, Santo Domingo Soriano, and Montevideo procured large numbers of captives from neighboring tolderías: 339 were taken to Santa Fe, 124 were taken to Montevideo, and fifty-three were distributed among the campaign's participants.[7] These raids also constituted the first Spanish effort at explicit territorial removal, and the desire to "clean" and "order" the countryside supplanted religious justifications or the desire to access resources. Despite describing each military foray as small scale and retributive,

TABLE 5 Spanish and mission raids. This table demonstrates the recorded numbers of Native captives (men [M], women [W], and children [CH]) taken in raids launched by Spanish settlements or the Guaraní missions compared to the numbers of Spanish captives rescued during Spanish attacks on tolderías. Destinations refer to where captives were taken following their abduction, and numbers do not include those killed in battle or executed immediately after

Year	Captives	M	W	CH	Total	Rescued	Destination
1697	Charrúas, Machados, others		2	2	4		Chile
1702	Mbojas, Mbatidas, Yaros, others				500		San Borja, Jesús
1707*	Charrúas				n/a		Guaraní missions
1707*	Yaros				100		Yapeyú, other Guaraní missions
1708*	Bohanes, Guenoas, Yaros				n/a		Guaraní missions
1715	Bohanes, Charrúas Machados, Yaros				2		Yapeyú
1728	Charrúas				n/a		Guaraní missions
1750	"Infieles"				150	1	Vivoras, Guaraní missions
1750	Charrúas				339		Cayastá
1751	Minuanes				124		Montevideo
1751	Charrúas			7	7	3	n/a
1752	Charrúas				53		Military officials
1752**	Minuanes				60		Military officials
1758	Minuanes	4	4		8		Montevideo
1785	Tapes	46	31	21	98		Guaraní missions
1798	"Infieles"				n/a		n/a
1797	"Infieles"				8		n/a

1798	Charrúas, Minuanes				133	13	Guaraní missions
1798	Charrúas, Minuanes				164		n/a
1800	Minuanes				32	3	San Miguel (Yapeyú)
1800	Charrúas	4	2		6	1	Buenos Aires
1801	n/a	30			30	5	Quartel del Yacuy
1801	Charrúas	4	23	25	52	3	Buenos Aires
1801	Charrúas, Minuanes	3	13	11	27	4	Buenos Aires
1805	"Infieles"				70		n/a
1805	"Infieles"				23		n/a
1806	Charrúas, Minuanes				67	2	Buenos Aires
Total		57	107	68	2057	35	

* The raids reported in 1707 and 1708 may have been one and the same; Bohanes and Yaros present for the raids against Guenoas fled eastward toward Corrientes, where the raids against Charrúas and Yaros occurred.

** The 1752 raid against Minuanes was a joint effort between Spain and Portugal during the Treaty of Madrid's boundary demarcations, but captives were taken into Spanish custody. Sources: AGNA, IX, 41-3-8, exp. 1; RAH, Mata Linares, t. 101, fs. 239–40; Cortesão, *Tratado de Madri*, 116, 144–45, 311, 321–22; Acosta y Lara, *La guerra de los charrúas*, 1:40–48; Trelles, "Vandalismo misionero," 22–25; ANA, Actas Capitulares, copias, carpeta 21, Sección Histórica, v. 108 (Acuerdo del 1723-08-07); Telesca, *Documentos Jesuíticos del siglo XVIII*, 79; Vianna, *Jesuítas e Bandeirantes no Uruguai*, 236–43; Latini, "Relatos del conflicto interétnico," 12; AGI, Buenos Aires, 235, fs. 12, 31v, 70v, 89v, 108, 130–30v, 150v, 172, 191, 214v, 239v, 259v, 276v, 296, 320–20v, 345v, 371v–72, 385v, 405v–6, 429v; AGNA, IX, 4-3-1 (Campo del Bloqueo; 1749-10-29, 1757-04-26); AGNU, Falcao Espalter, 1:46–48, 88–89, 110–15, 184–88; AGPSF, Actas de Cabildo de 1750-01-14, 1750-02-03, 1750-11-03, 1752-01-19; AGNU, Falcao Espalter, 4:127–30, 229; AGNA, IX, 2-1-4 (Montevideo, 1751-05-07); IEB, YAP-011, fs. 9v, 11v–12; *Revista del Archivo General Administrativo*, 28–29; AGI, Buenos Aires, 70 (Buenos Aires, 1785-06-08); AGNA, IX, 11-6-4 (Cuchilla de Tacuarembó, 1797-09-25); *Archivo Artigas*, 2:27–29, 411–14; AGNA, IX, 28-7-7 (Montevideo, 1803-10-24); AGNA, IX, 2-9-7 (San Miguel, 1798-12-18); AGNA, IX, 18-2-4 (Yapeyú, 1798-08-15); AGNA, IX, 3-9-2 (Colonia, 1798-08-23); AGNU, Manuscritos Originales Relativos a la Historia del Uruguay, 50-1-3, carpeta 10, no. 1, fs. 24–30; AGNA, IX, 10-6-1 (Río Queguay, 1800-05-28; Estancia de Román, 1801-05-25; Campamento en el Ibirapuita-guazú, 1806-04-24; Batoví chico, 1801-08-20); MM, Archivo Colonial, Arm. B, C28, P1, no. 3, fs. 1–3; *Telégrafo Mercantil*, 252 (282); AGNA, IX, 32-5-6 (Campamento de Tacuarembó Chico, 1805-03-20); AGNA, IX, 13-6-4 (Campamento de Tacuarembó Chico, 1805-06-02).

TABLE 6 Tolderia raids. This table demonstrates the numbers of captives (men [M], women [W], and children [CH]) abducted in tolderia raids or apprehended in the countryside, as well as the number of horses and livestock extracted from ranches or *vaquerías* during the same raids. It does not include numbers of people killed during the raids

Year	Location	Captors	M	W	CH	Total	Cattle
1703	Colônia	n/a	1	1	1	3	70 mares and 2 horses
1708	La Cruz, Yapeyú	Bohanes, Guenoas, allies				26	2,400 sheep and several horses
1716	Itatí	Bohanes, Charrúas, Yaros		1	2	3	n/a
1750	Santo Domingo Soriano	"Infieles"			1	1	cows and mares
1751	Santa Fe	Charrúas				16	horses and cattle
1751	Río Queguay	Bohanes, Charrúas, Minuanes	2	2		4	n/a
1751	Calera del Rey (Maldonado)	Minuanes				2	80–100 horses and 500 cattle
1758	Rosario	Charrúas, Tapes	1		2	3	"many horses"
1759	Río Ibira-puitá	Charrúas, Minuanes	2	2	3	7	n/a
1776	Mission ranches	Minuanes		2		2	cows and oxen
1798	Mission ranches	Charrúas, Minuanes				20	3,000 horses
1799	Paysandú	Charrúas, Minuanes				n/a	horses
1800	Paysandú	Charrúas, Minuanes			3	3	n/a
1800	Mission ranches	"Infieles"		6		9	n/a
1800	Mission ranches	Charrúas, Minuanes		2		2	900 horses
		Total	6	16	12	101	

Sources: AGNA, IX, 41-3-8, exp. 4, fs. 4–11v; Cortesão, *Tratado de Madri*, 5:321–22; Vianna, *Jesuítas e Bandeirantes no Uruguai*, 4:237–39; AGI, Charcas, 382, Informe del fiscal (1716–10–17) y resolución del Consejo (1716–10–20); RAH, Mata Linares, t. 102, f. 55; AGNU, Falcao Espalter, 1:46–48, 88–89, 110–15; AGNA, IX, 2-1-4, f. 794 (Montevideo, 1751–11–13); AGNA, IX, 4-3-2 (Campo del Bloqueo, 1758–03–03, 1758–04–26; Buenos Aires, 1758–05–11); AGI, Buenos Aires, 536 (Buenos Aires, 1759–07–02); AGNA, IX, 4-3-8 (Campamento de las Puntas de Chuniteri, 1776–06–04); AGNA, IX, 4-3-4 (Montevideo, 1798–03–20); AGNA, IX, 3-9-2 (Montevideo, 1798–03–20); AGNA, IX, 10-6-1 (Paysandú, 1799–11–04, 1800–04–23; Concepción del Uruguay, 1799–11–05); AGNU, Manuscritos Originales Relativos a la Historia del Uruguay, 50-1-3, carpeta 10, no. 5, fs. 122–23, no. 6, fs. 124–27.

Spanish officials frequently extended their raids to tolderías uninvolved in the initial conflict, subsequently articulating the benefits of removing mobile Native peoples from the countryside. The objective of extirpation permeated postexpeditionary reports as well, with ranking officers boasting that they had achieved complete territorial removal of entire ethnic communities.[8] Spanish captive taking occurred intermittently during the century's second half—most notably via a 1785 raid against two tolderías of refugees from the Guaraní missions—but accelerated again after the San Ildefonso demarcations, as the formation of a regiment of mounted guards in Montevideo systematized campaigns of territorial removal.[9]

While Spanish and mission raids on tolderías were a way to appropriate territory, tolderías' raids generally responded to military aggression or the encroachments of ranchers. In this way, raids by tolderías resembled the punitive attacks (*malones*) undertaken by Native peoples of the Pampas, Araucanía, and the Chaco.[10] Extant sources are insufficient to draw definitive connections between imperial raids and Native responses, yet a temporal correlation existed (tables 5 and 6). Toldería raids occurred in 1708 (following raids from Yapeyú), 1715 (after a campaign from Yapeyú and Santa Fe), 1728 (after Jesuit-Guaraní raids), 1750–51 (after campaigns from Santa Fe, Santo Domingo Soriano, and Montevideo), 1758 (after the Guaraní War), 1798 (following attacks by farmworkers), and 1799–1800 (following blandengue attacks). Imperial officials, amid broader discourses of Indigenous aggression, acknowledged the retributive nature of Native raids. In 1750, Santo Domingo Soriano's magistrate expressed concern over Minuanes joining nearby Charrúa tolderías because "the majority of [our] captives are Minuanes and they always set out to seek vengeance."[11] Likewise, a 1797 report revealed that Charrúas and Minuanes had attacked ranchers because "their tolderías were sacked and set on fire not once, but many times, and their occupants were killed like livestock in a slaughterhouse."[12]

Indigenous raiders targeted property rather than people in their assaults. The number of captives taken in these raids paled in comparison to those of their Spanish and mission counterparts, and many raids did not include captive taking at all. In most instances, tolderías took less than a dozen captives and instead extracted livestock, scorched crops and buildings, or killed ranch hands. Based on recorded visits to tolderías, captives do not appear to have constituted a substantive portion of their populations, and captives were occasionally offered to nearby settlements in exchange for commodities or to procure peace.[13] Captive taking may have been principally a wartime measure for some tolderías, as indicated by the bishop of Buenos Aires during a 1743 visit to Santa Fe: "[Nearby Charrúas] stole all of the cattle during peacetime, which were uncared for in the countryside, saying that the peace agreement served only to prohibit the killing of men and women, but not to stop robbing cattle."[14] Regardless, in targeting livestock, Native raiders challenged settlers' presumptions of property rights. Minuanes attacks on Guaraní ranches in 1776 and 1785 occurred in a context of ranchers' accelerated slaughtering of feral livestock and lapses in tribute payments to Indigenous authorities, a pattern analogous to raids by Comanches and other Native peoples in Texas and northern Mexico.[15]

In the back and forth of raiding, imperial and ecclesiastical authorities took measures to transform Native captives into Christian subjects. During the first half of the eighteenth century, most captives were taken to Jesuit-Guaraní missions, but beginning in the 1750s, as Spanish armed forces supplanted Guaraní militias, more and more captives were remitted to Spanish cities and forts in the south of the region. Captives arriving at non-mission settlements were divided and placed in the custody of military personnel, bureaucrats, or elite families, who in turn signed agreements that outlined the terms of captivity.[16] These agreements initially resembled tributary labor grants (*encomiendas*) and contracts of indentured servitude, as they established a finite period for service, prohibited captives' transfer or sale, and mandated religious instruction. Over time, however, officials placed fewer restrictions on captors. Following a 1752 expedition, the governor of Buenos Aires authorized the distribution of captives among the expedition's participants "to serve for ten years, with an obligation [for their captor] to teach them the mysteries of our Holy Catholic Faith. . . . The sale of these prisoners is not permitted since they should be treated as free people with only a pension of ten years of service."[17] By contrast, the agreement that governed the distribution of captives in Buenos Aires in 1801 neither restricted the duration of captivity nor prohibited captives' transfer or sale. It simply stated that "the Indian shall be turned over to the supplicant who solicited them, obliging [the supplicant] . . . to maintain, dress, and educate them, instructing them in the mysteries of our Sacred Religion without employing him in hard or excessive labors."[18]

Although most Indigenous captives ultimately worked in unfree conditions, imperial raids on tolderías were designed principally for the appropriation of territory and the exile of tolderías' residents. Resembling strategies employed elsewhere in the Americas, Spanish agents sought to extirpate tolderías from newly possessed lands, yet in the Río de la Plata this effort did not correlate with specific labor demands.[19] Given the availability of thousands of workers from the Guaraní missions following the 1767 Jesuit expulsion and the influx of enslaved Africans toward the end of the century—over seventy thousand slaves disembarked in the region between 1777 and 1812—captives from tolderías would have been unnecessary as a workforce.[20] Nor did officials point to labor demands when justifying raids. Rather, the transfer of Charrúas and Minuanes who lived near the border to Buenos Aires or Montevideo was an effort to prevent their escape and return to the countryside.[21] Thus, when the leader of an 1800 expedition against tolderías received instructions to take captives to one of Yapeyú's ranches, he suggested that they instead be sent to a distant town, because "anything to the contrary and they will all run away. . . . They will be more secure [in the town] because in the [ranch] they remain exposed to the invasion of others from their nation."[22]

Since imperial raiders frequently killed or executed adult men in the tolderías they attacked, most Indigenous exiles were women and children. During the systematic raids near the border that began in 1797, a steady flow of Charrúa and Minuán captives disembarked in Buenos Aires, where they were detained at a former Jesuit residence known as the *Casa de la Reclusión*.[23] Unlike Native captives from Buenos Aires's southern frontiers, who were often held at the residence as ransom for Spanish captives, Charrúas and Minuanes were subsequently distributed among the city's military officers, priests, and elite families, who employed them as domestic servants. Approximately one woman and one or two children were assigned to each petitioner, but mothers and children also faced separation at times. Captives arrived in great enough numbers that in 1801, a resident of Buenos Aires wrote a letter to the editor of one of the city's newspapers, *Telégrafo Mercantil*, stating, "Every day we see Indians around us and living in our own houses: I am speaking of the Pampas and Charrúas."[24]

Being bound to military officers or households made captives subject to changing residences and dislocation. Such was the case for Francisca, the lone Minuana in the household of a lieutenant colonel who took her from Maldonado to Buenos Aires; she was stabbed to death in 1774 after an altercation with an enslaved woman from Benguela who lived in the same household. Likewise, following the 1751 distribution in Montevideo, a surgeon took a Minuana and her daughter to Buenos Aires, while Montevideo's governor offered another woman as a gift to the wife of his counterpart in Buenos Aires. After the 1801 distribution in Buenos Aires, one Minuana was taken as far as Luján, a settlement along the Viceroyalty of the Río de la Plata's southern frontier.[25] The few men taken captive faced different circumstances. Those who were caciques tended to be exiled to other locales, as occurred in 1751 when the Minuán cacique Manuá was sent to Buenos Aires. Others were sent to public works projects, as occurred with a Ranquel cacique named Toroñan, likely from the Pampas or Patagonia, who was sentenced to perpetual labor in Montevideo in 1774.[26]

Not all captives found themselves in the households of petitioning families, as was the case with the 339 Charrúas captives from the 1750 Santa Fe campaigns, who were marched across the Río Paraná to establish a reducción named Nuestra Señora de la Concepción de Cayastá (hereafter Cayastá). Much like settlements populated by *genízaros* in the north of New Spain, Cayastá was designed as a buffer between Santa Fe and Abipón and Mocoví tolderías from the Chaco. Unlike the genízaros, the Charrúas taken there constituted an exile community whose members could not claim any legal right to return to their homeland.[27] Cayastá included a walled exterior and an adjacent fort, which would "enable the residents [of Santa Fe] to recover their former possessions" by providing a first line of defense against Abipón and Mocoví raiders. Indeed, within five years of Cayastá's founding, its inhabitants found themselves subject to raids from "rebels from [neighboring] nations, many of whom remain dispersed and unsubjugated."[28] During the next forty years, the reducción repeatedly endured attacks, droughts, plagues of locusts, and insufficient aid by residents of Santa Fe, who had initially agreed to support the settlement militarily and with livestock. By 1790, Cayastá's population totaled fewer than sixty adults, one-sixth the number of original inhabitants; and several years later, it was abandoned completely. Many of Cayastá's occupants fled to other tolderías, while others likely found employment in or around Santa Fe.[29]

Worlds Together

While the abduction and distribution of Indigenous captives generated long paper trails, there is limited documentation of the free Charrúas and Minuanes who also lived in settlements and adjacent ranches throughout the region. Few records exist of ethnonym-identified residents in these spaces, yet this paucity of sources derives more from imperial perceptions than from Indigenous absence, as ethnic identifiers ceased to be significant or perceptible to record keepers once a person was separated from their toldería or its lands. Instead, colonial writers employed generic terms to situate Indigenous people within the social milieu of the lettered city. Some writers indicated Native ancestry, such as Indian (*indio*) or Indian woman (*china*); others age, such as preadolescent child (*párvulo*) or infant (*criatura*); some occupation, such as domestic laborer (*criada*), peon (*peón*), or household dependent (*agregado*); and others skin color, such as mulatto (*mulato*). All identified perceived gender. These identifiers occasionally appeared alongside ethnonyms, yet they tended to supplant ethnonyms over the course of a person's lifetime or from one generation to the next. Records from farms and ranches on the outskirts of a settlement also make scant use of ethnonyms, despite evidence suggesting tolderías' inhabitants worked as seasonal laborers and traded with local settlers. There, Minuanes' and Charrúas' ostensible absence derived from the limited reach of the lettered city, as Christian baptism or marriage was not a prerequisite for participating in ranching activities, and the few censuses that included rural households did not account for nonresident laborers.[30]

This discursive disappearance derived from an ethnogeographic vision advanced by the Madrid and San Ildefonso boundary commissions. In their ethnographic accounts, members of these expeditions espoused a paradigmatic division between sedentary and mobile societies, which presumed that waning numbers of tolderías meant the complete disappearance of ethnic communities.[31] To be "Charrúa" or "Minuán" was to live in a toldería in the countryside, not on a ranch or within a walled settlement. This ideology undergirded captive distributions, which aimed to incorporate captives into a colonial social order via separation from their kin and Christian instruction. The principal exception was the Cayastá mission, where individuals continued to appear as "Charrúa" into the 1790s. In this instance, however, the reducción itself was associated with Charrúa captives, making "Charrúa" a catch-all term for its inhabitants, similar to "Guaraní" in the thirty Jesuit missions, "Abipón" in San Géronimo, or "Mocoví" in San Javier. Unlike the captive distributions, which sought acculturation, the aim here was to transform "infidels" into "mission Indians" through exile and separation from Spanish settlements.[32]

Individuals identified by ethnonym nonetheless appeared intermittently in civil and criminal records throughout the region, and their actions point to a broader presence of Charrúas and Minuanes than previously assumed. In Buenos Aires, Charrúas could be found even before blandengue raids swept the northern borderlands at the turn of the nineteenth century; and between 1776 and 1802, sixty-seven Charrúas and nine Minuanas were baptized in the city's La Merced and Concepción parishes.[33] In Santa Fe, decades after the purported expulsion of Charrúas from the city's hinterlands, Charrúa men appeared in prison for such offenses as drawing a knife on a priest, freeing a woman from prison, abducting a woman in the countryside, and theft.[34] In Colônia, numerous "Indians of the land" (*índios da terra*) were baptized between 1695 and 1704, followed by several Charrúa and Bohán women in the 1760s or 1770s, though many more likely received the sacrament in intermediate years.[35] In Rio Grande, neighboring Minuanes had their children baptized and had the sitting governor or a Portuguese resident serve as godparent. Half of the fifty-four Minuanes baptized in 1749 were children or grandchildren of caciques, and twenty-three more Minuanes received the sacrament in 1753. In the 1749 register, nearly all female recipients had godparents listed next to their names, while male recipients had none. Caciques presumably entrusted their daughters and other girls to Portuguese families to establish kinship ties.[36] In the decade following the baptisms, several Minuanes also married in Rio Grande, and others married or were baptized in San Borja, Colônia, and elsewhere.[37]

Civil and criminal records from in and around Montevideo, including four censuses between 1726 and 1773, provide the most voluminous accounts of Minuanes' and Charrúas' presence.[38] There, Minuanas married, served as witnesses in marriages, baptized their children, and used the legal system to settle civil disputes. Spouses included African descendants and Indigenous Americans, almost all of whom were migrants to Montevideo and none of whom were recorded as Minuán, indicating an effort to develop new familial ties and social networks. Witnesses and godparents also tended to be outsiders to the region.[39] Some of the Minuana women in Montevideo arrived via the midcentury raids from the city and were still attached to their original claimants' household when they married in the 1750s and 1760s. They then appeared in the 1770s living on farms or ranches belonging to third parties.[40] Several Charrúa and Minuán men appeared as well. A census of Montevideo's armed forces in 1772 and 1773 identified three Charrúa men within a military unit stationed on the outskirts of Montevideo's jurisdiction. The circumstances that led the men to join this unit are unclear, but their location placed them far away from any Charrúa tolderías, and their ages made them unlikely to have been captives of the midcentury raids.[41] Other men arrived via an agreement that Minuán caciques brokered with Montevideo's cabildo one decade before the censuses that allowed "the young men of their nation with license from their caciques to work on the ranches and farms . . . certain that the Lord Governor will compensate them for their work in the event that there is any neglect by the people who contracted them."[42] Despite a 1767 military campaign that supposedly expelled tolderías from the city's jurisdiction, a 1772 criminal case and a 1789 cabildo session confirm the sustained presence of Minuanes on Montevideo residents' ranches.[43]

By living within the jurisdiction of a specific settlement, Charrúas and Minuanes came under the watchful gaze of imperial authorities, which they alternatively evaded or put to use. In 1758, after a Charrúa woman living in the Rosario district near Santo Domingo Soriano was accused of drunkenness, authorities confiscated the woman's goods and "deposited her children in houses where they would be educated." The woman escaped, however, presenting Soriano's administrators with a conundrum, as they feared she would incite reprisal from nearby Charrúa tolderías.[44] Here and elsewhere, the proximity of tolderías threatened to undermine a settlement's authority over Indigenous residents. Captives separated from their territory and kin did not enjoy the same possibility of escape or retribution, and when two Minuanas found themselves embroiled in a 1770 scandal in Montevideo, they were unable to evade criminal proceedings and punishment.[45] Local legal systems could nonetheless provide recourse to address individual or collective grievances. In 1773, a Minuana named Juana Arnero filed a complaint against a man with whom she cohabited for falsely promising marriage and for mistreating her children; he was exiled to Buenos Aires the following month.[46] In 1782, residents of Cayastá filed a complaint to Franciscan authorities and requested that one of their caciques become administrator. Eight years later, a Charrúa named Cipriano Lencias petitioned directly to the viceroy regarding the reducción's poor conditions, inciting a royal investigation and Cayastá's dissolution.[47]

Movement to settlements was not always unidirectional or permanent, as some individuals traveled back and forth to make a living. Joseph Francisco, one of the children baptized in Rio Grande in 1749 and likely the son of the Minuán cacique Casildo, provides one example. Years after his baptism, Joseph worked as a bricklayer and later as a ranch hand near Rio Pardo before facing imprisonment in Maldonado, where his mother was said to have lived. Joseph eventually escaped, and by 1772, contrabandists hired him to help extract livestock from Santa Tecla and establish a new ranch on Portuguese lands. Joseph become so well known that when the San Ildefonso boundary commissions passed through Santa Tecla in 1787, they came across a river ford named after him.[48] A similar series of events unfolded with a Minuán boy named Francisco, who at twelve years of age was apprehended while transporting livestock for a contrabandist in Montevideo. Francisco had likely been captured as a young child and lived in the households of several Montevideo elites when not in the city's prison. Like Joseph, Francisco eventually escaped and moved between ranches and farmhouses before making a living with a Paraguayan contrabandist who transported livestock between Montevideo and Rio Pardo.[49] The movement of both Joseph Francisco and Francisco was facilitated by their use of informal economic networks incentivized by the interimperial border.

Other Native individuals positioned themselves as go-betweens for settlements and tolderías, appearing in nearly every recorded interaction between colonial and Indigenous authorities. Forays beyond the immediate reach of a settlement required guides who knew the countryside and nearby tolderías' current locations, particularly when the travelers sought to evade tolderías. In instances where colonial agents sought engagement, individuals knowledgeable in imperial languages, Guaraní, and other Native tongues were required.[50] Despite the ubiquity of intermediaries and interethnic engagement, written records provide only scant details of intermediaries' relationships with specific tolderías. One such instance was the 1749 baptism of Minuanes in Rio Grande, which may never have occurred if not for José Ladino, a Minuán who was fluent in Spanish. The Minuanes had supposedly hesitated to enter Portuguese settlements for fear of treachery, so the Portuguese governor sent a Jesuit priest and Ladino to meet them in the countryside. The Minuanes were "assured by the catechist Ladino that they would find good treatment with the [Jesuits]," and he convinced them to travel to Rio Grande. That Ladino was fluent in Spanish indicates he also had ties to Spanish settlements or Jesuit-Guaraní missions in the area, and his position as a catechist suggests a deeper tie to the Catholic religion.[51] Other intermediaries facilitated baptisms on a smaller scale, as occurred with a man from the Yapeyú mission who had been abducted by Charrúas only to return years later with a "gentile" wife, two children, and an old woman who had raised him. Several Guenoas also became residents of Yapeyú later that year.[52]

Native intermediaries were integral figures in diplomatic negotiations between settlements and tolderías, both for their linguistic skills and for their familiarity with both negotiating parties. Some had been taken captive years earlier, only to serve as negotiators in subsequent expeditions. In 1801, two Charrúas who lived in Buenos Aires—Antonio Ocalián and Vicente Adeltú—accompanied a commission from Yapeyú to nearby Charrúa and Minuán tolderías. Both men were purportedly Christian, and the latter was a cacique. Ocalián and Adeltú were appointed as "ambassadors" to the tolderías because they were "Indians from their same nation" who could "persuade [the Charrúas and Minuanes] to settle on a reducción and live in peace."[53] Rather than serving as mere guides or interpreters, Adeltú and Ocalián were to "go out and negotiate the peace propositions."[54] Upon arrival at the tolderías, they were the first to speak, offering a presentation to the caciques; after the expedition, Adeltú and Ocalián returned to Buenos Aires to provide an official report to the viceroy.[55] The ability to communicate in Spanish, Portuguese, or Guaraní also appears to have been a skill possessed by certain caciques: Moreira "knew the Paraguayan language well and even Spanish"; Juan Yasú spoke "in the language of Paraguay"; Juan Salcedo spoke Spanish; Pedro Ignacio Salcedo "[spoke] Spanish with much skill, and [spoke] Guaraní, Charrúa, and

Minuán perfectly"; and Vaimaca Pirú spoke Spanish and Portuguese.[56] Being multilingual might have even been a path to becoming a cacique. This would explain how an individual such as Miguel Ayala Caraí, who was the son of a Spanish man and a Minuán woman and who worked for years on Portuguese ranches, eventually became the principal cacique along the interimperial border.[57]

The 1763 peace negotiation between Minuanes and Montevideo perhaps best encapsulates the ties that linked settlements and tolderías. As Minuán caciques stood in the halls of the city's town council, their conversation with Spanish officials was translated and mediated by "Petrona, an Indian from the same nation, who lives among us since she is now a Christian, and also sister of the cacique Don Joseph. . . . [She is a] translator or interpreter for the said Indians, and speaker of our language."[58] Given Petrona's linguistic ability, she had probably inhabited the city for some time and was possibly the same Petrona who married a Pampa Indian in 1755. Regardless, she was the sister of both Joseph and the principal Minuán cacique, Cumandat. She was also one of numerous kin that the tolderías had in Montevideo, as Joseph requested to remain in the city after the negotiations because his wife lived there. The town council communicated that "if he wanted to do so, no violence would come upon him, to which [Cumandat] responded that he did not oppose this arrangement and of course he would concede it with pleasure."[59] By assuring Joseph's safe entrance and exit from the city, Montevideo's officials formally recognized a marriage that crossed the settlement-toldería divide, and individual ties persisted, even though official peace was cut short when the city attacked the tolderías in 1767.[60]

The End of the Line

Whereas the creation of an interimperial border intensified captive taking and movement between settlements and tolderías, the border's dissolution in the early nineteenth century ultimately led to the demise of tolderías that remained in the countryside. Late-eighteenth-century border making had provided opportunities for certain caciques and tolderías, but these benefits dissipated during the first three decades of the nineteenth century, as local rejection of imperial authority and the subsequent wars of independence undermined the border's legal weight. Once the border failed to restrict the movements of imperial agents, and alliances predicated on the border no longer guided imperial action, lands near the border became increasingly uninhabitable for tolderías. Tolderías' capacity to traverse and move livestock across the interimperial division ceased to be unique, leaving them exposed to an increasing amount of violence and bereft of economic opportunities. As caciques' success and their tolderías' survival had become intimately tied to borderline territorialities, the rupture of these arrangements undermined both. By 1834, tolderías disappeared altogether from written records.

This process began with the dissolution of the San Ildefonso line in 1801. That year, Charrúa and Minuán tolderías expelled Guaraní ranchers and Spanish settlers from their lands, after which Portuguese forces invaded and annexed the Siete Pueblos, Batoví, Santa Tecla, and other Spanish settlements along the border. This regional fighting took place within the broader imperial context of the War of the Oranges, which pitted Spain and France against Portugal and placed their South American borderlines in abeyance. Given that the war had ended and Iberian diplomats had signed the Treaty of Badajoz by the time of the tolderías' and Portugal's advancements in the Río de la Plata, colonial officials in the region were left to reconcile the incongruence between the extant San Ildefonso line and the new on-the-ground settlement patterns. Although the Treaty of Badajoz did not directly reference the Treaty of San Ildefonso, it promised Portugal "the conservation of its states and dominions" (Article 9) and obliged the Iberian crowns to "renew their treaties of defensive alliance" (Article 10).[61] Following the model set forth in the treaties of Madrid and San Ildefonso, regional officials deployed the concepts of uti possidetis and natural limits to reestablish a borderline in the Río de la Plata.[62] Yet unlike those earlier accords, tolderías' were taken into account when justifying the border's adjusted location.

Given that many of Portugal's newly claimed lands had been controlled by tolderías when the fighting broke out—specifically those south of the Río Ibicuí—Charrúas and Minuanes were thrust into regional debates about territorial possession, sovereignty, and Native autonomy. The governor of the Portuguese captaincy of Rio Grande declared that those lands "were abandoned by the Spanish nation before [the war], due to hostilities from Charrúa and Minuán Indians, [and] were explored during the war by our [Portugal's] repeated patrols . . . and also by militiamen, natives, and those undomesticated Indians who . . . are declared enemies of the Spanish."[63] This argument was built on a logic of occupation rights and Indigenous autonomy. The governor claimed possession on the grounds of Spanish abandonment and Portuguese occupation, thus employing the concept of uti possidetis to restore a functioning borderline. Yet Portuguese access was a byproduct of Native raids, and for the first time authorities considered tolderías when determining a border, if only as a proxy. The governor emphasized tolderías' presence and their enmity with the Spanish crown to simultaneously undercut Spanish claims to the lands via vassalage and fortify Portuguese claims of the same nature.[64]

In 1804, three years after the fighting began, Portuguese and Spanish officials came to an agreement on a new borderline. This time, the interimperial division was negotiated and defined by officials in Porto Alegre and Buenos Aires rather than authorities in Lisbon and Madrid. The 1804 status quo division, as initially proposed by the Spanish viceroy in Buenos Aires, took the Jaguarão and Ibicuí rivers as natural limits, thus marking the borderline south and west of the San Ildefonso line. But unlike previous borders, the status quo line was concretized by military occupation rather than collaborative mapping expeditions, and it was moved southwest to the Río Cuareim later that year to match the on-the-ground locations of Portuguese troops (figure 22).[65] Tolderías continued to exert effective territorial authority in the borderlands at this time, but the incorporation of much of their land into Portuguese dominions meant that they had to cross a new line—this time with no neutral zone—to gain refuge from Spanish blandengues. Tolderías continued to move livestock from Spanish ranches across the new border to Portuguese buyers, but they also confronted increasing numbers of Portuguese settlers and ranchers in their lands.[66]

If the 1801 invasion and the 1804 status quo line repositioned imperial soldiers, they did little to demilitarize the border. As occurred after the Madrid and San Ildefonso demarcations, officials in Buenos Aires and Porto Alegre established new forts along the borderline. Spanish forces sought to prevent further Portuguese advancements and to continue extermination campaigns against Charrúa and Minuán tolderías, while Portuguese forces aimed to consolidate their claims over land and livestock. In the 1780s and 1790s, Spanish authorities had used the presence of autonomous tolderías as a justification for more soldiers in the area, while their Portuguese counterparts accused the Spanish of encroaching on Portuguese dominions or neutral grounds under the guise of responding to tolderías' aggressions.[67] These formerly intermittent disputes became a fixture of borderline politics, and between 1801 and 1806, Portuguese officials repeatedly accused Spanish officials of using Charrúas and Minuanes as a pretext to reclaim lands lost in the war. The governor of Rio Grande complained in 1803 that the Spanish "keep troops in the countryside. Even though . . . they have assured me in two letters that [the troops] are for the Charrúa and Minuán Indians, I am nonetheless always suspicious that they are waiting for some orders from Europe."[68] The commanding officer of Rio Pardo was less circumspect: "[The Spanish] augment their forces little by little with the apparent motive of pursuing Infidel Indians, gauchos,

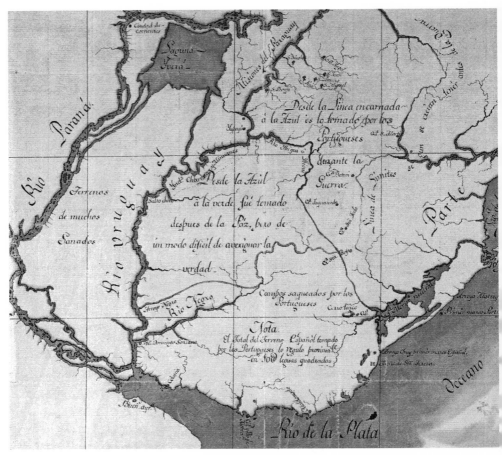

FIGURE 22 Agustín Ibáñez y Bojons, *Plano que sólo manifiesta lo indispensable*, 1804. Drawn by a Spanish engineer, this map identifies lands contested by Spain and Portugal following the 1801 invasion. It includes three lines, from right to left: the 1777 San Ildefonso line, the proposed 1804 status quo line, and the extent of Portuguese occupation. It also plots Charrúas and Minuanes but restricts them to the coast of the Río Uruguay rather than the entirety of disputed lands, which they occupied at the time. The status quo line would be adjusted later in 1804 to incorporate some of the occupied lands into Portuguese dominions. España. Ministerio de Cultura y Deporte. Archivo General de Indias. MP-Buenos Aires, 211.

and wrongdoers to the point that they occupy places that they want to add to their system of disputed lands."[69] Similar disputes occurred repeatedly in subsequent years, generating troves of diplomatic correspondence that highlight how imperial officials sought to rethink their engagement with tolderías without undermining borderline territorialities.[70]

Despite Portuguese apprehensions, Spanish officials initially respected the status quo borderline in their forays against tolderías and solicited Portuguese assistance once the tolderías crossed the border. Following the 1801 hostilities, the viceroy of the Río de la Plata demanded that the governor of Rio Grande "have the commanders of that district . . . not only pursue [tolderías] in common agreement with the Spanish chiefs and commanders, but take interest in their punishment and chastisement as any cultured nation should." For the Spanish viceroy, such collaboration was necessary "for the good harmony, union, and alliance that reigns between our august sovereigns. . . . Your government must conduct itself along the border between the two nations with circumspection and good faith."[71] Spanish authorities made similar requests through the end of 1805, and Portuguese officials repeatedly offered promises to patrol their side of the border. The Portuguese denied association with tolderías and pointed to their own attempts to expel them from certain territories, further contending that the countryside was too large to exercise complete control.[72]

Dissatisfaction with Portuguese efforts and the perpetuity of conflict with tolderías led the Spanish to level accusations that the Portuguese were acting in bad faith and violating the statutes of the borderline. An 1804 discovery of clandestine *vaquerías* that included Portuguese vassals and individuals from tolderías confirmed Spanish suspicions, and the Spanish decided to act unilaterally the following year.[73] Rather than crossing unannounced into Portuguese lands, however, they requested license. The commander of Spanish forces, Francisco Xavier de Viana, wrote to Paulo José da Silva Gama, the governor of Rio Grande: "Those barbarians, when they feel persecution [by Spanish forces], find asylum and security, crossing to the dominions of [the Portuguese Crown], aware or suspecting that the armies of the [Spanish] King cannot pursue them there." Since tolderías had made use of the borderline to foil Spanish forays, Viana concluded that it was necessary for Spanish troops to enter Portuguese lands. Yet he acknowledged that "it is necessary for me to give prior notice to Your Excellency of my intention to have you permit me in this case to enter into those dominions for the sole purpose of pursuing the infidels, extinguishing them, and finishing them."[74] This petition for access simultaneously recognized Portuguese territorial possessions and sought to temporarily suspend the agreed-on borderline in order to ultimately preserve its function.

Portuguese responses to Viana's request were invariably negative, and they grounded their opposition in precise definitions of imperial territorial possession and tolderías' natural rights. Silva Gama argued, "[It would] go against natural and human rights for me to concur in attacking the savage nations, embroiled in war with your government [if I do not have] a higher order or motives other than the pretext that they do not have any political representation." He flatly rejected the Spanish proposal, claiming that it "would be an injury to the [Portuguese] state, would violate its territory, and would harm human rights."[75] This two-pronged rejection simultaneously claimed Portuguese territorial possession over lands conquered in 1801 and positioned tolderías as autonomous actors protected by natural law. The argument for territorial integrity was clear—Portugal had the exclusive right to inflict punishment within its dominions—but the argument for natural rights was more nuanced. The governor suggested that any attack against tolderías was predicated on the idea that they "had no political representation," thus divorcing Indigenous vassalage from imperial land possession. Prior to the border, imperial officials often claimed tolderías' lands by declaring their vassalage, yet this required that they be accountable for tolderías' actions.[76] Silva Gama instead presented tolderías as autonomous, landless peoples for whose actions he had no responsibility if they occurred on the Spanish side of the border. Since there was no direct conflict between the tolderías and Portuguese authorities, he saw no justification for attacking them.

Silva Gama instead offered neutrality. In writing to Viana, he determined that "consent should not be given to Spanish troops breaking [Portugal's] sovereignty and territorial independence, entering with an armed force beyond our guards . . . In the same way, all kinds of help and favor to the savages should be denied."[77] A position of neutrality enabled Silva Gama to honor his duty to maintain the border without antagonizing Charrúa and Minuán tolderías, who were useful allies. Nonetheless, Porto Alegre's town council betrayed this neutrality by making a pact with a Charrúa cacique named Gaspar the following year. Despite his promise to the Spanish, Silva Gama reasoned that "such an alliance is of utmost interest to the State, in the event of any breaking [of peace] with the bordering nation, since these individuals are the most dexterous in the handling of horses and the most practiced in this countryside." Since Gaspar's tolderías and others were located south of the Río Ibicuí, they would serve as a cost-effective buffer to protect Portugal's newest territorial claims: "In this way, during times of peace, they will serve us as a formidable barrier against any surprises by our neighbors, and in [times of] war, without expenditures of the royal coffers, they will augment the number of [fighters on our side]." Portuguese officials also made pacts with Minuanes during these same years, as they saw their tolderías as useful allies that could harry Spanish neighbors without Portugal having to claim responsibility.[78]

Despite pacts with Charrúa and Minuán tolderías, Portuguese officials in Porto Alegre were unable to enforce the borderline among subordinates, and the border thus ceased to be a means of protection for tolderías. Given that the 1801 invasion and 1804 status quo line placed many tolderías on the Portuguese side of the border, some local Portuguese officials and ranchers sought their liquidation. San Borja's chief administrator prohibited the mission's residents from trading with nearby tolderías, while the administrator of the San Luis mission solicited support from José Saldanha—then governor of the newly acquired Siete Pueblos (Sete Povos in Portuguese)—to commission an expedition to "kill all of them." Portuguese agents also attempted a raid against the tolderías around 1804, but they later "came to an understanding" with the nearby caciques—including Masalana, who had been attacked by Spanish blandengues three years prior—and four to six hundred of their kin. Some individuals from these tolderías moved to San Borja, San Juan Bautista, and other missions; some continued to trade with mission inhabitants; some harried Spanish patrols; and others permitted or aided Portuguese settlers' cattle roundups and drives.[79] This subsequent collaboration did not ameliorate the broader shift in borderline dynamics, as tolderías now found themselves with enemies on both sides of the border. Peace would ultimately be short lived.

While Silva Gama and Viana debated the legality of a Spanish raid against tolderías in Portuguese lands, field agents took matters into their own hands. In 1806, Spanish blandengue Jorge Pacheco procured support from Portuguese captain Antonio Adolfo and a contingent of gauchos for a joint raid on tolderías on the Portuguese side of the border, offering fourteen thousand heads of cattle to Adolfo and six pesos to each gaucho. Since at least the previous year, Pacheco and others had been making appeals for a collaborative campaign; and in April 1806, Pacheco reported that he had raided three tolderías, killing forty-three inhabitants and capturing sixty-seven more, whom he remitted to Buenos Aires.[80] He continued his raids for another year and claimed to have closed in on seven of nine remaining tolderías, though it appears that he never engaged them. His expedition soon ended, as British invasions of Buenos Aires in 1806 and Montevideo in 1807 diverted the attention of Spanish officials and armed forces toward the coast.[81] Though incomplete, Pacheco's raids constituted an unprecedented rupture of the borderline arrangement that tolderías had come to manage efficiently. Whereas late eighteenth-century borderlines had produced predictable territorial practices on the part of imperial officials, Pacheco's breach restructured power dynamics and undermined standing pacts.

By 1806, attempts to map the status quo borderline also fell by the wayside. Following the 1801 conflict, officials on both sides sought to formalize the new interimperial division via renewed boundary commissions. The Portuguese, desiring legal recognition of conquered lands, suggested that the viability of the entire border depended on the formal adjustment of this portion of the line. Francisco João Roscio, the former demarcation officer who had become governor of Rio Grande, complained that his Spanish counterparts wanted to "alter the entire system and order of the legislation of limits," and expressed frustration that the former head of the Spanish demarcation teams had returned to Spain, leaving the results of the previous mapping expeditions unclear. After agreeing on a status quo border in 1804, however, the Spanish viceroy in Buenos Aires replied that he too wanted to formalize the provisional line to avoid future conflicts.[82] But in the end, the proposed bilateral mapping expeditions never came to fruition, as the ranking officers of the San Ildefonso boundary commissions were unavailable—two had died (Sebastião Xavier da Veiga Cabral da Câmara, 1801, and João Francisco Roscio, 1805), three had returned to Iberia (José Varela y Ulloa, 1791; Félix de Azara, 1801; and Diego de Alvear, 1805), and others had been assigned to different projects. It would not be until 1852, as part of an agreement between the Brazilian Empire and Uruguay, that mapping teams would join one another on the border.

If the shifting borderlines and joint raids in Portuguese dominions in 1806 upended tolderías' use of the border, the following quarter century undermined borderline territorialities altogether. Amid crises of imperial sovereignty—the Napoleonic Wars resulted in Portugal's royal court moving to Brazil in 1807 and the abdication of the Spanish throne in 1808—two movements for republican independence emerged in the Río de la Plata. The United Provinces of the Río de la Plata, based in Buenos Aires, sought to form a new government out of the former Viceroyalty of the Río de la Plata, while the Federal League, known also as the League of Free Peoples and based in the countryside, sought regional autonomy.[83] Between 1811 and 1820, these two movements alternatively collaborated with and fought against each other, while Spanish armies struggled to maintain a foothold in Montevideo, and Portuguese imperial forces pushed southward to expand their territorial claims. Meanwhile, provincial and municipal governments in Santa Fe, Corrientes, and numerous towns east of the Río Uruguay, seeking to preserve their own autonomy, reacted equivocally to these four armies.[84] These wars for independence produced borderlines governed not by law but by force, and despite peace agreements in 1812, 1819, 1821, and 1828, the precise location of the border remained ambiguous.[85]

Given the persistent militarization of the Río de la Plata's countryside during these years, most records regarding tolderías relate to their role in armed campaigns. Most notably, hundreds of Charrúas and Minuanes joined the Federal League to resist Portuguese invasions in 1811 and 1816, to blockade Montevideo and Mandisoví in 1813, and to defeat United Provinces forces between the Río Negro and the Río Yí in 1814. They were also present when the Federal League met definitive defeat in 1820.[86] Rather than clients of or unwavering loyalists to the league or its leader, José Gervasio Artigas, Charrúa and Minuán tolderías generally acted of their own accord. They maintained their own encampments and often refused to follow the league's army when it traveled outside their lands, as occurred in 1811, 1814, and 1820. These tolderías acted against the league's interests at times, whether in avoiding battles or raiding ranches, and as occurred during the 1813 blockade of Montevideo, the league's army sometimes sought to repress tolderías' actions. Some Charrúas and Minuanes built relationships with bands of gauchos, and some even sought pacts with Portuguese forces or guarded the countryside for the Portuguese, ostensibly forsaking ties held with the league.[87]

Relations with the Federal League or Portuguese officials occasionally proved beneficial, as several caciques and tolderías who had previously accepted reducciones or abandoned certain lands reappeared to stake claims over contested grounds. Masalana, whose tolдería had been continuously harried by blandengues, appeared alongside Artigas in 1812, as did Caciquillo, whose tolderías had previously settled on missions.[88] Moreover, for the first time in approximately fifty years, Minuán tolderías returned to Montevideo to participate in the city's siege. Upon visiting the rebel encampment outside Montevideo, the priest Dámaso Antonio Larrañaga observed, "I had the opportunity to speak with the Minuán caciques. . . . One of them ate with his wife at the General's [Artigas] table." Meanwhile, Charrúas joined Guaraní fighters to take control of Belén, the settlement founded originally as part of blandengue extermination campaigns, and then lands west of the Río Uruguay, making it as far as the city of Corrientes.[89]

But the breakdown of the border during the wars of independence ultimately made the countryside uninhabitable for tolderías. No longer able to cross the border for refuge, tolderías instead relied on pacts with unreliable allies, who envisioned an outcome devoid of mobile peoples. Portuguese officers made plans to "destroy them [Charrúas] without offering quarter" because "it is necessary that they cease to exist on the eastern side [of the Río Uruguay] or even on the western side, if possible," breaking with long-standing policies and echoing refrains often spoken by Spanish officials during the late eighteenth century.[90] The Portuguese also employed similar discourses of Indigenous aggression, as the advancing Portuguese army sought to protect new ranchers who entered tolderías' lands, particularly those between the Río Ibicuí and the Río Negro. Furthermore, the Portuguese employed different standards when dealing with tolderías than with the Federal League. In June 1812, at the same time as he agreed to an armistice with the Federal League, Portuguese colonel Joaquín de Oliveira Alvares claimed he "was obliged to shoot down and dispel" Charrúas who supported the league's army. This was despite having parleyed only a few days earlier with Masalana, Caciquillo, and the Charrúa cacique Gaspar, the last who had made a pact with the Portuguese governor in 1806. Citing a fear of treachery, the Portuguese subsequently raided these caciques' tolderías and burned their fields, killing as many as eighty people and taking sixty-six captives, whom they distributed among participants in the raid. Left with few options, Gaspar again attempted peace with the Portuguese, while Caciquillo joined gauchos on the other side of the Río Negro.[91]

Republican writers and fighters also pursued futures devoid of tolderías. Representatives of the United Provinces sought to use tolderías as evidence of the Federal League's savagery, wielding claims that Artigas had recruited Charrúas and Minuanes by granting them permission to plunder rural residences or that Charrúas who supported Artigas had "bound, beaten to a pulp, and fed to the dogs" three people in the countryside. When the Federal League held a congressional assembly in the town of Mercedes in 1815, elites in Buenos Aires and Montevideo derided this event by suggesting that Artigas hoped to form a "Minuán Republic."[92] Tolderías' role in the Federal League was also unclear. Artigas's landmark *Reglamento Provisorio*, a regulatory document to govern the countryside, sought to promote sedentism via the repartition of lands and to provide security by remitting vagrants to armed service. Though this document privileged subaltern peasants—free blacks, people of mixed race, Indigenous Americans, and poor creoles (in that order)—its ideals of sedentism and order mirrored those discussed since the boundary commissions.[93] This distinction between sedentary and mobile actors occasionally permeated the formation of the Federal League's armies, as troop registries reveal that Charrúas and Minuanes were clustered with regiments of Guaycurú fighters from the Chaco or with bands of gauchos, both mobile groups.[94] It was likely with this vision in mind that the priest José Bonifacio Redruello sought to garner royalist support for the Federal League's fight against the United Provinces. He argued that Artigas could "conserve [Minuanes and Charrúas] in order . . . and with the example of these infidels, [we] will be able to reduce [*reducir*] others." Bonifacio Redruello added that without Artigas's support, "it will be many years of work to reduce them to order." Whatever differences existed between imperial and republican armies, they agreed that postwar territories should be devoid of mobile peoples.[95]

Indeed, the end of the wars of independence brought little relief for tolderías, as armistices between rival factions neither allocated lands to them nor resolved border disputes. Spain was the first to retreat from the Río de la Plata's countryside, followed by the United Provinces in 1819 and the Federal League in 1820. Portugal thus incorporated the region—which it termed the "Cisplatine Province"—into Brazil, leaving tolderías bereft of a border. Accordingly, the Minuán caciques Rondeau and Caciquillo sought peace with Portuguese authorities and reportedly signed an agreement to accept vassalage.[96] Those tolderías who maintained autonomy had complex relations with administrators, as they both apprehended and returned deserters for payments and impeded the establishment of ranching estates. By the time a new wave of republican resistance expelled Portuguese authorities in 1828, the number of tolderías in the countryside had dwindled dramatically. The government of the newly formed republic of Uruguay adopted the same vision of territorial order as its predecessors and renewed raids against tolderías from 1831 through 1834.[97] Captives were sent to Montevideo, and for those who remained in the countryside, autonomy was no longer an option.

Conclusion

In the months following the 1831 captive distribution in Montevideo, many of the Charrúas in the custody of elite families soon found themselves imprisoned or overcome by grief. Some were deemed "useless" by the families that had claimed them and returned to the police or cast to the city's streets.[98] Others attempted escape, sometimes making it to nearby towns, only to be returned to their assigned families or the city's jail. One young Charrúa named Felipa was discovered with "burn marks on her face and scars on her body . . . saying that she preferred death to returning to her master who had treated her with great cruelty." Nonetheless, Montevideo's police chief deployed a soldier with an order for Felipa's return.[99] During these same months, many Charrúa mothers who had been separated from their children "cried for hours on end, clamored for their children, and sometimes pulled out their own hair," as reported in a letter to *El Universal*, one of Montevideo's newspapers.[100]

These events occurred far away from the border yet were nonetheless shaped by it. Captives were wrenched from their homelands in the name of territorial order, while the families to whom they were assigned were part of an effort to transform autonomous Native peoples into subservient citizens.

Although a paucity of source materials has impeded discussions of Charrúa and Minuán self-identification, remaining records reveal these individuals' presence in lands beyond those associated with their tolderías. In fact, baptismal records as late as the 1860s include individuals deemed Charrúa.[101] By tracing the movement of individuals from tolderías to settlements, this chapter has shown that far more people from Charrúa and Minuán tolderías lived in and around the region's settlements than civil and criminal records indicate. This contradiction suggests that Minuanes' and Charrúas' purported disappearance was more about imperial and republican imaginings than Indigenous absence. Particularly important to this imperial discourse were the notions that tolderías were incompatible with territorial order and that ethnicity derived from one's connection to a tolderías, ideas that were reinforced by the Madrid and San Ildefonso boundary commissions. As for those tolderías that remained in the countryside in the early nineteenth century, the replacement of a legal line with fluctuating borders determined by rival armies proved devastating. Whatever enmity existed between imperial and republican adversaries, they all agreed that tolderías had no place as autonomous actors in the region. Much like the demarcation officials and military personnel who preceded them, republican agents planned for Minuanes' and Charrúas' disappearance even as tolderías continued to exist in the countryside and former tolderías residents stretched across the region.[102]

Conclusion

In the early months of 1849, the Brazilian Empire sent a topographic team to survey its southernmost border in preparation for an anticipated joint boundary demarcation with Uruguay. The surveyors set out to define the borderline from the Atlantic coast to Bagé, a town near the ruins of Santa Tecla. They carried "two maps of [Rio Grande], accompanied by a note containing the positions of important points in the province, as determined by the [San Ildefonso] Commission of Limits," to guide their work.[1] As they moved inward from the coast, they came upon the remaining walls of the former São Miguel fort, where they paused to survey the local landscape. The expedition's ranking officer, Cândido Batista de Oliveira, climbed a nearby hill to gain a better vantage point, where he noted "an abundance of certain plants that generally appear in lands fertilized by animal remains, as is generally observed in cemeteries." He asked a local resident about this anomaly, and the man replied that this mound and others nearby were "cemeteries of the savage Indians who used to wander around this part of the countryside" and that "any digging done there uncovered human bones."[2] Oliveira calculated that there were hundreds of human remains beneath his feet and concluded that it must have been a mass grave dug after a battle with the fort.

Oliveira's diary resembled those of Spanish and Portuguese officials in the 1750s and 1780s. It interspersed historical anecdotes and topographical measurements with an itinerant account of place names and descriptive observations. Oliveira dedicated a large portion of his text to narrating the history of this international border, beginning with the 1750 Treaty of Madrid. He recounted the numerous attempts to "definitively demarcate Brazil's frontier," seamlessly assembling earlier demarcations in a century-long history that culminated in his efforts. This diary nonetheless differed from prior accounts, since it expunged tolderías from its narration entirely. Despite standing atop a mound of Indigenous remains along the borderline, Oliveira deemed tolderías' actions irrelevant to his teleological narrative of the realization of contemporary territorial order, a pattern that would characterize diplomatic debates and historical retellings thereafter.[3] Death and disappearance were all that were visible in his account.

Postindependence narratives of the Río de la Plata's colonial past mirrored Oliveira's in divorcing diplomatic disputes from tolderías' territorialities. For most of the nineteenth century, writers from and travelers to the region disregarded tolderías in histories of Ibero-American territorial advancement. Diplomats referenced or transcribed the works of imperial boundary commissions to fortify contemporary claims of national borders, while travelers deployed information from imperial ethnographies in narrating tolderías' evacuation of national spaces.[4] It was not until international territorial disputes were largely resolved in the late nineteenth century that tolderías began to receive significant literary attention, as writers began to use national boundaries as spatial frames for examining Indigenous pasts. Anthropologists revived the taxonomical efforts of San Ildefonso demarcation officials yet replaced imperial geographical containers with national or subnational ones and recast tolderías as cultural forebears rather than existential enemies.[5] Writers from the Brazilian state of Rio Grande do Sul posited Guenoas and Minuanes as prehistorical occupants of state lands, agglutinating all tolderías in the region into a "Guenoa macro-ethnicity," while Uruguayan scholars espoused a "Charrúa macroethnicity" as part of their national patrimony.[6] Historians too imagined tolderías via the retrospective gaze of postcolonial territorial units. They endeavored to "[enumerate] the Indigenous nations that inhabited Rio Grande," identify the "origin of the Indians that populated Uruguay," or narrate the "displacement of hunter Indians, who populated lands that would come to be Uruguayan." As Native peoples ("our Indians") moved on and off territories addressed in public archival collections ("our lands"), they moved in and out of nationally inspired histories.[7]

This shift toward appropriating Indigenous pasts while marginalizing contemporary Native peoples was ubiquitous with emergent nationalist and regionalist discourses throughout the Americas. Elite writers reproduced pre-Columbian symbols to espouse patrimonial heritage, "salvage ethnographers" recorded or collected elements of Native cultures they deemed destined to disappear, and artists mythologized Indigenous peoples that they considered to have been doomed to defeat; collectively, they biologized indigeneity, divorced it from modernity, and overlooked the persistence of Native societies.[8] In most of the Americas, this mindset prompted governmental efforts at territorial dispossession of, provincializing of, or genocidal campaigns against contemporary Indigenous communities, but the primary outcome in the Río de la Plata was to render invisible the descendants of Charrúas, Minuanes, and other autonomous peoples. Much like northeastern North America, where colonial-era dispossession and violence engendered postcolonial imaginings of Indigenous absence, national and local writers in southeastern

South America appropriated romanticized imaginations of vanquished Native societies in the past as descriptors of ostensibly Euro-American societies in the present.[9]

The nation- or state-bounded geographical imaginings that undergirded these studies engendered parallel and often contradictory accounts of Indigenous pasts in the Río de la Plata. Between 1850 and 2009, at least forty-seven published works made explicit claims regarding the historical locations or movements of Charrúas, Minuanes, Bohanes, Guenoas, or Yaros. They either situated one of the aforementioned groups in a fixed location throughout the colonial period or narrated ostensible ethnic migrations from the sixteenth through the eighteenth centuries. While these assertions conceivably made logical sense within isolated national or subnational conversations, mapping them together reveals impossible geographies. The bounded spaces that anthropologists used to define ethnic communities appear in disparate locales throughout the region rather than in the restricted sites posited by one author or another (map 11). Historical narratives of ethnic migration produced similar discrepancies; nearly every account purported that Charrúas or Minuanes had evacuated present-day national or state territories, yet these assertions were in diametric opposition to similar claims made from neighboring countries (maps 12 and 13).

The incongruent ethnogeographical assumptions shown in these composite maps more readily reflect imperial visions than Indigenous actions. Following the logics advanced by the Madrid and San Ildefonso boundary commissions, postcolonial scholars reified borders and ethnic categories, conflated colonial settlements with their claimed jurisdictions, and placed sedentary and mobile peoples in diametric opposition to each other. Moreover, they imagined colonial jurisdictions as protonational spaces. Reading from nearby public archives and from published sources, they stitched together ethnic histories that mischaracterized migration. If a purported ethnic community disappeared from the local records, it was assumed that it had been vanquished or had emigrated from a settlement's entire jurisdiction and the postcolonial jurisdiction that emerged from it. Minuanes' disappearance from Montevideo's records or Charrúas' disappearance from Santa Fe's was interpreted as evidence of Indigenous absence from the countryside rather than a lack of imperial access to it or the emergence of other forms of identification for the same Native communities. But the geographical movement of recorded ethnonyms over time did not always indicate the movement of humans; it often reflected changing patterns of ethnic classification among colonial writers derived from shifting colonial geographic imaginations. Reconsidering interethnic relations

MAP 11 Purported ethnic geographies. This map represents the collective ethnic geographies of authors who cataloged tolderías according to a fixed locale. Native peoples are plotted according to their ascribed ethnonym and the approximate area where authors situated them throughout the colonial period. Label weights correspond with the number of authors who made a particular claim: 12-point type for one author, increasing incrementally by 2 points per additional author, and reaching a maximum of 36 points for thirteen authors. Argentine historian Manuel Cervera argued that Bohanes also lived near the Tebicuarí River in Paraguay, beyond this map's frame to the north. Sources: Cervera, *Historia de la ciudad*, 193–95, 230, 237, 241–42, 481, 491–94, 499–500; Doblas, "Memoria histórica," 55; Azara, *Viajes por la América del Sur*, 181; d'Orbigny, *El Hombre Americano*, 276–77; Isabelle, *Voyage a Buénos-Ayres*, 98; José H. Figueira, "Los primitivos habitantes," 138; Martínez, *Cartografía histórica de República Argentina*, maps 3 and 5; Ambruzzi, *Mapa Histórico*; Biedma, *Atlas histórico de la República*, maps 5 and 9; Torres, *Los primitivos habitantes del delta*, 423, 429, 466; Araújo, *Etnología salvaje*, 35–39; Schuller, *Sobre el oríjen*, 39-41; Teschauer, *História do Rio Grande*, 65–66; Ferreira Rodrigues, *Almanak litterario*, 226-28; Vergara y Martín, *Diccionario etnográfico americano*, 36, 70, 100, 212–13; Penino and Sollazzo, "El paradero charrúa del Puerto," 153–54; Luedeke, "Os primitivos habitantes," 62;

in the Río de la Plata has therefore required a reassessment of the spatial assumptions that undergird regional archives and historiography.

Imperial Borders, Indigenous Brokers

Building on recent scholarship on borderlands and cartography in the Río de la Plata and elsewhere, this book has examined the relationship between borderline territorialities, interethnic relations, and historical memory. It suggested that prior to the invention of an interimperial border in the Río de la Plata, stationary colonial settlements and mobile Indigenous encampments developed local ties that often superseded imperial or ethnic allegiances. Colonial settlements were limited to isolated nodes around the region's perimeter, while tolderías arbitrated travel through the region's interior and access to its resources. These regional territorialities interacted dialectically with global juridical debates among Iberian and other European empires over territorial possession. Portuguese- and Spanish-American administrators sought pacts with tolderías to prevent the establishment of foreign settlements and solicited tolderías' vassalage as a means to claim possession of lands that tolderías effectively controlled. Given the ephemerality and contingency of these agreements, by the eighteenth century Iberian and Ibero-American officials began to place their faith in the latest mapping technologies as a means to circumvent tolderías in claims over lands beyond imperial control. This change in legal thought culminated in the 1750 Treaty of Madrid, which commissioned massive mapping expeditions to devise a border to partition the two empires' South American dominions.

The Treaty of Madrid and the Treaty of San Ildefonso relied on teams of trained mapmakers to transform an abstract borderline devised by royal courts into a usable legal geography for local administrators. These mapping expeditions constituted the meeting point of extant and idealized territorial

Lothrop, "Indians of the Paraná Delta," 111–13; Oliveira de Freitas, *A invasão de São Borja*, 22–25; Pérez Colman, *Historia de Entre Ríos*, 43; Perea y Alonso, *Apuntes para la Prehistoria Indígena*, 8; Canals Frau, *Las poblaciones indígenas*, 238–41; Serrano, *Los Pueblos y Culturas Indígenas*, 59–60, 88; Sosa, *La nación charrúa*, 49–60; Aparacio and Difrieri, *La Argentina suma de geografía*, 29, 44; Cordero, *Los charrúas*, 181–83; Imbelloni, "Lenguas indígenas del territorio argentino," 60; López Monfiglio, *El totemismo entre los charrúas*, 1, 5–7, 10; Cesar, *História do Rio Grande do Sul*, 20–25; Vidart, "Prólogo," 22–25; Antón, *El pueblo Jaguar*, 54; Basile Becker, *Os índios charrua e minuano*, 43–45; Fonseca, *Tropeiros de mula*, 32; Klein, "El destino," 1, 6; Maeder and Gutiérrez, *Atlas territorial y urbano*, map 1.

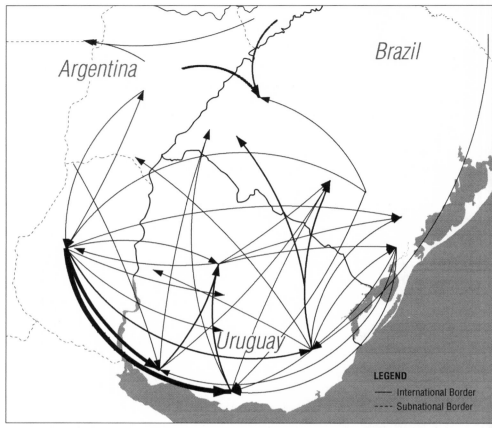

MAP 12 Purported migrations (Minuanes). This map represents the collective ethnic geographies of authors who articulated Minuán migrations. Arrows represent the before and after of purported migrations, which authors described as unidirectional from the sixteenth through the eighteenth centuries. Arrows are weighted at 1 point per author, and range from 1 to 7. Sources: Azara, *Viajes por la América del Sur*, 182–83; Dreys, *Notícia descriptiva*, 182–83; d'Orbigny, *El Hombre Americano*, 276–77; José H. Figueira, "Los primitivos habitantes," 138; Ambruzzi, *Mapa Histórico*; Cervera, *Historia de la ciudad*, 195, 230, 237, 241–42, 481, 491–94, 500; Biedma, *Atlas histórico de la República*, maps 5 and 9; Araújo, *Etnología salvaje*, 35–39; Teschauer, *História do Rio Grande*, 66–69; Ferreira Rodrigues, *Almanak litterario*, 226-28; Vergara y Martín, *Diccionario etnográfico americano*, 136–37; Saldanha, "Diário resumido," 236–37; Lothrop, "Indians of the Paraná Delta," 102–9; Caldas, "Etnologia Sul-Riograndense," 308, 319, 321; Canals Frau, *Las poblaciones indígenas*, 238–41; Sosa, *La nación charrúa*, 49–60; Cordero, *Los charrúas*, 181–83; José Joaquín Figueira, *Breviario*, 12; Ponce de León, "Minuanes o Guenoas," 24; Pi Hugarte, *Los indios de Uruguay*, 65–67; Vidart, "Prólogo," 22–25; Vidart, *El mundo de los Charrúas*, 17–21; Antón, *El pueblo Jaguar*, 157–60.

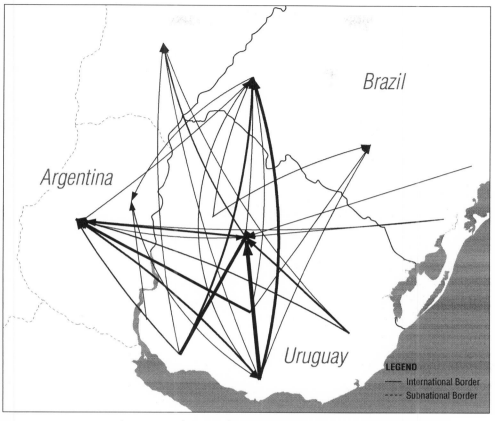

MAP 13 Purported migrations (Charrúas). This map represents the collective ethnic geographies of authors who articulated Charrúa migrations. The same methodology and symbology have been applied as in map 12, with arrow weight ranging from 1 to 6. Sources: Azara, *Viajes por la América del Sur*, 173–74, 181–83; Isabelle, *Voyage a Buénos-Ayres*, 98; Dreys, *Notícia descriptiva*, 182–83; d'Orbigny, *El Hombre Americano*, 276–77; José H. Figueira, "Los primitivos habitantes," 138; Schuller, *Sobre el oríjen*, 39–41; Cervera, *Historia de la ciudad*, 193–95, 230, 237, 241–42, 481, 491–94, 499–500; Teschauer, *História do Rio Grande*, 58–61; Ferreira Rodrigues, *Almanak litterario*, 226-28; Vergara y Martín, *Diccionario etnográfico americano*, 70, 100; Lothrop, "Indians of the Paraná Delta," 102, 110–17; Pérez Colman, *Historia de Entre Ríos*, 60–61; Caldas, "Etnologia Sul-Riograndense," 308, 319, 321; Canals Frau, *Las poblaciones indígenas*, 238–41; Cordero, *Los charrúas*, 181–83; José Joaquín Figueira, *Breviario*, 11–18; Pi Hugarte, *Los indios de Uruguay*, 65–67; Vidart, *El mundo de los Charrúas*, 17–21; Timó, "Las Relaciones Interétnicas y Etnicidad," 48; Klein, "El destino," 1, 6.

orders, thereby inciting responses from Indigenous communities through whose lands the border ran. The mapmakers' diaries and correspondence demonstrate continued Indigenous control amid imperial claims, while their maps and ethnographic taxonomies reveal an effort to naturalize tolderías, to distinguish them from imperial agents, and to promote a future in which they were absent. The boundary commissions thus marked a shift in Ibero-American interethnic policy in borderland spaces. In the Río de la Plata, as most tolderías fell on the Spanish side of the border, Spanish administrators began to treat them as obstacles to territorial order, while Portuguese officials built ties with them to access lands allocated to Spain. Tolderías near the borderline leveraged imperial desire to operationalize or subvert the line as a means to advance their own interests. Some incorporated migrants, extracted payments in exchange for policing the border (or undermining the policing of it), and built commercial networks across it. But if the development of a borderline territoriality provided opportunities to certain tolderías, its dissolution in the early nineteenth century undermined their autonomy. As the countryside became uninhabitable and tolderías no longer sustainable, many individuals sought opportunities elsewhere, and the ethnic identities once ascribed to them in colonial records were no longer meaningful to colonial and republican writers.

This focus on territoriality—the dialectic between the ways people imagined and acted in space—reveals a new role for collaborative, interimperial mapmaking in the Americas during the eighteenth century. Unlike fifteenth- and sixteenth-century imperial claims of territorial possession in contested borderlands, which were vaguely defined in engraved maps and restricted to narrow coastlines and corridors abroad, eighteenth-century border making aimed at on-the-ground precision and totalizing claims over terrestrial interiors. Maps produced by boundary commissions were both cultural texts and territorial templates that empowered local officials to exert legal claims and to advance new notions of on-the-ground order. Shifts in mapmaking dovetailed with discursive transformations in imperial law, ethnographic accounts, and historical renderings. They also corresponded with changing patterns of interaction between imperial, ecclesiastical, and Indigenous authorities, and those in between. As imperial officials, many of whom participated in the boundary commissions, prioritized the materialization of the borderline, they promoted new settlement patterns, policed trade in new places, and pursued new relations with tolderías. These borderline territorialities persisted thereafter and even intensified in the nineteenth century as colonial regimes splintered into republican governments. Postcolonial archives, in naturalizing the spatial visions of colonial authors, occluded the histories of autonomous Native peoples living beyond colonial spaces of control.

Imperial officials and subjects living in the Americas were central to this transformation, but so too were autonomous Indigenous societies. The actions of administrators, settlers, and traders elicited responses from tolderías, whose myriad replies were not easily classified along lines of resistance or accommodation yet ultimately reinforced the borderline as a meaningful territorial order. It was not until after the boundary demarcations that tolderías tended to concentrate themselves in lands adjacent to the imaginary line, when for many it became a regional center. Despite devastating effects for tolderías farthest from the interimperial boundary, Ibero-American border making did not imply overall Native decline. For many tolderías near the border, the late eighteenth century was a moment of expanding power, not another step in a long march toward defeat and disappearance. As border making augmented imperial needs and, in turn, dependency on Native communities, the development of borderline territorialities simultaneously advanced Iberian order and increased Indigenous authority in certain spaces. The limits of imperial power and the persistent autonomy of many Native communities did not undermine the materialization of the border but instead made it operative and meaningful. Recognizing this allows for broader understandings of Indigenous agency and the contingency of border-making efforts.

To identify the interplay between divergent territorial imaginings and changing interethnic relations, this book adopted a regional approach. Consequently, it identified certain contextual factors that may not have extended to other places and times. The Río de la Plata's mapped borderlines were backed by treaties, without which they would not have had sufficient legal weight for property claims, land titling, and borderline policing. The Amazon and the Pantanal appear to have been analogous cases, yet lines drawn in areas where only one European empire was present, such as Patagonia, the Chaco, or northern New Spain, might not have offered the same opportunities to Native agents. Moreover, since Indigenous polities throughout the Americas enforced their own borders and limited outsiders' access to their homelands, more work is required to understand the relationship between these borders and those devised by European mapmakers. This book's regional scale and rural focus intentionally provincialized traditional areas of study in the Río de la Plata, such as coastal cities and the Guaraní mission complex, sometimes at the expense of detailed analysis of singular sites of interaction. More work is thus necessary to evaluate regional processes from the vantage point of local settlements and tolderías and to trace the trajectories of migrants from tolderías in urban societies. A closer analysis of ecological conditions and change would likewise add material weight to discussions of regional territorialities, migration, and tolderías' eventual dispossession. Lastly, while the present study has attempted to read past the ethnogeographic visions espoused in colonial records and national histories, a reassessment of the significance of ethnonyms to both tolderías and imperial writers would deepen the discussion. Tethering together Indigenous and imperial territorialities and emphasizing spatial context over ethnic or colonial affiliations enables new readings of historical archives and new interpretative frameworks for studies to come.

THE TEMPORAL ARC of this book ended in the early nineteenth century, yet the changing territorialities discussed here continue to reverberate in the region. After the final raids against tolderías and subsequent captive distributions in Montevideo in the 1830s, several Charrúas faced a unique fate. A French schoolmaster in Montevideo received permission from the Uruguayan government to transport four captives—Vaimaca Pirú, Senaqué, Tacuabé, and Guyunusa—to Paris, where he presented them to members of the Academy of Sciences and then to the public via an ethnological exhibition. Pirú and Senaqué died soon after, and their bodies were taken to the Museum of Natural History (*Muséum national d'histoire naturelle*), also in Paris, and examined by phrenologists and other natural scientists. Tacuabé, Guyunusa, and Guyunusa's daughter, who was born in captivity, survived the human zoo and were eventually transported to Lyon, where the latter two died soon after.[10] Pirú's body remained in France's Museum of Man (*Musée de l'Homme*) until the Uruguayan government procured its repatriation in 2002. He was buried in Uruguay's National Pantheon (*Panteón Nacional*), the same resting place as the architects of his demise, and scientists took DNA samples from his body against vehement opposition by Charrúa activists, who eventually secured their return.[11]

Pirú's repatriation and the treatment of his remains were a significant moment for Indigenous reemergence in the Río de la Plata. In 1989, the Association of Descendants of the Charrúa Nation (ADENCH) became the first nationally recognized Indigenous social organization in Uruguay—a country where entrenched public and academic discourse denied their existence—and mobilized around the return of Pirú's remains. By 2005, ADENCH had joined numerous Charrúa communities throughout Uruguay to form the Council of the Charrúa Nation (CONACHA), which lobbied successfully for the national government to join the Fund for the Development of the Indigenous Peoples of Latin America and the Caribbean (FILAC), to declare April 11 the "Day of the Charrúa Nation and of Indigenous Identity," and to include ethnic self-identification as a census category.[12] Increased political visibility, community organization, the sharing of family histories, and the symbolic weight of DNA studies showing Indigenous ancestry have led approximately five percent of Uruguay's population to self-identify as Indigenous or of Indigenous descent, a sharp turn from previous years.[13] In Argentina's 2010 census, over 3,500 people in the province of Entre Ríos self-identified as Charrúa, and nearly 100 people in neighboring Corrientes did as well.[14] Meanwhile, in 2007 in Rio Grande do Sul, Brazil, a Charrúa community gained official recognition by Brazil's Fundação Nacional do Índio (FUNAI), which had previously denied their existence, and they formed a village outside Porto Alegre.[15]

Despite the increased visibility of contemporary Charrúas in Uruguay, northeastern Argentina, and southern Brazil, the entrenched ethnogeographical imaginings developed during the eighteenth century have impeded Indigenous efforts at reclaiming lands. Most notably, Uruguay remains one of the few countries in Latin America that has still not signed the International Labor Organization's Convention 169, the strongest recourse in international law for Native peoples when dealing with national governments. As a result, burial grounds similar to the one described by Oliveira remain national historical monuments, with the national government as the principal arbiter of access to these lands, thereby impeding present-day Charrúas' efforts to reconstitute their ecological and cosmological visions.[16] While these conditions are in part due to the rejection of current processes of ethnogenesis by scholarly, political, and public detractors, the collective focus on national or state arenas to discuss indigeneity has allowed for the persistence of colonial territorial frames. Critics have reiterated nation-centric narratives of Native disappearance and drawn on reified ethnic geographies to minimize the identities claimed by present-day communities.[17] In response, present-day Charrúas have mostly drawn on national or state contexts to assert ethnic identity, make public claims, and reconstruct historical lineages.[18]

Considering the persistent weight of territorial imaginings that emerged in the eighteenth century reveals deeper connections between colonialism, land, and indigeneity. Native claims and control over regional lands were more extensive than previously suggested, were acknowledged by colonial agents, and coexisted with overlapping imperial and ecclesiastical jurisdictions. The discursive erasure of autonomous Indigenous peoples from the region coincided with the drawing of an interimperial border, yet numerous tolderías were able to leverage border making to their own benefit. The story of colonialism in the Río de la Plata was therefore not simply a story of Native decline, and Indigenous agents were integral to the formation of regional societies. Likewise, the break marked between colonial and national periods was less significant than commonly assumed. The violence against tolderías that inaugurated republican independence was part of a deeper story of shifting territorialities, and a focus on its eighteenth-century emergence reveals a much larger scale than was previously accounted for. Because national claims to sovereignty were built on the inheritance of late-colonial spatial frames, they cannot be disentangled from the efforts at Native dispossession and disappearance that defined that moment. Lastly, as shifting forms of Indigenous identification corresponded with changing territorialities, the reemergence of Charrúa communities today is evidence of continued patterns of identity formation rather than an aberration. Looking at and across borders at their moment of creation allows for more precise renderings of the past and denaturalized discussions in the present, thereby opening space for the construction of new territorialities in the future.

Notes

Introduction

1. ANB 86, Secretário de Estado, cod. 104, v. 9, fs. 22–23, 87–88; Saldanha, "Diário resumido," 231, 235, 239, 241, 261, 281.

2. Eighteenth-century mapmakers did not record the precise length of the borders, but their semblance to Brazil's present-day international boundaries allows for a rough estimate. This border was five times longer than the present division between Mexico and the United States and nearly double the border between the United States (including Alaska) and Canada.

3. I differentiate the concepts of "possession" (claims over land) and "sovereignty" (claims over subjects) in order to demonstrate the interplay between them. Prior to the invention of an interimperial border, a sovereign's claim to territorial possession generally derived from ownership of lands belonging to imperial subjects; afterward, claims to sovereignty over imperial subjects more often derived from the subject's occupation of lands possessed by a given crown.

4. Sahlins, *Boundaries*, 5–7, 93–102; Stagg, *Borderlines in Borderlands*, 5; Prescott and Triggs, *International Frontiers*, 120, 318–22; Dunbabin, "Red Lines on Maps"; Rosen, *Border Law*, 12–20; Pedley, "Map Wars"; Postnikov, "Cartography and Boundary-Making."

5. The first collaborative boundary demarcation of this type occurred from 1699 to 1703 between the Hapsburg and Ottoman empires. Abou-el-Haj, "Formal Closure," 467; Veres, "Redefining Imperial Borders." Another early example is the Belgorod line near the Black Sea steppes. But despite Russia's construction of a line of fortifications in 1635 and prohibition of movement across the border in 1670, no mapping expedition occurred. Boeck, "Containment vs. Colonization." For a comprehensive summary of nineteenth-century border agreements in the Americas, see Prescott and Triggs, *International Frontiers*, 233–64.

6. Recent works have demonstrated the patchwork, nodal nature of imperial settlement patterns in the Americas, describing them as "a scattering of cities, isolated and practically out of communication with one another" (Rama, *The Lettered City*, 10); "islands of relative security" (Harris, *Resettlement of British Columbia*, 34, cited in Saler and Podruchny, "Glass Curtains," 296–97); "small slivers along the coast" (Ethridge, "Introduction," 40); "corridors" and "enclaves" (Benton, *Search for Sovereignty*, 2, 10–23); "outposts and footholds" Deloria, "From Nation to Neighborhood," 349, cited in Barr, "Geographies of Power" 9); "nodal" (Hämäläinen, "What's in a Concept?," 86–87); "territorial nodes" (Enrique, "Paisajes coloniales"); "archipelagos of colonization" (Russell-Wood, "Políticas de fixação e integração," 136); "a land-locked archipelago" (Jones, "International Relations in the Americas," 121); "islands of occupation" (Herzog, *Frontiers of Possession*, 1, 42); "islands (an archipelago) in a sea of grass or green forests" (Karasch, *Before Brasília*, 303); and "little more than a collection of pales" (Lennox, *Homelands and Empires*, 3).

7. For more on legal debates regarding land, labor, and Native peoples' positions within Iberian epistemologies, see Benton, *Search for Sovereignty*, 1–39; Herzog, *Frontiers of Possession*, 25–133; Van Deusen, *Global Indios*, 192–218; Davies, *Renaissance Ethnography*, 65–108.

8. Costa, "Viajes en la frontera," 121; Azara, "Correspondencia oficial e inédita," 6; Lucena Giraldo, *Laboratorio tropical*, 165–66, 274–75; Silva Pontes, "Diário histórico e físico," 362–63; Domingues, *Quando os índios eram vassalos*, 231–32.

9. Costa, "Viajes en la frontera," 121–23; Alvear, "Diario," 3:447–51; Silva Pontes, "Diário histórico e físico," 354–55; Quarleri, *Rebelión y guerra*. While the Guaraní and their allies halted the southern expeditions in greater Paraguay, Native peoples in the Orinoco delayed the northern expeditions for two years. Altic, "Missionary Cartography," 77, 80. Rather than analyzing interethnic engagement, most scholarship on the demarcations has focused on interimperial diplomacy, cartographic production, or the careers of commissioned mapmakers. Domingues, *Viagens de exploração geográfica*; Lucena Giraldo, *Laboratorio tropical*; Souza Torres, "Dominios y fronteras"; Raminelli, *Viagens ultramarinas*; Penhos, "En las fronteras del arte"; Bertocchi Moran, "El piloto Andrés de Oyarvide"; Gentinetta, "Sourrière de Souillac, un matemático ilustrado"; Bastos, "Às vésperas das demarcações"; Siquiera Bueno and Kantor, "A outra face das expedições"; Garcia, *Fronteira iluminada*. Recent research has nonetheless begun to examine Indigenous collaboration with or subversion of the expeditions. Zárate Botía, "Pueblos indígenas"; Langavant, "La frontera del Alto Paraguay."

10. Barr, "Geographies of Power"; McDonnell, *Masters of Empire*, 13–17; Witgen, *Infinity of Nations*, 3, 6; Saler and Podruchny, "Glass Curtains," 292; Lennox, *Homelands and Empires*, 3–6, 9–12, 42; Roller, *Amazonian Routes*, 21–22.

11. The use of "territoriality" follows David Delaney, who defines it as "an aspect of how humans as embodied beings organize themselves with respect to the social and material world." Territories are historically produced "human social creations" that "reflect and incorporate features of the social order that creates them." Delaney, *Territory*, 10–12. Whereas territoriality generally refers to power relations embedded in bordered enclosures, I use it to encompass other sociospatial dialectics as well, including place making, networking, and scaling. Lefebvre, *The Production of Space*; Soja, "The Socio-Spatial Dialectic"; Harvey, *Condition of Postmodernity*, 201–326; Brenner, "Critical Sociospatial Theory"; Gupta and Ferguson, "Beyond 'Culture.'"

12. ANB, 86, Secretário de Estado, cod. 104, v. 11, fs. 109v–12, 205–6, 215, 277–77v; Santos, "Uma vida dedicada ao Real Serviço," 517; Neumann, "Fronteira e identidade," 89–90.

13. Recent scholarship has shown that Native geographical visions often included dynamic borders or temporary rights to exclusive access to land. Contreras Painemal, "Los tratados mapuche"; Barr, "Geographies of Power"; Lennox, *Homelands and Empires*, 9–12, 21–22, 42; Edelson, *New Map of Empire*, 141–95.

14. Mignolo, *Darker Side of the Renaissance*, 219–313; Brotton, *Trading Territories*, 46–86; Burnett, *Masters of All They Surveyed*; Arias and Meléndez, *Mapping Colonial Spanish America*; Buisseret, "Spanish Colonial Cartography, 1450–1700"; Meléndez, "Cultural Production of Space"; Bleichmar et al., *Science in the Spanish and Portuguese Empires*; Magalhães, "Mundos em miniatura"; Portuondo, *Secret Science*; Vargas and Lois, *Historias de la Cartografía*; Kantor, "Cartografia e diplomacia"; Scott, *Contested Territory*; Dym and Offen, *Mapping Latin America*; El Jaber, *Un país malsano*, 282–324; Furtado, *O mapa que inventou o Brasil*.

15. Brody, *Maps and Dreams*; Gartner, "Mapmaking in the Central Andes"; Leibsohn, "Colony and Cartography"; Mundy, *Mapping of New Spain*; Lewis, *Cartographic Encounters*; Whitehead, "Indigenous Cartography"; Kagan, *Urban Images*, 45–70; Waselkov, "Indian Maps"; Carrasco and Sessions, *Cave, City, and Eagle's Nest*; Muñoz Arbelaez, "'Medir y amojonar'"; Offen, "Creating Mosquitia"; Safier, *Measuring the New World*; Heidi V. Scott, *Contested Territory*; Barcelos, "A cartografia indígena"; Brückner, *Early American Cartographies*, pt. 2; Castañeda de la Paz, "Nahua Cartography"; Steinke, "'Here Is My Country'"; Enrique and Pensa, "Mapas sobre el Cono Sur"; Hidalgo, *Trail of Footprints*.

16. Critical histories of cartography initially focused on contexts of identifiable state power during the nineteenth and twentieth centuries or within expanding capitalist world systems. Foucault, "Questions of Geography"; Anderson, *Imagined Communities*, 163–85; Harley, "Deconstructing the Map"; Radcliffe and Westwood, *Remaking the Nation*; Winichakul, "Siam Mapped"; Edney, *Mapping an Empire*, 77–118; James C. Scott, *Seeing Like a State*, 11–52; Woodward, "'Theory' and the History of Cartography"; Craib, *Cartographic Mexico*; Pickles, *History of Spaces*; Carrera, *Traveling from New Spain*; Mezzadra and Neilson, *Border as Method*, 27–59.

17. While the term "borderlands" has acquired myriad meanings, I use it narrowly to refer to contested, permeable, and changing sites of multidirectional exchange between Indigenous and colonial agents. For a deeper discussion of this term, see Hämäläinen and Truett, "On Borderlands," 338–45

18. Bukowczyk, *Permeable Border*, 2–4; Langfur, *Forbidden Lands*, 47; Hele, "Introduction," xiii, xvi; Barr and Countryman, "Introduction," 4; Lennox, *Homelands and Empires*, 3–4, 18, 45. Most contemporary studies have tacitly accepted a temporal distinction between "borderlands" (imperial) and "bordered lands" (national) and considered borderlines a nineteenth-century phenomenon. This temporal division was most explicitly articulated in Adelman and Aron, "From Borderlands to Borders." Critiques of this temporality have emphasized the persistence of permeable borderlands in national contexts rather than the earlier emergence of borderlines in colonial contexts. See, for example, LaDow, *Medicine Line*, 161, 216-17; Taylor, *Divided Ground*, 8–9; Reid, *The Sea Is My Country*, 13–14; Readman, Radding, and Bryant, "Borderlands in a Global Perspective," 3.

19. While subregional context has shaped where specific works fall on such a spectrum, Richard White's "middle ground" (1991) and Kathleen DuVal's "Native ground" (2006) frameworks represent paradigmatic anchor points. Examples of the former include White, *Middle Ground*; Binnema, *Common and Contested Ground*; Taylor, *Divided Ground*. Examples of the latter include DuVal, *Native Ground*; Hämäläinen, *Comanche Empire*; Witgen, *Infinity of Nations*; McDonnell, *Masters of Empire*; Berthelette, "'Frères et Enfants'." Recent work has sought to develop new frameworks to address enslaved peoples alienated from both European and Native worlds. Rushforth, *Bonds of Alliance*, 11-12; Miles, *Dawn of Detroit*, 255-57.

20. Scholarship on and from Latin America, in distinguishing *fronteras/fronteiras* (borderlands) from *límites* (borderlines), has described diverse borderlands as "zones rather than lines" (Weber, *Spanish Frontier in North America*, 9); "zones of historical interaction" (Guy and Sheridan, "On Frontiers," 10); "interaction zones" (Prado, *Edge of Empire*, 9–11, 109–26); "spaces of interaction" (Lucaioli and Nacuzzi, *Fronteras*); "zones of contact, conflict, and interaction" (Langfur, *Forbidden Lands*, 5); "contact zones" (Pratt, *Imperial Eyes*, 6–7;

Gándara, "Representaciones de un territorio," 63); "gray zones" (Pinto Rodríguez, *La formación del estado*, 16–17); "porous space" (Langavant, "La frontera del Alto Paraguay," 357); "porous frontiers" (Ortelli, "Vivir en los márgenes"); "economic zones" (Santamaría, "Fronteras indígenas," 199); and "ecological and cultural transition zones" (Readman, Radding, and Bryant, "Borderlands in a Global Perspective," 14). By focusing on Indigenous territorialities and ecological spaces, scholars have provided alternatives to imperial spatial frameworks and elucidated how knowledge about Native lands (*tierra adentro/campanha/sertão*) was produced in colonial enclaves. Nacuzzi, "La cuestión del nomadismo"; Radding, *Wandering Peoples*, 21–46; Hackel, *Children of Coyote, Missionaries of Saint Francis*, 65–123; Enrique, "La movilidad como estrategia"; Pérez Zavala and Tamagnini, "Dinámica territorial y poblacional," 198–205; Farberman and Ratto, "Actores, políticas e instituciones"; Herrera Ángel, *Ordenar para controlar*, 325–98; Lucaioli, "Los contextos de producción"; Erbig and Latini, "Across Archival Limits." Likewise, a long-standing emphasis on mestizaje, hybridity, interethnic exchange, and mediation has undergirded scholarship throughout the region. Rausch, *Tropical Plains Frontier*, 150; Claudia García, "Hibridación, interacción social y adaptación"; Ganson, *Guaraní under Spanish Rule*; Radding, *Landscapes of Power and Identity*, 117–61; Metcalf, *Go-Betweens*; Maria Regina Celestino de Almeida, "Índios e mestiços no Rio de Janeiro"; Acuña and Gutiérrez, "Territorios, gentes y culturas libres," 17–34; Yaremko, "'Frontier Indians,'" 226, 232; Sommer, "Amazonian Native Nobility." The distinction between fronteras and límites has often led to the conceptual separation of "internal" and "external" borders, the former referring to frontiers between Iberian settlers and neighboring Native peoples and the latter referring to spatial divisions between competing imperial projects. This conceptual gesture, likely deriving from the enormity of Spanish and Portuguese geographical claims vis-à-vis British, French, or Dutch colonial projects in the Americas, divorces interimperial borders from interethnic relations and, by extension, subordinates Indigenous peoples within imperial or republican national frames. Examples and historiographical summaries of this conceptual division include Barcelos, "Os Jesuítas e a ocupação," 102–4; Schröter, "La frontera," 373–74; Roulet, "Fronteras de papel," 11–13; Quarleri, *Rebelión y guerra*, 70–71; Langfur, "Frontier/Fronteira," 844, 848; Herzog, *Frontiers of Possession*, 2–4.

21. Turner Bushnell, "Indigenous America"; Chang, *Pacific Connections*; Weaver, *Red Atlantic*; Prado, *Edge of Empire*; Reid, *Sea Is My Country*; Lipman, *Saltwater Frontier*; Truchuelo and Reitano, *Las fronteras en el Mundo Atlántico*.

22. Similar critiques to resistance versus accommodation paradigms have provided new avenues for exploring Native power, agency, and ethnogenesis that decenter colonial order and chronologies. Boccara, "Colonización, resistencia y etnogénesis," 47, 71; Deeds, *Defiance and Deference*, 6–7, 202; Sommer, "Colony of the Sertão," 405; DuVal, *Native Ground*, 4–5; Hämäläinen, *Comanche Empire*, 6–9; Heidi V. Scott, *Contested Territory*, 49–74; Sidbury and Cañizares-Esguerra, "Mapping Ethnogenesis," 197–98; Monteiro, "Rethinking Amerindian Resistance and Persistence"; Salomón Tarquini and Casali, "Los pueblos indígenas," 37–38. Yet opportunities for Native agents were always context based, colonial spaces were always violent, and not all could adapt amid colonial power imbalances. Sweet, "Quiet Violence of Ethnogenesis"; Hämäläinen, "Lost in Transitions"; Griffin, "Plea"; Craib, "Cartography and Decolonization," 32.

23. This notion of borderlines as propositions that gained meaning via repeated responses to them derives from Wood, *Rethinking the Power of Maps*, 39–66; Kaiser and Nikiforova, "Performativity of Scale," 538–45.

24. Border making operated in contexts of "multiterritoriality," albeit ones in which imperial and Indigenous authority intersected in "zones of plural sovereignty." Haesbaert, "Del mito de la desterritorialización," 34–39; DeLay, "Introduction," 3.

25. Regional narratives of Native disappearance resemble those recounted elsewhere in North and South America, whereby postcolonial writers drew on Native pasts to articulate modern national or regional identities while denying the persistence of contemporary Indigenous Americans. Lepore, *Name of War*, 200; O'Brien, *Firsting and Lasting*; Earle, *Return of the Native*; Witgen, *Infinity of Nations*, 7–11.

26. *Río de la Plata* as used here refers to lands north and east of the eponymous estuary, an area that corresponds with present-day Uruguay, northeastern Argentina, and the far south of Brazil. Whereas Río de la Plata has long functioned as a catchall name for a much larger region—including the Argentine Pampas, Paraguay, or the entire Spanish viceroyalty of the Río de la Plata—this narrower use is meant to eschew common territorial frames for southeastern South America that privilege Spanish (*Banda Norte, Otra Banda*), Portuguese (*Capitania de El Rey, Rio Grande de São Pedro*), Jesuit-Guaraní (*estancias de los Siete Pueblos, Provincia jesuítica del Paraguay*), or nationalist (*Banda Oriental, Mesopotamia Argentina*) perspectives over tolderías' territorialities. For more on geographical frames and historical referents in the region, see Verdesio, *La invención del Uruguay*; Frega, "Uruguayos y orientales"; Prado, *Edge of Empire*, 107–30.

27. Articles that did not specify the borderline's location instead regulated commerce and other activities along the border.

28. Erbig and Latini, "Across Archival Limits."

29. While eighteenth-century tolderías' names for the region remain elusive, many Charrúa communities in Argentina and Uruguay now refer to their homelands as *Onkaiujmar*. Onkaiujmar is a combination of terms derived from remnants of the Charrúa and Guenoa languages, along with the related Chaná language. It could be translated as "the Great Father-Mother," and includes not only land but also rivers and the sky or heavens. "On" means father in Guenoa, "kai" comes from the "ukay," which is a feminine synonym, "uj" is a Chaná connector, and "mar" means much, many, or large in Charrúa. Whereas Onkaiujmar encompasses land, rivers, and the sky or heavens, the term *Beadá*, which means "grandmother," is used by Charrúas nowadays to refer to the land. Comunidad Charrúa Basquadé Inchalá, in discussion with the author, July 28, 2019; Delgado Cultelli, email message to author, October 20, 2019.

30. Poenitz, *Los infieles minuanes y charrúas*; Maeder, "El conflicto"; Wilde, "Guaraníes, 'gauchos' e 'indios infieles'"; Levinton, "Las estancias"; Azpiroz Perera and Dávila Cuevas, "Indios 'Infieles' y 'Potreadores'"; Wucherer, "Disputas a orillas del río Uruguay." Studies on Portuguese settlements include Prado, *A Colônia do Sacramento*, 84, 117, 125; Hameister, "'No princípio era o caos,'" 115. Studies on Spanish settlements include Castro, *Los Indios Mansos*; Fucé, "Ceremonia persuasiva." Studies of interethnic relations between Santa Fe and Charrúas are unique in their longevity. Cervera, *Historia de la ciudad*, 422–23; Sallaberry, *Los charrúas y Santa Fe*; Zapata Gollan, *Los chaná*; Livi, "El Charrúa en Santa Fe"; Areces et al., "Santa Fe la Vieja"; Lucaioli and Latini, "Fronteras permeables."

31. Cabrera Pérez, "Los 'indios infieles' de la Banda Oriental"; Verdesio, *Forgotten Conquests*, 93–109; Gil, "O contrabando na fronteira"; Wilde, "Orden y ambigüedad"; Bracco, *Charrúas, guenoas y guaraníes*; Sirtori, "Nos limites"; Frühauf Garcia, *As diversas formas*; Andrés Aguirre, "La Banda Oriental y Rio Grande."

32. Ethnohistorical scholarship on Jesuit-Guaraní missions in the region, in emphasizing the role of Guaraní agents vis-à-vis Portuguese and Spanish rivals, have centered mission space as a historical stage where tolderías entered as outsiders. Neumann, "Fronteira e identidade," 81–83; Barcelos, "Os Jesuítas e a ocupação," 102–4; Wilde, "Los guaraníes después de la expulsión," 74, 97–102; Quarleri, *Rebelión y guerra*, 70–71, 87, 90, 97–98, 100, 104, 106–7; Levinton, "Guaraníes y Charrúas"; Sarreal, "Globalization and the Guaraní," 79, 323–24; Ferreira Acruche, "De 'rebeldes, traidores, infieles, desleales y desobedientes.'"

33. Some recent works have indicated this dynamic by centering tolderías in regional framings. Latini, "Repensando," 69–71, 74, 85, 90, 93; Verdesio, "Forgotten Territorialities," 91–103.

34. This includes manuscripts from Argentina, Brazil, Paraguay, Uruguay, Portugal, Spain, and the United States. For more on archival records and tolderías in the region, see Erbig and Latini, "Across Archival Limits."

35. Recent efforts to interpret Indigenous action as a means to look beyond the spatial limits of imperial sources include Witgen, *Infinity of Nations*, 15; Miles, *Dawn of Detroit*, 12–16.

Chapter One

1. Cortesão, *Tratado de Madri*, 314; Cortesão, *Antecedentes do Tratado de Madri*, 164–71.

2. AGI, Charcas, 214 (Buenos Aires, 1731-04-31); AGNU, Ex Museo y Archivo Histórico Nacional, caja 1, n. 19, fs. 1–9; AHU, Nova Colónia do Sacramento (012), caixa 2, doc. 226; Azarola Gil, *Los Orígenes de Montevideo*, 125–28.

3. Cortesão, *Antecedentes do Tratado de Madri*, 165–70. In one letter from Ximénez, he claims that the Guenoas referred to Yapelman as their "Quirembà," which based upon similar Indigenous terms in lowland South America, may have signified that he was a military leader. BNE, MSS 12.977/34, fs. 26v–28; Combès and Villar, "Os mestiços mais puros," 54n3. Here and elsewhere, the names of caciques derive from historical sources and thus reflect how the caciques were referred to by Guaraní, Portuguese, and Spanish writers and interpreters, and not necessarily by residents of the tolderías.

4. Cortesão, *Antecedentes do Tratado de Madri*, 162, 166–68, 247–48. During these years, the missions sought to establish cattle reserves near Yapeyú and San Miguel, which required that they pass through toldería-controlled lands. Sarreal, *Guaraní and Their Missions*, 65–92.

5. Cortesão, *Antecedentes do Tratado de Madri*, 164–65.

6. Cortesão, *Antecedentes do Tratado de Madri*, 165–66, 168–70; Cortesão, *Tratado de Madri*, 314.

7. The archipelagic spatial organization of Indigenous and imperial polities was not unique to the Río de la Plata. Scholars have used archipelagos as a spatial metaphor to discuss Indigenous sociopolitical organization from the Andes to mainland North America. Murra, "An Aymara Kingdom in 1567," 123; Edelson, *New Map of Empire*, 147.

For examples of the term applied to imperial settlement patterns, see note 6 of the Introduction.

8. This early-modern structure of governance was seen throughout the Iberian empires. Nader, *Liberty in Absolutist Spain*; Herzog, *Upholding Justice*; Cañeque, *King's Living Image*; Cardim et al., *Polycentric Monarchies*.

9. Beginning in 1617, the Spanish grouped their settlements in the region into the governorship of the Río de la Plata, administered from Buenos Aires, and the governorship of Paraguay, administered from Asunción. Both pertained to the viceroyalty of Peru. The Portuguese founded Colônia in 1680, and it pertained to the captaincy of Rio de Janeiro, while Rio Grande, founded in 1737, pertained first to the captaincy of São Paulo and later to the captaincy of São Vicente. During the second half of the eighteenth century, this administrative arrangement would change dramatically.

10. In 1731, the San Nicolás mission counted 7,690 inhabitants, while the Loreto mission counted 7,048. Jackson, "La población y tasas vitales"; Sarreal, *Guaraní and Their Missions*, 2–3, 48–49, 239; Johnson, Socolow, and Seibert, "Población y espacio," 331; Foschiatti del Dell'Orto and Bolsi, "La Población," 76; Pollero Beheregaray, "Historia demográfica de Montevideo," 157–59; Prado, *Edge of Empire*, 18. Santa Fe's population likely totaled between two thousand and five thousand inhabitants during the eighteenth century, but estimates are based on travel accounts and general reports rather than systematic censuses. Suárez and Tornay, "Poblaciones, vecinos y fronteras rioplatenses," 535–36, 555; Calvo, *Vivienda y ciudad colonial*, 67–69. Likewise, travelers calculated Rio Grande's population to be fourteen hundred inhabitants in 1744. Queiroz, "A Vila do Rio Grande," 96.

11. Bluteau, *Vocabulário Português e Latino*, 665–66; *Diccionario de autoridades*, vol. 5; Prado, *A Colônia do Sacramento*, 86. *Plaza* and *praça*, much like the English term *place*, derive from the Latin *platĕa* (courtyard, broad street), which comes from the Greek *plateîa* (broad street) and the Proto-Indo-European (PIE) root *plat-* (to spread), thus carrying connotations of a site, a pathway, and expansion. Online Etymology Dictionary, s.v. "plaza," accessed December 13, 2018, https://www.etymonline.com/classic/search?q=plaza. There are even examples of *plaza* being used to denote Indigenous towns in sixteenth-century Central America. Bolaños, "Place to Live," 276–77, 291n4.

12. By as early as 1735, mission inhabitants held the perpetual right to arms and performed regular military exercises in their main square. Avellaneda and Quarleri, "Las milicias guaraníes," 109–32, esp. 117; Di Stefano and Zanatta, *Historia de la iglesia argentina*, 117–18; Sarreal, *Guaraní and Their Missions*, 33–34, 41, 65–92.

13. AGNA, IX, 4-3-1 (Santo Domingo Soriano, 1746-02-13; Vívoras, 1746-09-16; Campo de Bloqueo, 1752-10-19, 1757-08-06); AGNA, IX, 24-3-2 (Campo del Bloqueo, 1758-04-26). While wild cattle were the region's most lucrative resource, there was also a significant amount of small-scale farming, particularly around Montevideo and Colônia. Gelman, *Campesinos y estancieros*.

14. González, *Diario de viaje a las vaquerías*, 20, 23–25; Coni, *Historia de las vaquerías*, 66–75; Porto, *História das Missões Orientais*, 3:315–19; Barrios Pintos, *De las vaquerías al alambrado*, 107; Asúa, *Science in the Vanished Arcadia*, 202.

15. In an effort to claim herds of livestock, ranchers frequently branded them. These claims over property, while recognizable by tolderías, most likely did not constitute legitimate possession from their vantage point.

16. Sallaberry, *Los charrúas y Santa Fe*, 222–32; Livi, "El Charrúa en Santa Fe," 35–36; Lucaioli and Latini, "Fronteras permeables"; Cortesão, *Jesuítas e Bandeirantes no Tape*, 175–77; Levinton, "Guaraníes y Charrúas"; Wilde, "Guaraníes, 'gauchos' e 'indios infieles,'" 104; Oyarvide, *Memoria geográfica*, 10:43.

17. These purported ethnic divisions were likely products of Spanish travelers who positioned themselves between tolderías. Travelers moving up and down the Río Paraná potentially used the river to distinguish the numerous tolderías that frequented it, naming those on the western side (Banda Occidental) of the river Abipones and Mocovíes and those on the eastern side (Banda Oriental) Charrúas.

18. A detailed analysis of the Battle of the Yí can be found in Bracco, *Charrúas, guenoas y guaraníes*, 197–262.

19. RAH, Mata Linares, t. 101, fs. 239–40; Cortesão, *Tratado de Madri*, 143. Guenoas also aided the Spanish *maestre del campo* Francisco García de Piedrabuena's 1715 expedition against Charrúa tolderías in Entre Ríos. In this instance, Piedrabuena paid Guenoas in yerba maté, tobacco, and cloth in exchange for their aid. Latini, "Relatos del conflicto interétnico," 3–5. Recent scholarship has shown that this pattern of strategic alliances occurred throughout the Americas, belying earlier historiographical binaries of colonizer and colonized. Metcalf, *Go-Betweens*; DuVal, *Native Ground*; Matthew and Oudijk, *Indian Conquistadors*; Gose, *Invaders as Ancestors*, 7–14.

20. Funes, *Ensayo*, 1:329–30; Cortesão, *Tratado de Madri*, 224; Latini and Lucaioli, "Las tramas."

21. González, *Diario de viaje a las vaquerías*, 11–18, 25. Although the Battle of the Yí occurred in February 1702, armed engagements between Guaraní militias and confederated tolderías began the previous year, leading to González's calculation of four years.

22. AGI, Charcas, 384, "Petición del Procurador de la Compañía de Jesús, padre Juan José Rico" (n/d), visto en consejo (1743-10-17); Pereira, "'Y hoy están en paz,'" 22.

23. MM, Archivo Colonial, Arm. B, C17, P9, no. 36 (San Borja, 1708-12-20); AGI, Charcas, 263 (Madrid, 1716-05-12); "Memoria para las generaciones venideras," 547–49; Funes, *Ensayo*, 1:329–30; Sota, *Historia del Territorio Oriental*, 1:160–61.

24. Cortesão, *Tratado de Madri*, 321–22; Vianna, *Jesuítas e Bandeirantes no Uruguai*, 234, 241; Porto, *História das Missões Orientais*, 4:44–47. One of the principal Minuán caciques involved in these events was Yaguareté, who received gifts from Spanish officials in 1714 and who was among the caciques that received Miguel Ximénez in 1731. AGI, Charcas, 264, fs. 11–13; "Memoria para las generaciones venideras," 549.

25. Lozano, *Historia de las revoluciones*, 273. Attacks occurred along roadways and the Paraná and Uruguay rivers. AGPSF, Actas de Cabildo de Santa Fe de 1708-02-24 and 1709-06-26; RAH, Mata Linares, t. 102, fs. 55–56v; AGI, Charcas, 382, "Informe del fiscal" (Madrid, 1716-10-17); Funes, *Ensayo*, 1:334.

26. AGI, Buenos Aires, 235, "Responses to question #116 of inquiry," fs. 12, 31v, 50v–51, 70v, 89v, 108, 130–30v, 150v, 172, 191, 214v, 239v, 259v, 276v, 296, 320–20v, 345v, 371v–72, 385v, 405v–6, 429v. Although these testimonies, taken as part of an investigation into the Comunero Rebellion in Paraguay, were likely influenced by deponents' explicit enmity against the Jesuits, they nonetheless point to the fragility of settlements and tolderías' rationales behind intercepting riverine travelers.

27. Sepp von Rechegg, *Viagem às Missões Jesuíticas*, 50–51, 107–8; *Cartas anuas*, 20:370.

28. Fortes, "Velhos caminhos," 210–15; Fortes, *Rio Grande de São Pedro*, 35; Acosta y Lara, *La guerra de los charrúas*, 1:34. The rise in the demand for cattle and the establishment of the Sorocaba market were linked to the growth of diamond and gold mining in Minas Gerais. The Caminho da Costa was the only terrestrial route between Colônia and Rio Grande and was a forty-day journey. IEB, AL-068-004; BA, 51-v-37, f. 134.

29. Brito Peixoto, "Relação," 299–300; AHU, São Paulo-Mendes Gouveia (023-01), caixa 3, docs. 293, 371 and 374; AHU, Brasil Geral (003), caixa 5, doc. 464; "Coleção de documentos," 4–6; "Carta do Brigadeiro Jose da Silva Paes"; "Memoria dos serviços prestados," 245–46; "Carta de Cristovão Pereira"; Fortes, "Velhos caminhos," 219; Vellinho, *Capitania d'El-Rei*, 142–43, 148.

30. ANB, D9, Vice-Reinado, caixa 746, pac. 2 (Lisboa, 1715-10-17); AHU, Rio de Janeiro (017), caixa 10, doc. 1122; Fernandes Pinheiro, *Anais da Província de São Pedro*, 196–200; Fortes, *Rio Grande de São Pedro*, 15–18; Brito Peixoto, "Correspondencia do Capitão-Mór da Laguna," 290; Frühauf Garcia, "Quando os índios escolhem," 617.

31. Bulkeley and Cummins, *Voyage to the South Seas*, 173–76.

32. IHGB, Conselho Ultramarino, Arq. 1.1.26, fs. 68–68v.

33. IHGB, Conselho Ultramarino, Arq. 1.1.26, f. 71.

34. AGI, Charcas, 263 (Buenos Aires, 1718-07-04). These communities presumably included women, despite their lack of mention in the records. For similar cases, see AGI, Charcas, 264 (Buenos Aires, 1723-03-14); Cattáneo, "Relación del viaje," 184–85.

35. BNP, F.R. 909, f. 64.

36. IHGB, Conselho Ultramarino, Arq. 1.1.26, f. 68v; Archivo do Estado de São Paulo, *Documentos relativos ao "bandeirismo" paulista*, 121–22.

37. In addition to proposing future trade, the Spaniards also requested license to sell the eight hundred livestock they had with them. Fortes, *Rio Grande de São Pedro*, 16–17; Brito Peixoto, "Relação," 299. For more on trans-imperial trade in the Río de la Plata during the first half of the eighteenth century, see Prado, *Edge of Empire*, 15–23.

38. AHU, São Paulo-Mendes Gouveia (023-01), caixa 3, doc. 293; Brito Peixoto, "Correspondencia do Capitão-Mór da Laguna," 282–90; Fortes, *Rio Grande de São Pedro*, 13–18; Fonseca Galvão, *Notas geográficas e históricas*, 29. These tolderías were associated with the Minuán caciques Agostinho, Manoel, Nicolão, and Casildo, who exercised control over lands from Rio Grande to at least the south of the Lagoa Mirim. This relationship appears to have continued over time, as the Portuguese officers in Rio Grande reaffirmed their pact in 1737 and the caciques brought kin for baptism in 1749. Acosta y Lara, *La guerra de los charrúas*, 1:33, 52–53; IEB, AL-072-042; Hameister, "'No princípio era o caos,'" 114; Kühn, *Breve história do Rio Grande*, 20–21.

39. Archaeologists have identified over 250 sites, most of which are concentrated along the Paraná and Uruguay rivers and in the highlands in the north and east of the region. Mounds served a wide range of purposes, including flood protection, agriculture, animal domestication, care and burial of ancestors' remains, and geographical marking. Their precise locations may have also been influenced by seasonal movement and long-distance networks of communication. Bonomo and Barboza, "Arqueología del Litoral," 217; Bonomo, Politis, and Castro, "Los indígenas de Entre Ríos"; Gianotti, "Procedimientos," 272–73, 280–81.

40. The Spanish city of Santa Fe in the west frequently purchased captives from Charrúa traders, while Portuguese-led raiders (*bandeirantes*) from São Paulo sought captives in the

north. Areces, López, and Regis, "Relaciones interétnicas en Santa Fe"; Lucaioli and Latini, "Fronteras permeables"; Acosta y Lara, *La guerra de los charrúas*, 1:25–26; Monteiro, *Negros da terra*; Sarreal, *Guaraní and Their Missions*, 27–34. For more on southeastern North America's shatter zone and petite nations, see Ethridge and Shuck-Hall, *Mapping the Mississippian Shatter Zone*; Ellis, "Petite Nation with Powerful Networks."

41. The term *toldería* was commonly used in lowland South America, including the Chaco, the Pampas, and Patagonia. It was one of the principal identifiers used to denote autonomous Native peoples in the Río de la Plata, alongside other labels such as Indians of the land (*índios da terra*), infidels (*infieles*), barbarians (*bárbaros*), and pagans (*gentio*), most of which were pejorative. Much like *parcialidades*, a term commonly used in present-day scholarship from the region, *tolderías* referred to communities organized around kin-based authority. A toldería was also a physical site, much like the *rancherías* of northern New Spain, Chiquitanía, and elsewhere, but whereas rancherías were "semipermanent settlements," tolderías tended to be seasonally itinerant. Radding, *Landscapes of Power and Identity*, 41–43; Barr, "Geographies of Power," 34–35.

42. IHGB, Conselho Ultramarino, Arq. 1.1.25, f. 60v; AGI, Chile, 153 (Montevideo, 1724-08-29); AGI, Buenos Aires, 304 (Buenos Aires, 1749-09-05); AGI, Charcas, 264 (Buenos Aires, 1721-08-31); Cortesão, *Antecedentes do Tratado de Madri*, 64; Lucaioli and Latini, "Fronteras permeables," 123.

43. The existence of cemeteries within tolderías indicates that Native peoples in the region had certain locales that they returned to periodically. When mentioned in recorded accounts, these cemeteries tended to be located in highland areas, which also served as spiritual centers. For example, a 1752 map by Jesuit Bernardo Nusdorffer marked the Cerro Aceguá as a site where Guenoas "bring their dead from many leagues away to bury them" and the Cerro Ybití María as a site where their spiritual leaders (*hechiceros*) "pierce their bodies and do thousands of devilries until the demon appears to them in a visible form there on top of the mountain." Fúrlong Cárdiff, *Cartografía jesuítica*, vol. 2, Lámina XXIV. See also Saldanha, "Diário resumido," 233, 236; Lozano, *Historia de la conquista*, 1:411; Cortesão, Antecedentes do Tratado de Madri, 6:166; Pereira, *Minuanos/Guenoas*, 183.

44. Nacuzzi, *Identidades impuestas*.

45. Lozano, *Historia de la conquista*, 1:26; Sepp von Rechegg, *Viagem às Missões Jesuíticas*, 104; AGI, Charcas, 199 (Lima, 1751-02-15), fs. 8–9; Charlevoix, *Historia del Paraguay*, 2:264–65. For a detailed discussion of contradictory and shifting uses of ethnonyms in the region, see Arce Asenjo, "Etnónimos indígenas"; Erbig and Latini, "Across Archival Limits."

46. The colonial tendency to view distinct Native polities as a centralized ethnic empire was not unique to the Río de la Plata, as similar patterns were evident in southeastern North America. Galloway, "'So Many Little Republics,'" 513–15.

47. Wucherer, "Disputas a orillas del río Uruguay," 5. Lidia Nacuzzi has conceptualized Tehuelche movements in a similar way, focusing on fixed stopping points that Tehuelches frequented in Patagonia. Nacuzzi, "La cuestión del nomadismo." In other instances, tolderías' movements responded to human threats or served as a quarantine against smallpox epidemics. For example, Cattáneo, "Relación del viaje," 187; Oyarvide, *Memoria geográfica*, 8:212.

48. AGI, Charcas, 237, (San Lorenzo, 1720-11-08); AGNA, IX, 2-1-4 (Montevideo, 1750-01-27). See also Luís Ferrand de Almeida, "A Colónia do Sacramento," 429; AHU, Rio de Janeiro, Castro e Almeida (017-01), caixa 13, doc. 2568.

49. Cortesão, *Antecedentes do Tratado de Madri*, 164–66.

50. AGNA, IX, 4-3-1 (Vívoras, 1746-09-16, 1746-09-23).

51. AGNU, Ex Museo y Archivo Histórico Nacional, caja 1, no. 19, f. 3; AGI, Charcas, 214 (Buenos Aires, 1731-04-30).

52. Rodolfo Garcia, *Anais da Biblioteca Nacional*, 52:418; Alvear, "Diario," 2:353–54; Levinton, *El espacio jesuítico-guaraní*, 110.

53. Montevideo and Maldonado are two of the principal natural harbors along the Río de la Plata's northern coast. From at least the late seventeenth century, Minuanes traded with European ships at these sites. For a detailed list of these exchanges, see table 1.

54. AGNU, Falcao Espalter, 15:94-95.

55. Schröder, "Batoví," 111. As travelers moved through the region, they found other cemeteries as well, often in highland areas between watersheds. BNB, 09,02,003, f. 2; Saldanha, "Diário resumido," 183.

56. Cortesão, *Antecedentes do Tratado de Madri*, 169.

57. "Memoria para las generaciones venideras," 549; Cortesão, *Antecedentes do Tratado de Madri*, 165; BNE, MSS 12.977-34, f. 26v; AGI, Charcas, 264, fs. 11–13.

58. Other Charrúa leaders had shorter geographical ranges of influence—a cacique named Carabí operated between Yapeyú and lands southwest, while the Yasú family moved between Santa Fe and Corrientes—yet the pattern of principal caciques exercising authority over numerous tolderías appeared consistent throughout. Latini, "Relatos del conflicto interétnico," 4; Sallaberry, *Los charrúas y Santa Fe*, 234.

59. Cortesão, *Antecedentes do Tratado de Madri*, 165–66.

60. Azarola Gil, *Los Orígenes de Montevideo*, 128–29; Fucé, "Ceremonia persuasiva," 166–68.

61. AGI, Charcas, 382 (Madrid, 1716-10-17); AGI, Charcas, 226 (Buenos Aires, 1721-09-10); AGPSF, Acta de Cabildo de Santa Fe de 1732-01-22; AHU, Rio Grande (019), caixa 1, doc. 18; Archivo do Estado de São Paulo, *Documentos relativos ao "bandeirismo" paulista*, 92; Lozano, *Historia de las revoluciones*, 273; Sepp von Rechegg, *Viagem às Missões Jesuíticas*, 50–51; *Acuerdos del Extinguido Cabildo*, 4:313; Cortesão, *Tratado de Madri*, 126–27; Coni, *Historia de las vaquerías*, 72–73; Fernandes Pinheiro, *Anais da Província de São Pedro*, 196–200.

62. Examples of pacts between the Portuguese and the Minuanes near Rio Grande include AHU, Rio de Janeiro, Castro e Almeida (017-01), caixa 39, doc. 9058; AHU, São Paulo (023), caixa 1, doc. 67; AHU, São Paulo-Mendes Gouveia (023-01), caixa 3, docs. 371, 374 and 457; Brito Peixoto, "Correspondencia do Capitão-Mór da Laguna," 290; Fortes, *Rio Grande de São Pedro*, 16–18; "Memoria dos serviços prestados."

63. Funes, *Ensayo*, 1:329–30; AGI, Charcas, 263 (Madrid, 1716-05-12).

64. Toledo's report named the Charrúas' enemies "Indios Yanuas." This was likely a reference to Guenoas, given the phonetic proximity of the two words. It may have meant "plains Indians" (*indios llanuras*), though based on the geographical locations of the people in question, this would also indicate that they were Guenoas. AGI, Charcas, 262, fs. 7v-8, 16.

65. AGI, Charcas, 262, fs. 16–16v.

66. Bracco, *Charrúas, guenoas y guaraníes*, 58, 267.

67. AGI, Charcas, 262, fs. 1v–3v, 7v–8. Guenoas also acquired European trade goods, including textiles, from French ships in Montevideo and harbors farther east. Vianna, *Jesuítas e Bandeirantes no Uruguai*, 237. For details on tolderías' trade with foreign ships, see chapter 2.

68. Cabral, *Descrição Corográfica e Coleção Histórica*, 19; AHU, Nova Colónia do Sacramento (012), caixa 1, doc. 26; AHU, Rio de Janeiro, Castro e Almeida (017-01), caixa 13, doc. 2568; Luís Ferrand de Almeida, "A Colónia do Sacramento," 426; Bauzá, *Historia de la Dominación Española*, 1:414.

69. Sepp von Rechegg, *Viagem às Missões Jesuíticas*, 50–53.

70. Scholars often argued for a bilateral division between the Portuguese/Minuanes and the Spanish/Guaraní, with Charrúas falling on either side. Such divisions have presupposed hierarchies between imperial patrons and Indigenous clients and the uniformity of imperial or ethnic categories. Recent scholarship has challenged this tendency by focusing on the temporality of pacts or Native peoples' ability to negotiate between empires. See Levinton, "Guaraníes y Charrúas"; Frühauf Garcia, "Quando os índios escolhem."

71. Areces, López, and Regis, "Relaciones interétnicas en Santa Fe," 159–67; Lucaioli and Latini, "Fronteras permeables"; AGNA, IX, 41-3-8, exp. 1.

72. RAH, Mata Linares, t. 102, f. 402v; AGPSF, Acta de Cabildo de Santa Fe de 1710-10-11, 1713-12-30, 1715-12-07, 1715-12-08, 1715-12-10; MM, Archivo Colonial, Arm. B, C17, P1, no. 40; Vianna, *Jesuítas e Bandeirantes no Uruguai*, 230–35; Lucaioli and Latini, "Fronteras permeables." Santa Fe also opposed a 1735 expedition against Charrúas. Sallaberry, *Los charrúas y Santa Fe*, 190, 232.

73. AGI, Buenos Aires, 235, fs. 12, 31v, 50v–51, 70–70v, 89-89v, 107v–8, 130–30v, 150–50v, 171v–72, 191, 214v, 239–39v, 259v, 276v, 296, 319–20v, 345v, 371v–72, 385v, 405v–6, 429–29v.

74. AGI, Buenos Aires, 235, f. 89.

75. Sá, *Historia topographica*, 18–19; Acosta y Lara, *La guerra de los charrúas*, 1:29; Cabral, *Descrição Corográfica e Coleção Histórica*, 55–56, 68–70; Pont, *Campos Realengos*, 138; Frühauf Garcia, "Quando os índios escolhem," 617; Prado, *A Colônia do Sacramento*, 117.

76. AGI, Charcas, 263 (Buenos Aires, 1715-12-16). Tapes also broke the blockade on occasion. AGI, Buenos Aires, 533 (Buenos Aires, 1736-03-20).

77. AGI, Charcas, 278 (Madrid, 1683-12-17).

78. AGI, Charcas, 264 (Buenos Aires, 1722-05-31), fs. 11–13; López Mazz and Bracco, *Minuanos*, 101; AGI, Charcas, 237 (San Lorenzo, 1720-11-08); AGI, Charcas, 221 (Buenos Aires, 1721-09-12); AGI, Contaduría, 1937 (Buenos Aires, 1722-01-13); *Acuerdos del Extinguido Cabildo*, 4:313; *Acuerdos del Extinguido Cabildo*, 5:222–23.

79. BNP, F. 1445, f. 56. Other examples of tolderías participating in attacks on Colônia include AHU, Serviço de Partes (030), caixa 4, doc. 611; "Documentos sobre a Colônia do Sacramento," 41–42.

80. AGI, Charcas, 264 (Buenos Aires, 1722-05-31); Frühauf Garcia, "Quando os índios escolhem," 621–27.

81. IHGB, Conselho Ultramarino, Arq. 1.1.23, fs. 79v–80; Cortesão, *Tratado de Madri*, 130; AHU, Rio de Janeiro, Castro e Almeida (017-01), caixa 13, doc. 2568; Luís Ferrand de Almeida, "A Colónia do Sacramento," 426–30.

82. AGNA, IX, 4-3-1 (Campo de Bloqueo, 1748-03-26 and 1748-05-21; Buenos Aires, 1748-04-16); "Registro de atos oficiais," 258; Leite, *História da Companhia de Jesús,* 528–30. In 1749, Charrúas also faced military campaigns coordinated by the governor of Buenos Aires, which may have led Charrúa tolderías to forge peaceful ties with Minuanes rather than to seek refuge in Spanish or missionary plazas. AGNA, IX, 4-3-1 (Santo Domingo Soriano, 1750-01-16); Bracco, "Los errores Charrúa y Guenoa-Minuán," 132–33.

83. The term *reducción* (*redução* in Portuguese) was used broadly in the Río de la Plata to refer to any ecclesiastical settlement, including the large-scale Jesuit-Guaraní missions and the Franciscan village of Santo Domingo Soriano. Given important differences in size and longevity, the present text uses the term exclusively to refer to the small, short-lived settlements that appeared between tolderías and missionaries. For details on reducciones in the region, see chapter 2.

84. AGNA, IX, 41-1-3, exp. 4 (Buenos Aires, 1703-10-08).

85. Quiroga, *Mapa de las Misiones;* Fúrlong Cárdiff, *Cartografía jesuítica,* vol. 2, Lámina XVI.

86. AGNA, VII, Biblioteca Nacional 289, doc. 4390/2, #5.

87. *Acuerdos del Extinguido Cabildo,* 6:286–87, 645-48; Coni, *Historia de las vaquerías,* 77; AGNU, Ex Museo y Archivo Histórico Nacional, caja 1, n. 19, fs. 3–4.

88. *Acuerdos del Extinguido Cabildo,* 6:399. The deal with Charrúa tolderías was brokered by Domingo Monzón, who in return received a land title (*merced*). AGNU, Escribano de Gobierno y Hacienda, 1823, exp. 46, fs. 16v–18v; Barrios Pintos, *De las vaquerías al alambrado,* 20. Buenos Aires had implemented similar strategies in the past, when dealing with tolderías closer to its own city walls. In 1725, amid another British request for leather under the real asiento, Buenos Aires reached out to one hundred Indigenous allies in order to procure safe access to its immediate countryside. *Acuerdos del Extinguido Cabildo,* 5:516.

89. *Acuerdos del Extinguido Cabildo,* 6:433–35, 459–61, 465–70, 645–48; Acosta y Lara, *La guerra de los charrúas,* 1:55–58; Azarola Gil, *Los Orígenes de Montevideo,* 129–33; Fucé, "Ceremonia persuasiva," 166–69. Verbal agreements were made regarding the enactment of justice in future wrongdoings, but there is little evidence to show that such an arrangement was ever enforced.

90. Argentine and Uruguayan national histories often reference this event to demonstrate the military might of mission forces or the cunning diplomacy of Spanish officers. In these retellings, Minuanes have served as aggressors whose defeat was inevitable. Funes, *Ensayo,* 2:53–55; Bauzá, *Historia de la Dominación Española,* 2:16–19; Azarola Gil, *Los Orígenes de Montevideo,* 123-33; Sota, *Historia del Territorio Oriental,* 2:26–28; Acosta y Lara, *La guerra de los charrúas,* 1:51–59; Fucé, "Ceremonia persuasiva"; Wucherer, "Disputas a orillas del río Uruguay," 8–12.

Chapter Two

1. AGNA, IX, 41-3-8, exp. 4, fs. 4–46v, 64–65, 71–83.

2. AGNA, IX, 41-3-8, exp. 4, fs. 18–47.

3. AGNA, IX, 41-3-8, exp. 4, fs. 46–53v.

4. AGNA, IX, 41-3-8, exp. 4, fs. 49–50v.

5. AGNA, IX, 41-3-8, exp. 4, fs. 54–59, 67–83, 86–87.

6. Possession refers to legal rights over land, including the right to trade, extract resources, settle, or proselytize. In pre-eighteenth-century borderlands, where multiple European crowns competed, it did not necessarily imply sovereignty over all inhabitants of a particular territorial unit or ownership of their property. A crown might claim the right to police a given geographical area, but that right did not imply exclusivity of access or signify that foreigners or Native peoples living within such a space were vassals of that crown. Sahlins, *Boundaries*, 61–102.

7. Sixteenth- and seventeenth-century travelers in the Americas used river estuaries as markers for claiming possession of inland territories. Controlling river estuaries did not always imply control or even access to interior lands, however, as Iberians depended on the knowledge and goodwill of local guides in order to possess lands beyond the coast. Benton, *Search for Sovereignty*, 41–59; Metcalf, *Go-Betweens*, 75–88.

8. The Iberian Union was the joining of the Portuguese and Spanish crowns, along with their overseas domains, under the Spanish Hapsburg dynasty.

9. During the Iberian Union, almost forty-five thousand enslaved Africans disembarked in Buenos Aires via Brazilian ports, after which this inter-American trade declined significantly. Borucki, *From Shipmates to Soldiers*, 5–6; Borucki, Eltis, and Wheat, "Atlantic History and the Slave Trade," 440, 444–45. See also Schultz, "Interwoven"; Bandeira, *O expansionismo brasileiro*, 55; Owens, "Spanish-Portuguese Territorial Rivalry," 19; Prado, *A Colônia do Sacramento*, 23–35, 44; Possamai, "De núcleo de povoamento," 23.

10. Edney, "Knowledge and Cartography," 87–90; Owens, "Spanish-Portuguese Territorial Rivalry," 15–17; Cortesão, *História do Brasil nos velhos mapas*, 1:154–55; Benton, *Search for Sovereignty*, 22–23. For the various interpretations of the Tordesillas meridian in South America and the Río de la Plata, see Garcia, *Fronteira iluminada*, 31–38.

11. Benton, *Search for Sovereignty*, 2–23, 30–38; Herzog, *Frontiers of Possession*, 33–133; Standen and Power, *Frontiers in Question*; Branch, "Mapping the Sovereign State," 9–19.

12. Jesuits also competed with the Spanish settlers and Franciscans from Paraguay, who sought to incorporate Guaraní people in villages and as tribute laborers (*encomendados*). Austin, "Guaraní Kinship and the Encomienda." Itatín was located near the present-day border of Paraguay and the Brazilian state of Mato Grosso do Sul, Guayrá within the Brazilian state of Paraná, and Tape within the state of Rio Grande do Sul. Other Jesuit-Guaraní mission clusters subject to bandeirante raids included Iguazú Acaray (Paraguay and Paraná) and the area between the upper Paraná and Uruguay rivers. Maeder and Gutiérrez, *Atlas territorial y urbano*, 20–21.

13. The Battle of Mbororé (1641) served as a turning point in relations between missions and bandeirantes, as the Spanish crown began to arm mission dwellers. Quarleri, *Rebelión y guerra*, 81–91. The de facto division along the Río Uruguay appeared in contemporary maps. See, for example Bowen, *A New and Accurate Map*.

14. ANB, 86, Secretário de Estado, cod. 920, v. 1, "Autos Acordados Entre as Coroas da Espanha e Portugal Sôbre Limites da América (1681)"; BA, 51-v-37, fs. 17v, 44v–50; BA, 54-xiii-16, no. 157, fs. 1–8; Cortesão, *História do Brasil nos velhos mapas*, 1:111–59.

15. The Laguna de los Xarayes corresponds with present-day Pantanal, located in Bolivia, Brazil, and Paraguay. While the notion of a Brazil Island dates to at least Gaspar Viegas's 1519 *Atlas de Lopo Homem*, its juridical weight reached its apex during the middle of

the next century. It was particularly prevalent in Dutch maps, yet also figured regularly in the works of Jesuit mapmakers until the Treaty of Madrid. Cortesão, *História do Brasil nos velhos mapas*, 1:339–63; Buarque de Holanda, *Visão do Paraíso*, 178; Kantor, "Usos diplomáticos da ilha-Brasil," 71; Costa, "De Xarayes ao Pantanal"; Asúa, *Science in the Vanished Arcadia*, 189.

16. Kantor, "Usos diplomáticos da ilha-Brasil," 77–79; Mariluz Urquijo, "La valoración de la bulas"; Caamaño-Dones, "La concesión a Castilla," 13–18; Benton, *Search for Sovereignty*, 234–35; Moretti, *International Law and Nomadic People*, 3–44.

17. *Uti posseditis*, which in Latin means "as you possess," is a concept of international law that suggests that extant settlements take priority over earlier accords when determining territorial possession.

18. The Siete Pueblos included San Borja, San Nicolás, San Luis, San Lorenzo, San Miguel, San Juan Bautista, and Santo Ángel. For more on connections between settlements and legal claims to possession in the region, see "Registro de atos oficiais," 261–72; IHGB, Conselho Ultramarino, Arq. 1.1.26, 40v–41v, 217v–20v; MM, Archivo Colonial, Arm. B, C18, P1, no. 12; Camargo, "Las relaciones luso-hispánicas en torno," 240; Quarleri, *Rebelión y guerra*, 103–4; Barcelos, "Os Jesuítas e a ocupação," 107–9.

19. BA, 54-xiii-16, no. 157; IHGB, Conselho Ultramarino, Arq. 1.2.21, f. 144; IHGB, Conselho Ultramarino, Arq. 1.1.25, f. 281; Sylva, *Relação do sitio*, 1–5; AHU, Nova Colónia do Sacramento (012), caixa 3, doc. 325; IEB, Projeto Brasil Ciência, 14 C 4, L 19 700, "Tratado de limites das conquistas"; BA, 51-v-37, fs. 43v–44v; BA, 54-xiii-16, fs. 1–11v; BA, 51-v-37, fs. 43v–44v. For more on ceremonial acts and historical narratives to claim possession, see Keller, Lissitzyn, and Mann, *Creation of Rights of Sovereignty*, 23–48; Seed, *Ceremonies of Possession*, *69-148*; Benton, *Search for Sovereignty*, 54–55n40; Herzog, *Frontiers of Possession*, 25–33; Verdesio, *Forgotten Conquests*, 75; El Jaber, *Un país malsano*, 17-20.

20. ANB, 86, Secretário de Estado, cod. 728, v. 1, fs. 10–11. Portuguese royal authorities made similar complaints regarding Montevideo, the Guardia de San Juan, and Spanish attempts to populate Maldonado. AHU, Nova Colónia do Sacramento (012), caixa 1, docs. 27 and 78; BA, 49-x-7, fs. 138–39v; BA, 51-v-37, f. 138; BUC, MS 509; IHGB, Conselho Ultramarino, Arq. 1.3.3, fs. 86–93; Sylva, *Relação do sitio*, 1–5.

21. Pagden, "Law, Colonization, Legitimation," 9.

22. From 1529 to 1534, the Spanish crown issued four charters in South America: Nueva Castilla, Nueva Léon, Nueva Toledo, and Nueva Andalucía. Each measured two hundred leagues from north to south and stretched eastward from the Pacific to the Atlantic Ocean or the Tordesillas meridian. Aranda, *Colección de los tratados*, 61; Becú, "Las capitulaciones rioplatenses," 90. The Charter of Massachusetts Bay, issued by the English crown in 1629, stretched from 40° to 48° north latitude. Avalon Project at the Yale Law School, "The Charter of Massachusetts Bay, 1629."

23. Muratori, *Jesuit's Travels*, 5.

24. In 1721, representatives from Buenos Aires, Santa Fe, and various missions agreed to construct boundary stones near the Río Uruguay and near Colônia, which defined each settlement's rights to access cattle. AGI, Charcas, 221, "Reunión de los apoderados" (Buenos Aires, 1721-01-28).

25. A cannon shot at this time would measure approximately three miles. IHGB, Conselho Ultramarino, Arq. 1.1.23, f. 86; IHGB, Conselho Ultramarino, Arq. 1.1.25, fs.43v–47v;

IHGRGS, Arquivo Visconde de São Leopoldo, fs. 10v–12; RAH, Mata Linares, t. 107, f. 29; BA, 54-xiii-16, no. 155, fs. 1–15.

26. "Tratado Provisional de Lisboa"; IEB, AL-046-091, fs. 183v–85; BUC, MS 548, fs. 243–45; IHGRGS, Arquivo Visconde de São Leopoldo, fs. 10v–16; Sylva, *Relação do sitio*, 72–73; Sá, *Historia topographica*, 98–99.

27. Many eighteenth-century writers believed that Jesuit missionaries had discovered gold and silver mines in the area, which the missionaries supposedly hid from foreigners. The prospect of discovering mines heightened exchange between Minuán and Guenoa tolderías and foreign ships. AHU, Nova Colónia do Sacramento (012), caixa 1, doc. 20; BA, 51-v-37, fs. 25v, 137; IHGB, Conselho Ultramarino, Arq. 1.1.25, f. 280; IHGB, Conselho Ultramarino, Arq. 1.2.21, fs. 180v–81, 182, 185v. Knowledge of mines occasionally appeared in discussions between tolderías and settlements as well. AHU, Rio de Janeiro, Castro e Almeida (017-01), caixa 13, doc. 2568; Luís Ferrand de Almeida, "A Colónia do Sacramento," 426.

28. Brito Peixoto, "Relação," 299.

29. IHGB, Conselho Ultramarino, Arq. 1.1.25, fs. 59v–62, 280–90; AHU, Rio de Janeiro, Castro e Almeida (017-01), caixa 17, doc. 3580; Frühauf Garcia, "Quando os índios escolhem," 618–19.

30. Bulkeley and Cummins, *Voyage to the South Seas*, 166.

31. See, for example, *Croquis de la costa*.

32. Prado, *A Colônia do Sacramento*, 94; Owens, "Spanish-Portuguese Territorial Rivalry," 20.

33. From the first years of the founding of Colônia, authorities in Buenos Aires sought to separate local tolderías from the Portuguese in Colônia, mostly to no avail. AGI, Charcas, 278, "Parecer y voto dado al gobernador de Buenos Aires" (1683-02-03); Cortesão, *Alexandre de Gusmão*, 352. See also AHU, Nova Colónia do Sacramento (012), caixa 3, doc. 325; BNP, F. 1445, f. 56; ANB, D9. Vice-Reinado, caixa 746, pac. 2, fs. 4–4v; Thun, Cerno, and Obermeier, *Guarinihape tecocue*, 102, 118, 126–27, 130; Vianna, *Jesuítas e Bandeirantes no Uruguai*, 231.

34. MM, Archivo Colonial, Arm. B, C18, P1, no. 2, fs. 4, 6v–7; Sylva, *Relação do sitio*, 72–75.

35. AHU, Nova Colónia do Sacramento (012), caixa 3, docs. 304 and 312; Sylva, *Relação do sitio*, 23–40, 85–101; Sá, *Historia topographica*, 116–18. Following the Treaty of Utrecht in 1715, Portuguese diplomats began to advance their own claims of jurisdictional exclusivity. IEB, AL-136-27-11; IHGB, Conselho Ultramarino, Arq. 1.1.25, f. 281v; IHGB, Conselho Ultramarino, Arq. 1.3.3, fs. 86–93; BA, 49-x-7, fs. 138–39v; Cortesão, *Alexandre de Gusmão*, 481.

36. Cortesão, *História do Brasil nos velhos mapas*, 2:135; Portuondo, *Secret Science*.

37. Blaeu, *Nova et accurata Brasiliae*; Wit, *Novissima et Accuratissima*; Fer, *Partie La Plus Meridionale De L'Amerique*; Homann, *Typus geographicus Chili Paraguay*.

38. This changing representation may have been due to D'Anville's correspondence with the Portuguese secretary of state for foreign affairs, leading up to negotiations for the 1750 Treaty of Madrid. Furtado, *O mapa que inventou o Brasil*, 324–26.

39. Safier, *Measuring the New World*, 76–81; Magalhães, "Mundos em miniatura," 80–84; André Ferrand de Almeida, *A formação do espaço brasileiro*, 100–12.

40. The Soares expedition produced the first measurements of longitude in the Río de la Plata region in 1730, followed by the Spanish Jesuit Miguel Quiroga in 1748. Cortesão, *História do Brasil nos velhos mapas*, 2:198–200.

41. AGN-A, IX, 4-3-2, (San Borja, 1759-01-28).

42. Buisseret, "Spanish Colonial Cartography," 1148, 1168; Fúrlong Cárdiff, *Cartografía jesuítica*; Barcelos, "A cartografia indígena."

43. AHU, Rio de Janeiro, Castro e Almeida (017-01), caixa 33, doc. 7623; Cortesão, *História do Brasil nos velhos mapas*, 2:202–3. Soares communicated with Cristóvão Pereira, a military officer whose close relations with Minuanes enabled him to chart a pathway between Colônia and Rio Grande. "O Rio Grande do Sul na cartografia antiga," 297.

44. Vitoria's writings were part of a broader attempt to regulate the standards of territorial possession in the Americas, which included the Laws of Burgos (1512) and the Requerimiento (1513). Vitoria contended that even if the pope had dominion over peoples throughout the world, he was not authorized to claim their property, including lands. Vitoria, *Political Writings*, 233–92, esp. 258; Hanke, *Spanish Struggle for Justice*, 1–36; Mariluz Urquijo, "La valoración de la bulas," 170–71; Caamaño-Dones, *La concesión a Castilla*, 15–16; Amith, *Möbius Strip*, 77–85; Muldoon, "John Wyclif and the Rights"; Seed, *Ceremonies of Possession*, 88; Schwartz, "Principle of the Defence of the Innocent."

45. Van Deusen, *Global Indios*, 194–7, 205–11; Davies, *Renaissance Ethnography*, 65–108.

46. Muriel, *Elementos de derecho natural*, 99. Despite offering primacy to sedentary peoples, Grotius did acknowledge mobile peoples' claims. Moretti, *International Law and Nomadic People*, 25–30.

47. Sutton, *Capitalism and Cartography*, 73–99; Amith, *Möbius Strip*, 71–75, 98–103; Herzog, "Colonial Law and 'Native Customs,'" 311.

48. The act of forming a reducción, to *reducirse* (*reduzir-se* in Portuguese), literally meant "to be ordered," "to be brought to reason," or "to be brought back." Rappaport and Cummins, *Beyond the Lettered City*, 221. Examples of the use of this concept in the Río de la Plata include AGNA, IX, 4-3-1 (Campo del Bloqueo, 1750-11-15; Las Vívoras, 1746-07-14); IHGB, Conselho Ultramarino, Arq. 1.1.25, 49v, 60–61; Muriel, *Elementos de derecho natural*, 104, 313; BNB, I-28,28,19, f. 11v; AGI, Chile, 153 (Montevideo, 1724-08-29); AGNA, VII, Biblioteca Nacional 183, doc. 1188; Ferrufino, *Relacion del martirios*, 33v; AGI, Contaduría, 1931 (Buenos Aires, 1710-03-04), f. 25; *Cartas anuas*, 20:367; AGPSF, Acta de Cabildo de Santa Fe de 1750-02-03. For more on Indigenous conversion or vassalage as an avenue to claim territorial possession, see Herzog, *Frontiers of Possession*, 70–95; Ellis, "Petite Nation with Powerful Networks," 172–74.

49. Imperial subjects did not necessarily share this juridical perspective. While individuals or communities may have accepted the authority of a royal court, this did not imply the cession of land rights. Owensby, *Empire of Law and Indian Justice*, 90–129.

50. Buchan and Heath, "Savagery and Civilization," 7–11; Fitzmaurice, "Genealogy of Terra Nullius"; Mariluz Urquijo, *El régimen de la tierra*, 28–29.

51. Muriel, *Elementos de derecho natural*, 99, 128, 131, 315, 348–49; Moretti, *International Law and Nomadic People*, 24–30, 39; Levinton, *El espacio jesuítico-guaraní*, 138n417.

52. AGI, Charcas, 264 (Buenos Aires, 1721-08-31).

53. AGI, Charcas, 263 (Buenos Aires, 1699-12-19, 1715-12-16).

54. AGI, Charcas, 264 (Buenos Aires, 1721-08-31).

55. Fucé, "Ceremonia persuasiva." A transcription of the peace accords is available in Acosta y Lara, *La guerra de los charrúas*, 1:57–58. For details on the 1732 agreement, see chapter 1.

56. Records of these exchanges do not include or indicate Indigenous perceptions, but intercultural exchanges frequently produced misunderstandings in which both sides interpret an action through their own cultural norms. White, *Middle Ground*, x; Lockhart, *Of Things of the Indies*, 98–119; David Murray, *Indian Giving*, 1, 12–13.

57. AGI, Charcas, 263 (1ª carta, Buenos Aires, 1716-05-13).

58. AGI, Charcas, 263 (2ª carta, Buenos Aires, 1716-05-13).

59. IHGB, Conselho Ultramarino, Arq. 1.1.25, fs. 49–49v.

60. IHGB, Conselho Ultramarino, Arq. 1.1.25, fs. 59–62; AHU, Rio de Janeiro, Castro e Almeida (017-01), caixa 17, doc. 3580; AHU, Nova Colónia do Sacramento (012), caixa 1, doc. 52.

61. IHGB, Conselho Ultramarino, Arq. 1.1.25, fs. 237–38; AHU, Nova Colónia do Sacramento (012), caixa 2, doc. 180. For more on baptisms and Minuán caciques, see Hameister, "'No princípio era o caos,'" 114–15, 125.

62. AGNA, VII, Biblioteca Nacional 289, docs. 4390/1 and 4390/2; Levinton, *El espacio jesuítico-guaraní*, 111–12.

63. Santa Fe and Corrientes were exceptions to this rule, likely because by the 1715 Treaty of Utrecht, Portugal no longer claimed dominion over territories west of the Río Uruguay.

64. "Carta de Cristovão Pereira"; "Copia da carta de Cristovão Pereira"; Fortes, "O Brigadeiro José da Silva," 49, 62; BNP, F. 1445, f. 56; "Coleção de documentos," 16–17.

65. AGI, Chile, 153 (Montevideo, 1724-08-29, 1726-09-15).

66. AGI, Charcas, 384, "Petición del Procurador de la Compañía de Jesús, padre Juan José Rico" (n/d), pero visto en consejo (1743-10-17); Bracco, *Charrúas, guenoas y guaraníes*, 266–67; Acosta y Lara, *La guerra de los charrúas*, 1:81–96.

67. AGNA, VII, Biblioteca Nacional 183, docs. 1182 and 1188.

68. IHGB, Arquivo, lata 168, doc. 4, f. 64. Numerous Portuguese diplomats also expressed this distrust toward Spanish-sponsored mapping expeditions. IHGB, Arquivo, lata 50, doc. 7; IHGB, Conselho Ultramarino, Arq. 1.2.1, f. 30v.

69. Juan and Ulloa, *Disertación histórica y geográfica*, 71–72.

70. "Tratado firmado en Madrid."

71. Luís Ferrand de Almeida, *Alexandre de Gusmão, o Brasil*; Ferreira, "O Mapa das Cortes"; Furtado, *O mapa que inventou o Brasil*.

72. Cortesão, *Alexandre de Gusmão*, 474-82; Block, *Mission Culture*, 49–50; Ferreira Acruche, "De rebeldes," 153. For more on the primacy of uti possidetis over the Tordesillas meridian or natural limits in the negotiation of the Treaty of Madrid, see Alden, *Royal Government in Colonial Brazil*, 88; Camargo, "Las relaciones luso-hispánicas en torno," 237–38, 244–46; Kantor, "Soberania e territorialidade colonial"; Magalhães, "Mundos em miniatura," 85; Furtado, *O mapa que inventou o Brasil*, 332–41.

73. "Registro de atos oficiais," 235–36, 258; Leite, *História da Companhia de Jesús*, 6:528–30; Hameister, "Para dar calor," 22–23, 190–91, 279–89, 299; Hameister, "'No princípio era o caos,'" 100–2, 109–16.

74. Montevideo was prepared to offer 265 cows, 510 sheep, 110 silver pesos, yerba maté, and eight months' worth of jerky if the toldería would accept a settlement; Cortesão, *Antecedentes do Tratado de Madri*, 301–2; AGNA, IX, 2-1-4 (Montevideo, 1750-07-22, 1750-09-06); AGNU, Falcao Espalter, 1:182–84; AGI, Charcas, 378 (Buenos Aires, 1751-04-26).

75. AGNA, IX, 4-3-1 (Buenos Aires, 1750-10-12; Las Vívoras, 1750-11-09; Campo del Bloqueo, 1750-11-15); AGNA, IX, 2-1-4 , f. 794 (Montevideo, 1751-11-13); Bracco, *Charrúas, guenoas y guaraníes,* 266; Bracco, "Los errores Charrúa y Guenoa-Minuán," 133.

76. AGNU, Ex Archivo General Administrativo, caja 2, carpeta 19, no. 3.

77. Cortesão, *Antecedentes do Tratado de Madri,* 298; AGPSF, Acta de Cabildo de Santa Fe de 1750-11-03.

78. Administrators in numerous Spanish settlements demonstrated a desire to replace pact making with aggressive military engagement. AGNA, IX, 2-1-4 (Montevideo, 1751-07-11); AGNU, Falcao Espalter, 1:86–87, 117; AGNU, Falcao Espalter, 4:127–30; Sallaberry, *Los charrúas y Santa Fe,* 241–53.

79. AGNU, Falcao Espalter, 1:111–15, 182–86; AGNU, Falcao Espalter, 4:228–30; AGPSF, Actas de Cabildo de Santa Fe de 1750-02-03, 1750-03-07, 1750-08-03, 1750-09-10, 1750-09-25, 1750-11-03 (several), 1750-11-09, 1750-11-26, 1751-01-07, 1752-01-19, 1755-09-09; AGI, Charcas, 378 (Buenos Aires, 1751-04-26).

80. AGNA, IX, 4-3-1 (Vívoras, 1748-02-14; Campo del Bloqueo, 1749-05-22, 1749-07-21, 1756-02-24, 1757-08-06); AGNA, IX, 2-1-4, (Montevideo, 1750-10-27, 1751-01-19); AGNU, Falcao Espalter, 1:47, 88–89, 111–13, 185; AGNU, Falcao Espalter, 4:129; AGI, Charcas, 215 (Santo Domingo Soriano, 1750-09-07).

81. AGPSF, Acta de Cabildo de Santa Fe de 1752-02-17; IEB, AL-068-002; AGNU, Falcao Espalter, 1:86–87; AGNU, Falcao Espalter, 4:228–30, 235–41; Sallaberry, *Los charrúas y Santa Fe,* 232, 234, 249, 262–64, 287–89; Poenitz, *Los infieles minuanes y charrúas,* 1–2.

82. Leite, *História da Companhia de Jesús,* 6:528–29.

83. AGNA, IX, 4-3-1 (Santo Domingo Soriano, 1750-01-16).

84. Bracco, *Charrúas, guenoas y guaraníes,* 270; AGNA, IX, 4-3-1 (Santo Domingo Soriano, 1750-01-16, 1750-09-06, 1750-09-29; Vívoras, 1750-10-13, 1750-11-09); AGNA, IX, 2-1-4 (Montevideo, 1750-12-30, 1751-01-26, 1751-11-13); AGNU, Falcao Espalter, 1:47; AGNU, Ex Archivo General Administrativo, caja 2, carpeta 35, no. 8; AGI, Charcas, 221 (Buenos Aires, 1752-09-07).

85. Azara, *Viajes por la América del Sur,* 182. For more on tolderías' realignments, see chapter 4.

Chapter Three

1. Saldanha, "Diário resumido," 231–39; Varela y Ulloa, *Diario de la primera partida,* 2:151, 178; Oyarvide, *Memoria geográfica,* 8:197–98.

2. Varela y Ulloa, *Diario de la primera partida,* 2:178; Saldanha, "Diário resumido," 241.

3. Saldanha, "Diário resumido," 234–36; Varela y Ulloa, *Diario de la primera partida,* 2:151, 177-78; Oyarvide, *Memoria geográfica,* 8:196–98; Cabrer, "Diario," 6, 9; Alvear, "Diario," 2:343–44; ANB, 86, Secretário de Estado, cod. 104, v. 9, fs. 87–87v; Acosta y Lara, *La guerra de los charrúas,* 1:111–12, 121-25; Poenitz, *Los infieles minuanes y charrúas,* 8; AGNA, IX, 17-7-2 (San Nicolás, 1785-04-13; San Luis, 1785-04-15); AGNA, IX, 23-2-6 (Santa Tecla, 1775-05-26).

4. Saldanha, "Diário resumido," 234; Varela y Ulloa, *Diario de la primera partida,* 2:177.

5. Oyarvide, *Memoria geográfica,* 8:212.

6. Oyarvide, *Memoria geográfica,* 8:191; Alvear, "Diario," 2:348.

7. Safier, *Measuring the New World*, 5–9.

8. In the Amazon and along the Mato Grosso–Paraguay borderlands, the boundary commissions never completed their efforts. Rausch, *Tropical Plains Frontier*, 81; Souza Torres, "Dominios y fronteras," 186; Zárate Botía, "Pueblos indígenas," 29; Langavant, "La frontera del Alto Paraguay," 332, 334.

9. ANB, 86, Secretário de Estado, cod. 104, v. 11, fs. 362–62v; IHGB, Arquivo, lata 108, doc. 20, f. 1. For a similar series of events in the Amazon, see Souza Torres, "Dominios y fronteras," 198–214.

10. Furtado, *O mapa que inventou o Brasil*; Ferreira, "O Mapa das Cortes"; André Ferrand de Almeida, "O Mapa Geográfico de América"; Martín-Merás, "Fondos cartográficos y documentales," 3.

11. AHU, Brasil Limites (059), caixa 2, doc. 127; ANB, 86, Secretário de Estado, cod. 104, v. 5, fs. 63–66; IHGB, Arquivo, lata 109, doc. 8, f. 9; IHGB, Conselho Ultramarino, Arq. 1.3.7, f. 28v.

12. Rodolfo Garcia, *Anais da Biblioteca Nacional*, 53:302; BA, 51-vii-48, fs. 59–59v. The same issue of scale occurred with Great Britain's 1763 "Proclamation Line" in mainland North America. Edelson, *New Map of Empire*, 158–59.

13. "Tratado firmado en Madrid," 4.

14. "Tratado preliminar," 4–6; Golin, *A Fronteira*, 172.

15. For the Treaty of Madrid's northern commission alone, Spain employed over eight hundred laborers, while Portuguese teams totaled over one thousand laborers. Lucena Giraldo, *Laboratorio tropical*, 267–82; Mendonça, *A Amazônia na era pombalina*, 631. Precise numbers for other subdivisions are uneven, given that many laborers were hired along the way and thus not accounted for in the roll sheets drafted prior to demarcation. The overall estimates employed here draw on the following records. For the Treaty of Madrid's southern commission: BNB, 09,3,012, fs. 1–5; IEB, YAP-011, fs. 3-3v, 31v. For the Treaty of San Ildefonso: IHGB, Conselho Ultramarino, Arq. 1.1.1, fs. 107, 121–26; IHGB, Conselho Ultramarino, Arq. 1.3.7, fs. 401–8; ANB, 86, Secretário de Estado, cod. 104, v. 5, fs. 72–73v, 157–60; BNB, 04,4,003, fs. 5–8, 20; AGNA, VII, Biblioteca Nacional 46, fs. 29–30; Varela y Ulloa, *Diario de la primera partida*, 1:154–56; Domingues, *Viagens de exploração geográfica*, 30–32; Siquiera Bueno and Kantor, "A outra face das expedições," 253–57; Souza Torres, "Dominios y fronteras," 212.

16. The third and fourth Portuguese subdivisions traveled inland from São Paulo toward Paraguay and did not pass through the Río de la Plata region.

17. BNB, 09,3,012, fs. 35–36; ANB, 86, Secretário de Estado, cod. 104, v. 11, fs. 37–37v. Demarcation officials carried maps drawn by Jesuits, frontierspeople, and European engravers, and the San Ildefonso subdivisions also consulted the maps and diaries produced by the Madrid demarcations. BNB, 04,4,003, 12v–13; IEB, AL-136-27-12, fs. 56–57; IEB, YAP-011, fs. 41–42v; Rodolfo Garcia, *Anais da Biblioteca Nacional*, 53:249, 285.

18. AGNA, XIII, 15-4-4; AGNA, XIII, 15-4-5; AGNA, XIII, 15-4-6; AGNA, XIII, 15-5-1; AGNA, XIII, 15-5-2; BA, 51-vii-48, f. 60; BNB, 09,3,012, fs. 85, 104; BNB, 09,4,14, fs. 81–81v; IHGB, Conselho Ultramarino, Arq. 1.1.1, fs. 107, 121–26; IHGB, Conselho Ultramarino, Arq. 1.2.19, fs. 72v–73. In the Río de la Plata, many laborers were from the Guaraní missions and drew lower wages. Sarreal, *Guaraní and Their Missions*, 152.

19. Saldanha, "Diário resumido," 229, 246, 258. In contemporary Guaraní orthography, these terms would be written as "Ka'ayvate," "Ka'aguasu," "Ybyra-jepiro," and "Apikasuro."

20. ANB, 86, Secretário de Estado, cod. 104, v. 10, f. 54v. At least one Guaraní guide accompanied the demarcation teams through Charrúa and Minuán lands during the San Ildefonso expedition. AGNA, XIII. 15-5-1, fs. 147–47v.

21. Oyarvide, *Memoria geográfica*, 8:218–19.

22. Azara, "Correspondencia oficial e inédita," 26–31.

23. Azara, "Correspondencia oficial e inédita," 3–7.

24. ANB, 86, Secretário de Estado, cod. 104, v. 8, f. 306.

25. ANB, 86, Secretário de Estado, cod. 104, v. 10, f. 129; BNB, 09,3,012, f. 60.

26. AGI, Buenos Aires, 70 (Buenos Aires, 1785-03-26, 1785-04-01, 1785-04-07, 1785-05-24; Rio Grande 1784-11-06); AGI, Buenos Aires, 73 (Charqueada en el Piratini, 1786-02-02; Campamento do Pavaó, 1786-01-12); ANB, 86, Secretário de Estado, cod. 104, v. 8, fs. 65–78v, 86–91v, 94–99, 307v; BNB, 09,4,14, fs. 31–39, 54v–56v; Varela y Ulloa, *Diario de la primera partida*, 1:123–47; Gil, "Sobre o comércio ilícito."

27. Oyarvide, *Memoria geográfica*, 8:196, 221–22.

28. ANB, 86, Secretário de Estado, cod. 104, v. 8, fs. 354, 364, 371, 395v; ANB, 86. Secretário de Estado, cod. 104, v. 9, f. 22; BNB, 09,02,003, f. 2; IEB, YAP-011, fs. 13, 15v–16; Roscio, "Compêndio Noticioso," 107; Saldanha, "Diário resumido," 183, 187, 204, 301; Fúrlong Cárdiff, *Cartografía jesuítica*, vol. 2, Lámina XXIV; Porto, "O minuano na toponímia" 105.

29. IEB, YAP-011, fs. 9v, 11v–12; "Diário compilado da 1ª tropa," 47.

30. IEB, YAP-011, fs. 25–27.

31. Traditional retellings of the war argued that Jesuits orchestrated the uprising and that their subsequent expulsions were its principal outcome; revisionist accounts have focused on Guaraní leadership and action, often in defiance of the missionaries' conciliatory attitude. Mörner, *Expulsion of the Jesuits*; Golin, *A Guerra Guaranítica*; Ganson, *Guaraní under Spanish Rule*; Quarleri, *Rebelión y guerra*; Neumann, "Fronteira e identidade," Gálvez, *De la tierra sin mal*, 283-310. Still, some work has centered tolderías' actions by focusing on their resistance to the Siete Pueblos' transmigration or their later alliance with mission forces. Poenitz, *Los infieles minuanes y charrúas*, 2–3; Cabrera Pérez, "Los 'indios infieles'"; Bracco, *Charrúas, guenoas y guaraníes*, 276–85; Pereira, "'Y hoy están en paz,'" 25–26.

32. Cortesão, *Do Tratado de Madri*, 142–47, 164-65, 168–69, 175–80, 193, 197, 207–8; Rodolfo Garcia, *Anais da Biblioteca Nacional*, 52:143, 386, 405; Bauzá, *Historia de la Dominación Española*, 2:84–88, 93–94.

33. Cortesão, *Do Tratado de Madri*, 144–45, 164–69, 176–79.

34. Poenitz, *Los infieles minuanes y charrúas*, 2; Levinton, "Las estancias," 44.

35. Ganson, *Guaraní under Spanish Rule*, 95; Levinton, *El espacio jesuítico-guaraní*.

36. IHGB, Conselho Ultramarino, Arq. 1.2.31, 25–26v.

37. For more on these campaigns, see chapter 2.

38. Frühauf Garcia, "Quando os índios escolhem," 620–21; Rodolfo Garcia, *Anais da Biblioteca Nacional*, 52:510.

39. Rodolfo Garcia, *Anais da Biblioteca Nacional*, 52:417–18, 429–30; Cortesão, *Do Tratado de Madri*, 230–31.

40. AHU, Rio de Janeiro, Castro e Almeida (017-01), caixa 73, docs. 16897 and 16898; AHU, Rio de Janeiro, Castro e Almeida (017-01), caixa 78, doc. 18205; Rodrigues da Cunha, "Diário da expedição," 188; Rodolfo Garcia, *Anais da Biblioteca Nacional*, 52:475, 497–98; Henis, "Diario histórico," 4, 21–22.

41. AGNU, Falcao Espalter, 3:127, 130–31.

42. AGNU, Falcao Espalter, 3:126.

43. AHU, Rio de Janeiro, Castro e Almeida (017-01), caixa 78, doc. 18218; Cortesão, *Do Tratado de Madri*, 137, 188; "Diário compilado da 1ª tropa," 72; Rodolfo Garcia, *Anais da Biblioteca Nacional*, 52:505, 510–11, 519–20; Henis, "Diario histórico," 40–41; Acosta y Lara, *La guerra de los charrúas*, 1:102–3; Frühauf Garcia, "Quando os índios escolhem," 622.

44. Rodolfo Garcia, *Anais da Biblioteca Nacional*, 52:430, 502–3; AHU, Brasil Limites (059), caixa 1, doc. 90.

45. IEB, AL-068-002; AGNA, IX, 4-3-1, (1757-05-18; Campo del Bloqueo, 1757-04-26, 1757-06-09, 1757-08-05, 1757-08-06; Santo Domingo Soriano, 1757-07-01); AGNA, IX, 4-3-2, (1757-02-24; Campo del Bloqueo, 1758-02-27, 1758-09-10, 1758-11-06; 1760-01-22, 1760-04-24; Buenos Aires, 1760-03-06, 1760-08-09); Rodolfo Garcia, *Anais da Biblioteca Nacional*, 52:418–20, 445, 519–20, 535, 541; Henis, "Diario histórico," 40–41, 53; Graell, "Diario del capitán," 464, 469.

46. AHU, Brasil Limites (059), caixa 1, docs. 42 and 74; AHU, Brasil Limites (059), caixa 2, docs. 116 and 142.

47. Rodolfo Garcia, *Anais da Biblioteca Nacional*, 53:246, 249, 263, 318–19.

48. For more on migrants incorporating into tolderías, see chapter 4.

49. See Article 1 of the treaty. Colaboradores de Wikisource, "Tratado de El Pardo (1761)."

50. AGNA, IX, 3-2-1 (Montevideo, 1761-08-25); AGNA, IX, 16-6-5 (Cuartel General del Rio Grande, 1763-08-31); Herzog, *Frontiers of Possession*, 45–48; Golin, *A Fronteira*, 167; IHGB, Arquivo, lata 168, doc. 4, fs. 63–65.

51. Côlonia was returned to Portugal in the 1763 Treaty of Paris. Examples of other Luso-Hispanic borderline conflicts during these years include Langavant, "La frontera del Alto Paraguay," 335; Block, *Mission Culture*, 49–52; Rausch, *Tropical Plains Frontier*, 78.

52. In the Amazon, the Portuguese were able to gain a more favorable location of the San Ildefonso line because of their establishment of forts and of fixed settlements with Native communities in the 1760s and 1770s, yet there, too, the boundary commissions negotiated the exchange of settlements to accommodate the border. Siquiera Bueno and Kantor, "A outra face das expedições," 244; Souza Torres, "Dominios y fronteras," 194–95.

53. BNB, 09,3,012, fs. 127–30; IHGB, Conselho Ultramarino, Arq. 1.2.19, 73v, 84; IHGB, Arquivo, lata 762, pasta 31, fs. 1–5; Costa, "Viajes en la frontera," 121; Bertocchi Moran, "El piloto Andrés de Oyarvide," 750–51.

54. ANB, 86, Secretário de Estado, cod. 104, v. 13, f. 142; AGNA, IX, 4-3-4 (Cerro Largo, 1800-02-13).

55. Latini, "Repensando," 86.

56. The Relaciones Geográficas were a series of questionnaires sent to Spain's American colonies during the late sixteenth century. Despite numerous responses from Mesoamerica, which included maps produced by Native painters, the questionnaires completed in South America were almost entirely from the central and northern Andes, with no responses from Chile, Paraguay, the Guianas, the Río de la Plata, or Brazil. Mundy, *Mapping of New Spain*, 29–59; Edwards, "Geographical Coverage," 78.

57. Diego García, "Memoria," 122–23; Ortiz de Vergara, "Declaración," 118; Schmidl, "Viaje al Río de la Plata," 6–12; Rela, *Portugal en las exploraciones*, 257, 263.

58. Fúrlong Cárdiff, *Cartografía jesuítica*, vol. 2.

59. ANB, 86, Secretário de Estado, cod. 104, v. 10, f. 131. Some subdivisions also drew watercolors to represent the events of their expeditions and the landscapes they encountered. Siquiera Bueno and Kantor, "A outra face das expedições," 252–61.

60. ANB, 86, Secretário de Estado, cod. 104, v. 10, f. 131.

61. ANB, 86, Secretário de Estado, cod. 104, v. 11, fs. 111–12; ANB, D9, Vice-Reinado, caixa 749, pac. 2 (Buenos Aires, 1793-07-10); Azara, "Correspondencia oficial e inédita," 8–10.

62. "Tratado preliminar," 4–5.

63. ANB, 86, Secretário de Estado, cod. 104, v. 8, fs. 13, 20v, 65–78v.

64. AGNA, IX, 24-2-4, exp. 37, fs. 39, 48v-54; AHRS, Informações sobre pedidos de terras, maço 1, no. 62 (Rio Pardo, 1792-04-14); AHRS, F1246, 140–42v, 190–91v; AHRS, F1247, 60–61, 100–101v, 183–84v, 189v–90, 250v–52, 257v–59, 288–89; AHRS, F1248, 1–2v, 22–23, 188v–90v, 216v–18, 277–79v, 289v–90; AHRS, F1249, fs. 259v–61; AGNU, Ex AGA, caja 134, carpeta 2, no. 85; RAH, Mata Linares, t. 78, f. 1,172.

65. ANB, D9, Vice-Reinado, caixa 494, pac. 1, fs. 2–3; "Informe del Virrey Arredondo."

66. See also Blasco, *Traslado do Mappa* (BNB, 049,02,024, no. 12). On Enlightenment geography, see Livingstone, *Geographical Tradition*, 102–38; Edney and Pedley, *History of Cartography*.

67. Oyarvide, *Memoria geográfica*, 8:213.

68. Saldanha, "Diário resumido," 231; Azara, *Geografía, física y esférica*, 392; Alvear, "Relacion geográfica é histórica," 8.

69. Wilde, "Orden y ambigüedad," 114–17; Frühauf Garcia, *As diversas formas*.

70. Saldanha, "Diário resumido," 236.

71. Varela y Ulloa, *Diario de la primera partida*, 1:36; Alvear, "Diario," 2:343. See also Juan and Ulloa, *Voyage to South America*, 172–73.

72. Juan Francisco de Aguirre, "Diario," 7:341–42.

73. Saldanha, "Diário resumido," 233.

74. See, for example, Azara, *Viajes por la América del Sur*, 39–42; Azara, *Geografía, física y esférica*, 368.

75. Alvear, "Diario," 1:341; Azara, *Descripción é historia*, 2:211–12.

76. Juan Francisco de Aguirre, "Diario," 7:38; Azara, *Geografía, física y esférica*, 197.

77. Juan Francisco de Aguirre, "Diario," 4:144.

78. Alvear, "Diario," 2:344–45.

79. Azara, *Descripción é historia*, 1:165; Azara, *Geografía, física y esférica*, 368.

80. Saldanha, "Diário resumido," 235–36; ANB, 86, Secretário de Estado, cod. 104, v. 9, 87–87v. For more on state ethnographies and imperial differences, see Wilde, "Orden y ambigüedad," 109–17; Sirtori, "Nos limites," 14–25.

81. ANB, 86, Secretário de Estado, cod. 104, v. 10, 194–95.

82. ANB, 86, Secretário de Estado, cod. 104, v. 11, fs. 109v–12, 205–5v, 215, 277–77v, 338–39v.

83. AGNA, XIII, 15-4-4, f. 334; Azara, "Correspondencia oficial e inédita," 3–7, 14–17; BNB, 09,3,012, 127–30; Leite, *História da Companhia de Jesús*, 9:148; Lucena Giraldo and Pedro, *La frontera caríbica*, 58–60, 66; Altic, "Missionary Cartography," 77, 80–82; Siquiera Bueno and Kantor, "A outra face das expedições," 248.

Chapter Four

1. ANB, 86, Secretário de Estado, cod. 104, v. 7, f. 743; BNB, 09,4,14, f. 511; "Autos principaes ao Conselho de Guerra," 497; AGI, Buenos Aires, 70 (Buenos Aires, 1785-06-08); AGNA, IX 23-2-6 (Santa Tecla, 1785-01-26).

2. AHU, Rio de Janeiro (017), caixa 128, doc. 10244; ANB, 86, Secretário de Estado, cod. 104, v. 8, fs. 101–2v.

3. ANB, 86, Secretário de Estado, cod. 104, v. 8, fs. 204–7; Frühauf Garcia, "Quando os índios escolhem," 623–25.

4. For details on Caraí's tolderías taxing the San Ildefonso demarcations, see chapter 3.

5. Segarra, *Frontera y límites*, 22; Golin, *A Fronteira*, 227–37, 249–58.

6. ANB, D9, Vice-Reinado, caixa 749, pac. 1 (Viamão, 1772-02-12; Porto Alegre, 1804-10-01); "Relatorio apresentado ao governo de Lisboa," 26; IHGB, Conselho Ultramarino, Arq. 1.2.19, fs. 144–48v; ANB, 86, Secretário de Estado, cod. 104, v. 5, fs. 170–70v.

7. Azara, *Descripción é historia*, 2:259–60. See also Langavant, "La frontera del Alto Paraguay," 340–41.

8. IEB, YAP-035, fs. 6–9.

9. Officers in the northern commission followed similar political trajectories and led similar settlement initiatives as their southern counterparts. Siquiera Bueno and Kantor, "A outra face das expedições," 251–52; Lucena Giraldo and Pedro, *La frontera caríbica*, 64–81; Rausch, *Tropical Plains Frontier*, 78–79.

10. Lynch, *Spanish Colonial Administration*, 62–89; Prado, *Edge of Empire*, 83–130; Rüdiger, *Colonização e propriedade de terras*, 54–65; De Província de São Pedro, 49–50; Eugénio dos Santos, "A administração portuguesa no sul," 388–90; Almeida Santos, "Poder e territorialização."

11. Borucki, *From Shipmates to Soldiers*, 25–56; Sarreal, *Guaraní and Their Missions*, 75–82; Fortes, "Velhos caminhos," 250–54; Fonseca, *Tropeiros de mula*, 67.

12. Azara, *Memoria sobre el estato rural*, 10, 23–24; Barrios Pintos, *De las vaquerías al alambrado*, 127. Other goods, such as yerba maté from Paraguay, were channeled through the Río de la Plata. Whigham, *Politics of River Trade*, 11–20.

13. These initiatives were known as the Arreglo de los Campos. For a detailed discussion, see Sala de Touron, de la Torre, and Rodríguez, *Evolución económica de la Banda Oriental*, 81–121.

14. BNB, 09,4,14, 32v, 208–9v.

15. Herzog, "Naming, Identifying and Authorizing Movement," 195.

16. AGNA, IX, 23-2-6 (1793-09-30; 1794-03-15); Gil, "O contrabando na fronteira," 12; "Informe del Virrey Arredondo," 30–31, 33–34; AHRS, F1243, fs. 163–64.

17. "Tratado firmado en Madrid," 10; "Tratado preliminar," 11–12.

18. ANB, 86, Secretário de Estado, cod. 104, v. 9, fs. 132–36v; ANB, 86, Secretário de Estado, cod. 104, v. 11, fs. 440–40v; ANB, D9, Vice-Reinado, caixa 749, pac. 2 (Montevideo, 1799-04-17; Buenos Aires, 1791-07-21; Rio Grande de São Pedro, 1791-10-12); AGNA, IX, 1-3-5 (1798-01-26, 1798-02-01, 1798-02-11); AGNA, IX, 18-2-4 (San Miguel, 1799-07-18, 1799-09-18; San Nicolás, 1799-10-20); AGNA, IX, 23-2-6 (1780-05-16, 1794-11-09); AGNA, IX, 1-5-3 (1760-05-04; Puesto de Santiago, 1759-06-26); AGNA, IX, 4-3-1 (1753-06-01); AGNA, IX, 4-3-2 (Campo del Bloqueo, 1758-06-27; Buenos Aires, 1758-07-07, 1760-11-30; San Borja,

1759-12-13, 1759-03-21; Salto, 1759-09-24); AGNA, IX, 4-3-3 (Campo del Bloqueo, 1761-06-26, 1761-07-09, 1761-07-10, 1761-08-21, 1761-08-31, 1761-09-23, 1761-09-27, 1761-11-23); AGNA, IX, 4-3-8 (Colonia, 1777-06-20); AGNA, VII, Lamas 32 [2635], fs. 113v–15v.

19. Gil, *Infiéis Trangressores*; Prado, "A carreira transimperial"; Langavant, "La frontera del Alto Paraguay," 349–55.

20. ANB, 86, Secretário de Estado, cod. 104, v. 8, 17–23, 79–83v, 109, 111v, 113v–14v, 233–35v, 301; ANB, 86, Secretário de Estado, cod. 104, v. 11, fs. 161–69v; ANB, D9, Vice-Reinado, caixa 749, pac. 2 (Buenos Aires, 1791-07-21); Oyarvide, "Memoria geográfica," 8:181–86; IHGB, Arquivo, lata 110, doc. 28, fs. 18–37; BNB, 09,4,14, fs. 24–25.

21. "Demarcação do sul do Brasil," 49–295; AHRS, F1244, 171v–72; AHRS, F1246, 140v–42, 190–91v, 197v–98, 216v–17v; AHRS, F1247, 60–61, 100–104, 147–48v, 183–84v, 189v–90, 250v–52, 257v –59, 288–89; AHRS, F1248, 1–2v, 22–23, 37v–38v, 67–68, 188v–90v, 216v–18, 263–65, 277–79v, 289v–90; AHRS, F1249, 69–70v, 76–78, 111v–13, 200–201v, 259v–61, 263v; AHRS, Sesmarias, Maço 2, nos. 28 and 45; AHRS, Sesmarias, Maço 3, no. 62; AHRS, Sesmarias, Maço 5, no. 106; AHRS, Sesmarias, Maço 6, no. 118; AHRS, Sesmarias, Maço 7, nos. 137 and 148; Porto, "Fronteira do Rio Pardo"; Aguirre, "La Banda Oriental y Rio Grande," 60–61.

22. Azara, *Memoria sobre el estado rural*, 6–7, 18–19; Roscio, "Compêndio Noticioso," 139.

23. ANB, 86, Secretário de Estado, cod. 104, v. 9, fs. 132–36v.

24. Poska, *Gendered Crossings*, 151–61; Frühauf Garcia, *As diversas formas*, 125–71; Mariluz Urquijo, *La expedición contra los charrúas*, 31–33; Mariluz Urquijo, *La fundación de San Gabriel*, 21–25; Eugénio dos Santos, "A administração portuguesa no sul," 392–93, 396–98.

25. ANB, D9, Vice-Reinado, caixa 749, pac. 2 (Porto Alegre, 1773-09-02); Azara, *Memoria sobre el estado rural*, 18–19.

26. AGNA, IX, 23-2-6 (1795-02-26).

27. ANB, 86, Secretário de Estado, cod. 104, v. 11, f. 442v; AHRS, F1244, fs. 171v–72; Djenderedjian, "Roots of Revolution," 650–61; Gil, *Infiéis Trangressores*; Prado, "A carreira transimperial."

28. IHGB, Conselho Ultramarino, Arq. 1.1.29, fs. 71–72v; AGNA, IX, 4-3-2 (Buenos Aires, 1760-08-09).

29. IHGB, Conselho Ultramarino, Arq. 1.2.1, f. 267v; Segarra, *Frontera y límites*, 18.

30. AGNA, IX, 1-3-5 (Cerro Largo, 1798-11-25); AGNA, IX, 4-3-8 (Colonia, 1775-09-26; Real de San Carlos, 1775-09-30); AGNA, IX, 37-8-5, exp. 1, fs. 15–18; AHRS, Autoridades Militares, Maço 1 (Rio Grande, 1795-10-26; Erval, 1800-11-09); ANB, D9, Vice-Reinado, caixa 749, pac. 1 (Rio Grande, 1792-06-02); ANB, 86, Secretário de Estado, cod. 93, v. 1 (1779-10-04; Buenos Aires, 1779-04-28); IHGB, Conselho Ultramarino, Arq. 1.2.19, fs. 28v.

31. AGNA, IX, 1-3-5 (Cerro Largo, 1800-06-30, 1805-10-01).

32. Barrios Pintos, *De las vaquerías al alambrado*, 70, 188; Lastarria, *Colonias orientales del Río Paraguay*, 352.

33. IHGB, Conselho Ultramarino, Arq. 1.2.1, fs. 344v–45.

34. Sarreal, *Guaraní and Their Missions*, 192–216. Examples include AGNA, IX, 4-3-1 (Las Vívoras, 1750-11-09); AGNA, IX, 4-3-2 (Campo del Bloqueo, 1758-10-03); AGNA, IX, 4-3-4 (Vívoras, 1798-09-28); AGNA, IX, 3-9-2 (Montevideo, 1798-03-20); IHGB, Conselho Ultramarino, Arq. 1.2.19, f. 261v; Lastarria, *Colonias orientales del Río Paraguay*, 139.

35. Examples of the use of the word *castigar* include AGNA, IX, 2-1-4 (Montevideo, 1751-01-26); AGNA, IX, 4-3-1 (Campo de Bloqueo, 1749-10-29, 1752-10-19, 1757-07-19, 1757-08-06;

San Salvador, 1746-05-16, 1746-09-20; Santo Domingo Soriano, 1750-01-16); AGNA, IX, 10-6-1 (Arroyo de la Virgen, 1797-12-27); AGNA, IX, 24-3-6, leg. 30, exp. 8 (Las Vívoras, 1800-02-18); AGNA, IX, 28-7-7 (Montevideo, 1803-10-24). Examples of the word *exterminar* include ANHA, Enrique Fitte, III-75; AGNA, IX, 4-3-4 (San Salvador, 1799-09-24); AGNA, IX, 10-6-1 (Buenos Aires, 1806-05-23); AGNU, Ex AGA, caja 10, carpeta 2, nos. 1–2; "Memoria de Juan José de Vértiz," 117.

36. Doblas, "Memoria histórica," 56; Levinton, "La burocracia administrativa."

37. After a spike in hostilities in earlier decades, Spanish authorities began to pursue peace, commerce, and integration with Native communities in other parts of the viceroyalty and in Chile during the late eighteenth century, particularly after the 1780s. Levaggi, *Paz en la frontera*; Weber, *Bárbaros*; Roulet, "Fronteras de papel," 2–3; Pérez Zavala and Tamagnini, "Dinámica territorial y poblacional," 196, 202; Mandrini, "Transformations"; Gándara, "Representaciones de un territorio," 68. These strategies were not universal, however, as military fortifications lined interethnic borderlands and shifting contexts sometimes generated more conflict than collaboration. Lucaioli, *Abipones en las fronteras*, 95–176, 227–99; Nesis, *Los grupos mocoví*, 87–97, 114–18; Buscaglia, "Indígenas, Borbones y enclaves coloniales," 10–13, 22–24; Salomón Tarquini and Casali, "Los pueblos indígenas," 24. Similar turns toward peaceful diplomacy and incorporation could be seen in other eighteenth-century Spanish American borderlands as well. Ávila, "Conquista, control y convicción"; Yaremko, "'Frontier Indians,'" 219; Vázquez Pino, "Los yndios infieles," 19; Morgan, "Funcionarios borbónicos," 141.

38. Herzog, "Naming, Identifying and Authorizing Movement," 194; Langfur, *Forbidden Lands*, 76–78; Roller, *Amazonian Routes*, 165–90; Ferreira Acruche, "De rebeldes," 153–59, 166.

39. *Diccionario de autoridades*, vol. 6; Moraes Silva, *Diccionario da lingua portugueza, recompilado*, 826.

40. AGNA, IX, 4-3-4, "Undated Letter to Viceroy." Other examples include AGNA, IX, 4-3-8 (Campamento de Chunireri, 1776-06-04 [x2], 1776-10-27; San Nicolás, 1776-04-01, 1776-04-04, 1776-04-09; San Borja, 1776-05-06).

41. AGNU, Ex AGA, caja 2, carpeta 24, no 2, f. 1; Levinton, *El espacio jesuítico-guaraní*, 112; AGI, Buenos Aires, 333, "Copia del informe sobre arreglo de campos," (Buenos Aires, 1785-08-04). For details on the midcentury campaigns, see chapter 2.

42. RAH, Mata Linares, t. 102, fs. 54–59v; AGPSF, Acta de Cabildo de 1713-12-30.

43. Acosta y Lara, *La guerra de los charrúas*, 1:77–153. If nearly all these expeditions were in response to "hostilities" by tolderías, most tolderías' raids were against newly founded ranches in tolderías' lands. AGNU, Ex AGA, caja 10, carpeta 2, nos. 1–2; RAH, Mata Linares, t. 11, fs. 38v–39; AGNU, Ex AGA, caja 229, carpeta 7, no. 57.

44. AGNA, IX, 2-9-7 (San Miguel, 1798-12-18); AGNA, IX, 18-2-4 (Yapeyú, 1798-08-17, 1799-09-17, 1799-10-17; Santo Tomé, 1799-07-20; San Borja, 1799-07-19; Salto Chico, 1798-08-29, 1798-09-26 [x2], 1798-10-13; Capilla Mandizoby, 1798-08-25); AGNA, IX, 4-3-4 (Montevideo, 1798-03-20). The blandengues of Montevideo modeled similar military orders that operated along Buenos Aires's southern frontier and in Santa Fe. Fradkin, "Las milicias de caballeria," 140–41; Alemano, "Los Blandengues de la Frontera," 64–69. For more on raids, see AGNA, IX, 21-2-5 (Buenos Aires, 1797-10-02, 1801-07-21).

45. AGNU, Manuscritos Originales Relativos a la Historia del Uruguay, 50-1-3, carpeta 10, no. 1, fs. 20–20v.

46. AGNU, Manuscritos Originales Relativos a la Historia del Uruguay, 50-1-3, carpeta 10, no. 1, f. 6; Lastarria, *Colonias orientales del Río Paraguay*, 51.

47. AGNU, Manuscritos Originales Relativos a la Historia del Uruguay, 50-1-3, carpeta 10, no. 1, , fs. 29–30, nos. 2–11; AGNA, IX, 10-6-1 (Concepción del Uruguay, 1799-11-12, 1800-03-24; Paysandú, 1800-04-23, 1800-11-14, 1801-01-03, 1801-01-17; Buenos Aires, 1800-10-04; Quartel General del Yacuy, 1801-03-21; Batoví chico, 1801-08-20); MM, Archivo Colonial, Arm. B, C28, P1, no. 3; MM, Archivo Colonial, Arm. B, C29, P1, no. 20; *Archivo Artigas*, 2:296, 300, 304–5; Bauzá, *Historia de la Dominación Española*, 2:337–53.

48. AGNA, IX, 37-8-5, exp. 1, fs. 20–23; Azara, *Memoria sobre el estato rural*, 19; Lastarria, *Colonias orientales del Río Paraguay*, 268. Pacheco's plan also stipulated four settlements, although he was only successful in founding Belén. Bauzá, *Historia de la Dominación Española*, 2:338; Mariluz Urquijo, *La expedición contra los charrúas*; Azpiroz Perera and Dávila Cuevas, "Indios 'Infieles' y 'Potreadores,'" 2–7.

49. ANHA, Enrique Fitte, III-75; AHRS, Autoridades Militares, Maço 1 (Acampamento do Santa Maria, 1801-11-29; Acampamento da Conceição, 1801-11-29).

50. Almeida, *O Diretório dos índios*, 149–226; Domingues, *Quando os índios eram vassalos*, 135–98; Roller, *Amazonian Routes*, 16–56; Langfur, *Forbidden Lands*, 60–67, 163–90; Karasch, "Catechism and Captivity"; Ferreira Acruche, "De rebeldes," 159. Divergent policies engendered divergent responses, as Indigenous leaders in Amazônia threatened to undermine the border as a means of extracting concessions from Portuguese authorities. Sampaio, "'Vossa Excelência mandará.'"

51. Poenitz, *Los infieles minuanes y charrúas*, 7–8. Payaguá and Mbayá traders along the Paraguay–Mato Grosso border developed similar trade relationships. Langavant, "La frontera del Alto Paraguay," 349–50.

52. ANB, 86, Secretário de Estado, cod. 104, v. 13, f. 68.

53. "Documentos relativos á incorporação do território," 56–57, 72; IHGB, Conselho Ultramarino, Arq. 1.2.19, fs. 257–60v, 261v; *Archivo Artigas*, 2:406; Acosta y Lara, *La guerra de los charrúas*, 1:213–40; Poenitz, *Los infieles minuanes y charrúas*, 13; Frühauf Garcia, *As diversas formas*, 251–52. For details on adjustment of the San Ildefonso line, see chapter 5.

54. AGNA, IX, 4-3-8 (San Nicolás, 1776-04-01, 1776-04-04, 1776-04-09, 1776-04-15; San Ignacio, 1776-04-08; Santo Tomé, 1776-05-02; San Borja, 1776-05-06; Campamento de Chunireri, 1776-06-04, 1776-10-27; San Miguel, 1776-07-04); "Autos principaes ao Conselho de Guerra," 124–25; Poenitz, *Los infieles minuanes y charrúas*, 3–5.

55. IHGB, Conselho Ultramarino, Arq. 1.2.19, fs. 252–52v, 286–88; AHU, Rio Grande (019), caixa 11, doc. 667; caixa 121, docs. 720 e 754; Frühauf Garcia, *As diversas formas*, 258–63.

56. BNB, 09,4,14, fs. 111v–19, 199–200, 500–503v; "Relatorio apresentado ao governo de Lisboa," 12.

57. "Autos principaes ao Conselho de Guerra," 124–25; Silva, "Rafael Pinto Bandeira"; Gil, "O contrabando na fronteira," 5.

58. "Officio do vice-rei Luiz de Vasconcellos," 46.

59. Alvear, "Diario," 2:343.

60. Saldanha, "Diário resumido," 236–37.

61. Gelman, *Campesinos y estancieros*, 102–35.

62. Azpiroz Perera and Dávila Cuevas, "Indios 'Infieles' y 'Potreadores'"; Alvear, "Diario," 2:343; AGI, Buenos Aires, 107 (Montevideo, 1789-03-05).

63. For more on individuals from tolderías in and around settlements, see chapter 5.

64. AGNA, IX, 4-3-1 (1757-05-18, 1757-06-09; Buenos Aires, 1757-05-02; Santo Domingo Soriano, 1757-07-01; Campo del Bloqueo, 1757-03-10, 1757-04-14, 1757-08-05); AGNA, IX, 4-3-2 (Campo del Bloqueo, 1758-02-27, 1758-04-01, 1758-09-10, 1758-11-06; Buenos Aires, 1760-08-09).

65. AGNU, Ex AGA, caja 11, carpeta 3, no. 1; AGNU, Ex AGA, caja 12, carpeta 7, no. 1; *Revista del Archivo General Administrativo*, 357–59, 390–93; Acosta y Lara, *La guerra de los charrúas*, 1:109–25; AGI, Buenos Aires, 214 (Arroyo de Pintado, 1770-04-11; Montevideo, 1770-05-14).

66. For Moreira and Salteinho, see AGNA, IX, 23-2-6 (1775-05-26, 1775-08-19); *Revista del Archivo General Administrativo*, 357–59, 390–93; Saldanha, "Diário resumido," 234–35; Acosta y Lara, *La guerra de los charrúas*, 1:111–12. For Ignacio, see AGNA, IX, 36-2-6, exp. 38 (Candelaria, 1794-03-24, 1794-04-25, 1794-05-23); Poenitz, *Los infieles minuanes y charrúas*, 9–11; AGNA, IX, 10-6-1 (Rio Queguay, 1800-05-28).

67. AGNA, IX, 24-2-6, exp. 27; AGNA, IX, 36-2-6 (Candelaria, 1794-03-24, 1794-04-25, 1794-05-23); AGNA, IX, 10-6-1 (Batoví chico, 1801-08-20); Poenitz, *Los infieles minuanes y charrúas*, 9–11; Cabrera Pérez, "La incorporación del indígena," 16.

68. AGNA, IX, 10-6-1 (Arroyo de la Virgen, 1797-12-27); IHGB, Conselho Ultramarino, Arq. 1.3.7, fs. 273–80v, 289–89v, 327–31v; Poenitz, *Los infieles minuanes y charrúas*, 6–8; Azpiroz Perera and Dávila Cuevas, "Indios 'Infieles' y 'Potreadores,'" 6.

69. AGNA, IX, 4-3-1 (Campo del Bloqueo, 1757-04-26, 1757-05-02); AGNA, IX, 1-3-5 (Guardia de Melo, 1796-02-12).

70. *Archivo Artigas*, 2:396; Frühauf Garcia, *As diversas formas*, 253–54.

71. AGNA, IX, 10-6-1 (Concepción del Uruguay, 1799-10-13).

72. AGNA, IX, 23-2-6 (1775-05-26, 1775-06-17, 1775-08-19, 1775-10-20, 1775-11-15); AGNA, IX, 4-3-8 (San Nicolás, 1776-04-01, 1776-04-04, 1776-04-09, 1776-04-15; San Ignacio, 1776-04-08; Santo Tomé, 1776-05-02; San Borja, 1776-05-06; Campamento de Chunireri, 1776-10-27, 1776-06-04; San Miguel, 1776-07-04).

73. AGNA, IX, 4-3-8 (Campamento de Chunireri, 1776-06-04); AGNA, IX, 23-2-6 (1778-02-09).

74. "Autos principaes ao Conselho de Guerra," 124–25. In addition to sharing a name with the cacique, Miguel Antonio de Ayala frequently served as an intermediary between Caraí and Santa Tecla and provided regular gifts to Minuán tolderías. It is possible that he was the cacique's father. AGNA, IX, 17-4-6 (1776-04-09); AGNA, IX, 23-2-6 (1775-10-20, 1776-04-08); AGNA, IX, 4-3-8 (San Nicolás, 1776-04-01, 1776-04-09); Levinton, *El espacio jesuítico-guaraní*, 110.

75. In Guaraní, *karai* means, among other things, "Lord," "Spanish," "white," or "baptized." The rough antonym of the word would be *ava*, which means "savage" or "unconverted Indian." The word *karai* was also used as a title for Bartolomeo in his letter to Pinto Bandeira.

76. AGNA, IX 4-3-8 (San Nicolás, 1776-04-01, 1776-04-04, 1776-04-09); ANB, 86, Secretário de Estado, cod. 104, v. 8, fs. 101–2v, 204–7; ANB, 86, Secretário de Estado, cod. 104, v. 9, fs. 87–87v; Alvear, "Diario," 2:343; Porto, *História das Missões Orientais*, 3:70–71; Frühauf Garcia, "Quando os índios escolhem," 628–29. For similar cases of mestizos occupying positions of authority within Native polities, see Sidbury and Cañizares-Esguerra, "Mapping Ethnogenesis," 192–93.

77. Mariluz Urquijo, "Los guaraníes después de la expulsión"; Wilde, "Los guaraníes después de la expulsion," 102; Ganson, *Guaraní under Spanish Rule,* 117–63; Jackson, "Post-Jesuit Expulsion Population"; Frühauf Garcia, *As diversas formas,* 125–71; Sarreal, *Guaraní and Their Missions,* 156–57. Although most outward migration from the missions occurred after 1767, the trend began during the crisis over the Siete Pueblos. Garcia, *Anais da Biblioteca Nacional,* 52:147, 203, 207–8; AGNA, IX, 3-3-3 (Salto, 1758-01-13, 1758-09-25, 1758-09-30); AGNU, Ex AGA, caja 10, carpeta 2, no. 1, fs. 1–2; Di Stefano and Zanatta, *Historia de la iglesia argentina,* 125–27.

78. AGNA, IX, 4-3-2 (Campo del Bloqueo, 1758-04-26); AGNA, IX, 17-7-2 (San Luis, 1785-05-11); AGI, Buenos Aires, 70 (Buenos Aires, 1785-06-08); IHGB, Conselho Ultramarino, Arq. 1.3.7, fs. 276v, 278–79v; Wilde, "Orden y ambigüedad," 112–17. Similar efforts occurred on Buenos Aires's southern frontier, where settlers voluntarily living among tolderías faced the death penalty. Lastarria, *Documentos para la historia del Virreinato,* 304–5.

79. AGNA, IX, 17-7-2 (San Nicolás, 1785-04-13); Wilde, "Guaraníes, 'gauchos' e 'indios infieles,'" 105, 107.

80. Borucki, *From Shipmates to Soldiers,* 10.

81. AGNA, IX, 4-3-1 (Santo Domingo Soriano, 1750-01-16); AGNA, IX, 2-1-4 (Montevideo, 1750-12-30); Azara, *Descripción é historia,* 1:145, 160–61; Lastarria, *Colonias orientales del Río Paraguay,* 200; Verdesio, *Forgotten Conquests,* 99–107; Bracco, *Charrúas, guenoas y guaraníes,* 270.

82. For relationships between ethnogenesis and preexistent cultural ties, see Mandrini and Ortelli, "Repensando viejos problemas," 142–43; Boccara, *Los vencedores*; Ethridge, "Introduction," 40–42; Saunt, "The Indians' Old World." For tribalization and the connections between ethnogenesis and ethnocide in contexts of violence, see Ferguson and Whitehead, "Violent Edge of Empire," 12–16; Chappell, "Ethnogenesis and Frontiers," 271–72; Whitehead, "Ethnogenesis and Ethnocide," 21, 34–35; Monteiro, "Tupis, tapuias e historiadores,'" 53–78; Hämäläinen, "Lost in Transitions"; Griffin, "Plea for a New Atlantic History," 237; Vázquez Pino, "Los yndios infieles," 17–18. For incongruences between Native self-identification, imperial ethnic classifications, and territoriality, see Nacuzzi, *Identidades impuestas*; Ortelli, *Trama de una guerra conveniente*; Giudicelli, "Encasillar la frontera"; Pérez Zavala and Tamagnini, "Dinámica territorial y poblacional," 204–5; Roulet, *Huincas en tierras de indios*; Giudicelli, *Luchas de clasificación,* 11–12, 19–104; Erbig and Latini, "Across Archival Limits."

83. Similar realignments occurred throughout the Americas at this time. Weber, *Bárbaros,* 78; Sidbury and Cañizares-Esguerra, "Mapping Ethnogenesis," 193–94.

84. Oyarvide, "Memoria geográfica," 8:212; *Revista del Archivo General Administrativo,* 357.

85. Sarreal, *Guaraní and Their Missions,* 192–216; AGNA, IX, 10-6-1 (Arroyo de la Virgen, 1797-12-27).

86. AGNA, IX, 22-8-2, exp. 3, f. 13.

87. ANB, 86, Secretário de Estado, cod. 104, v. 9, fs. 22–23.

88. AGNA, IX, 4-3-8 (Campamento de Chunireri, 1776-06-04; San Borja, 1776-05-06); "Autos principaes ao Conselho de Guerra" 174–77; "Documentos relativos á incorporação do território," 71–74; IHGB, Conselho Ultramarino, Arq. 1.2.19, fs. 286–88; Poenitz, *Los infieles minuanes y charrúas,* 5–7.

Chapter Five

1. Acosta y Lara, *La guerra de los charrúas*, 2:73 (Document U1).

2. Acosta y Lara, *La guerra de los charrúas*, 2:51–72, 78, 101, 105–6 (Documents G1-S1, Z1, N, S); Curel, *Reseña sobre la tribu*, 46. For a summary of research on the Charrúas sent to Paris, see Arce Asenjo, "Nuevos datos sobre el destino." At least five Charrúa men were banished to the Malvinas (Falkland) Islands, where they participated in an uprising against British officials in August 1834. *El episodio ocurrido en Puerto de la Soledad*, 37, 81, 84, 135, 145, 168.

3. Answers to the first question have emphasized imperial military might, the outbreak of pathogens, acculturation via mestizaje, and declining reproductive capacity; answers to the second have examined administrative strategies for incorporating Indigenous captives and captives' struggles to integrate into Spanish colonial society. Bauzá, *Historia de la Dominación Española*, vol. 2; Vidal, *La leyenda de la destrucción*; Acosta y Lara, *La guerra de los charrúas*, vol. 2, pt. 2; Basile Becker, *Os índios charrua e minuano*, 231–37; Padrón Favre, *Los Charrúas-Minuanes*, 60–79; Cabrera Pérez and Messano, "El ocaso del mundo indígena"; Klein, "El destino," 7; Consens, *Extinción de los indígenas*; Laroque, "Os nativos charrua/minuano," 20–1; Garcia and Milder, "Convergências e divergências," 45; Houot, *El trágico fin*, 13–16; Bracco, *Con las armas en la mano*, 150–75.

4. José de Herrera y Sotomayor, "Expediente iniciado el 28 de abril de 1690," transcribed in Lucaioli and Latini, "Fronteras permeables," 124; Sallaberry, *Los charrúas y Santa Fe*, 132–49; Areces, López, and Regis, "Relaciones interétnicas en Santa Fe"; Bracco, *Cautivas entre indígenas y gauchos*, 24–25. Imperial prohibitions on Indigenous slavery, tributary labor grants, and captive taking included the Leyes Nuevas (1542); the Ordenanzas de Alfaro (1612), which Hapsburg King Felipe III decreed in 1618; and the Recopilación de Leyes de las Indias (1680). Mirow, *Latin American Law*, 85–91. A 1737 Real Cédula also prohibited the enslavement of Indigenous captives, with the exception of those believed to practice cannibalism and who therefore were not protected by natural law. Aguirre, "Cambiando de perspectiva," 3–4. The Portuguese crown placed legal restrictions on Indigenous slavery in 1570, 1609, 1680, and 1728, but the practice nonetheless persisted in Brazil until at least 1758. Stuart Schwartz, *Sugar Plantations*, 53; Nazzari, "Transition," 138, 152–53; Monteiro, *Negros da terra*, 41–42; Francisco Ribeiro da Silva, "A legislação seiscentista portuguesa," 16–21.

5. AGNA, IX, 41-3-8, exp. 1.

6. Acosta y Lara, *La guerra de los charrúas*, 1:42, 46, 47–48; RAH, Mata Linares, t. 101, fs. 239–40; Cortesão, *Tratado de Madri*, 116, 144–45, 311, 321–22; AGNA, VII, Colección Segurola. Reales Órdenes y Cédulas, libro 181, doc. 938 (Madrid, 1706-11-26); AGI, Buenos Aires, 235, fs. 12, 31v, 50v–51, 70v, 89v, 108, 130–30v, 150v, 172, 191, 214v, 239v, 259v, 276v, 296, 320–20v, 345v, 371v–72, 385v, 405v–406, 429v; Trelles, "Vandalismo misionero," 22–25; Vianna, *Jesuítas e Bandeirantes no Uruguai*, 231, 235–43; Porto, *História das Missões Orientais*, 4:39–48; Latini, "Relatos del conflicto interétnico."

7. AGPSF, Actas de Cabildo de 1750-01-14, 1750-02-03, 1750-11-03, 1752-01-19; AGNA, IX, 4-3-1 (Campo del Bloqueo, 1749-10-29); AGNU, Falcao Espalter, 1:46–48, 88–89, 110–15, 184–87; AGNU, Falcao Espalter, 4:229.

8. AGNA, IX, 4-3-1 (Las Vívoras, 1746-07-02); MM, Archivo Colonial, Arm. B, C28, P1, no. 3, f. 3; AGNU, Falcao Espalter, 1:112; AGNU, Falcao Espalter, 4:229.

9. AGI, Buenos Aires, 70 (Buenos Aires, 1785-06-08). For details on these campaigns, see chapter 4.

10. *Malones* in other areas of the Río de la Plata, and the subsequent sale or return of captives, have been studied in terms of ritual, reproduction, tribute, and pact making. Mayo, "El cautiverio y sus funciones"; Socolow, "Los cautivos españoles"; Villar and Jiménez, "'Para servirse de ellos'"; Boccara, *Los vencedores*; Operé, *Indian Captivity in Spanish America*; Mandrini, "Transformations"; Lucaioli and Latini, "Fronteras permeables," 125–26.

11. AGNA, IX, 4-3-1 (Santo Domingo Soriano, 1750-01-16).

12. AGNA, IX, 10-6-1 (Arroyo de la Virgen, 1797-12-27).

13. AGNA, IX, 4-3-1 (Las Vívoras, 1750-11-09); AGNA, IX, 2-1-4, f. 794 (Montevideo, 1751-11-13); AGI, Buenos Aires, 536 (Buenos Aires, 1759-07-02).

14. AGI, Charcas, 373, f. 2.

15. For mission ranches in tolderías' lands, see chapter 4. For raids in Texas and northern Mexico, see DeLay, *War of a Thousand Deserts*.

16. Susana Aguirre, "Cambiando de perspectiva," 8–9.

17. AGPSF, Acta de Cabildo de 1752-01-19.

18. AGNA, IX, 21-2-5 (Buenos Aires, 1801-07-21).

19. Recent scholarship connecting Indigenous captivity with imperial efforts at territorial removal includes Susana Aguirre, "Cambiando de perspectiva," 2–3; Bracco and López Mazz, *Charrúas, pampas y serranos, chanáes*, 7–9; Babcock, "Rethinking the Establecimientos"; Conrad, "Captive Fates"; Cramaussel, "Forced Transfer of Indians," 186–87; Karasch, "Catechism and Captivity," 198–210. Other scholars have demonstrated the ubiquity of Native slavery with European imperialism in the Americas, and current estimates suggest that between two and five million Indigenous Americans were enslaved from the sixteenth through the nineteenth centuries. Rushforth, *Bonds of Alliance*, 9; Reséndez, *Other Slavery*, 5–6; Bialuschewski and Fisher, "New Directions," 2. Indigenous enslavement reached all corners of the Americas, albeit with regional idiosyncrasies, and Native captives were frequently deracinated and shipped to distant places, often overseas or across empires. Monteiro, *Negros da terra*; Maria Beatriz Nizza da Silva, *Brasil*, 15–56; Domingues, *Quando os índios eram vassalos*, 25–62; Sousa, "Mão-de-obra indígena na Amazônia Colonial"; Sommer, "Colony of the Sertão"; Brooks, *Captives and Cousins*; Barr, "From Captives to Slaves"; Gallay, *Indian Slavery in Colonial America*; Ethridge, "Introduction," 10–26; Van Deusen, *Global Indios*; Weaver, *Red Atlantic*, 35–85; Yaremko, "'Frontier Indians,'" 222–32; Offen, "Mapping Amerindian Captivity"; Lipman, *Saltwater Frontier*, 217–22; Miles, *Dawn of Detroit*.

20. Borucki, "Slave Trade to the Río de la Plata"; Rosal, "El tráfico de esclavos."

21. Susana Aguirre, "Cambiando de perspectiva," 6.

22. AGNU, Manuscritos Originales Relativos a la Historia del Uruguay, 50-1-3, carpeta 10, no. 1, fs. 29–29v.

23. AGNA, IX, 18-2-4 (Yapeyú, 1798-08-15, 1798-08-17; Capilla de Mandizoby, 1798-08-25; Salto Chico del Uruguay, 1798-08-29, 1798-09-26, 1798-10-13; Buenos Aires, 1798-09-06, 1798-08-16); AGNA, IX, 10-6-1 (Puerto de S. José, 1797-09-26; Cuchilla de Tacuarembó, 1797-10-14; Buenos Aires, 1797-10-02); Lastarria, *Colonias orientales del Río Paraguay*, 273–74. For more on the Casa de la Reclusión, see Pérez Baltasar, "Orígenes de los recogimientos," 20–21; Susana Aguirre, "Cambiando de perspectiva," 5–8.

24. *Telégrafo Mercantil*, 6:85–86 (115–16). See also AGNA, IX, 21-2-5 (Buenos Aires, 1801-07-21); AGNA, IX, 9-2-9, transcribed in Cabrera Pérez, "La incorporación del indígena," 10.

25. AGNA, IX, 39-8-8, exp. 13; AGNA, IX, 4-3-3 (Campo de las Vacas, 1761-06-02); AGNA, IX, 2-1-4 (Montevideo, 1751-05-19, 1751-07-11); AGNU, Falcao Espalter, 1:187–88; Susana Aguirre, "Cambiando de perspectiva," 10.

26. AGNU, Falcao Espalter, 1:188; AGNU, Ex AGA, caja 37, carpeta 6, no. 6 (Buenos Aires, 1774-09-22); Alemano, "La prisón de Toroñan."

27. AGPSF, Acta de Cabildo de 1756-04-10; Sallaberry, *Los charrúas y Santa Fe*, 266–78. For more on *genízaros*, see Brooks, "'We Betray Our Own Nation,'" 322, 324, 326, 331, 337.

28. AGPSF, Actas de Cabildo de 1750-09-25, 1750-11-09, 1755-09-09; RAH, Mata Linares, t. 102, f. 402v. Other missions in the Chaco also had walled exteriors as protection from raids. Saeger, "Jesuit Missions (Reducciones)," 630.

29. AGNA, IX, 7-2-1 (Buenos Aires, 1782-05-21, 1792-01-13); AGNA, IX, 37-5-3 (Pueblo de la Concepción, 1790-06-30; Santa Fe, 1790-10-19; Cayastá, 1793-04-29).

30. Messano, "Padrones y archivos parroquiales."

31. For more on the boundary commissions' ethnographic accounts, see chapter 3.

32. Wilde, "Indios misionados"; Lucaioli, *Abipones en las fronteras*, 107–21; Nesis, *Los grupos mocoví*, 89–97.

33. "Argentina, Capital Federal, registros parroquiales, 1737–1977," index and images, FHL microfilm 611,230, FamilySearch; "Argentina, Capital Federal, registros parroquiales, 1737–1977," index and images, FHL microfilm 1,102,295, FamilySearch; "Argentina, Capital Federal, registros parroquiales, 1737–1977," index and images, FHL microfilm 1,096,676, FamilySearch; "Argentina, Capital Federal, registros parroquiales, 1737–1977," index and images, FHL microfilm 611,230, FamilySearch; Susana Aguirre, "Cambiando de perspectiva," 5.

34. AGPSF, Actas de Cabildo de 1772-04-11, 1779-03-27, 1802-04-10; Sallaberry, *Los charrúas y Santa Fe*, 249.

35. Baptismal, marriage, and death records of many Indigenous captives, slaves, and freedpeople in Colônia were separated by record keepers, and have largely been omitted from recent transcriptions. Some cases have nonetheless appeared. Buys de Barros, *Colônia do Sacramento*, 1:26, 31, 35–36, 345; 2:324–25, 339, 359, 367.

36. "Brasil, Rio Grande do Sul, Registros da Igreja Católica, 1738–1952," images, FamilySearch. A partial transcription is available in López Mazz and Bracco, *Minuanos*, 146–51. See also "Registro de atos oficiais," 235–36; Hameister, "'No princípio era o caos,'" 110–15.

37. UFRGS, Centro de Documentação Histórica, Microfilme 16, cited in López Israel, "As relações de fronteira," 53, 62; AGI, Charcas, 384, "Petición del Procurador de la Compañía de Jesús, padre Juan José Rico (n/d), pero visto en consejo (1743-10-17)"; Porto, *História das Missões Orientais*, 4:44.

38. Messano, "Padrones y archivos parroquiales," 100.

39. Apolant, *Génesis de la familia uruguaya*, 176–78, 351–52, 384, 369, 387, 406, 467–71, 480, 512–13, 534, 609–11, 630–31, 661–62, 802.

40. Apolant, *Génesis de la familia uruguaya*, 176–78, 369, 609–11, 512–13.

41. Apolant, *Padrones olvidados de Montevideo*, 117.

42. *Revista del Archivo General Administrativo*, 392.

43. AGNU, Archivos Judiciales, civil 1, caja 26, no. 43; AGI, Buenos Aires, 107 (Montevideo, 1789-03-05).

44. AGNA, IX, 4-3-2 (Campo del Bloqueo, 1758-12-05).

45. Apolant, *Génesis de la familia uruguaya*, 630–31.

46. AGNU, Archivos Judiciales, civil 1, caja 28, no. 31. This may have been the same woman—Juana de Rivas—who had gained autonomy from the man to whom she was entrusted upon captivity. Apolant, *Génesis de la familia uruguaya*, 176–78, 369, 609–11.

47. AGNA, IX, 7-2-1 (Buenos Aires, 1782-05-21); AGNA, IX, 37-5-3, fs. 1–28v, 36–36v; AG-PSF, Acta de Cabildo de 1790-10-05.

48. AGI, Buenos Aires, 540, fs. 24–27v, 66v–67, 88v; Saldanha, "Diário resumido," 187.

49. AGI, Buenos Aires, 542 (Santa Teresa, 1778-01-22; Buenos Aires, 1778-01-29).

50. Metcalf, *Go-Betweens*; Yannakakis, *Art of Being In-Between*. While the concept of a "go-between" can apply to a wide variety of actors, the focus here is on Native intermediaries. For examples of Indigenous guides and translators, see chapter 1.

51. Leite, *História da Companhia de Jesús*, 6:528–29. Ladino may have arrived in Rio Grande and been baptized earlier that year. Hameister, "Para dar calor," 284–85.

52. Cortesão, *Antecedentes do Tratado de Madri*, 164–71, 247–48.

53. AGNU, Manuscritos Originales Relativos a la Historia del Uruguay, 50-1-3, carpeta 10, no. 1, f. 19.

54. AGNU, Manuscritos Originales Relativos a la Historia del Uruguay, 50-1-3, carpeta 10, no. 1, fs. 34–34v.

55. AGNU, Manuscritos Originales Relativos a la Historia del Uruguay, 50-1-3, carpeta 10, no. 1, fs. 19, 34–34v, 38, 42–43v, 45; Acosta y Lara, *La guerra de los charrúas*, 1:163.

56. "The Paraguayan language" here referred to Guaraní. Sepp von Rechegg, *Viagem às Missões Jesuíticas*, 105; Vianna, *Jesuítas e Bandeirantes no Uruguai*, 230; AGPSF, Acta de Cabildo de 1715-12-07; Poenitz, *Los infieles minuanes y charrúas*, 9; AGNA, IX, 10-6-1 (Batoví Chico, 1801-08-20); Barrios Pintos, "Caciques Charrúas en Territorio Oriental," 88.

57. Frühauf Garcia, "Quando os índios escolhem," 628–29. In other regions, such as the Pampas and Patagonia, tolderías sometimes had multiple caciques, each of whom held a different function—caciques of war, caciques of peace, and ceremonial caciques. Nacuzzi, "Repensando y revisando el concepto," 77–78.

58. *Revista del Archivo General Administrativo*, 391.

59. Apolant, *Génesis de la familia uruguaya*, 406; *Revista del Archivo General Administrativo*, 289, 293; Acosta y Lara, *La guerra de los charrúas*, 1:112.

60. AGNU, Ex AGA, caja 14, carpetas 3 and 4.

61. Colaboradores de Wikisource, "Tratado de Badajoz (1801)." In most of South America, the San Ildefonso line was reaffirmed, and Ibero-American officials treated the 1777 accord as operative in subsequent diplomatic correspondence. Portugal and France adjusted their border in northern South America via Article 4 of the Treaty of Madrid, which they signed in September 1801. "Tratado de paz," 431.

62. Segarra, *Frontera y límites*, 22; Golin, *A Fronteira*, 227–37, 249–58.

63. "Documentos relativos á incorporação do território," 72.

64. Portuguese diplomats employed a similar strategy with regard to the missions, claiming that Guaraní residents of the Siete Pueblos had greeted them as liberators. "Documentos relativos á incorporação do território," 71; Segarra, *Frontera y límites*, 22; Frühauf Garcia, *As diversas formas*, 201–2.

65. Quesada, *La política del Brasil*, 29–65; Segarra, *Frontera y límites*, 22; Pérez Martínez, "Los límites del Estado Oriental," 305; Golin, *A Fronteira*, 233, 249–53.

66. *Archivo Artigas*, 3:471–72; Frühauf Garcia, *As diversas formas*, 254–58.

67. Disputes over Spanish breaches of the agreed-upon line occurred in 1783, 1785, and 1792. ANB, 86, Secretário de Estado, cod. 104, v. 5, fs. 170–70v; ANB, D9, Vice-Reinado, caixa 749, pac. 1 (Rio Grande, 1792-06-02); BNB, 09,4,14, fs. 111v–119, 508v.

68. IHGB, Conselho Ultramarino, Arq. 1.2.19, fs. 63–63v.

69. IHGB, Conselho Ultramarino, Arq. 1.2.19, fs. 255v–56.

70. AHU, Brasil Limites (059), caixa 4, doc. 272; AHU, Rio de Janeiro (017), caixa 208, doc. 14559; ANB, 86, Secretário de Estado, cod. 104, v. 13, fs. 151–52, 155; IHGB, Conselho Ultramarino, Arq. 1.2.19, fs. 65v–66, 208–9v, 237, 258–59v, 261v.

71. IHGB, Conselho Ultramarino, Arq. 1.2.19, fs. 240v–41.

72. IHGB, Conselho Ultramarino, Arq. 1.2.19, fs. 65v–66v, 247–48; IHGB, Conselho Ultramarino, Arq. 1.3.7, fs. 158–62.

73. IHGB, Conselho Ultramarino, Arq. 1.3.7, fs. 273–79v, 289–89v, 292–95, 327–31v, 365–74. Portuguese prisoners denied toldería involvement with the vaquería yet affirmed that the tolderías were trading partners. *Archivo Artigas*, 2:281–324.

74. IHGB, Conselho Ultramarino, Arq. 1.2.19, f. 263v.

75. IHGB, Conselho Ultramarino, Arq. 1.2.19, fs. 265–65v.

76. See, for example, the actions of the Spanish governor of Buenos Aires after the death of Jesuit Manuel González in 1703, discussed in chapter 2.

77. IHGB, Conselho Ultramarino, Arq. 1.2.19, fs. 265–65v, 270–70v; IHGB, Conselho Ultramarino, Arq. 1.3.7, fs. 271–72.

78. IHGB, Conselho Ultramarino, Arq. 1.2.19, fs. 252–53, 268v–71, 286–88. For more on the pacts between tolderías and Portuguese authorities in Porto Alegre, see Frühauf Garcia, *As diversas formas*, 258–63; Golin, *A Fronteira*, 219, 254–55.

79. *Archivo Artigas*, 2:281–324, esp. 305–6, 310.

80. AGNA, IX, 10-6-1 (Tacuarembó Chico, 1806-01-20, 1806-02-01, 1806-03-28; Buenos Aires, 1806-03-15, 1806-04-12; Pontos de Nhandei, 1806-02-25; Chacra, 1806-02-17; Campamento en el Ibirapuita-guazú, 1806-04-24); IHGB, Conselho Ultramarino, Arq. 1.2.19, fs. 241v–44v, 267–86v; IHGB, Conselho Ultramarino, Arq. 1.3.7, fs. 156–57, 159–62; Acosta y Lara, *La guerra de los charrúas*, 1:222; Frühauf Garcia, *As diversas formas*, 254–58.

81. AGNA, IX, 18-3-7 (Belén, 1807-07-29), cited in Wilde, "Guaraníes, 'gauchos' e 'indios infieles,'" 115. Spanish military endeavors along Buenos Aires's southern frontier were likewise diverted by the British invasions. Pérez Zavala and Tamagnini, "Dinámica territorial y poblacional," 217.

82. IHGB, Conselho Ultramarino, Arq. 1.3.7, fs. 205, 210, 366; ANB, D9, Vice-Reinado, caixa 749, pac. 1 (Porto Alegre, 1805-04-10, 1805-10-10, 1805-10-21; Rio Grande, 1801-11-08); ANB, 86, Secretário de Estado, cod. 104, v. 12, fs. 98–109; IHGB, Conselho Ultramarino, Arq. 1.2.19, 1.2.19, fs. 212–45v; Mones and Klappenbach, *Un ilustrado aragonés*; Bertocchi Moran, "El piloto Andrés de Oyarvide"; Zweifel, "De Palas a Minerva," 309–16.

83. For connections between Iberian sovereignty, the Napoleonic Wars, and American independence, see Guerra, "La desintegración de la monarquía"; Adelman, *Sovereignty and Revolution*; Paquette, *Imperial Portugal*.

84. Rao, "Arbiters of Change"; Frega, "Los 'infelices'"; Kühn, "Una frontera en convulsión."

85. Segarra, *Frontera y límites*, 22–25; Castellanos, *La Cisplatina*, 9, 17, 81.

86. Mandisoví was a town along the western shoreline of the Río Uruguay from which rival forces sought to control movement up and down the river. *Archivo Artigas*, 6:30, 188, 206–7, 390–91, 523–25; *Archivo Artigas*, 7:260; *Archivo Artigas*, 11:361–62, 388–89, 411; *Archivo Artigas*, 13:249, 255; *Archivo Artigas*, 17:151–52, 306–8, 336, 397; *Archivo Artigas*, 18:162–66; *Archivo Artigas*, 19:160–67, 256; *Archivo Artigas*, 31:66, 80–84, 116–20, 264–66; *Archivo Artigas*, 33:9–10, 14–19; *Archivo Artigas*, 36:294–95; Acosta y Lara, *La guerra de los charrúas*, 2:2:3, 5–6, 8, 19–21, 57; Padrón Favre, *Los Charrúas-Minuanes*, 38.

87. *Archivo Artigas*, 6:320–21, 390–91, 446–48, 471–76; *Archivo Artigas*, 7:280–81, 285–88; *Archivo Artigas*, 8:280–81; *Archivo Artigas*, 10:26–28, 194–95; *Archivo Artigas*, 12:276–77; *Archivo Artigas*, 13:147, 238, 255; *Archivo Artigas*, 14:194–95; *Archivo Artigas*, 18:5–7, 27–29, 32–33, 86–87; *Archivo Artigas*, 33:7; *Archivo Artigas*, 36:294–95, 308–9, 322–23, 330–32. See also Acosta y Lara, *La guerra de los charrúas*, 2:2:57; Padrón Favre, *Los Charrúas-Minuanes*, 81–130, 157–58; Frega, "Los 'infelices,'" 172–73.

88. Acosta y Lara, *La guerra de los charrúas*, 1:164–66. The cacique most closely associated with Artigas in historical texts was Manuel Artigas, "El Caciquillo." It is possible that this was the same "Caciquillo" who had moved his tolderías to San Borja in 1794. AGNA, IX, 36-2-6, exp. 38 (Candelaría, 1794-03-24, 1794-04-25, 1794-05-23); Poenitz, *Los infieles minuanes y charrúas*, 9–10.

89. Larrañaga, *Selección de escritos*, 28–30; *Archivo Artigas*, 11:289, 340–43; *Archivo Artigas*, 20:201.

90. *Archivo Artigas*, 6:390–91, 426–28; *Archivo Artigas*, 10:13–14.

91. *Archivo Artigas*, 7:384–85; *Archivo Artigas*, 8:280–83; *Archivo Artigas*, 10:18–19, 26–28, 32–36, 194–95; Barrios Pintos, "Caciques Charrúas en Territorio Oriental," 88; Padrón Favre, *Los Charrúas-Minuanes*, 40.

92. *Archivo Artigas*, 11:300–302; *Archivo Artigas*, 23:462; *Archivo Artigas*, 28:158; *Archivo Artigas*, 34:333 (57).

93. *Archivo Artigas*, 21:93–96. See also Frega, "El Reglamento de Tierras," 506–12.

94. Colaboradores de Wikisource, "Reglamento de Artigas"; *Archivo Artigas*, 20:32–33; *Archivo Artigas*, 31:116–20; *Archivo Artigas*, 33:21, 286.

95. *Archivo Artigas*, 18:256.

96. *Archivo Artigas*, 36:308–9, 322–23; Rao, "Arbiters of Change," 540–43; Frega, "Los 'infelices,'" 172.

97. AGNU, Ministrio de Gobierno, caja 805, fs. 403–4; AGNU, Ministrio de Gobierno, caja 807, f. 428; Padrón Favre, *Los Charrúas-Minuanes*, 43–60; Acosta y Lara, *La guerra de los charrúas*, 2:81–113, 151–53.

98. Acosta y Lara, *La guerra de los charrúas*, 2:74–75 (Documents W1 and X1).

99. Acosta y Lara, *La guerra de los charrúas*, 2:73, 77–78, 107–8 (Documents V1, Z1, X).

100. Acosta y Lara, *La guerra de los charrúas*, 2:72–73 (Document T1).

101. "Uruguay, bautismos, 1750–1900," index, FHL microfilm 625,269, FamilySearch; "Uruguay, bautismos, 1750–1900," index, FHL microfilm 625,479, FamilySearch.

102. *Archivo Artigas*, 26:383; Curel, *Reseña sobre la tribu*, 39.

Conclusion

1. Candido Baptista de Oliveira, *Reconhecimento topográphico*, 7.
2. Candido Baptista de Oliveira, *Reconhecimento topográphico*, 12–13.
3. Candido Baptista de Oliveira, *Reconhecimento topográphico*, 20–25; José Joaquim Machado de Oliveira, *Memória histórica sobre a questão*.
4. National territorial narratives include: Sota, *Historia del Territorio Oriental*, vols. 1–2; Funes, *Ensayo de la historia civil de Buenos Aires* vols. 1–2; Bauzá, *Historia de la Dominación Española*, vols. 1–2; Trelles, "Degollacion de Charruas"; Luis Alberto de Herrera, *La tierra charrúa*, 32–35. Notable colonial-era ethnographies published at this time include Hervás, *Saggio pratico delle lingue*, 85, 228; Doblas, "Memoria histórica"; Azara, *Viajes por la América del Sur*; Saldanha, "Diário resumido"; Charlevoix, *Historia del Paraguay*. Nineteenth-century travelers, many of whom drew on Azara's work, included d'Orbigny, *El Hombre Americano*, 32, 38, 80–81, 276–80; Saint-Hilaire, *Voyage a Rio-Grande do Sul*, 248–49, 277–78; Curel, *Reseña sobre la tribu*; Isabelle, *Voyage a Buénos-Ayres*, 98, 107–10, 303, 315, 369–71; Dreys, *Notícia descriptiva*, 182–83, 191–92; John Hale Murray, *Travels in Uruguay, South America*, 65–66.
5. Most notable among these works was José Figueira's presentation at the 1892 Exposición Histórica-Americana in Madrid, which celebrated the four hundredth anniversary of Columbus's arrival to the Americas. José H. Figueira, "Los primitivos habitantes." Earlier ethnographic efforts include Díaz, *Apuntos varios sobre los indios*; Vilardebó, *Noticias sobre los charrúas*; Ameghino, *La antigüedad del hombre*, 254, 257–260; José Joaquín Figueira, *Contribución al estudio*, 33–40.
6. The idea of a "macro-etnia guenoa" appeared in such texts as Southey, *História do Brazil*, 531; Porto, *História das Missões Orientais*, 3:66–67. The idea of a "macro-etnia charrúa" permeated Argentine scholarship as well and appeared in such texts as Lafone Quevado, "Los indios chanases y su lengua"; Serrano, "Filiação Linguística Serrana"; Imbelloni, "Lenguas indígenas del territorio argentino," 60, 75; Vidart, *El mundo de los Charrúas*, 16–17. Other scholars subsumed both groups into broader categorizations of "Guaraní," "Guaycurús," or "Pampas." For more on the relationship between national imaginaries and the ascription of ethnonyms, see Basini Rodríguez, "Índios num país sem índios," 96, 363, 376.
7. Oliveira de Freitas, *A invasão de São Borja*, 14–15; Sosa, *La nación charrúa*, 53; Pi Hugarte, *Los indios de Uruguay*, 13–14; Penino and Sollazzo, "El paradero charrúa del Puerto," 153–55; Luis Alberto de Herrera, *La tierra charrúa*, 35; Cordero, *Los charrúas*, 11; Vidart, "Prólogo," 11, 18. Other examples include Quesada, *Los indios en las Provincias*, 41–45; Otero, *La orden franciscana en el Uruguay*, 2–6, 10–13, 47–48; Fortes, *Rio Grande de São Pedro*, 9–24, 35; Azarola Gil, *Los Orígenes de Montevideo*, 29–30, 123–33; Leite, *História da Companhia de Jesús*, 6:453, 493–97, 525–26, 528–30; Pivel Devoto, *Raíces coloniales de la Revolución*, 50, 59, 66, 81; Mariluz Urquijo, *El Virreinato del Río de la Plata*, 363–436; Vellinho, *Brazil South*, 76, 129, 135; Acosta y Lara, *La guerra de los charrúas*, vol. 1; Villegas, "La evangelización del indio."
8. Monteiro, "Tupis, tapuias e historiadores"; Castro-Klarén, "Nation in Ruins"; Sanders, *Contentious Republicans*; Craib, *Cartographic Mexico*, 19–53; Earle, *Return of the Native*; Andermann, *Optic of the State*; Caplan, *Indigenous Citizens*; Devine Guzmán, *Native and Na-*

tional, 31–104; Appelbaum, *Mapping the Country of Regions*; Roller, "On the Verge of Total Extinction"; Achugar, "Foundational Images of the Nation," 21–24.

9. Verdesio, "Amnesic Nation"; Houot, *Guaraníes y charrúas*, 167–340; Azpiroz, "De 'salvajes' a heroicos." Analyses of similar patterns in northeastern North America include Lepore, *Name of War*; O'Brien, *Firsting and Lasting*.

10. Flourens, "Recherches anatomiques"; Saint-Hilaire, "Extrait d'un mémoire," 584. For more on the Charrúa captives in France, see Rivet, *Los últimos charrúas*; José Joaquín Figueira, *Eduardo Acevedo Díaz y los Aborígenes*; Arce Asenjo, "Nuevos datos sobre el destino." Vaimaca Pirú was not the only Charrúa whose body was subject to racialized scientific investigation. One year earlier, a Charrúa named Ramón Mataojo was sent to France, but due to a lack of interest from the French academy and public, he reportedly remained on the ship and died soon afterward. Houot, *Un cacique charrúa en París*, 16–17. Another Charrúa cacique, Sepe, died in 1866, only to have his body exhumed and his cranium sent to Rio de Janeiro. Acosta y Lara, "Un linaje charrúa en Tacuarembó," 18.

11. López Mazz, "Sangre indígena en Uruguay," 190–91; Picerno, *¿Qué quieren estos hombres?*, 38–46.

12. April 11 marks the anniversary of the Salsipuedes massacre, which occurred in 1831. CONACHA does not encompass all Indigenous communities in Uruguay, and participating communities have changed over the years. For a detailed summary of Indigenous social movements in Uruguay, see Cultelli, "30 años del movimiento indígena."

13. Much of this increased visibility has come via collaboration among Charrúa communities, occasionally with scholars from other countries. See, for example, Michelena, "Mujeres charrúas"; Olivera, *Devenir Charrúa en el Uruguay*; Magalhães de Carvalho and Michelena, "Reflexiones sobre los esencialismos"; Verdesio, "Para repensar los estudios coloniales," 265–71. For more on DNA studies in the region and their limitations, see Sans, Figueiro, and Hidalgo, "New Mitochondrial C1 Lineage"; López Mazz, "Sangre indígena en Uruguay," 189, 196; Kent and Santos, "'Os charrúas vivem' nos gaúchos"; Hilbert, "Charruas e minuanos," 185. Other efforts to increase Indigenous visibility in Uruguay include Maggi, *Artigas y su hijo el Caciquillo*; Antón, *Uruguaypirí*; Abella, *Reconstruyendo nuestra raíz charrúa*.

14. *Censo Nacional de Población (Región Nordeste Argentino)* 32; *Censo Nacional de Población (Región Pampeana)* 51–53.

15. Víctora, "'A viagem de volta'"; Pouey Vidal, "Etnoarqueologia dos Charrua do Rio Grande."

16. Other Latin American countries that have not signed Convention 169 include Belize, El Salvador, Panama, Guyana, Suriname, and French Guiana. For more on land claims and Convention 169 in Uruguay, see Verdesio, "Un fantasma recorre el Uruguay"; Merenson, "Cuando ser indio no rinde"; Gómez Corte, "Em busca da memória," 142–67; Consejo de la Nación Charrúa, "Información básica." Rio Grande's Charrúa community, despite gaining land rights, has faced similar bureaucratic challenges. Víctora and Ruas-Neto, "Querem matar os 'últimos Charruas.'"

17. Critics who have derided Indigenous reemergence as "Charruamania" include academics and national leaders. Examples include Pi Hugarte, "Sobre el charruismo"; Padrón Favre, *Los Charrúas-Minuanes*, 84–87; Sanguinetti, "El Charruismo"; Cabrera, "La garra minuana"; Vidart, "No hay indios en el Uruguay." Some Uruguayans have emphasized

Guaraní or Guenoa-Minuán historical significance in order to dismiss Charrúa ancestry, while Riograndenses have used Charrúa ancestry as a way to dismiss modern-day Guaraní communities. For deeper analysis of this discourse, see Verdesio, "Un fantasma recorre el Uruguay"; Magalhães de Carvalho and Michelena, "Reflexiones sobre los esencialismos," 4; Delgado Cultelli, "Violaciones históricas"; Basini Rodríguez, "Índios num país sem índios"; Víctora, "'A viagem de volta.'"

18. Transnational collaboration among Charrúas in Uruguay and in Entre Ríos, Argentina, including the Union de Mujeres del Pueblo Charrúa (UMPCHA), is a notable exception to this rule. Olivera, "Charrúas urbanos en Uruguay," 104.

Bibliography

Manuscript Repositories

Academia Nacional de la Historia de la República Argentina (Buenos Aires, Argentina)
Archivo General de Indias (Seville, Spain)
Archivo General de la Nación, Argentina (Buenos Aires, Argentina)
Archivo General de la Nación, Uruguay (Montevideo, Uruguay)
Archivo General de la Provincia de Santa Fe (Santa Fe, Argentina)
Archivo General de Simancas (Simancas, Spain)
Archivo General Militar de Madrid (Madrid, Spain)
Arquivo Histórico do Rio Grande do Sul (Porto Alegre, Brazil)
Arquivo Histórico Ultramarino (Lisbon, Portugal)
Arquivo Nacional do Brasil (Rio de Janeiro, Brazil)
Biblioteca da Ajuda (Lisbon, Portugal)
Biblioteca Nacional de España (Madrid, Spain)
Biblioteca Nacional de Portugal (Lisbon, Portugal)
Biblioteca Nacional do Brasil (Rio de Janeiro, Brazil)
Biblioteca da Universidade de Coimbra (Coimbra, Portugal)
Bibliothèque nationale de France (Paris, France)
Instituto de Estudos Brasileiros (São Paulo, Brazil)
Instituto Histórico e Geográfico Brasileiro (Rio de Janeiro, Brazil)
Instituto Histórico e Geográfico do Rio Grande do Sul (Porto Alegre, Brazil)
John Carter Brown Library (Providence, RI)
Library of Congress (Washington, DC)
Museo Mitre (Buenos Aires, Argentina)
Museo Naval de Madrid (Madrid, Spain)
Newberry Library (Chicago, IL)
Oliveira Lima Library (Washington, DC)
Real Academia de la Historia (Madrid, Spain)
Universidade Federal do Rio Grande do Sul (Porto Alegre, Brazil)

Published Primary Sources

Acuerdos del Extinguido Cabildo de Buenos Aires. Serie II, vol. 4. Buenos Aires, 1927.
Acuerdos del Extinguido Cabildo de Buenos Aires. Serie II, vol. 5. Buenos Aires, 1928.
Acuerdos del Extinguido Cabildo de Buenos Aires. Serie II, vol. 6. Buenos Aires, 1928.
Aguirre, Juan Francisco de. "Diario de Aguirre." In *Anales de la Biblioteca: Publicación de documentos relativos al Río de la Plata con introducciones y notas.* Vol. 4, edited by Paul Groussac, 1–271. Buenos Aires: Imprenta y Casa Editora de Coni Hermanos, 1905.

———. "Diario de Aguirre." In *Anales de la Biblioteca: Publicación de documentos relativos al Río de la Plata con introducciones y notas.* Vol. 7, edited by Paul Groussac, 1–490. Buenos Aires: Imprensa de Coni Hermanos, 1911.

Alvear, Diego de. "Diario de la segunda partida demarcadora de límites en la América Meridional, 1783–1791." In *Anales de la Biblioteca: Publicación de documentos relativos al Río de la Plata con introducciones y notas.* Vol. 1, edited by Paul Groussac, 267–384. Buenos Aires: Imprenta y Casa Editora de Coni Hermanos, 1900.

———. "Diario de la segunda partida demarcadora de límites en la América Meridional." In *Anales de la Biblioteca: Publicación de documentos relativos al Río de la Plata con introducciones y notas.* Vol. 2, edited by Paul Groussac, 288–360. Buenos Aires: Imprenta y Casa Editora de Coni Hermanos, 1902.

———. "Diario de la segunda partida demarcadora de límites en la América Meridional." In *Anales de la Biblioteca: Publicación de documentos relativos al Río de la Plata con introducciones y notas.* Vol. 3, edited by Paul Groussac, 373–464. Buenos Aires: Imprenta y Casa Editora de Coni Hermanos, 1904.

———. "Relacion geográfica é histórica de la provincia de Misiones." In *Colección de obras y documentos relativos a la historia antigua y moderna de las provincias del Río de la Plata.* Vol. 4, edited by Pedro de Angelis, 1–106. Buenos Aires: Imprenta del Estado, 1836.

Aranda, Ricardo, ed. *Colección de los tratados, convenciones, capitulaciones, armisticios y otros actos diplomáticos y políticos.* Lima: Imprenta del Estado, 1890.

Archivo Artigas. Vol. 2. Montevideo: Monteverde, 1951.

Archivo Artigas. Vol. 3. Montevideo: Monteverde, 1952.

Archivo Artigas. Vol. 6. Montevideo: Monteverde, 1965.

Archivo Artigas. Vol. 7. Montevideo: Monteverde, 1966.

Archivo Artigas. Vol. 8. Montevideo: Monteverde, 1967.

Archivo Artigas. Vol. 10. Montevideo: Monteverde, 1969.

Archivo Artigas. Vol. 11. Montevideo: Monteverde, 1974.

Archivo Artigas. Vol. 12. Montevideo: Monteverde, 1974.

Archivo Artigas. Vol. 13. Montevideo: Monteverde, 1975.

Archivo Artigas. Vol. 14. Montevideo: Monteverde, 1976.

Archivo Artigas. Vol. 17. Montevideo: Monteverde, 1980.

Archivo Artigas. Vol. 18. Montevideo: Monteverde, 1981.

Archivo Artigas. Vol. 19. Montevideo: Monteverde, 1981.

Archivo Artigas. Vol. 20. Montevideo: Monteverde, 1981.

Archivo Artigas. Vol. 21. Montevideo: Monteverde, 1987.

Archivo Artigas. Vol. 23. Montevideo: Monteverde, 1990.

Archivo Artigas. Vol. 26. Montevideo: Monteverde, 1992.

Archivo Artigas. Vol. 28. Montevideo: Monteverde, 1994.

Archivo Artigas. Vol. 31. Montevideo: Imprimex S.A., 1998.

Archivo Artigas. Vol. 33. Montevideo: Editorial Doble Emme, 2000.

Archivo Artigas. Vol. 34. Montevideo: Iconoprint, 2003.

Archivo Artigas. Vol. 36. Montevideo: Tarma, 2005.

Archivo do Estado de São Paulo, ed. *Documentos relativos ao "bandeirismo" paulista e questões connexas, no periodo de 1721 a 1740: Peças históricas existentes no Archivo Nacional, e copiadas, coordenadas e annotadas, de ordem do governo do estado.* Publicação official de documentos interessantes para a história e costumes de São Paulo. Vol. 50. São Paulo: Estabelecimento Graphico Irmãos Ferraz, 1929.

"Argentina, Capital Federal, registros parroquiales, 1737–1977." Index and images. Josef Maria Charrua, 16 December 1797. Nuestra Señora de la Piedad, Ciudad de Buenos Aires, Capital Federal, Argentina, parroquias Católicas, Buenos Aires. FamilySearch.

"Argentina, Capital Federal, registros parroquiales, 1737–1977." Index and images. Maria Mercedes Charrua, 1 December 1796. Nuestra Señora de La Merced, Ciudad de Buenos Aires, Capital Federal, Argentina, parroquias Católicas, Buenos Aires. FamilySearch.

"Argentina, Capital Federal, registros parroquiales, 1737–1977." Index and images. Juana Manuela Benita Peralta, 24 June 1797. Inmaculada Concepción, Ciudad de Buenos Aires, Capital Federal, Argentina, parroquias Católicas, Buenos Aires. FamilySearch.

"Argentina, Capital Federal, registros parroquiales, 1737–1977." Index and images. Josef Ramos Isidro Charrua, 23 April 1794. Inmaculada Concepción, Ciudad de Buenos Aires, Capital Federal, Argentina, parroquias Católicas, Buenos Aires. FamilySearch.

Avalon Project at the Yale Law School. "The Charter of Massachusetts Bay, 1629." Accessed October 21, 2016. http://avalon.law.yale.edu/17th_century/mass03.asp.

Azara, Félix de. "Correspondencia oficial e inédita sobre la demarcación de límites entre el Paraguay y el Brasil." In *Colección de obras y documentos relativos a la historia antigua y moderna de las provincias del Río de la Plata*. Vol. 4, edited by Pedro de Angelis, 3–68. Buenos Aires: Imprenta del Estado, 1836.

———. *Descripción é historia del Paraguay y del Río de la Plata*. 2 vols. Madrid: Imprenta de Sanchiz, 1847.

———. *Geografía, física y esférica de las provincias del Paraguay y misiones guaraníes*. Montevideo: Museo Nacional, 1904.

———. *Memoria sobre el estado rural del Río de la Plata y otros informes*. Buenos Aires: Editorial Bajel, 1943.

———. *Viajes por la América del Sur*. 2nd ed. Montevideo: Biblioteca del Comercio del Plata, 1850.

Betagh, William. *A Voyage Round the World: Being an Account of a Remarkable Enterprize, begun in the Year 1719, chiefly to cruise on the Spaniards in the great South Ocean*. London: Printed for T. Combes, J. Lacy, and J. Clarke, 1728.

Bluteau, Raphael. *Vocabulário Português e Latino*. Vol. 6. Coimbra: Colégio das Artes da Companhia de Jesus, 1728.

Bracco, Diego, and José M. López Mazz. *Charrúas, pampas y serranos, chanáes y guaraníes: La insurrección del año 1686*. Montevideo: Linardi y Risso, 2006.

"Brasil, Rio Grande do Sul, Registros da Igreja Católica, 1738–1952." Images. Paróquias Católicas, Rio Grande do Sul, Rio Grande, São Pedro, Batismos 1738, Jul-1755. FamilySearch.

Brito Peixoto, Francisco de. "Correspondencia do Capitão-Mór da Laguna, Francisco de Brito Peixoto." In *Documentos interessantes para a história e costumes de São Paulo*. Vol. 32, 270–95. São Paulo: Typographia Andrade & Mello, 1901.

———. "Relação que remette o capitão-mór da Laguna ao governador general da capitania de São Paulo." In *Documentos interessantes para a história e costumes de São Paulo*. Vol. 32, 296–300. São Paulo: Typographia Andrade & Mello, 1901.

Bulkeley, John, and John Cummins. *A Voyage to the South Seas, in the Years 1740–1.* London: Printed for Jacob Robinson, 1743.

Buys de Barros, Dalmiro da Mota. *Colônia do Sacramento: Batizados, Casamentos e Óbitos, 1690–1777.* 2 vols. Rio de Janeiro: Vermelho Marinho, 2012.

Cabral, Sebastião da Veiga. *Descrição Corogràfica e Coleção Histórica do Continente da Nova Colônia da Cidade do Sacramento.* Montevideo: Imprenta Nacional, 1965.

Cabrer, José María. "Diario de la segunda sub-division de limites española [. . .]." In *El límite oriental del territorio de Misiones (República Argentina).* Vol. 2, edited by Melitón González, 3–255. Montevideo: Imp. a vapor de El Siglo, 1883.

"Carta de Cristovão Pereira de Abreu para Gomes Fr.e de Andrada datada do Rio Grande de S. Pedro 29 de Setembro de 1736." *Revista do Instituto Histórico e Geográfico do Rio Grande do Sul* 26, no. 104 (1946): 357–58.

"Carta do Brigadeiro Jose da Silva Paes, datada de 24 de Setembro de 1736, para o Gn.l Gomes Freire de Andrada (Idem, fl. 139)." *Revista do Instituto Histórico e Geográfico do Rio Grande do Sul* 26, no. 104 (1946): 387–88.

Cartas anuas de la Provincia del Paraguay, Chile y Tucumán, de la Compañía de Jesús (1609–1614). Vol. 19 of *Documentos para la Historia Argentina.* Buenos Aires: Talleres S. A. Casa Jacobo Peuser, 1927.

Cartas anuas de la Provincia del Paraguay, Chile y Tucumán, de la Compañía de Jesús (1615–1637). Vol. 20 of *Documentos para la Historia Argentina.* Buenos Aires: Talleres S. A. Casa Jacobo Peuser, 1929.

Cattáneo, Cayetano. "Relación del viaje realizado de Buenos Aires a la Misiones Orientales." In *La cruz y el lazo,* edited by Esteban F. Campal, 175–94. Montevideo: Ediciones de la Banda Oriental, 1994.

Charlevoix, Pierre François-Xavier. *Historia del Paraguay.* 2 vols. Madrid: Libraría General de Victoriano Suárez, 1910–12.

Colaboradores de Wikisource. "Reglamento de Artigas para el fomento de la campaña (1815)." *Wikisource, La Biblioteca Libre.* Accessed August 12, 2017. https://es.wikisource .org/w/index.php?title=Reglamento_de_Artigas_para_el_fomento_de_la _campa%C3%B1a_(1815)&oldid=752818.

———. "Tratado de Badajoz (1801)." *Wikisource, La Biblioteca Libre.* Accessed November 26, 2018. https://es.wikisource.org/w/index.php?title=Tratado_de _Badajoz_(1801)&oldid=220007.

———. "Tratado de El Pardo (1761)." *Wikisource, La Biblioteca Libre.* Accessed December 13, 2018. https://es.wikisource.org/w/index.php?title=Tratado_de_El _Pardo_(1761)&oldid=472186.

"Coleção de documentos sôbre o Brigadeiro José da Silva Paes: Documentos sôbre a Colonia do Sacramento e expedição que foi a socorrer em 1737." *Revista do Instituto Histórico e Geográfico do Rio Grande do Sul* 28, 1–4 quarters (1948): 3–145.

"Copia da carta de Cristovão Pereira de Abreu a Jose da Silva Paes, datada do Rio Grande de Sam Pedro aos 5 de Dezembro de 1736." *Revista do Instituto Histórico e Geográfico do Rio Grande do Sul* 26, no. 104 (1946): 416–19.

Cortesão, Jaime, ed. *Antecedentes do Tratado de Madri: Jesuítas e Bandeirantes no Paraguai (1703–1751).* Vol. 6 of *Manuscritos da Coleção De Angelis.* Rio de Janeiro: Biblioteca Nacional, 1955.

————, ed. *Do Tratado de Madri à conquista dos Sete Povos (1750–1802)*. Vol. 7 of *Manuscritos da Coleção De Angelis*. Rio de Janeiro: Biblioteca Nacional, 1969.

————, ed. *Jesuítas e Bandeirantes no Itatim (1596-1760)*. Vol. 2 of *Manuscritos da Coleção De Angelis*. Rio de Janeiro: Biblioteca Nacional, 1952.

————, ed. *Jesuítas e Bandeirantes no Tape (1615–1641)*. Vol. 3 of *Manuscritos da Coleção De Angelis*. Rio de Janeiro: Biblioteca Nacional, 1969.

————, ed. *Tratado de Madri: Antecedentes—Colônia do Sacramento (1669-1749)*. Vol. 5 of *Manuscritos da Coleção De Angelis*. Rio de Janeiro: Biblioteca Nacional, 1954.

Curel, François de. *Reseña sobre la tribu de los indios charrúas*. Montevideo: Vintén Editor, 1996.

De Província de São Pedro a Estado do Rio Grande do Sul: Censos do RS, 1803–1950. Porto Alegre: Fundação de Economia e Estatística, 1981.

"Demarcação do sul do Brasil: Pelo Governador e Capitão General Gomes Freire de Andrada, 1752–1757." *Revista do Arquivo Público Mineiro* 24, no. 1 (1933): 43–344. "Diário compilado da 1ª tropa." In *Collecção de notícias para a história e geografia das nações ultramarinas que vivem nos dominios portuguezes ou lhes são visinhas*, Vol. 7, 45–123. Lisboa: Academia Real das Sciencias, 1841.

Diccionario de autoridades. Vol. 5. Madrid: Real Academia Española, 1737.

Diccionario de autoridades. Vol. 6. Madrid: Real Academia Española, 1739.

Doblas, Gonzalo de. "Memoria histórica, geográfica, política y económica sobre la Provincia de Misiones de Indios Guaranis." In *Colección de obras y documentos relativos a la historia antigua y moderna de las provincias del Río de la Plata*. Vol. 3, edited by Pedro de Angelis, 3–116. Buenos Aires: Imprenta del Estado, 1836.

"Documentos relativos á incorporação do território das Missões ao domínio portugues no anno de 1801." *Revista do Archivo Público do Rio Grande do Sul* 1 (1921): 20–75.

"Documentos sobre a Colônia do Sacramento: Cópia feita em 1938 por Artur da Motta Alves e propriedade da Biblioteca Riograndense, da Cidade do Rio Grande." *Revista do Instituto Histórico e Geográfico do Rio Grande do Sul* 25, no. 99 (1945): 41–117.

d'Orbigny, Alcide Dessalines. *El Hombre Americano*. Colección Eurindia. Buenos Aires: Editorial Futuro, 1944.

Dreys, Nicolào. *Notícia descriptiva da Província do Rio-Grande de S. Pedro do Sul*. Rio de Janeiro: Na Typ. Imp. e Const. de J. Villeneuve e Comp., 1839.

El episodio ocurrido en Puerto de la Soledad de Malvinas el 26 de Agosto de 1833: Testimonios documentales. Vol. 3 of *Serie Documental*. Buenos Aires: Academia Nacional de la Historia, 1967.

Ferrufino, Juan B. *Relacion del martirio de los padres Roque Gonçalez de Santacruz, Alonso Rodriguez, Iuan del Castillo, de la Compañia de Iesus. Padecido en el Paraguay, a 16. de Noviembre de 1628*. Madrid, 1629.

Flourens, Jean Pierre. "Recherches anatomiques sur les corps muqueux, ou appareil pigmental de la peau, dans l'Indien Charrua, le nègre et le mulâtre." In *Comptes rendus hebdomadaires des séances de l'Académie des sciences*. Vol. 3, 699–706. Paris: L'Académie des Sciences, 1836.

García, Diego. "Memoria." In *Revista de la Biblioteca Pública de Buenos Aires*. Vol. 1, edited by Manuel Ricardo Trelles, 114–23. Buenos Aires: Imprenta y Librería de Mayo, 1879.

González, Silvestre. *Diario de viaje a las Vaquerías del Mar (1705).* Montevideo: Artes Gráficas Covadonga, 1966.

Graell, Francisco. "Diario del capitán D. Francisco Graell en la expedición contra los siete pueblos rebeldes de la banda oriental del Uruguay (1755–1756)." In *Colección de documentos inéditos para la historia de España,* 449–84. Madrid: Imprenta de José Perales y Martínez, 1892.

Henis, Tadeo Xavier. "Diario histórico de la rebellion y guerra de los pueblos guaranís, situados en la costa oriental del Río Uruguay, del año de 1754." In *Colección de obras y documentos relativos a la historia antigua y moderna de las provincias del Río de la Plata,* Vol. 5, edited by Pedro de Angelis, 3–60. Buenos Aires: Imprenta del Estado, 1836.

Hervás, Lorenzo. *Catálogo de las lenguas de las naciones conocidas, y numeracion, division, y clases de estas segun la diversidad de sus idiomas y dialectos.* Vol 1. Madrid: Ranz, 1800.

———. *Saggio pratico delle lingue: con prolegomeni, e una raccolta di orazioni dominicali in piu di trecento lingue e dialetti [. . .].* Cesena: Gregorio Biasini, 1787.

"Informe del Virrey Arredondo á su sucesor D. Pedro Melo de Portugal y Villena, sobre el estado de la cuestion de límites en 1795." In *Colección de obras y documentos relativos a la historia antigua y moderna de las provincias del Río de la Plata.* Vol. 4, edited by Pedro de Angelis, 1–38. Buenos Aires: Imprenta del Estado, 1836.

Isabelle, Arsène. *Voyage a Buénos-Ayres et a Porto-Alègre par la Banda-Oriental, les Missions D'Uruguay et la Province de Rio-Grande-do-Sul (de 1830 a 1834).* Havre: Imprimerie de J. Morlent, 1835.

Jarque, Francisco. *Insignes missioneros de la Compañía de Jesus en la provincia de Paraguay: Estado presente de sus missiones en Tucuman, Paraguay y Rio de la Plata que comprende su distrito.* Pamplona: Juan Micòn, 1687.

Juan, Jorge, and Antonio de Ulloa. *A Voyage to South America: Describing at Large the Spanish Cities, Towns, Provinces, &c. on that Extensive Continent.* 1758. London: Printed for John Stockdale, R. Faulder, Longman, and Lackington, 1772.

———. *Disertación histórica y geográfica sobre el meridiano de demarcación.* 1749. Madrid: Instituto Histórico de Marina, 1972.

Larrañaga, Dámaso Antonio. *Selección de escritos.* Montevideo: Ministerio de Instrucción Pública y Previsión Social, 1965.

Lastarria, Miguel, ed. *Colonias orientales del Río Paraguay ó de la Plata.* Vol. 3 of *Documentos para la Historia Argentina.* Buenos Aires: Compañía Sud-Americana de Billetes de Banco, 1914.

———, ed. *Documentos para la historia del Virreinato del Río de la Plata.* Vol. 1. Buenos Aires: Compañía Sud-Americana de Billetes de Banco, 1912.

Latini, Sergio Hernán, "Relatos del conflicto interétnico: Francisco García de Piedrabuena contra los 'charrúas y otros infieles,' 1715." *Corpus. Archivos virtuales de la alteridad americana* 2, no. 2 (2012): 1–12.

Lozano, Pedro. *Historia de la conquista del Paraguay, Rio de la Plata y Tucuman.* Biblioteca del Rio de la Plata. Vol. 1. Buenos Aires: Casa Editora "Imprenta Popular," 1873.

———. *Historia de la conquista del Paraguay, Rio de la Plata y Tucuman.* Biblioteca del Rio de la Plata. Vol. 3. Buenos Aires: Casa Editora "Imprenta Popular," 1874.

————. *Historia de las revoluciones de la Provincia del Paraguay (1721–1735).* Vol. 1. Buenos Aires: Cabaut y Cía, 1905.

"Mémoire pour servir d'addition & d'éclairciffiment à la Relation abrégée, & qu'on vient de donner au public, sur l'abominable conduite des Jésuites, dans les pays et domaines d'outre-mer dépendans des royaumes d'Espagne et de Portugal." 1712. Holland, 1756.

"Memoria de Juan José de Vértiz y Salcedo a su sucesor." In *Memorias de los virreyes del Río de la Plata*, edited by Julio César González. Buenos Aires: Editorial Bajel, 1945.

"Memoria dos serviços prestados pelo Mestre de Campo André Ribeiro Coutinho no Governo do Rio Grande de S. Pedro, dirigida a Gomes Freire de Andrada, em 1740." *Revista do Instituto Histórico e Geográfico do Rio Grande do Sul* 16, no. 64 (1936): 237–46.

"Memoria para las generaciones venideras, de los indios misioneros del pueblo de Yapeyú." In *Misiones del Paraguay: Organización social de las doctrinas guaraníes de la Compañía de Jesús*, edited by Pablo Hernández, 546–49. Barcelona: Gustavo Gili, 1913.

Moraes Silva, Antonio de. *Diccionario da lingua portugueza—recompilado dos vocabularios impressos ate agora, e nesta segunda edição novamente emendado e muito acrescentado.* Vol. 2. Lisboa: Typographia Lacerdina, 1789.

Muratori, Lodovico Antonio. *The Jesuit's Travels in South America, Paraguay, Chili &c.* London: Printed for Jeffrey and Sael, No. 11, Pall-Mall, 1788.

Muriel, Domingo. *Elementos de derecho natural y de gentes.* Buenos Aires: Imprenta de Coni Hermanos, 1911.

Murray, John Hale. *Travels in Uruguay, South America: Together with an Account of the Present State of Sheep-Farming and Emigration to That Country.* London: Longmans, 1871. "Officio do vice-rei Luiz de Vasconcellos, sobre o Rio Grande do Sul." *Revista do Instituto Histórico e Geográfico do Rio Grande do Sul* 9, no. 33 (1929): 41–48.

Oliveira, Candido Baptista de. *Reconhecimento topográphico da fronteira do império, na Província de São Pedro.* Rio de Janeiro: Na Typographia Nacional, 1850.

Oliveira, José Joaquim Machado de. *Memória histórica sobre a questão de limites entre o Brasil e Montevidéo.* São Paulo: Typ. Liberal de J.R. de A. Marques, 1852.

Ortiz de Vergara, Francisco. "Declaración de Francisco Ortiz de Vergara." In *Documentos históricos y geográficos relativos a la conquista rioplatense*, edited by José Torre Revello. Buenos Aires: Tallares Casa Jacobo Peuser, 1941.

Oyarvide, Andrés de. *Memoria geográfica de los viajes practicados desde Buenos Aires hasta el Salto Grande del Paraná.* In *Colección histórica completa de los tratados, convenciones, capitulaciones, armisticios, cuestiones de límites . . . de todos los estados.* Vol. 8, edited by Carlos Calvo, 1–442. Paris: A. Durand, 1862.

————. *Memoria geográfica de los viajes practicados desde Buenos Aires hasta el Salto Grande del Paraná.* In *Colección histórica completa de los tratados, convenciones, capitulaciones, armisticios, cuestiones de límites . . . de todos los estados.* Vol. 10, edited by Carlos Calvo, 1–383. Paris: A. Durand, 1866.

"Registro de atos oficiais no presídio do Rio Grande (1737–1753)." *Anais do Arquivo Histórico do Rio Grande do Sul* 1 (1977): 25–328.

"Relatorio apresentado ao governo de Lisboa pelo vice-rei Luiz de Vasconcellos, em Outubro de 1784, sobre o Rio Grande do Sul." *Revista do Instituto Histórico e Geográfico do Rio Grande do Sul* 9, no. 33 (1929): 3–40.

Revista del Archivo General Administrativo: Colección de Documentos para Servir al Estudio de la Historia de la República del Uruguay. Vol. 3. Montevideo: Imprenta "El Siglo Ilustrado," 1887.

Rodrigues da Cunha, Jacinto. "Diário da expedição de Gomes Freire de Andrada às Missões do Uruguay." *Revista do Instituto Histórico e Geográphico do Brazil* 16 (1853): 138–321.

Roscio, Francisco João. "Compêndio Noticioso." In *O Capitalismo Pastoril*, edited by Décio Freitas, 105–40. Porto Alegre: Escola Superior de Teologia São Lourenço de Brindes, 1980.

Sá, Simão Pereira de. *Historia topographica e bellica da Nova Colonia do Sacramento do Rio da Prata.* Rio de Janeiro: Typographia Leuzinger, 1900.

Saint-Hilaire, Auguste de. *Voyage a Rio-Grande do Sul (Brésil).* Orléans: H. Herluioson, Libraire-Éditeur, 1887.

Saint-Hilaire, Étienne Geoffroy. "Extrait d'un mémoire sur l'orang-outang, vivant actuellement à la Ménagerie." In *Comptes rendus hebdomadaires des séances de l'Académie des sciences.* Vol. 2, 581–602. Paris: L'Académie des Sciences, 1836.

Saldanha, José de. "Diário resumido." In *Anais da Biblioteca Nacional do Rio de Janeiro*, Vol. 51, edited by Rodolfo Garcia, 135–301. Rio de Janeiro: M.E.S.—Serviço Gráfico, 1929.

Schmidl, Ulrich. "Viage al Rio de la Plata y Paraguay." In *Colección de obras y documentos relativos a la historia antigua y moderna de las provincias del Río de la Plata.* Vol. 3, edited by Pedro de Angelis, 3–61. Buenos Aires: Imprenta del Estado, 1836.

Sepp von Rechegg, Anton. *Viagem às Missões Jesuíticas e Trabalhos Apostólicos.* Biblioteca Histórica Brasileira. São Paulo: Livraria Martins Editora; Editora da Universidade de São Paulo, 1972.

Silva Pontes, Antônio Pires da. "Diário histórico e físico da viagem dos oficiais da demarcação que partiram do quartel geral de Barcelos para a capital de Vila Bela da Capitania de Mato Grosso, em 1 de Setembro de 1781." *Revista do Instituto Histórico e Geográfico Brasileiro* 262 (1964): 344–406.

Sylva, Silvestre Ferreira da. *Relação do sitio, que o Governador de Buenos Aires D. Miguel de Salcedo poz no anno de 1735 à Praça da Nova Colonia do Sacramento.* Lisboa: Impres. da Congregaçaõ Camer. da S. Igreja de Lisboa, 1748.

Techo, Nicolás del. *Historia de la Provincia del Paraguay.* Vol. 3. Madrid: A. de Uribe y Compañía, 1897.

Telégrafo Mercantil: Rural, político-económico e historiógrafo del Río de la Plata (1801–1802), Vol. 6. Buenos Aires: Compañía Sud-Americana de Billetes de Banco, 1914.

Thun, Harald, Leonardo Cerno, and Franz Obermeier, eds. *Guarinihape tecocue—lo que pasó en la guerra (1704–1705).* Fontes Americanae. Vol. 5. Kiel: Westensee, 2015.

"Tratado de paz entre la república francesa y el reino de Portugal, celebrado en Madrid á 29 de setiembre de 1801." In *Cuenta dada de su vida política*, edited by Manuel Godoy, 429–32. Madrid: Imprenta de I. Sancha, 1856.

"Tratado firmado en Madrid á 13 de Enero de 1750, para determinar los límites de los estados pertenecientes á las Coronas de España y Portugal, en Asia y América." In

Colección de obras y documentos relativos a la historia antigua y moderna de las provincias del Río de la Plata. Vol. 4, edited by Pedro de Angelis, 3–14. Buenos Aires: Imprenta del Estado, 1836.

"Tratado preliminar sobre los límites de los estados pertenecientes á las Coronas de España y Portugal, en la América meridional, ajustado y concluido en San Lorenzo, á 11 de Octubre de 1777." In *Colección de obras y documentos relativos a la historia antigua y moderna de las provincias del Río de la Plata.* Vol. 4, edited by Pedro de Angelis, 3–15. Buenos Aires: Imprenta del Estado, 1836.

"Tratado Provisional de Lisboa de 7 de mayo de 1681." Accessed June 30, 2016. https://es .wikisource.org/wiki/Tratado_Provisional_de_Lisboa_del_7_de_mayo_de_1681.

"Uruguay, bautismos, 1750–1900." Index. Thomas Charrua, 16 March 1839. Nuestra Señora del Carmen, Salto, Uruguay. FamilySearch.

"Uruguay, bautismos, 1750–1900." Index. Candida Charruas, 4 September 1863. Nuestra Señora de las Mercedes, Mercedes, Soriano, Uruguay. FamilySearch.

Varela y Ulloa, José. *Diario de la primera partida de la demarcación de limites entre España y Portugal en América.* 2 vols. Madrid: Imprenta del Patronato de Huérfanos de Intendencia é Intervención Militares, 1920–25.

Vianna, Helio, ed. *Jesuítas e Bandeirantes no Uruguai (1611–1758).* Vol. 4 of *Manuscritos da Coleção De Angelis.* Rio de Janeiro: Biblioteca Nacional, 1970.

Vitoria, Francisco de. *Political Writings.* New York: Cambridge University Press, 1991.

Maps and Atlases

Ambruzzi, L. *Mapa Histórico de la República O. del Uruguay,* 1898.

Biedma, José J. *Atlas histórico de la República Argentina.* Buenos Aires: A. Estrada y Cia., 1909.

Blaeu, Joan, *Nova et accurata Brasiliae totius tabula.* Amsterdam: Joanne Blaev I.F., 1689.

Blasco, Miguel Angelo de. *Mappa remetido do Sr. Marquez a sua Exª o qual trazendo troccado o Ibicuy, ate agora conhecido, com o nome de Jaguary Guazu, e ao Rº da Serra do Mato Grosso denominado-o o Ibicuy, foi a baze, onde depois explicarão as prezentes duvidas e questoens,* 1758. BNB, Cartografia, Manuscritos 049,02,024, no 4.

———. *Mappa remetido ao Sr. Marquez, q demonstra a parage mais conveniente pª juntarem-se as tropas das primr.as partidas, e do caminho mais breve pª chegar ao ponto de sta. Tecla, onde se deixou parada a demarcação por cauza dos indios então rebeldes,* 1758. BNB, Cartografia, Manuscritos 049,02,024, no 3

———. *Traslado do Mappa que o Comissarº. Plenipotenciario de S. Mage. C. (feito pelos geographos) remeteo ao de S. Mage. Fma. em o qual são rezumidas parte das duvidas das quaes se trata nos escritos a parte, e no que se vai junto,* 1758. BNB, Cartografia, Manuscritos 049,02,024, no 12.

Bowen, Emanuel, *A New and Accurate Map of Paraguay, Rio de la Plata, Tucumania Guaria &c.* London: Printed for William Innys, Richard Ware, Aaron Ward, J. and P. Knapton, John Clarke, T. Longman and T. Shewell, Thomas Osborne, Henry Whitridge, 1747.

Croquis de la costa de la America del Sur donde proyectaban establecerse los ingleses, [1733?]. http://www.mcu.es/ccbae/es/consulta/registro.cmd?id=176782.

Fer, Nicolas de. *Partie La Plus Meridionale De L'Amerique, ou se Trouve Le Chili, Le Paraguay, et les Terres Magellaniques avec Les Fameux Detroits de Magellan et de Le Maire,* Paris, 1737.

Fúrlong Cárdiff, Guillermo. *Cartografía jesuítica del Rio de la Plata.* 2 vols. Buenos Aires: Talleres S. A. Casa Jacobo Peuser, 1936.

Homann, Johann Baptiste. *Typus Geographicus Chili Paraguay Freti Magellanici &c.* Nuremberg, 1733.

Plano del Rio de la Plata que comprende los Pueblos de Misiones y Linea que se puso para dividir las Jurisdiciones entre los dos Monarcas de España y Portugal aunque despues en el año 1759 se quedaron las cosas como se estavan, n.d. AGMM, ARG-8,2.

Quiroga, Joseph. *Mapa de las Missiones de/la Compañia de Jesvs en/los rios Paraná, y Vruguay.* 1749. Rome: Francheschelli, Ferdinandus, 1753.

Requena, Francisco. *Mapa geográfico de la mayor parte de la América Meridional que contiene los paises pordonde debe trazarse la línia divisoria que divida los dominios de España y Portugal.* Philadelphia, 1796. https://collections.leventhalmap.org/search /commonwealth:6t053s188.

Saldanha, José de. *Mappa Corographico da Capitania de S. Pedro,* 1801. BNB, Cartografia, ARC.023,13,003 http://objdigital.bn.br/objdigital2/acervo_digital/div_cartografia /cart168591/cart168591.html.

Varela y Ulloa, José. *Plano topografico que comprende la parte septentrional de la Laguna de Merin,* 1786. http://hdl.loc.gov/loc.gmd/g5622m.br000084.

———. *Plano topografico que comprende las vertientes del Arroyo Ycabaqua, las del Rio Negro y la cresta que divide aguas al Yacuy y al Uruguay hasta la Sierra de los Tapes o Montegrande,* 1787. http://hdl.loc.gov/loc.gmd/g5620.br000086.

———. *Plano topografico que comprende una parte del Montegrande, el Rio Yacuy, los establecimentos y misiones del Uruguay, los yervales que actualmento poseen los indios guaranias y el curso del mismo Uruguay desde la boca del verdadero Pepiri o Peguiri hasta el paso que llaman de Concepcion,* 1789. http://hdl.loc.gov/loc.gmd/g5202u .br000083.

Varela y Ulloa, José, and Sebastião da Veiga Cabral da Câmara. *Plano topografico que comprende la costa del mar,* 1789. http://hdl.loc.gov/loc.gmd/g5620.br000087.

Wit, Frederick de. *Novissima et Accuratissime Septentrionalis ac Meridionalis Americae.* Amsterdam, 1688.

Secondary Sources

Abella, Gonzalo. *Reconstruyendo nuestra raíz charrúa.* Montevideo: BetumSan, 2010.

Abou-el-Haj, Rifaat A. "The Formal Closure of the Ottoman Frontier in Europe: 1699–1703." *Journal of the American Oriental Society* 89, no. 3 (1969): 467–75.

Achugar, Hugo. "Foundational Images of the Nation in Latin America." In *Building Nineteenth-Century Latin America: Re-rooted Cultures, Identities, and Nations,* edited by William G. Acree Jr. and Juan Carlos González Espitia, 11–31. Nashville: Vanderbilt University Press, 2009.

Acosta y Lara, Eduardo F. *La guerra de los charrúas en la Banda Oriental.* 2 vols. Montevideo: Librería Linardi y Risso, 1989.

————. "Un linaje charrúa en Tacuarembó: A 150 años de Salsipuedes." *Revista de la Facultad de Humanidades y Ciencias, Serie Ciencias Antropológicas* 1, no. 2 (1981): 13–30.

Acuña, José Polo, and Ruth Gutiérrez. "Territorios, gentes y culturas libres en el Caribe continental Neo-Grandino 1700–1850: Una síntesis." In *Historia social del Caribe colombiano: Territorios, indígenas, trabajadores, cultura, memoria e historia*, edited by José Polo Acuña and Sergio Paolo, 9–41. Medellín: La Carreta, 2011.

Adelman, Jeremy. *Sovereignty and Revolution in the Iberian Atlantic*. Princeton, NJ: Princeton University Press, 2006.

Adelman, Jeremy, and Stephen Aron. "From Borderlands to Borders: Empires, Nation-States, and the Peoples in between in North American History." *American Historical Review* 104, no. 3 (1999): 814–41.

Aguirre, Andrés. "La Banda Oriental y Rio Grande en el siglo XVIII: ¿Periferia imperial o frontera colonial?" *Anuario PROEHAA*, no. 1 (2015): 47–76.

Aguirre, Susana. "Cambiando de perspectiva: Cautivos en el interior de la frontera." *Mundo Agrario. Revista de estudios rurales* 7, no. 13 (2006): 1–16.

Alden, Dauril. *Royal Government in Colonial Brazil, with Special Reference to the Administration of the Marquis of Lavradio, Viceroy, 1769–1779*. Berkeley: University of California Press, 1968.

Alemano, María Eugenia. "La prisión de Toroñan: Conflicto, poder y 'araucanización' en la frontera pampeana (1770-1780)." *Revista TEFROS* 11, no. 2 (2015): 27–55.

————. "Los Blandengues de la Frontera de Buenos Aires y los dilemas de la defensa del Imperio (1752–1806)." *Fronteras de la Historia* 22, no. 2 (2017): 44–74.

Almeida, André Ferrand de. *A formação do espaço brasileiro e o projeto do Novo Atlas da América Portuguesa (1713–1748)*. Lisboa: Comissão Nacional para as Comemorações dos Descobrimentos Portugueses, 2001.

————. "O Mapa Geográfico de América Meridional, de Juan de la Cruz Cano y Olmedilla." *Anais do Museu Paulista* 17, no. 2 (July–December 2009): 79–89.

Almeida, Luís Ferrand de. "A Colónia do Sacramento na época da Sucessão de Espanha." PhD diss., Universidade de Coimbra, 1973.

————. *Alexandre de Gusmão, o Brasil e o Tratado de Madrid (1735–1750)*. História Moderna e Contemporânea. Vol. 5. Coimbra: Universidade de Coimbra, 1990.

Almeida, Maria Regina Celestino de. "Índios e mestiços no Rio de Janeiro: Significados pluriais e cambiantes (séculos XVIII–XIX)." *Memoria Americana* 16, no. 2 (2008): 19–40.

Almeida, Rita Heloísa de. *O Diretório dos índios: Um projeto de "civilização" no Brasil do século XVIII*. Brasília: Editora UnB, 1997.

Altic, Mirela. "Missionary Cartography of the Amazon after the Treaty of Madrid (1750): The Jesuit Contribution to the Demarcation of Imperial Frontiers." *Terrae Icognitae* 46, no. 2 (2014): 69–85.

Ameghino, Florentino. *La antigüedad del hombre en la plata*. Buenos Aires: La Cultura Argentina, 1918.

Amith, Jonathan D. *The Möbius Strip: A Spatial History of Colonial Society in Guerrero, Mexico*. Stanford, CA: Stanford University Press, 2005.

Andermann, Jens. *The Optic of the State: Visuality and Power in Argentina and Brazil*. Pittsburgh: University of Pittsburgh Press, 2007.

Anderson, Benedict. *Imagined Communities: Reflections on the Origin and Spread of Nationalism*. 2nd ed. London: Verso, 1991.

Antón, Danilo J. *El pueblo Jaguar: Lucha y sobrevivencia de los charrúas a través del tiempo*. Montevideo: Piriguazú Ediciones, 1998.

———. *Uruguaypirí*. Montevideo: Rosebud Ediciones, 1994.

Aparacio, Francisco de, and Horacio A. Difrieri. *La Argentina suma de Geografía*. Vol. 7. Buenos Aires: Ediciones Peuser, 1958.

Apolant, Juan Alejandro. *Génesis de la familia uruguaya*. Montevideo: Instituto Histórico y Geográfico del Uruguay, 1966.

———. *Padrones olvidados de Montevideo del siglo XVIII*. Vol. 2: Separata de Boletín histórico del Estado Mayor del Ejército, nos. 108–111 and nos. 112–115. Montevideo: Imprensa Letras, 1966.

Appelbaum, Nancy. *Mapping the Country of Regions: The Chorographic Commission of Nineteenth-Century Colombia*. Chapel Hill: University of North Carolina Press, 2016.

Araújo, Orestes. *Etnología salvaje: Historia de los Charrúas y demás tribus indígenas del Uruguay (primera parte)*. Montevideo: José María Serrano, 1911.

Arce Asenjo, Darío. "Etnónimos indígenas en la historiografía uruguaya: Desensamblando piezas de diferentes puzzles." *Anuario de Antropología Social y Cultural en Uruguay* 13 (2015): 23–34.

———. "Nuevos datos sobre el destino de Tacuavé y la hija de Guyunusa." *Antropología Social y Cultural en Uruguay*, 2007, 51–71.

Areces, Nidia R., Silvana López, and Elida Regis. "Relaciones interétnicas en Santa Fe la Vieja: Rescate con charrúas." In *Reflexiones sobre el V Centenario*, edited by Nidia R. Areces, 155–69. Rosario: UNR Editoria, 1992.

Areces, Nidia R., Silvana López, Beatriz N. Regueiro, Elida Regis, and Tarragó Griselda. "Santa Fe la Vieja. Frontera abierta y de guerra. Los frentes Charrúa y Chaqueño." *Memoria Americana* 2 (1993): 7–40.

Arias, Santa, and Mariselle Meléndez, eds. *Mapping Colonial Spanish America: Places and Commonplaces of Identity, Culture, and Experience*. Lewisburg, PA: Bucknell University Press, 2002.

Asúa, Miguel. *Science in the Vanished Arcadia: Knowledge of Nature in the Jesuit Missions of Paraguay and Río de la Plata*. Leiden: Brill, 2014.

Austin, Shawn. "Guaraní Kinship and the Encomienda Community in Colonial Paraguay, Sixteenth and Early Seventeenth Centuries." *Colonial Latin American Review* 24, no. 4 (2015): 545–71.

Avellaneda, Mercedes, and Lía Quarleri. "Las milicias guaraníes en el Paraguay y Río de la Plata: Alcances y limitaciones (1659–1756)." *Estudos Ibero-Americanos* 33, no. 1 (2007): 109–32.

Ávila, Carlos Lázaro. "Conquista, control y convicción: El papel de los parlamentos indígenas en México, El Chaco y Norteamérica." *Revista de Indias* 59, no. 217 (1999): 645–73.

Azarola Gil, Luís Enrique. *Los Orígenes de Montevideo, 1607–1759*. Montevideo: Casa A. Barreiro y Ramos, 1940.

Azpiroz, Andrés. "De 'salvajes' a heroicos: La construcción de la voz y la imagen del 'indio Charrúa' desde 1830 a los inicios del siglo XX." *Almanack, Guarulhos*, no. 16 (2017): 1–38.

Azpiroz Perera, Andres, and Adriana Dávila Cuevas. "Indios 'Infieles' y 'Potreadores': Sociedad colonial y poblaciones indígenas en las fronteras de la Banda Oriental. La fundación de Belén 1801." Paper presented at II Jornadas de Investigación en Humanidades, Universidad de la República, Montevideo, 2009.

Babcock, Matthew. "Rethinking the Establecimientos: Why Apaches Settled on Spanish-Run Reservations, 1786–1793." *New Mexico Historical Review* 84, no. 3 (2009): 363–97.

Bandeira, Moniz. *O expansionismo brasileiro.* Rio de Janeiro: Philobiblion, 1985.

Barcelos, Artur H. F. "A cartografia indígena no Rio da Prata colonial." Paper presented at the X Encontro Estadual de História, Santa Maria, Rio Grande do Sul, July 2010, 1–15.

———. "Os Jesuítas e a ocupação do espaço platino nos séculos XVII e XVIII." *Revista Complutense de Historia de América* 26 (2000): 93–116.

Barr, Juliana. "From Captives to Slaves: Commodifying Indian Women in the Borderlands." *Journal of American History* 92, no. 1 (2005): 19–46.

———. "Geographies of Power: Mapping Indian Borders in the 'Borderlands' of the Early Southwest." *William and Mary Quarterly* 68, no. 1 (2011): 5–46.

Barr, Juliana, and Edward Countryman. "Introduction: Maps and Spaces, Paths to Connect, and Lines to Divide." In *Contested Spaces of Early America*, edited by Juliana Barr and Edward Countryman, 1–28. Philadelphia: University of Pennsylvania Press, 2014.

Barrios Pintos, Aníbal. "Caciques Charrúas en Territorio Oriental." *Almanaque del Banco de Seguros del Estado* 70 (1981): 86–89.

———. *De las vaquerías al alambrado: Contribución a la historia rural uruguaya.* Montevideo: Ediciones del Nuevo Mundo, 1967.

Basile Becker, Ítala Irene. *Os índios charrua e minuano na antiga banda oriental do Uruguai.* São Leopoldo, RS, Brasil: Editora Unisinos, 2002.

Basini Rodríguez, Jose Exequiel. "Índios num país sem índios: A estética do desaparecimento." Tese de Doutorado, Universidade Federal do Rio Grande do Sul, 2003.

Bastos, Carlos Augusto. "Às vésperas das demarcações: Expectativas luso-espanholas para as fronteiras imeriais no vale amazônico (1777–1780)." *Fronteiras y Debates* 1, no. 1 (2014): 9–24.

Bauzá, Francisco. *Historia de la Dominación Española en el Uruguay.* 2 vols. Montevideo: A. Barreiro y Ramos, Editor, 1895.

Becú, Ricardo Zorraquín. "Las capitulaciones rioplatenses." *Revista Chilena de historia del Derecho* 11 (1985): 85–108.

Benton, Lauren A. *A Search for Sovereignty: Law and Geography in European Empires, 1400–1900.* New York: Cambridge University Press, 2010.

Berthelette, Scott. "'Frères et Enfants du même Père': The French Illusion of Empire West of the Great Lakes, 1731–1743." *Early American Studies* 14, no. 1 (2016): 174–98.

Bertocchi Moran, Alejandro N. "El piloto Andrés de Oyarvide y su labor en el Río de la Plata." *Itsas Memoria. Revista de Estudios Marítimos del País Vasco* 6 (2009): 747–62.

Bialuschewski, Arne, and Linford D. Fisher. "New Directions in the History of Native American Slave Studies." *Ethnohistory* 64, no. 1 (2017): 1–17.

Binnema, Theodore. *Common and Contested Ground: A Human and Environmental History of the Northwest Plains*. Norman: University of Oklahoma Press, 2001.

Bleichmar, Daniela, Paula de Vos, Kristin Huffine, and Kevin Sheehan, eds. *Science in the Spanish and Portuguese Empires, 1500–1800*. Stanford, CA: Stanford University Press, 2009.

Block, David. *Mission Culture on the Upper Amazon: Native Tradition, Jesuit Enterprise and Secular Policy in Moxos, 1660–1880*. Lincoln: University of Nebraska Press, 1994.

Boccara, Guillaume. "Colonización, resistencia y etnogénesis en las fronteras americanas." In *Colonización, resistencia y mestizaje en las Américas, siglos XVI–XX*, edited by Guillaume Boccara, 47–82. Quito: Abya Yala; Instituto Francés de Estudios Andinos (IFEA), 2002.

———. *Los vencedores: Historia del pueblo mapuche en la época colonial*. San Pedro de Atacama: Línea Editorial IIAM, 2007.

Boeck, Brian J. "Containment vs. Colonization: Muscovite Approaches to Settling the Steppe." In *Peopling the Russian Periphery: Borderland Colonization in Eurasian History*, edited by Nicholas B. Breyfogle, Abby M. Schrader, and Willard Sunderland, 41–60. New York: Routledge, 2007.

Bolaños, Álvaro Félix. "A Place to Live, a Place to Think, and a Place to Die: Sixteenth Century Frontier Cities, Plazas, and 'Relaciones' in Spanish America." In *Mapping Colonial Spanish America: Places and Commonplaces of Identity, Culture, and Experience*, edited by Santa Arias and Mariselle Meléndez, 275–93. Lewisburg, PA: Bucknell University Press, 2002.

Bonomo, Mariano, and María C. Barboza. "Arqueología del Litoral: Introducción." *Revista del Museo de Antropología* 7, no. 2 (2014): 215–18.

Bonomo, Mariano, Gustavo G. Politis, and Juan Carlos Castro. "Los indígenas de Entre Ríos." In *Manual de Historia de Entre Ríos*, edited by Ministro de Cultura y Comunicación de la provincia de Entre Ríos, 45–75. Paraná: Editorial de Entre Ríos, 2014.

Borucki, Alex. *From Shipmates to Soldiers: Emerging Black Identities in the Río de la Plata*. Albuquerque: University of New Mexico Press, 2015.

———. "The Slave Trade to the Río de la Plata, 1777–1812: Trans-Imperial Networks and Atlantic Warfare." *Colonial Latin American Review* 20, no. 1 (2011): 81–107.

Borucki, Alex, David Eltis, and David Wheat. "Atlantic History and the Slave Trade to Spanish America." *American Historical Review* 120, no. 2 (2015): 433–61.

Bracco, Diego. *Cautivas entre indígenas y gauchos*. Montevideo: Ediciones de la Banda Oriental, 2016.

———. *Charrúas, guenoas y guaraníes: Interacción y destrucción, indígenas del Río de la Plata*. Montevideo: Linardi y Risso, 2004.

———. *Con las armas en la mano: Charrúas, guenoa-minuanos y guaraníes*. Montevideo: Planeta, 2013.

———. "Los errores Charrúa y Guenoa-Minuán." *Jahrbuch für Geschichte Lateinamerikas* 41 (2004): 117–36.

Branch, Jordan. "Mapping the Sovereign State: Technology, Authority, and Systemic Change." *International Organization* 65 (2011): 1–36.

Brenner, Neil. "Critical Sociospatial Theory and the Geographies of Uneven Spatial Development." In *The SAGE Handbook of Economic Geography*, edited by Andrew

Leyshon, Roger Lee, Linda McDowell, and Peter Sunley, 135–48. Thousand Oaks, CA: Sage, 2011.

Brody, Hugh. *Maps and Dreams.* New York: Pantheon Books, 1982.

Brooks, James. *Captives and Cousins: Slavery, Kinship, and Community in the Southwest Borderlands.* Chapel Hill: University of North Carolina Press, 2002.

———. "'We Betray Our Own Nation': Indian Slavery and Multi-Ethnic Communities in the Southwest Borderlands." In *Indian Slavery in Colonial America,* edited by Alan Gallay, 319–52. Lincoln: University of Nebraska Press, 2009.

Brotton, Jerry. *Trading Territories: Mapping the Early Modern World.* Ithaca, NY: Cornell University Press, 1998.

Brückner, Martin, ed. *Early American Cartographies.* Chapel Hill: University of North Carolina Press, 2011.

Buarque de Holanda, Sérgio. *Visão do Paraíso: Os motivos edênicos no descobrimento e colonização do Brasil.* 2nd ed. São Paulo: Companhia Editora Nacional, 1969.

Buchan, Bruce, and Mary Heath. "Savagery and Civilization: From Terra Nullius to the 'Tide of History.'" *Ethnicities* 6, no. 1 (2006).

Buisseret, David. "Spanish Colonial Cartography, 1450–1700." In *The History of Cartography: Cartography in the European Renaissance,* edited by David Woodward, 1143–71. Chicago: University of Chicago Press, 2007.

Bukowczyk, John J. *Permeable Border: The Great Lakes Basin as a Transnational Region, 1650–1990.* Pittsburgh, PA: University of Pittsburgh Press, 2005.

Burnett, D. Graham. *Masters of All They Surveyed: Exploration, Geography, and a British El Dorado.* Chicago: University of Chicago Press, 2000.

Buscaglia, Silvana. "Indígenas, Borbones y enclaves coloniales: Las relaciones interétnicas en el fuerte San José durante su primera década de funcionamiento (Chubut, 1779–1789)." *Corpus. Archivos viertuales de la alteridad americana* 5, no. 1 (2015): 1–37.

Caamaño-Dones, Josué. "La concesión a Castilla de la soberanía sobre las Indias y el deber de evangelizar." Unpublished manuscript, 2005. http://smjegupr.net/wp-content/uploads/2012/05/La-concesion-a-Castilla-de-la-soberania-sobre-las-Indias.pdf.

Cabrera, Sebastián. "La garra minuana." *Qué pasa,* April 6, 2013. http://www.elpais.com.uy/que-pasa/los-abuelos-indios.html.

Cabrera Pérez, Leonel. "La incorporación del indígena de la Banda Oriental a la sociedad colonial/nacional urbana." *Revista TEFROS* 9 (2011): 1–23.

———. "Los 'indios infieles' de la Banda Oriental y su participación en la Guerra Guaranítica." *Estudos Ibero-Americanos* 15, no. 1 (1989): 215–27.

Cabrera Pérez, Leonel, and Isabel Barreto Messano. "El ocaso del mundo indígena y las formas de integración a la sociedad urbana montevideana." *Revista TEFROS* 4, no. 2 (2006): 1–19.

Caldas, J. A. L. Tupí. "Etnologia Sul-Riograndense: Esboço fundamental." *Revista do Instituto Histórico e Geográfico do Rio Grande do Sul* 22, no. 86 (1942): 303–80.

Calvo, Luis María. *Vivienda y ciudad colonial: El caso de Santa Fe.* Santa Fe, NM: Universidad Nacional del Litoral, 2011.

Camargo, Fernando. "Las relaciones luso-hispánicas en torno a las Misiones Orientales del Uruguay: De los orígenes al Tratado de Madrid, 1750." *Fronteras de la Historia* 8 (2003): 217–48.

Canals Frau, Salvador. *Las poblaciones indígenas de la Argentina: Su origen, su pasado, su presente.* Buenos Aires: Editorial Sudamericana, 1953.

Cañeque, Alejandro. *The King's Living Image: The Culture and Politics of Viceregal Power in Colonial Mexico.* New York: Routledge, 2004.

Caplan, Karen D. *Indigenous Citizens: Local Liberalism in Early National Oaxaca and Yucatán.* Stanford, CA: Stanford University Press, 2010.

Cardim, Pedro, Tamar Herzog, José Javier Ruiz Ibañez, and Gaetano Sabatini, eds. *Polycentric Monarchies: How Did Early Modern Spain and Portugal Achieve and Maintain a Global Hegemony?* Eastbourne: Sussex Academic Press, 2012.

Carrasco, David, and Scott Sessions, eds. *Cave, City, and Eagle's Nest: An Interpretive Journey through the Mapa de Cuauhtinchan no. 2.* Albuquerque: University of New Mexico Press, 2007.

Carrera, Magali. *Traveling from New Spain to Mexico: Mapping Practices of Nineteenth-Century Mexico.* Durham, NC: Duke University Press, 2011.

Castañeda de la Paz, María. "Nahua Cartography in Historical Context: Searching for Sources on the Mapa de Otumba." *Ethnohistory* 61, no. 2 (2014): 301–27.

Castellanos, Alfredo. *La Cisplatina: La independencia y la república caudillesca.* Vol. 3 of Historia Uruguaya. Montevideo: Ediciones de la Banda Oriental, 1974.

Castro, Wilde E. M. *Los Indios Mansos de la Banda Oriental: Santo Domingo Soriano— Documentada.* Montevideo: Impresora Editorial, 2000.

Castro-Klarén, Sara. "The Nation in Ruins: Archaeology and the Rise of the Nation." In *Beyond Imagined Communities: Reading and Writing the Nation in Nineteenth-Century Latin America,* edited by Sara Castro-Klarén and John Charles Chasteen, 161–96. Washington, DC: Woodrow Wilson Center Press, 2003.

Censo Nacional de Población, Hogares y Viviendas 2010 Censo del Bicentenario: Pueblos Originarios (Región Nordeste Argentino). Buenos Aires: Instituto Nacional de Estadística y Censos - INDEC, 2015.

Censo Nacional de Población, Hogares y Viviendas 2010 Censo del Bicentenario: Pueblos Originarios (Región Pampeana). Buenos Aires: Instituto Nacional de Estadística y Censos - INDEC, 2015.

Cervera, Manuel. *Historia de la ciudad y provincia de Santa Fe, 1573–1583.* Vol. 1. Santa Fe: La Unión de Ramón Ibáñey, 1907.

Cesar, Guilhermino. *História do Rio Grande do Sul: Período Colonial.* 3rd ed. Pôrto Alegre: Martins Livreiro-Editor, 2002.

Chang, Kornel S. *Pacific Connections: The Making of the U.S.-Canadian Borderlands.* Berkeley: University of California Press, 2012.

Chappell, David A. "Ethnogenesis and Frontiers." *Journal of World History* 4, no. 2 (1993): 267–75.

Combès, Isabelle, and Diego Villar. "Os mestiços mais puros: Representações chiriguano e chané da mestiçagem." *Mana* 13, no. 1 (2007): 41–62.

Coni, Emilio A. *Historia de las vaquerías del Río de la Plata, 1555–1750.* Buenos Aires: Editorial Devenir, 1956.

Conrad, Paul Timothy. "Captive Fates: Displaced American Indians in the Southwest Borderlands, Mexico, and Cuba, 1500–1800." PhD diss., University of Texas at Austin, August 2011.

Consejo de la Nación Charrúa. "Información básica al relator para Uruguay del Comité para la Eliminación de la Discriminación Racial (CERD): Hacia el examen del informe de Uruguay en la 91ª Sesion." Unpublished manuscript, Geneva, 2016.

Consens, Mario. *Extinción de los indígenas en el Río de la Plata*. Montevideo: Linardi y Risso, 2010.

Contreras Painemal, Carlos. "Los tratados mapuche." *Estudios Latinoamericanos* 1, no. 2 (2009): 47–66.

Cordero, Serafín. *Los charrúas: Síntesis etnográfica y arqueológica del Uruguay*. Montevideo: Editorial "Mentor," 1960.

Cortesão, Jaime, ed. *Alexandre de Gusmão e o Tratado de Madrid (1750), Parte III: Antecedentes do Tratado*. Vol. 1. Rio de Janeiro: Ministério das Relações Exteriores, Instituto Rio Branco, 1951.

———. *História do Brasil nos velhos mapas*. 2 vols. Rio de Janeiro: Ministério das Relações Exteriores, Instituto Rio Branco, 1971.

Costa, Maria de Fátima. "De Xarayes ao Pantanal: A cartografia de um mito geográfico." *Revista do Instituto de Estudos Brasileiros*, no. 45 (2007): 21–36.

———. "Miguel Ciera: Um demarcador de limites no interior sul-americano (1750–1760)." *Anais do Museu Paulista* 17, no. 2 (2009): 189–214.

———. "Viajes en la frontera colonial: Historias de una expedición de límites en la América Meridional (1753–1754)." *Anales del Museo de América* 16 (2009): 113–26.

Craib, Raymond B. *Cartographic Mexico: A History of State Fixations and Fugitive Landscapes*. Durham, NC: Duke University Press, 2004.

———. "Cartography and Decolonization." In *Decolonizing the Map: Cartography from Colony to Nation*, edited by James R. Akerman, 11–71. Chicago: University of Chicago Press, 2017.

Cramaussel, Chantal. "Forced Transfer of Indians in Nueva Vizcaya and Sinaloa: A Hispanic Method of Colonization." In *Contested Spaces of Early America*, edited by Juliana Barr and Edward Countryman, 184–207. Philadelphia: University of Pennsylvania Press, 2014.

Davies, Surekha. *Renaissance Ethnography and the Invention of the Human: New Worlds, Maps, and Monsters*. Cambridge: Cambridge University Press, 2016.

Deeds, Susan M. *Defiance and Deference in Mexico's Colonial North: Indians under Spanish Rule in Nueva Vizcaya*. Austin: University of Texas Press, 2003.

Delaney, David. *Territory: A Short Introduction*. Oxford: Blackwell, 2005.

DeLay, Brian. "Introduction" to *North American Borderlands: Rewriting Histories*, edited by Brian DeLay, 1-8. New York: Routledge, 2013.

DeLay, Brian. *War of a Thousand Deserts: Indian Raids and the U.S.-Mexican War*. New Haven, CT: Yale University Press, 2008.

Delgado Cultelli, Martín. "30 años del movimiento indígena en Uruguay." *Zur*, October 12, 2019. http://www.zur.org.uy/content/30-a%C3%B1os-del-movimiento -ind%C3%ADgena-en-uruguay.

———. "Violaciones históricas a los derechos de los pueblos originarios en el Uruguay: Una mirada introspectiva." *Conversaciones del Cono Sur* 3, no. 1 (2017): 1–5.

Deloria, Philip J. "From Nation to Neighborhood: Land, Policy, Culture, Colonialism, and Empire in U.S.-Indian Relations," in *The Cultural Turn in U.S. History*, edited by

James W. Cook, Lawrence B. Glickman, and Michael O'Malley, 343–82. Chicago: University of Chicago Press, 2008.

Devine Guzmán, Tracy. *Native and National in Brazil: Indigeneity after Independence.* Chapel Hill: University of North Carolina Press, 2013.

Di Stefano, Roberto, and Loris Zanatta. *Historia de la iglesia argentina: Desde la conquista hasta fines del siglo XX.* Buenos Aires: Grijalbo Mondadori, 2000.

Díaz, Antonio. *Apuntos varios sobre los indios charrúas.* Montevideo: Estado Mayor del Ejército, Departamento de Estudios Históricos, División "Histórica," 1977.

Djenderedjian, Julio. "Roots of Revolution: Frontier Settlement Policy and the Emergence of New Spaces of Power in the Río de la Plata Borderlands, 1777–1810." *Hispanic American Historical Review* 88, no. 4 (2008): 639–68.

Domingues, Ângela. *Quando os índios eram vassalos: Colonização e relações de poder no norte do Brasil na segunda metade do século XVIII.* Lisboa: Comissão Nacional Comemorações dos Descobrimentos Portugueses, 2000.

———. *Viagens de exploração geográfica na amazónia em finais do século XVIII: Política, ciência e aventura.* Série Atlântica. Lisboa: Instituto de Historia de Além-Mar, 1991.

Dunbabin, J. P. D. "Red Lines on Maps: The Impact of Cartographical Errors on the Border between the United States and British North America, 1782–1842." *Imago Mundi* 50 (1998): 105–26.

DuVal, Kathleen. *The Native Ground: Indians and Colonists in the Heart of the Continent.* Philadelphia: University of Pennsylvania Press, 2006.

Dym, Jordana, and Karl Offen, eds. *Mapping Latin America: A Cartographic Reader.* Chicago: University of Chicago Press, 2011.

Earle, Rebecca. *The Return of the Native: Indians and Myth-Making in Spanish America, 1810–1930.* Durham, NC: Duke University Press, 2007.

Edelson, S. Max. *The New Map of Empire: How Britain Imagined America before Independence.* Cambridge, MA: Harvard University Press, 2017.

Edney, Matthew H. "Knowledge and Cartography in the Early Atlantic." In *The Oxford Handbook of the Atlantic World: 1450–1850*, edited by Nicholas Canny and Philip D. Morgan, 87–112. Oxford: Oxford University Press, 2011.

———. *Mapping an Empire.* Chicago: University of Chicago Press, 1997.

Edney, Matthew H., and Mary Sponberg Pedley, eds. *The History of Cartography: Cartography in the European Enlightenment.* Vol. 4. Chicago: University of Chicago Press, forthcoming.

Edwards, Clinton R. "Geographical Coverage of the Sixteenth-Century Relaciones de Indias from South America." *Geoscience and Man* 21 (1980): 75–82.

El Jaber, Loreley. *Un país malsano: La conquista del espacio en las crónicas del Río de la Plata (siglos XVI y XVII).* Buenos Aires: Beatriz Viterbo Editora, 2011.

Ellis, Elizabeth. "Petite Nation with Powerful Networks: The Tunicas in the Eighteenth Century." *Louisiana History: The Journal of the Louisiana Historical Association* 58, no. 2 (2017): 133–78.

Enrique, Laura Aylén. "La movilidad como estrategia en el uso del territorio norpatagónico a vines del siglo XVIII: Funcionarios coloniales y grupos indígenas." *Relaciones de la Sociedad Argentina de Antropología* 36 (2011): 361–68.

————. "Paisajes coloniales en las fuentes escritas: una propuesta para re-pensarlos mediante la idea de 'nodos territoriales.'" In *Fuentes y archivos para una nueva Historia socio-cultural,* edited by Silvina Jensen, Andrea Pasquaré, and Leandro A. Di Gresia, 139–48. Bahía Blanca: Hemisferio Derecho, 2015.

Enrique, Laura Aylén, and María Laura Pensa. "Mapas sobre el Cono Sur americano." In *Entre los datos y los formatos: Indicios para la historia indígena de las fronteras en los archivos coloniales,* edited by Lidia R. Nacuzzi, 116–36. Buenos Aires: Centro de Antropología Social IDES, 2018.

Erbig, Jeffrey A., Jr. "Borderline Offerings: Tolderías and Mapmakers in the Eighteenth-Century Río de la Plata." *Hispanic American Historical Review* 96, no. 3 (2016): 445–80.

Erbig, Jeffrey A., Jr., and Sergio Hernán Latini. "Across Archival Limits: Imperial Records, Changing Ethnonyms, and Geographies of Knowledge." *Ethnohistory* 66, no. 2 (2019): 249–73.

Ethridge, Robbie. "Introduction: Mapping the Mississippian Shatter Zone." In *Mapping the Mississippian Shatter Zone: The Colonial Indian Slave Trade and Regional Instability in the American South,* edited by Robbie Ethridge and Sheri-Marie Shuck-Hall, 1–62. Lincoln: University of Nebraska Press, 2009.

Ethridge, Robbie, and Sheri-Marie Shuck-Hall, eds. *Mapping the Mississippian Shatter Zone: The Colonial Indian Slave Trade and Regional Instability in the American South.* Lincoln: University of Nebraska Press, 2009.

Farberman, Judith, and Silvia Ratto. "Actores, políticas e instituciones en dos espacios fronterizos chaqueños: La frontera santiagueña y el litoral rioplatense entre 1630–1800." *Prohistoria* 17, no. 22 (2014): 3–31.

Ferguson, R. Brian, and Neil L. Whitehead. "The Violent Edge of Empire." In *War in the Tribal Zone: Expanding States and Indigenous Warfare,* edited by R. Brian Ferguson and Neil L. Whitehead, 1–30. Santa Fe, NM: School of American Research Press, 1992.

Fernandes Pinheiro, José Feliciano. *Anais da Província de São Pedro (História da Colonização Alemã no Rio Grande do Sul).* Quarta Edição. Petrópolis: Editora Vozes, 1978.

Ferreira, Mário Olímpio Clemente. "O Mapa das Cortes e o Tratado de Madrid: a cartografia a serviço da diplomacia." *Varia História* 23, no. 37 (June 2007): 51–79.

Ferreira Acruche, Hevelly. "De 'rebeldes, traidores, infieles, desleales y desobedientes' a vassalos d'El Rei: O princípio da devolução de índios no Rio da Prata colonial (1750–1763)." *Antiguos Jesuitas en Iberoamérica* 3, no. 2 (2015): 150–68.

Ferreira Rodrigues, Alfredo. *Almanak litterario e estatístico do Rio Grande do Sul.* Vol. 23. Pelotas: Pinto & C., 1911.

Figueira, José H. "Los primitivos habitantes del Uruguay." In *El Uruguay en la Exposición Histórico-Americana de Madrid: Memoria de los trabajos realizados por la Comisión Nacional encargada de organizar los elementos de concurrencia,* 121–219. Montevideo: Imprenta Artística de Dornaleche y Reyes, 1892.

Figueira, José Joaquín. *Breviario de etnología y arqueología del Uruguay.* Montevideo: Gaceta Comercial, 1965.

————. *Contribución al estudio de la bibliografía de los aborígenes del Uruguay: "Los charrúas" de Pedro Stagnero y "Cerros de las cuentas" por Mario Ísola.* Montevideo, 1957.

———. *Eduardo Acevedo Díaz y los Aborígenes del Uruguay.* Montevideo: Estado Mayor del Ejército, Departamento de Estudios Históricos, División "Histórica," 1977.

Fitzmaurice, Andrew. "The Genealogy of Terra Nullius." *Australian Historical Studies* 38, no. 129 (2007): 1–15.

Fonseca, Pedro Ari Veríssimo da. *Tropeiros de mula: A ocupação do espaço, a dilitação das fronteiras.* 2nd ed. Passo Fundo: Gráfica Editora Berthier, 2004.

Fonseca Galvão, Manoel do Nascimento da. *Notas geográficas e históricas sobre a Laguna desde sua fundação até 1750.* London: British Library, 2016.

Fortes, João Borges. "O Brigadeiro José da Silva Paes e a fundação do Rio Grande." *Revista do Instituto Histórico e Geográfico do Rio Grande do Sul* 13, no. 51 (1933): 3–119.

———. *Rio Grande de São Pedro: Povoamento e conquista.* Vol. 37. Rio de Janeiro: Biblioteca Militar, 1941.

———. "Velhos caminhos do Rio Grande do Sul." *Revista do Instituto Histórico e Geográfico do Rio Grande do Sul* 18, no. 72 (1938): 203–54.

Foschiatti del Dell'Orto, Ana María H., and Alfredo S. Bolsi. "La Población de la Ciudad de Corrientes entre 1588 y 1988: Análisis desde la Perspectiva Geográfica." *Revista Geográfica*, no. 118 (1993): 65–115.

Foucault, Michel. "Questions of Geography." In *Power/Knowledge: Selected Interviews and Other Writings, 1972–1977*, edited by Colin Gordon, 63–77. New York: Pantheon Books, 1980.

Fradkin, Raúl O. "Las milicias de caballería de Buenos Aires, 1752–1805." *Fronteras de la Historia* 19, no. 1 (2014): 124–50.

Frega, Ana. "El Reglamento de Tierras de 1815: Justicia revolucionaria y virtud republicana." In *Tierras, reglamento y revolución: Reflexiones a doscientos años del reglamento artiguiste de 1815*, edited by Gerardo Caetano and Ana Ribeiro, 487–533. Montevideo: Planeta, 2015.

———. "Los 'infelices' y el carácter popular de la revolución artiguista." In *¿Y el pueblo dónde está? Contribuciones para una historia popular de la revolución de independencia en el Río de la Plata*, edited by Raúl O. Fradkin, 151–75. Buenos Aires: Prometeo Libros, 2008.

———. "Uruguayos y orientales: Itinerario de una síntesis compleja." In *Crear la nación: Los nombres de los países de América Latina*, edited by José Carlos Chiaramonte, Carlos Marichal, and Aimer Granados, 95–112. Buenos Aires: Editorial Sudamericana, 2008.

Frühauf Garcia, Elisa. *As diversas formas de ser índio: Políticas indígenas e políticas indigenistas no extremo sul da América portuguesa.* Rio de Janeiro: Arquivo Nacional, 2009.

———. "Quando os índios escolhem os seus aliados: As relações de 'amizade' entre os minuanos e os lusitanos no sul da América portuguesa (c. 1750–1800)." *Varia História* 24, no. 40 (July/December 2008): 613–32.

Fucé, Pablo. "Ceremonia persuasiva: El Gobernador, el Cabildo y la paz con los indígenas minuanes (Montevideo, 1730–1732)." *BROCAR* 30 (2006): 159–71.

Funes, Gregorio. *Ensayo de la historia civil de Buenos Aires, Tucuman y Paraguay.* 2nd ed. 2 vols. Buenos Aires: Imprenta Bonaerense, 1856.

Furtado, Júnia Ferreira. *O mapa que inventou o Brasil.* Rio de Janeiro: Versal, 2013.

Gallay, Alan, ed. *Indian Slavery in Colonial America.* Lincoln: University of Nebraska Press, 2009.

Galloway, Patricia. "'So Many Little Republics': British Negotiations with the Choctaw Confederacy, 1765." *Ethnohistory* 41, no. 4 (1994): 513–37.

Gálvez, Lucía. *De la tierra sin mal al paraíso: Guaraníes y jesuitas.* Buenos Aires: Aguilar, 2013.

Gándara, Natalia. "Representaciones de un territorio: La frontera mapuche en los proyectos ilustrados del Reino de Chile en la sigunda mitad del siglo XVIII." *Historia Crítica,* no. 59 (2015): 61–80.

Ganson, Barbara A. *The Guaraní under Spanish Rule in the Río de la Plata.* Stanford, CA: Stanford University Press, 2003.

Garcia, Anderson Marques, and Saul Eduardo Seiguer Milder. "Convergências e divergências: Aspectos das culturas indígenas Charrua e Minuano." *Vivência* 39 (2012): 37–49.

García, Claudia. "Hibridación, interacción social y adaptación cultural en la Costa de Mosquitos, siglos XVII y XVIII." *Anuario de Estudios Americanos* 59, no. 2 (2002): 441–62.

Garcia, Fernando Cacciatore de. *Fronteira iluminada: História do povoamento, conquista e limites do Rio Grande do Sul a partir do Tratado de Tordesilhas (1420–1920).* 2nd ed. Porto Alegre: Editora Sulina, 2012.

Garcia, Rodolfo, ed. *Anais da Biblioteca Nacional do Rio de Janeiro.* Vol. 52. Rio de Janeiro: M.E.S.—Serviço Gráfico, 1930.

———. *Anais da Biblioteca Nacional do Rio de Janeiro.* Vol. 53. Rio de Janeiro: M.E.S.—Serviço Gráfico, 1931.

Gartner, William G. "Mapmaking in the Central Andes." In *The History of Cartography: Cartography in the Traditional Africa, America, Arctic, Australian, and Pacific Societies,* edited by David Woodward and G. Malcolm Lewis, 257–300. Chicago: University of Chicago Press, 1998.

Gelman, Jorge. *Campesinos y estancieros.* Buenos Aires: Editorial Los Libros del Riel, 1998.

Gentinetta, Martín Alejandro. "Sourrière de Souillac, un matemático ilustrado en el Río de la Plata: Su trayectoria y aportes a la monarquía borbónica a fines del siglo XVIII." *Escuela de Historia,* no. 25 (2013).

Gianotti, Camila. "Procedimientos para el análisis de la movilidad prehistórica entre los constructores de cerritos mediante el uso de tecnologías geoespaciales." *Revista del Museo de Antropología* 7, no. 2 (2014): 271–84.

Gil, Tiago. *Infiéis Trangressores: Os contrabandistas da "fronteira" (1760–1810).* Rio de Janeiro: Arquivo Nacional, 2007.

———. "O contrabando na fronteira: Uma produção social de mercadorias." *Revista de la ABPHE* 95 (2003).

———. "Sobre o comércio ilícito: A visão dos demarcadores de limites sobre o contrabando terrestre na fronteira entre os domínios lusos e espanhóis no Rio da Prata (1774–1801)." Artigo apresentado nas II Jornadas de História Regional Comparada Porto Alegre, October 12–15, 2005.

Giudicelli, Christophe. "Encasillar la frontera: Clasificaciones coloniales y disciplinamiento del espacio en el área Diaguito-Calchaquí, siglos XVI–XVII." *Anuario IEHS: Instituto de Estudios histórico sociales,* no. 22 (2007): 161–212.

———, ed. *Luchas de clasificación: Las sociedades indígenas entre taxonomía, memoria y reapropiación.* Rosario: Prohistoria Ediciones, 2018.

Golin, Tau. *A Fronteira: Governos e movimentos espontâneos na fixação dos limites do Brasil com o Uruguai e a Argentina*. Vol. 1. Porto Alegre: L&PM, 2002.

———. *A Guerra Guaranítica: Como os exércitos de Portugal e Espanha destruíram os Sete Povos dos jesuítas e índios guaranis no Rio Grande do Sul*. 3rd ed. Porto Alegre: Editora da Universidade, Universidade Federal do Rio Grande do Sul, 1998.

Gómez Corte, José Ignacio Gomeza. "Em busca da memória e da identidade: A resistência do povo charrua no Uruguai." MA thesis, Universidade Federal do Estado de Rio de Janeiro, 2017.

Gose, Peter. *Invaders as Ancestors: On the Intercultural Making and Unmaking of Spanish Colonialism in the Andes*. Toronto: University of Toronto Press, 2008.

Griffin, Patrick. "A Plea for a New Atlantic History." *William and Mary Quarterly* 68, no. 2 (2011): 236–39.

Guerra, François-Xavier. "La desintegración de la monarquía hispánica: Revolución de independencia." In *De los imperios a las naciones: Iberoamérica siglo XIX*, edited by Antonio Annino, Luis Castro Leiva, and François-Xavier Guerra, 195–227. Zaragoza: IberCaja, Obra Cultural, 1994.

Gupta, Akhil, and James Ferguson. "Beyond 'Culture': Space, Identity, and the Politics of Difference." In *Culture, Power, Place: Explorations in Critical Anthropology*, edited by Akhil Gupta and James Ferguson, 33–51. Durham: Duke University Press, 1997.

Guy, Donna J., and Thomas E. Sheridan. "On Frontiers: The Northern and Southern Edges of the Spanish Empire in the Americas." In *Contested Ground: Comparative Frontiers on the Northern and Southern Edges of the Spanish Empire*, edited by Donna J. Guy and Thomas E. Sheridan, 3–15. Tucson: University of Arizona Press, 1998.

Hackel, Steven W. *Children of Coyote, Missionaries of Saint Francis: Indian-Spanish Relations in Colonial California, 1769–1850*. Chapel Hill: University of North Carolina Press, 2005.

Haesbaert, Rogério. "Del mito de la desterritorialización a la multiterritorialidad." *Cultura y representaciones sociales* 8, no. 15 (2013): 9–42.

Hämäläinen, Pekka. *The Comanche Empire*. New Haven, CT: Yale University Press, 2008.

———. "Lost in Transitions: Suffering, Survival, and Belonging in the Early Modern Atlantic World." *William and Mary Quarterly* 68, no. 2 (2011): 219–23.

———. "What's in a Concept? The Kinetic Empire of the Comanches." *History and Theory* 52 (2013): 81–90.

Hämäläinen, Pekka, and Samuel Truett. "On Borderlands." *Journal of American History* 98, no. 2 (2011): 338–61.

Hameister, Martha D. "'No princípio era o caos': A formação de um povoado na fronteira americana dos Impérios Ibéricos através do estudo das relações do compadrio." *Revista de História Regional* 15, no. 2 (2010): 95–128.

———. "Para dar calor à nova povoação: Estudo sobre estratégias sociais e familiares a partir dos registros batismais da Vila do Rio Grande (1738–1763)." Tese de Doutorado, 2006.

Hanke, Lewis. *The Spanish Struggle for Justice in the Conquest of America*. Philadelphia: University of Pennsylvania Press, 1949.

Harley, J. Brian. "Deconstructing the Map." In *Writing Worlds: Discourse, Text and Metaphor in the Representation of Landscape*, edited by T. J. Barnes and J. S. Duncan, 277–89. London: Routledge, 1992.

Harris, Cole. *The Resettlement of British Columbia: Essays on Colonialism and Geographical Change.* Vancouver: UBC Press, 1997.

Harvey, David. *The Condition of Postmodernity: An Enquiry into the Origins of Cultural Change.* Cambridge, MA: Blackwell, 1990.

Hele, Karl S. "Introduction" to *Lines Drawn upon the Water: First Nations and the Great Lakes Borders and Borderlands,* edited by Karl S. Hele, xiii–xxiii. Waterloo: Wilfrid Laurier University Press, 2008.

Herrera, Luis Alberto de. *La tierra charrúa.* 1901. Montevideo: Arca Editorial, 1968.

Herrera Ángel, Marta. *Ordenar para controlar: Ordenamiento espacial y control político en las llanuras del Caribe y en los Andes Centrales Neograndinos.* 3rd ed. Bogotá: Ediciones Uniades, 2014.

Herzog, Tamar. "Colonial Law and 'Native Customs': Indigenous Land Rights in Colonial Spanish America." *Americas* 69, no. 3 (2013): 303–21.

———. *Frontiers of Possession: Spain and Portugal in Europe and the Americas.* Cambridge, MA: Harvard University Press, 2015.

———. "Naming, Identifying and Authorizing Movement in Early Modern Spain and Spanish America." In *Registration and Recognition: Documenting the Person in World History,* edited by Keith Breckenridge and Simon Szreter, 191–209. Oxford: Oxford University Press, 2012.

———. *Upholding Justice: Society, State, and the Penal System in Quito, 1650–1750.* Ann Arbor: University of Michigan Press, 2004.

Hidalgo, Alex. *Trail of Footprints: A History of Indigenous Maps from Viceregal Mexico.* Austin: University of Texas Press, 2019.

Hilbert, Klaus. "Charruas e minuanos: Entre ruptura e continuidade." In *Povos indígenas,* edited by Nelson Boeira and Tau Golin, 179–205. Passo Fundo: Méritos, 2009.

Houot, Annie. *El trágico fin de los indios charrúas.* Montevideo: Linardi y Risso, 2013.

———. *Guaraníes y charrúas en la literatura uruguaya del siglo XIX: Realidad y ficción.* Montevideo: Linardi y Risso, 2007.

———. *Un cacique charrúa en París.* Montevideo: Editorial Costa Atlántica, 2002.

Imbelloni, José. "Lenguas indígenas del territorio argentino." In *Historia de la Nación Argentina,* edited by Ricardo Levene, 57–75. Buenos Aires: Academia Nacional de la Historia, Editorial El Ateneo, 1961.

Jackson, Robert H. "La población y tasas vitales de las misiones jesuíticas de los Guaraní (Argentina, Brasil, Paraguay)." *Antiguos Jesuitas en Iberoamérica* 5, no. 2 (2017): 100–165.

———. "The Post-Jesuit Expulsion Population of the Paraguay Missions, 1768–1803." *Colonial Latin American Historical Review* 16, no. 4 (2007): 429–58.

Johnson, Lyman L., Susan M. Socolow, and Sibila Seibert. "Población y espacio en el Buenos Aires del siglo XVIII." *Desarrollo Económico* 20, no. 79 (1980): 329–49.

Jones, Charles. "International Relations in the Americas during the Long Eighteenth Century, 1663–1820." In *International Orders in the Early Modern World: Before the Rise of the West,* edited by Shogo Suzuki, Yongjin Zhang, and Joel Quirk, 118–37. New York: Routledge, 2013.

Kagan, Richard. *Urban Images of the Hispanic World, 1493–1793.* New Haven, CT: Yale University Press, 2000.

Kaiser, Robert, and Elena Nikiforova. "The Performativity of Scale: The Social Construction of Scale Effects in Narva, Estonia." *Environment and Planning D: Society and Space* 26 (2008): 537–62.

Kantor, Iris. "Cartografia e diplomacia: usos geopolíticos da informação toponímica (1750–1850)." *Anais do Museu Paulista* 17, no. 2 (2009): 39–61.

———. "Soberania e territorialidade colonial: Academia Real de História Portuguesa e a América Portuguesa (1720)." In *Temas Setecentistas: Governos e populações no império português*, edited by Andrea Doré and Antonio Cesar de Almeida Santos, 233–39. Curitiva: UFPR/SCHLA, 2009.

———. "Usos diplomáticos da ilha-Brasil: Polêmicas cartográficas e historiográficas." *Varia História* 23, no. 37 (2007): 70–80.

Karasch, Mary. *Before Brasília: Frontier Life in Central Brasil*. Albuquerque: University of New Mexico Press, 2016.

———. "Catechism and Captivity: Indian Policy in Goiás, 1780–1889." In *Native Brazil: Beyond the Convert and the Cannibal, 1500–1900*, edited by Hal Langfur, 198–224. Albuquerque: University of New Mexico Press, 2014.

Keller, Arthur S., Oliver J. Lissitzyn, and Frederick J. Mann. *Creation of Rights of Sovereignty through Symbolic Acts, 1400–1800*. New York: Columbia University Press, 1938.

Kent, Michael, and Ricardo Ventura Santos. "'Os charrúas vivem' nos gaúchos: A vida social de uma pesquisa de 'resgate' genético de uma etnia indígena extinta no sul do Brasil." *Horizóntes Antropológicos* 18, no. 37 (2012): 341–72.

Klein, Fernando. "El destino de los indígenas del Uruguay." *Nómadas. Revista Crítica de Cincias Sociales y Jurídicas* 15, no. 1 (2007).

Kühn, Fábio. *Breve história do Rio Grande do Sul*. 4th ed. Temas do novo século. Porto Alegre: RS Leitura XXI, 2011.

———. "Una frontera en convulsión: Rio Grande de São Pedro y la Banda Oriental durante el gobierno de don Diogo de Souza (1809–1814)." *Cuadernos del CILMA*, no. 18 (2013): 127–39.

LaDow, Beth. *The Medicine Line: Life and Death on a North American Borderland*. New York: Routledge, 2001.

Lafone Quevado, Samuel. "Los indios chanases y su lengua. Con apuntes sobre los querandíes, yaros, boanes, güenoas o minuanes." *Boletín del Instituto Geográfico Argentino* 18 (1897): 133–51.

Langavant, Benita Herreros Cleret de. "La frontera del Alto Paraguay a fines del siglo XVIII: Diplomacia, cartografía y cotidianidad." In *Las fronteras en el Mundo Atlántico (siglos XVI–XIX)*, edited by Susana Truchuelo and Emir Reitano, 331–60. La Plata: Universidad Nacional de La Plata, 2017.

Langfur, Hal. *The Forbidden Lands: Colonial Identity, Frontier Violence, and the Persistence of Brazil's Eastern Indians, 1750–1830*. Stanford, CA: Stanford University Press, 2006.

———. "Frontier/ Fronteira: A Transnational Reframing of Brazil's Inland Colonization." *History Compass* 12, no. 11 (2014): 843–52.

Laroque, Luís Fernando da Silva. "Os nativos charrua/minuano, guarani e kainkang: O protagonismo indígena e as relações interculturais em territórios de planície, serra e planalto do Rio Grande do Sul." In *Releituras da História do Rio Grande do Sul*, edited by Claudio Knierim and Sandra Careli, 15–42. Porto Alegre: CORAG, 2011.

Latini, Sergio Hernán. "Reducción de charrúas en la "Banda del Norte" a principios del siglo XVII: ¿Logro del poder colonial o estrategia indígena de adaptación?" *Memoria Americana* 21, no. 2 (2013): 203–33.

———. "Repensando la construcción de la cuenca del Plata como espacio de frontera." In *Fronteras: Espacios de interacción en las tierras bajas del sur de América*, edited by Carina P. Lucaioli and Lidia R. Nacuzzi, 69–99. Buenos Aires: Sociedad Argentina de Antropología, 2010.

Latini, Sergio Hernán, and Carina P. Lucaioli. "Las tramas de la interacción colonial en el Chaco y la "otra banda": Una campaña punitiva de principios del siglo XVIII." *Revista de Ciencias Sociales*, no. 26 (2014): 7–27.

Lefebvre, Henri. *The Production of Space*. Cambridge: Blackwell, 1991.

Leibsohn, Dana. "Colony and Cartography: Shifting Signs on Indigenous Maps of New Spain." In *Reframing the Renaissance: Visual Culture in Europe and Latin America, 1450–1650*, edited by Claire J. Farago, 265–81. New Haven, CT: Yale University Press, 1995.

Leite, Serafim. *História da Companhia de Jesús no Brasil*. Vol. 6. Rio de Janeiro: Imprensa Nacional, 1945.

———. *História da Companhia de Jesús no Brasil*. Vol. 9. Rio de Janeiro: Instituto Nacional do Livro, 1949.

Lennox, Jeffers. *Homelands and Empires: Indigenous Spaces, Imperial Fictions, and Competition for Territory in Northeastern North America, 1690–1763*. Toronto: University of Toronto Press, 2017.

Lepore, Jill. *The Name of War: King Philip's War and the Origins of American Identity*. New York: Knopf, 1998.

Levaggi, Abelardo. *Paz en la frontera: Historia de la relaciones diplomáticas con las comunidades indígenas en la Argentina (Siglos XVI–XIX)*. Buenos Aires: Universidad del Museo Social Argentino, 2000.

Levinton, Norberto. *El espacio jesuítico-guaraní: La formación de una región cultural*. Biblioteca de Estudios Paraguayos. Vol. 80. Asunción: Centro de Estudios Antropológicos de la Universidad Católica (CEADUC), 2009.

———. "Guaraníes y Charrúas: Una frontera exclusivista-inclusivista." *Revista de História Regional* 14, no. 1 (2009): 49–75.

———. "La burocracia administrativa contra la obra evangelizadora: Una reducción de Charrúas fundada por Fray Marcos Ortiz." *Primeras Jornadas de Historia de la Orden Dominicana en la Argentina* (August 2003): 245–57.

———. "Las estancias de Nuestra Señora de los Reyes de Yapeyú: Tenencia de la tierra por uso cotidiano, acuerdo interétnico y derecho natural (Misiones jesuíticas del Paraguay)." *Revista Complutense de Historia de América* 31 (2005): 33–51.

Lewis, G. Malcolm, ed. *Cartographic Encounters: Perspectives on Native American Mapmaking and Map Use*. Chicago: University of Chicago Press, 1998.

Lipman, Andrew. *The Saltwater Frontier: Indians and the Contest for the American Coast*. New Haven, CT: Yale University Press, 2015.

Livi, Hebe. "El Charrúa en Santa Fe." *Revista de la Junta Provincial de Estudios Históricos de Santa Fe*, no. 49 (1978): 33–45.

Livingstone, David N. *The Geographical Tradition: Episodes in the History of a Contested Enterprise*. Cambridge: Blackwell, 1993.

Lockhart, James. *Of Things of the Indies: Essays Old and New in Early Latin American History.* Stanford, CA: Stanford University Press, 1999.

López Israel, Carolina. "As relações de fronteira no início do século XVIII a partir de um estudo demográfico de Rio Grande." *Biblos* 20 (2006): 51–64.

López Mazz, José M. "Sangre indígena en Uruguay: Memoria y ciudadanías post nacionales." *Athenea Digital* 18, no. 1 (2018): 181–201.

López Mazz, José M., and Diego Bracco. *Minuanos: Apuntes y notas para la historia y la arqueología del territorio guenoa-minuán (Indígenas de Uruguay, Argentina y Brasil).* Montevideo: Linardi y Risso, 2010.

López Monfiglio, César M. *El totemismo entre los charrúas.* Vol. 1 of Cuadernos de antropología. Montevideo: Centro de Estudios Arqueológicos y Antropológicos Americanos, 1962.

Lothrop, Samuel Kirlkand. "Indians of the Paraná Delta, Argentina." *Annals of the New York Academy of Sciences* 33 (1932): 77–232.

Lucaioli, Carina P. *Abipones en las fronteras del Chaco: Una etnografía histórica sobre el siglo XVIII.* Buenos Aires: Sociedad Argentina de Antropología, 2011.

———. "Los contextos de producción de los documentos coloniales." In *Entre los datos y los formatos: Indicios para la historia indígena de las fronteras en los archivos coloniales,* edited by Lidia R. Nacuzzi, 6–28. Buenos Aires: Centro de Antropología Social IDES, 2018.

Lucaioli, Carina P., and Sergio Hernán Latini. "Fronteras permeables: Circulación de cautivos en el espacio santafesino." *Runa* 35, no. 1 (2014): 113–32.

Lucaioli, Carina P. and Lidia R. Nacuzzi, eds. *Fronteras: Espacios de interacción en las tierras bajas del sur de América.* Buenos Aires: Sociedad Argentina de Antropología, 2010.

Lucena Giraldo, Manuel. *Laboratorio tropical: La expedición de límites al Orinoco, 1750– 1767.* Caracas, Venezuela: CSIC-España, 1993.

Lucena Giraldo, Manuel, and Antonio E. de Pedro. *La frontera caríbica: Expedición de Límites al Orinoco, 1754/1761.* Caracas: Lagoven, 1992.

Luedeke, Hugo. "Os primitivos habitantes do Rio Grande do Sul." *Revista do Archivo Público do Rio Grande do Sul,* no. 20 (1928): 59–63.

Lynch, John. *Spanish Colonial Administration, 1782–1810: The Intendant System in the Viceroyalty of the Río de la Plata.* London: University of London, 1958.

Maeder, Ernesto J. A. "El conflicto entre charrúas y guaraníes de 1700: Una disputa por el espacio oriental de las misiones." *ICADE,* no. 20 (1992): 129–43.

Maeder, Ernesto J. A., and Ramón Gutiérrez. *Atlas territorial y urbano de las misiones jesuíticas de guaraníes. Argentina, Paraguay e Brasil.* Sevilla: Consejería de Cultura, 2009.

Magalhães, Joaquim Romero. "Mundos em miniatura: Aproximação a alguns aspectos da cartografia portuguesa do Brasil (séculos XVI a XVIII)." *Anais do Museu Paulista* 17, no. 1 (2009): 69–94.

Magalhães de Carvalho, Ana Maria, and Mónica Michelena. "Reflexiones sobre los esencialismos en la antropología uruguaya: Una etnografía invertida." *Conversaciones del Cono Sur* 3, no. 1 (2017): 1–10.

Maggi, Carlos. *Artigas y su hijo el Caciquillo: El mundo pensado desde el lejano norte o las 300 pruebas contra la historia en uso.* Montevideo: Editorial Fin del Siglo, 1991.

Mandrini, Raul. "Transformations: The Río de la Plata during the Bourbon Era." In *Contested Spaces of Early America,* edited by Juliana Barr and Edward Countryman, 142–62. Philadelphia: University of Pennsylvania Press, 2014.

Mandrini, Raúl, and Sara Ortelli. "Repensando viejos problemas: Observaciones sobre la araucanización de las pampas." *Runa* 22 (1995): 135–50.

Mariluz Urquijo, José María. *El régimen de la tierra en el derecho indiano.* Buenos Aires: Perrot, 1968.

————. *El Virreinato del Río de la Plata en la época del Marqués de Avilés (1799–1801).* 2nd ed. Colección del 5° Centenario. Buenos Aires: Plus Ultra, 1987.

————. *La expedición contra los charrúas en 1801 y la fundación de Belén.* Montevideo: El Siglo Ilustrado, 1952.

————. *La fundación de San Gabriel de Batoví.* Montevideo: Monteverde, 1953.

————. "La valoración de la bulas alejandrinas en el siglo XVIII." *Anuario Mexicano de Historia del Derecho,* no. 5 (1993): 167–77.

————. "Los guaraníes después de la expulsión de los jesuitas." *Estudios Americanos* 6, no. 25 (1953): 323–30.

Martínez, Benigno T. *Cartografía histórica de República Argentina.* Buenos Aires: Museo Plata, 1893.

Martín-Merás, Luisa. "Fondos cartográficos y documentales de la Comisión de Límites de Brasil en el siglo XVIII en el Museo Naval e Madrid." *Terra Brasilis (Nova Série)* 7–8–9 (2007): 1–58.

Matthew, Laura E., and Michel R. Oudijk, eds. *Indian Conquistadors: Indigenous Allies in the Conquest of Mesoamerica.* Norman: University of Oklahoma Press, 2007.

Mayo, Carlos A. "El cautiverio y sus funciones en una sociedad de frontera: El caso de Buenos Aires (1750–1810)." *Revista de Indias* 45, no. 175 (1985): 235–43.

McDonnell, Michael A. *Masters of Empire: Great Lakes Indians and the Making of America.* New York: Hill and Wang, 2015.

Meléndez, Mariselle. "The Cultural Production of Space in Colonial Latin America: From Visualizing Difference to the Circulation of Knowledge." In *The Spatial Turn: Interdisciplinary Perspectives,* edited by Barney Warf and Santa Arias. London: Routledge, 2009.

Mendonça, Marcos. *A Amazônia na era pombalina: Correspondência inédita do governador e capitão-general do estado do Grão Pará e Maranhão.* Vol. 2. Rio de Janeiro: Instituto Histórico e Geográfico Brasileiro, 1963.

Merenson, Silvina. "Cuando ser indio no rinde: Sociedad política, particularismo y excepción en las narrativas nacionales del Uruguay." *Espaço Ameríndio* 4, no. 2 (2010): 172–90.

Messano, Isabel Barreto. "Padrones y archivos parroquiales en el Uruguay: Desafíos y alternativas en el estudio de las poblaciones históricas." In *Poblaciones históricas: Fuentes, métodos y líneas de investigación,* 95–115. Rio de Janeiro: Asociación Latinoamericana de Población, 2009.

Metcalf, Alida C. *Go-Betweens and the Colonization of Brazil, 1500–1600.* Austin: University of Texas Press, 2005.

Mezzadra, Sandro, and Brett Neilson. *Border as Method, or, The Multiplication of Labor.* Durham, NC: Duke University Press, 2013.

Michelena, Mónica. "Mujeres charrúas: Rearmando el gran quillapí de la memoria en Uruguay." Universidad Indígena Intercultural, 2011.

Mignolo, Walter. *The Darker Side of the Renaissance: Literacy, Territoriality, and Colonization.* Ann Arbor: University of Michigan Press, 1995.

Miles, Tiya. *The Dawn of Detroit: A Chronicle of Slavery and Freedom in the City of the Straits.* New York: New Press, 2017.

Mirow, Matthew C. *Latin American Law: A History of Private Law and Institutions in Spanish America.* Austin: University of Texas Press, 2004.

Mones, Alvaro, and Miguel A. Klappenbach. *Un ilustrado aragonés en el Virreinato del Río de la Plata, Félix de Azara (1742–1821): Estudios sobre su vida, su obra y su pensamiento.* Montevideo: Museo Nacional de Historia Natural, 1997.

Monteiro, John M. *Negros da terra: Índios e bandeirantes nas origens de São Paulo.* São Paulo: Companhia das Letras, 1994.

———. "Rethinking Amerindian Resistance and Persistence in Colonial Portuguese America." In *New Approaches to Resistance in Brazil and Mexico*, edited by John Gledhill and Patience A. Schell, 25–43. Durham, NC: Duke University Press, 2012.

———. "Tupis, tapuias e historiadores: Estudos de História Indígena e do Indigenismo." Tese Apresentada para o Concurso de Livre Docência, IFCH-Unicamp, 2001.

Moretti, Marco. *International Law and Nomadic People.* Central Milton Keynes: Author House, 2012.

Morgan, Muriel L. "Funcionarios borbónicos y espacios de frontera: Objetivos de las políticas de población entre las reducciones de Moxos y Chiquitos." *Memoria Americana* 23, no. 1 (2015): 129–57.

Mörner, Magnus. *The Expulsion of the Jesuits from Latin America.* New York: Knopf, 1965.

Muldoon, James. "John Wyclif and the Rights of the Infidels: The Requerimiento Re-examined." *Americas* 36, no. 3 (1980): 301–16.

Mundy, Barbara E. *The Mapping of New Spain: Indigenous Cartography and the Maps of the Relaciones Geográficas.* Chicago: University of Chicago Press, 1996.

Muñoz Arbelaez, Santiago. "'Medir y amojonar': La cartografía y la producción del espacio colonial en la Provincia de Santa Marta, siglo XVIII." *Historia Crítica*, no. 34 (2007): 208–31.

Murra, John V. "An Aymara Kingdom in 1567." *Ethnohistory* 15, no. 2 (1968): 115–51.

Murray, David. *Indian Giving: Economies of Power in Indian-White Exchanges.* Amherst: University of Massachusetts Press, 2000.

Nacuzzi, Lidia R. *Identidades impuestas: Tehuelches, aucas y pampas en el norte de la Patagonia.* 2nd ed. Buenos Aires: Sociedad Argentina de Antropología, 2005.

———. "La cuestión del nomadismo entre los tehuelches." *Memoria Americana*, no. 1 (1991): 103–34.

———. "Repensando y revisando el concepto de cacicazgo en las fronteras del sur de América (Pampa y Patagonia)." *Revista Española de Antropología Americana* 38, no. 2 (2008): 75–95.

Nader, Helen. *Liberty in Absolutist Spain: The Habsburg Sale of Towns, 1516–1700.* Baltimore, MD: Johns Hopkins University Press, 1990.

Nazzari, Muriel. "Transition toward Slavery: Changing Legal Practice regarding Indians in Seventeenth-Century São Paulo." *Americas* 49, no. 2 (1992): 131–55.

Nesis, Florencia Sol. *Los grupos mocoví en el siglo XVIII*. Buenos Aires: Sociedad Argentina de Antropología, 2005.

Neumann, Eduardo Santos. "Fronteira e identidade: Confrontos luso-guarani na Banda Oriental, 1680–1757." *Revista Complutense de Historia de América* 26 (2000): 73–92.

———. "O Rio Grande do Sul na cartografia antiga." *Revista do Instituto Histórico e Geográfico do Rio Grande do Sul* 26, no. 103 (1946): 293–97.

O'Brien, Jean M. *Firsting and Lasting: Writing Indians Out of Existence in New England*. Minneapolis: University of Minnesota Press, 2010.

Offen, Karl. "Creating Mosquitia: Mapping Amerindian Spatial Practices in Eastern Central America, 1629–1779." *Journal of Historical Geography* 33 (2007): 254–82.

———. "Mapping Amerindian Captivity in Colonial Mosquitia." *Journal of Latin American Geography* 14, no. 3 (2015): 35–65.

Oliveira de Freitas, Osorio Tuyuty. *A invasão de São Borja*. Pôrto Alegre: Do globo, 1935.

Olivera, Andrea. "Charrúas urbanos en Uruguay: ¿Un proceso de etnogénesis?" In *Sujetos emergentes: Nuevos y viejos contextos de negociación de las identidades en América Latina*, edited by Carlos Alberto Casas Mendoza, José Guadalupe Rivera González, and Leonardo Ernesto Márquez Mireles, 95–110. San Luis Potosí: Ediciones Eón, 2013.

———. *Devenir Charrúa en el Uruguay: Una etnografía junto con colectivos urbanos*. Montevideo: Fondation pour l'Université de Lausanne, 2016.

Operé, Fernando. *Indian Captivity in Spanish America: Frontier Narratives*. Charlottesville: University of Virginia Press, 2008.

Ortelli, Sara. *Trama de una guerra conveniente: Nueva Vizcaya y la sombra de los apaches, 1748–1790*. México DF: Centro de Estudios Históricos, El Colegio de México, 2007.

———. "Vivir en los márgenes: Fronteras porosas y circulación de población en la Nueva Vizcaya tardo colonial." *Anuario de Historia Regional y de las Fronteras* 19, no. 1 (2014): 39–57.

Otero, Pacífico. *La orden franciscana en el Uruguay: Crónica histórica del Convento de San Bernardino de Montevideo*. Buenos Aires: Cabaut y Cía, 1908.

Owens, David James. "Spanish-Portuguese Territorial Rivalry in Colonial Río de la Plata." *Yearbook, Conference of Latin Americanist Geographers* 19 (1993): 15–24.

Owensby, Brian. *Empire of Law and Indian Justice in Colonial Mexico*. Stanford, CA: Stanford University Press, 2008.

Padrón Favre, Oscar. *Los Charrúas-Minuanes en su etapa final*. Durazno, Uruguay: Tierradentro Ediciones, 2004.

Pagden, Anthony. "Law, Colonization, Legitimation, and the European Background." In *The Cambridge History of Law in America*, edited by Michael Grossberg and Christopher L. Tomlins, 1–31. Cambridge: Cambridge University Press, 2008.

Paquette, Gabriel. *Imperial Portugal in the Age of Atlantic Revolutions: The Luso-Brazilian World, c. 1770–1850*. Cambridge: Cambridge University Press, 2013.

Pedley, Mary Sponberg. "Map Wars: The Role of Maps in the Nova Scotia/Acadia Boundary Disputes of 1750." *Imago Mundi* 50 (1998): 96–104.

Penhos, Marta. "En las fronteras del arte: Topografía, cartografía y pintura en la Expedición de la América Meridional a fines del siglo XVIII." In *Historias de la Cartografía de Iberamérica: Nuevos caminos, viejos problemas*, edited by Héctor Mendoza Vargas and Carla Lois, 329–49. México DF: Instituto de Geografía, UNAM; INEGI, 2009.

Penino, Raúl, and Alfredo F. Sollazzo. "El paradero charrúa del Puerto de las Tunas y su alfarería." *Revista de la Sociedad de Amigos de la Arqueología* 1 (1927): 151–60.

Perea y Alonso, S. *Apuntes para la Prehistoria Indígena del Río de la Plata y especialmente de la Banda Oriental del Uruguay.* Montevideo: Imprenta de A. Monteverde y Cía., 1937.

Pereira, Cesar Castro. "'Y hoy están en paz': Relações entre os índios 'infiéis' da Banda Oriental e guaranis missioneiros no período colonial tardio (1737–1801)." Trabalho de Conclusão de Curso, Universidade Federal do Rio Grande do Sul, dezembro de 2008.

Pereira, Claudio Corrêa. *Minuanos/Guenoas: Os Cerritos de bacia da lagoa Mirim e as origens de uma nação pampiana.* Porto Alegre: Fundação Cultural Gaúcha, 2008.

Pérez Baltasar, María Dolores. "Orígenes de los recogimientos de mujeres." *Cuadernos de Historia Moderna y Contemporánea* 6 (1985): 13–24.

Pérez Colman, César Blás. *Historia de Entre Ríos: Epoca colonial (1520–1810).* Vol. 1. Paraná: Imprensa de la Provincia, 1936–37.

Pérez Martínez, Ruperto. "Los límites del Estado Oriental y el Tratado de 12 de Octubre de 1851." *La Revista de Derecho, Jurisprudencia y Administración* 7, no. 19 (1901): 303–8.

Pérez Zavala, Graciana, and Marcela Tamagnini. "Dinámica territorial y poblacional en el Virreinato del Río de la Plata: Indígenas y cristianos en la frontera sur de la gobernación intendencia de Córdoba del Tucumán, 1779–1804." *Fronteras de la Historia* 17, no. 1 (2012): 195–225.

Pi Hugarte, Renzo. *Los indios de Uruguay.* Madrid: Editorial MAPFRE, 1993.

———. "Sobre el charruismo: La antropología en el sarao de las seudociencias." *Antropología Social y Cultural en Uruguay* (2002–2003), 103–21.

Picerno, José E. *¿Qué quieren estos hombres?* Montevideo: Tradinco, 2003.

Pickles, John. *A History of Spaces: Cartographic Reason, Mapping and the Geo-Coded World.* New York: Routledge, 2004.

Pinto Rodríguez, Jorge. *La formación del estado y la nación, y el pueblo mapuche: De la inclusión a la exclusión.* Santiago, Chile: Dirección de Bibliotecas, Archivos y Museos: Centro de Investigaciones Diego Barros Arana, 2003.

Pivel Devoto, Juan E. *Raíces coloniales de la Revolución Oriental de 1811.* Montevideo, 1952.

Poenitz, Erich L. W. Edgar. *Los infieles minuanes y charrúas en territorio misionero durante la época virreinal.* Posadas, Argentina: Universidad Nacional de Misiones, Facultad de Ciencias Sociales, 1985.

Pollero Beheregaray, Raquel. "Historia demográfica de Montevideo y su campaña (1757–1860)." Tesis de Doctorado, Universidad de la República, 2016.

Ponce de León, Luis R. "Minuanes o Guenoas: Eran nuestros indígenas en la época de fundación de Montevideo." *Boletín Histórico del Estado Mayor General de Ejército*, 112–15 (1967): 23–40.

Pont, Raul. *Campos Realengos: Formação da Fronteira Sudoeste do Rio Grande do Sul.* Vol. 1. Porto Alegre: Renascença, 1986.

Porto, Aurélio. "Fronteira do Rio Pardo: Penetração e fixação de povoadores." *Revista do Instituto Histórico e Geográfico do Rio Grande do Sul* 9, no. 33 (1929): 49–64.

———. *História das Missões Orientais do Uruguai (Primeira Parte).* Vol. 3 of *Jesuítas no Sul do Brasil.* Porto Alegre: Livraria Selbach, 1954.

————. *História das Missões Orientais do Uruguai (Segunda Parte)*. Vol. 4 of *Jesuítas no Sul do Brasil*. Porto Alegre: Livraria Selbach, 1954.

————. "O minuano na toponímia rio-grandense." *Revista do Instituto Histórico e Geográfico do Rio Grande do Sul* 18, no. 71 (1938): 103–11.

Portuondo, María M. *Secret Science: Spanish Cosmography and the New World*. Chicago: University of Chicago Press, 2009.

Poska, Allyson M. *Gendered Crossings: Women and Migration in the Spanish Empire*. Albuquerque: University of New Mexico Press, 2016.

Possamai, Paulo César. "De núcleo de povoamento à praça de guerra: A Colônia do Sacramento de 1735 a 1777." *Topoi* 11, no. 21 (2010): 23–36.

Postnikov, Alexei. "Cartography and Boundary-Making on the Pamir (Eighteenth and Nineteenth Centuries)." *Terrae Icognitae* 30, no. 1 (1998): 72–89.

Pouey Vidal, Viviane. "Etnoarqueologia dos Charrua do Rio Grande do Sul: História, construção e ressignificação étnica." *Estudios Históricos* 7, no. 15 (2015): 1–30.

Prado, Fabrício Pereira. "A carreira transimperial de don Manuel Cipriano de Melo no Rio da Prata do século XVIII." *Topoi* 13, no. 25 (2012): 168–84.

————. *A Colônia do Sacramento: O extremo sul da américa portuguesa no século XVIII*. Porto Alegre: F.P. Prado, 2002.

————. *Edge of Empire: Atlantic Networks and Revolution in Bourbon Río de la Plata*. Oakland: University of California Press, 2015.

Pratt, Mary Louise. *Imperial Eyes: Travel Writing and Transculturation*. New York: Routledge, 1992.

Prescott, John Robert Victor, and Gillian D. Triggs. *International Frontiers and Boundaries: Law, Politics and Geography*. Leiden: Martinus Nijhoff, 2008.

Quarleri, Lía. *Rebelión y guerra en las fronteras del Plata: Guaraníes, jesuitas e imperios coloniales*. Buenos Aires: Fondo de la Cultura Económica, 2009.

Queiroz, Maria Luiza Bertulini. "A Vila do Rio Grande de São Pedro, 1737–1822." Universidade Federal de Santa Catarina, 1985.

Quesada, Vicente G. *La política del Brasil con las repúblicas del Río de la Plata*. Vol. 2 of *Historia diplomática latino-americana*. Buenos Aires: La Cultura Argentina, 1919.

————. *Los indios en las Provincias del Río de la Plata: Estudio Histórico*. Buenos Aires: Compañía Sud-Americana de Billetes de Banco, 1903.

Radcliffe, Sarah A., and Sallie Westwood, eds. *Remaking the Nation: Place, Identity and Politics in Latin America*. London: Routledge, 1996.

Radding, Cynthia M. *Landscapes of Power and Identity: Comparative Histories in the Sonoran Desert and the Forests of Amazonia from Colony to Republic*. Durham, NC: Duke University Press, 2005.

————. *Wandering Peoples: Colonialism, Ethnic Spaces, and Ecological Frontiers in Northwestern Mexico, 1700–1850*. Durham, NC: Duke University Press, 1997.

Rama, Ángel. *The Lettered City*. Durham, NC: Duke University Press, 1996.

Raminelli, Ronald. *Viagens ultramarinas: Monarcas, vassalos e governo à distância*. São Paulo: Alameda, 2008.

Rao, Sujay. "Arbiters of Change: Provincial Elites and the Origins of Federalism in Argentina's Littoral, 1814–1820." *Americas* 64, no. 4 (2008): 511–46.

Rappaport, Joanne, and Tom Cummins. *Beyond the Lettered City: Indigenous Literacies in the Andes*. Durham, NC: Duke University Press, 2012.

Rausch, Jane M. *A Tropical Plains Frontier: The Llanos of Colombia, 1531–1831*. Albuquerque: University of New Mexico Press, 1984.

Readman, Paul, Cynthia Radding, and Chad Bryant. "Borderlands in a Global Perspective." In *Borderlands in World History, 1700–1914*, edited by Paul Readman, Cynthia Radding, and Chad Bryant, 1–23. Basingstoke: Palgrave Macmillan, 2014.

Reid, Joshua L. *The Sea Is My Country: The Maritime World of the Makahs, An Indigenous Borderlands People*. New Haven, CT: Yale University Press, 2015.

Rela, Walter. *Portugal en las exploraciones del Río de la Plata*. Montevideo: Academia Uruguaya de Historia Maritima y Fluvial, 2002.

Reséndez, Andrés. *The Other Slavery: The Uncovered Story of Indian Enslavement in the America*. Boston: Houghton Mifflin Harcourt, 2016.

Rivet, Paul. *Los últimos charrúas*. Montevideo: Ediciones de la Plaza, 2003.

Roller, Heather F. *Amazonian Routes: Indigenous Mobility and Colonial Communities in Northern Brazil*. Stanford, CA: Stanford University Press, 2014.

———. "On the Verge of Total Extinction? From Guaikurú to Kadiwéu in Nineteenth-Century Brazil." *Ethnohistory* 65, no. 4 (2018): 647–70.

Rosal, Miguel Ángel. "El tráfico de esclavos hacia el Río de la Plata." In *La ruta del esclavo en el Río de la Plata: Aportes para el diálogo intercultural*, edited by Marisa Pineau, 131–51. Caseros: Editorial de la Universidad Nacional de Tres de Febrero, 2011.

Rosen, Deborah. *Border Law: The First Seminole War and American Nationhood*. Cambridge, MA: Harvard University Press, 2015.

Roulet, Florencia. "Fronteras de papel: El periplo semántico de una palabra en la documentación relativa a la frontera sur rioplatense de los siglos XVIII y XIX." *Revista TEFROS* 4, no. 2 (2006): 1–20.

———. *Huincas en tierras de indios: Mediaciones e identidades en los relatos de viajeros tardocoloniales*. Buenos Aires: EUDEBA, 2016.

Rüdiger, Sebalt. *Colonização e propriedade de terras no Rio Grande do Sul (século XVIII)*. Porto Alegre: Instituto Estadual do Livro Divisão de Cultura, 1965.

Rushforth, Brett. *Bonds of Alliance: Indigenous and Atlantic Slaveries in New France*. Chapel Hill: University of North Carolina Press, 2012.

Russell-Wood, A.J.R. "Políticas de fixação e integração." In *História da Expansão Portuguesa*, edited by Francisco Bethencourt and Kirti Chaudhuri, 136. Lisboa: Círculo de Leitores, 1998.

Saeger, James S. "Jesuit Missions (Reducciones)." In *Encyclopedia of Latin American History and Culture*, edited by Jay Kinsbruner and Erick D. Langer, 629–32. Detroit, MI: Charles Scribner's Sons, 2008.

Safier, Neil. *Measuring the New World: Enlightenment Science and South America*. Chicago: University of Chicago Press, 2008.

Sahlins, Peter. *Boundaries: The Making of France and Spain in the Pyrenees*. Berkeley: University of California Press, 1989.

Sala de Touron, Lucía, Nelson de la Torre, and Julio Carlos Rodríguez. *Evolución económica de la Banda Oriental*. 2nd ed. Montevideo: Ediciones Pueblos Unidos, 1968.

Saler, Bethel, and Carolyn Podruchny. "Glass Curtains and Storied Landscapes: The Fur Trade, National Boundaries, and Historians." In *Bridging National Borders in North America: Transnational and Comparative Histories*, edited by Benjamin H. Johnson and Andrew R. Graybill, 275–302. Durham, NC: Duke University Press, 2010.

Sallaberry, Juan Faustino. *Los charrúas y Santa Fe*. Montevideo: Gómez y Compañía, 1926.

Salomón Tarquini, Claudia, and Romina Casali. "Los pueblos indígenas de Pampa y Patagonia, siglos XVIII–XX: Un breve estado de las investegaciones." *Papeles de Trabajo* 9, no. 16 (2015): 22–55.

Sampaio, Patrícia Maria Melo. "'Vossa Excelência mandará o que for servido . . .': Políticas indígenas e indigenistas na Amazônia Portuguesa do final do século XVIII." *Tempo* 12, no. 23 (2007): 39–55.

Sanders, James. *Contentious Republicans: Popular Politics, Race, and Class in Nineteenth-Century Colombia*. Durham, NC: Duke University Press, 2004.

Sanguinetti, Julio María. "El Charruismo." *El País*, April 19, 2009. http://historico.elpais .com.uy/09/04/19/predit_411886.asp.

Sans, Monica, Gonzalo Figueiro, and Pedro C. Hidalgo. "A New Mitochondrial C1 Lineage from the Prehistory of Uruguay: Population Genocide, Ethnocide, and Continuity." *Human Biology* 84, no. 3 (2012): 287–305.

Santamaría, Daniel J. "Fronteras indígenas del oriente boliviano: La dominación colonial en Moxos y Chiquitos, 1675–1810." *Boletín Americanista*, no. 36 (1986).

Santos, Eugénio dos. "A administração portuguesa no sul do Brasil durante o período pombalino: Denúncias ao abuso do poder. A questão indígena." *Revista da Faculdade de Letras*, no. 13 (1996): 387–402.

Santos, Fabiano Vilaça dos. "Uma vida dedicada ao Real Serviço: João Pereira Caldas, dos sertões do Rio Negro à nomeação para o Conselho Ultramarino (1753–1790)." *Varia História* 26, no. 44 (2010): 499–521.

Sarreal, Julia. "Globalization and the Guaraní: From Missions to Modernization in the Eighteenth Century." PhD diss., Harvard University, 2009.

———. *The Guaraní and Their Missions: A Socioeconomic History*. Stanford, CA: Stanford University Press, 2014.

Saunt, Claudio. "The Indians' Old World." *William and Mary Quarterly* 68, no. 2 (2011): 215–18.

Schröder, Celso Martins. "Batoví." *Revista do Instituto Histórico e Geográfico do Rio Grande do Sul* 16, no. 61 (1936): 109–19.

Schröter, Bernd. "La frontera en hispanoamérica colonial: Un estudio historiográfico comparativo." *Colonial Latin American Historical Review* 10, no. 3 (2001): 351–85.

Schuller, Rodolfo R. *Sobre el oríjen de los Charrúa: Réplica al doctor Jorge Friederici, de Leipzig*. Santiago, Chile: Imprenta Cervantes, 1906.

Schultz, Kara. "Interwoven: Slaving in the Southern Atlantic under the Union of the Iberian Crowns, 1580–1640." *Journal of Global Slavery* 2, no. 3 (2017): 248–72. https:// doi.org/10.1163/2405836X-00203003.

Schwartz, Daniel. "The Principle of the Defence of the Innocent and the Conquest of America: 'Save Those Dragged towards Death.'" *Journal of the History of International Law* 9, no. 2 (2007): 263–91.

Schwartz, Stuart. *Sugar Plantations in the Formation of Brazilian Society: Bahia, 1550–1835.* Cambridge: Cambridge University Press, 1985.

Scott, Heidi V. *Contested Territory: Mapping Peru in the Sixteenth and Seventeenth Centuries.* Notre Dame, IN: University of Notre Dame Press, 2009.

Scott, James C. *Seeing Like a State: How Certain Schemes to Improve the Human Condition Have Failed.* New Haven, CT: Yale University Press, 1998.

Seed, Patricia. *Ceremonies of Possession in Europe's Conquest of the New World, 1492–1640.* New York: Cambridge University Press, 1995.

Segarra, Enrique M. *Frontera y límites.* Montevideo: Nuestra Tierra, 1969.

Serrano, Antônio. "Filiação Linguística Serrana." *Revista do Instituto Histórico e Geográfico do Rio Grande do Sul* 16, no. 61 (1936): 103–8.

———. *Los Pueblos y Culturas Indígenas del Litoral.* Santa Fe: El Litoral, 1955.

Sidbury, James, and Jorge Cañizares-Esguerra. "Mapping Ethnogenesis in the Early Modern Atlantic." *William and Mary Quarterly* 68, no. 2 (2011): 181–208.

Silva, Augusto da. "Rafael Pinto Bandeira: De bandoleiro a governador. Relações entre os poderes privado e público no Rio Grande de São Pedro." MA thesis, 1999.

Silva, Francisco Ribeiro da. "A legislação seiscentista portuguesa e os índios do Brasil." In *Brasil: Colonização e escrividão,* edited by Maria Beatriz Nizza da Silva, 15–27. Rio de Janeiro: Editora Nova Fronteira, 1999.

Silva, Maria Beatriz Nizza da, ed. *Brasil: Colonização e escrividão.* Rio de Janeiro: Editora Nova Fronteira, 2000.

Siquiera Bueno, Beatriz Piccolotto, and Iris Kantor. "A outra face das expedições científico-demarcatórias na Amazônia: O coronel Francisco Requena y Herrera e a comitiva castelhana." In *Cartógrafos para toda a Terra: Produção e circulação do saber cartográfico ibero-americano. Agentes e contextos,* edited by Francisco Roque de Oliveira, 243–64. Lisboa: Biblioteca Nacional de Portugal, 2015.

Sirtori, Bruna. "Nos limites do relato: Indígenas e demarcadores na fronteira sul da América Ibérica no século XVIII." *Fundação Biblioteca Nacional, Programa Nacional de Apoio à Pesquisa* (2008), 1–28.

Socolow, Susan. "Los cautivos españoles en las sociedades indígenas: El contacto cultural a través de la frontera argentina." *Anuario del IEHS* 2 (1987): 99–136.

Soja, Edward W. "The Socio-Spatial Dialectic." *Annals of the Association of American Geographers* 70, no. 2 (1980): 207–25.

Sommer, Barbara A. "The Amazonian Native Nobility in Late-Colonial Pará." In *Native Brazil: Beyond the Convert and the Cannibal, 1500–1900,* edited by Hal Langfur, 108–31. Albuquerque: University of New Mexico Press, 2014.

———. "Colony of the Sertão: Amazonian Expeditions and the Indian Slave Trade." *Americas* 61, no. 3 (2005): 401–28.

Sosa, Rodolfo M. *La nación charrúa.* Montevideo: Editorial "Letras," 1957.

Sota, Juan Manuel de la. *Historia del Territorio Oriental del Uruguay.* 2 vols. Montevideo: Ministerio de la Instrucción Pública y Previsión Social, 1965.

Sousa, James O. "Mão-de-obra indígena na Amazônia Colonial." *Em Tempo de Histórias,* no. 6 (2002): 1–18.

Southey, Robert. *História do Brazil.* Vol. 5. Rio de Janeiro: Livraria de B. L. Garnier, 1862.

Souza Torres, Simei Maria de. "Dominios y fronteras en la Amazonía colonial: El Tratado de San Ildefonso (1777–1790)." *Fronteras de la Historia*, no. 8 (2003): 185–216.

Stagg, J. C. A. *Borderlines in Borderlands: James Madison and the Spanish-American Frontier, 1776–1821.* New Haven, CT: Yale University Press, 2009.

Standen, Naomi, and Daniel Power, eds. *Frontiers in Question: Eurasian Borderlands, 700–1700.* New York: St. Martin's Press, 1999.

Steinke, Christopher. "'Here Is My Country': Too Né's Map of Lewis and Clark in the Great Plains." *William and Mary Quarterly* 71, no. 4 (2014): 589–610.

Suárez, Teresa, and María Laura Tornay. "Poblaciones, vecinos y fronteras rioplatenses: Santa Fe a fines del siglo XVIII." *Anuario de Estudios Americanos* 60, no. 2 (2003): 521–55.

Sutton, Elizabeth A. *Capitalism and Cartography in the Dutch Golden Age.* Chicago: University of Chicago Press, 2015.

Sweet, James. "The Quiet Violence of Ethnogenesis." *William and Mary Quarterly* 68, no. 2 (2011): 209–14.

Taylor, Alan. *The Divided Ground: Indians, Settlers, and the Northern Borderland of the American Revolution.* New York: Knopf, 2006.

Telesca, Ignacio, ed. *Documentos Jesuíticos del siglo XVIII en el Archivo Nacional de Asunción.* Paraguay: CEPAG, 2006.

Teschauer, Carlos. *História do Rio Grande do Sul dos dois primeiros séculos.* 2nd ed. Vol. 1. São Leopoldo, RS: Editora Unisinos, 2002.

Timó, Enrique. "Las Relaciones Interétnicas y Etnicidad en la Provincia de Entre Ríos." Tesis Doctoral, Universidad de Buenos Aires, 29 September 2004.

Torres, Luis María. *Los primitivos habitantes del delta del Paraná.* Vol. 4. Buenos Aires: Imprenta de Coni Hermanos, 1911.

Trelles, Manuel Ricardo. "Degollacion de Charruas." *Revista de la Biblioteca Pública de Buenos Aires* 2 (1880): 219–35.

———. "Vandalismo misionero." In *Revista Nacional*, 18–34. Buenos Aires: Imprenta Europa, 1886.

Truchuelo, Susana and Emir Reitano, eds. *Las fronteras en el Mundo Atlántico (siglos XVI–XIX).* La Plata: Universidad Nacional de La Plata, 2017.

Turner Bushnell, Amy. "Indigenous America and the Limits of the Atlantic World, 1493–1825." In *Atlantic History: A Critical Appraisal*, edited by Jack Greene and Philip D. Morgan, 191–222. Oxford: Oxford University Press, 2009.

Van Deusen, Nancy. *Global Indios: The Indigenous Struggle for Justice in Sixteenth-Century Spain.* Durham, NC: Duke University Press, 2015.

Vargas, Héctor Mendoza, and Carla Lois, eds. *Historias de la Cartografía de Iberamérica: Nuevos caminos, viejos problemas.* Colección Geografía para el siglo XXI, Serie Libros de investigación, vol. 4. México DF: Instituto de Geografía, UNAM; INEGI, 2009.

Vázquez Pino, Daniela. "'Los yndios infieles han quebrantado la paz': Negociaciones entre agentes europeos, chocoes y cunas en el Darién, 1739–1789." *Fronteras de la Historia* 20, no. 2 (2015): 14–42.

Vellinho, Moysés. *Brazil South: Its Conquest and Settlement.* New York: Knopf, 1968.

———. *Capitania d'El-Rei: Aspectos Polêmicos da Formação Rio-Grandense.* Rio de Janeiro: Editôra Globo, 1964.

Verdesio, Gustavo. "An Amnesic Nation: The Erasure of Indigenous Pasts by Uruguayan Expert Knowledges." In *Beyond Imagined Communities: Reading and Writing the Nation in Nineteenth-century Latin America*, edited by Sara Castro-Klarén and John Charles Chasteen, 196–224. Washington, DC: Woodrow Wilson Center Press, 2003.

———. *Forgotten Conquests: Rereading New World History from the Margins*. Philadelphia: Temple University Press, 2001.

———. "Forgotten Territorialities: The Materiality of Indigenous Pasts." *Nepantla: Views from South* 2, no. 1 (2001): 85–114.

———. *La invención del Uruguay: La entrada del territorio y sus habitantes a la cultura occidental*. Montevideo: Editorial Graffiti/Editorial Trazas, 1996.

———. "Para repensar los estudios coloniales: Sobre la relación entre el campo de estudios, las disciplinas, y los pueblos indígenas." *Telar* 9, 11–12 (2014): 257–72.

———. "Un fantasma recorre el Uruguay: La reemergencia charrúa en un 'pais sin indios.'" *Cuadernos de Literatura* 18, no. 36 (2014): 86–107.

Veres, Madalina Valeria. "Redefining Imperial Borders: Marking the Eastern Border of the Habsburg Monarchy in the Second Half of the Eighteenth Century." In *History of Cartography*, edited by Elri Liebenberg, Imre Josef Demhardt, and Zsolt Gyözö Török, 3–23. Berlin: Springer-Verlag, 2014.

Vergara y Martín, Gabriel María. *Diccionario etnográfico americano*. Madrid: Sucesores de Hernando, 1922.

Víctora, Ceres. "'A viagem de volta': O reconhecimento de indígenas no sul do Brasil como um evento crítico." *Sociedade e Cultura* 14, no. 2 (2011): 299–309.

Víctora, Ceres, and Antonio Leite Ruas-Neto. "'Querem matar os 'últimos Charruas': Sofrimento social e 'luta' dos indígenas que vivem nas cidades." *Revista Antropológicas* 15, no. 22 (2011): 37–59.

Vidal, Ángel. *La leyenda de la destrucción de los charrúas por el General Fructuoso Rivera*. Montevideo: El Siglo Ilustrado, 1933.

Vidart, Daniel. *El mundo de los Charrúas*. 3rd ed. Montevideo: Ediciones de la Banda Oriental, 1996.

———. "Prólogo." In *Reseña sobre la tribu de los indios charrúas*. by François de Curel, 9–38. Montevideo: Vintén Editor, 1996.

———. "No hay indios en el Uruguay contemporáneo." *Anuario de Antropología Social y Cultural en Uruguay* 10 (2012): 251–57.

Vilardebó, Teodoro M. *Noticias sobre los charrúas (Códice Vilardebó)*. 2nd ed. Montevideo: Artes Gráficas Covadonga, 1963.

Villar, Daniel, and Juan Francisco Jiménez. "'Para servirse de ellos': Cautiverio, ventas a la usanza del pays y rescate de indios en las pampas y araucania (siglos XVII–XIX)." *Relaciones de la Sociedad Argentina de Antropologia* 26 (2001).

Villegas, Juan. "La evangelización del indio de la Banda Oriental del Uruguay (siglos XVI–XVIII)." In *Cristianismo y mundo colonial: Tres estudios acerca de la evangelización de hispanoamérica*, edited by Johannes Meier, 69–112. Münster: Aschendorff Verlagsbuchhandlung GmbH, 1995.

Waselkov, Gregory A. "Indian Maps of the Colonial Southeast." In *Powhatan's Mantle: Indians in the Colonial Southeast*, edited by Gregory A. Waselkov, Peter H. Wood, and Tom Hatley, 435–502. Lincoln: University of Nebraska Press, 2006.

Weaver, Jace. *The Red Atlantic: American Indigenes and the Making of the Modern World, 1000–1927*. Chapel Hill: University of North Carolina Press, 2014.

Weber, David J. *Bárbaros: Spaniards and Their Savages in the Age of Enlightenment*. New Haven, CT: Yale University Press, 2005.

———. *The Spanish Frontier in North America: The Brief Edition*. New Haven, CT: Yale University Press, 2009.

Whigham, Thomas L. *The Politics of River Trade: Tradition and Development in the Upper Plata, 1780–1870*. Albuquerque: University of New Mexico Press, 1991.

White, Richard. *The Middle Ground: Indians, Empires, and Republics in the Great Lakes Region, 1650–1815*. Cambridge: Cambridge University Press, 1991.

Whitehead, Neil L. "Ethnogenesis and Ethnocide in the European Occupation of Native Surinam, 1499–1681." In *History, Power, and Identity: Ethnogenesis in the Americas, 1492–1992*, edited by Jonathan D. Hill, 20–35. Iowa City: University of Iowa Press, 1996.

———. "Indigenous Cartography in Lowland South America and the Caribbean." In *The History of Cartography: Cartography in the Traditional Africa, America, Arctic, Australian, and Pacific Societies*, edited by David Woodward and G. Malcolm Lewis, 301–26. Chicago: University of Chicago Press, 1998.

Wilde, Guillermo. "Guaraníes, 'gauchos' e 'indios infieles' en el proceso de disgregación de las antiguas doctrinas jesuíticas del Paraguay." *Universidad Católica Revista del Centro de Estudios Antropológicos* 38, no. 2 (December 2003): 73–128.

———. "Indios misionados y misioneros indianizados en las tierras bajas de América del Sur: Sobre los límites de la adaptación cultural." In *La indianización: Cautivos, renegados, "hommes libres" y misioneros en los confines americanos (s. XVI–XIX)*, edited by Salvador Bernabéu Albert, Christophe Giudicelli, and Gilles Havard, 291–310. Madrid y Paris: Ediciones Doce Calles; Écoles des Hautes Études en Sciences Sociales, 2012.

———. "Los guaraníes después de la expulsión de los jesuitas: Dinámicas políticas y transacciones simbólicas." *Revista Complutense de Historia de América* 27 (2001): 69–106.

———. "Orden y ambigüedad en la formación territorial del Río de la Plata a fines del siglo XVIII." *Horizontes Antropológicos* 9, no. 19 (2003): 105–35.

Winichakul, Thongchai. "Siam Mapped: The Making of Thai Nationhood." *Ecologist* 26, no. 5 (1996): 215–21.

Witgen, Michael J. *An Infinity of Nations: How the Native New World Shaped Early America*. Philadelphia: University of Pennsylvania Press, 2012.

Wood, Denis. *Rethinking the Power of Maps*. New York: Guilford Press, 2010.

Woodward, David. "'Theory' and the History of Cartography." In *Approaches and Challenges in a Worldwide History of Cartography*, edited by David Woodward, Catherine Delano-Smith, and Cordell D. K. Yee, 23–29. Catalunya: Institut Cartogràfic de Catalunya, 2001.

Wucherer, Pedro Miguel Omar Svriz. "Disputas a orillas del río Uruguay: Guerra y paz con los minuanes en el siglo XVIII." *Gazeta de Antropología* 2, no. 27 (2011).

Yannakakis, Yanna. *The Art of Being In-Between: Native Intermediaries, Indian Identity, and Local Rule in Colonial Oaxaca*. Durham, NC: Duke University Press, 2008.

Yaremko, Jason M. "'Frontier Indians': 'Indios Mansos,' 'Indios Bravos,' and the Layers of Indigenous Existence in the Caribbean Borderlands." In *Borderlands in World History*,

1700–1914, edited by Paul Readman, Cynthia Radding, and Chad Bryant, 217–36. Basingstoke: Palgrave Macmillan, 2014.

Zapata Gollan, Agustín. *Los chaná en el territorio de la provincia de Santa Fe.* Publaciónes del Departamento de Estudios Etnográficos y Coloniales no. 4. Santa Fe: Ministerio de Gobierno e Instrucción Pública, 1945.

Zárate Botía, Carlos Gilberto. "Pueblos indígenas y expediciones de límites en el noroeste amazónico." *Fronteiras y Debates* 1, no. 1 (2014): 25–40.

Zweifel, Teresa. "De Palas a Minerva: Panorama de la representación técnica en el Río de la Plata 1789–1866." In *Historias de la Cartografía de Iberamérica: Nuevos caminos, viejos problemas*, edited by Héctor Mendoza Vargas and Carla Lois, 307–28. México DF: Instituto de Geografía, UNAM; INEGI, 2009.

Index

Abipón Indians, 17, 33, 84, 99, 102, 105, 146, 147, 182n17. *See also* tolderías
Adeltú, Vicente, 150
ADENCH, 172
aguardiente, 1, 21, 30
Aguirre, Francisco de, 103, 111
Alvear, Diego de, 102–3, 104, 110, 124, 158
Amazon (region), 1, 4, 65, 105, 122, 171, 201n50
Amazon River, 23, 43, 44, 45, 55, 76, 79
Amazônia. *See* Amazon
Andrade, Gomes Freire de, 110
archaeology, 23–24, 183n39
Argentina, 166, 168, 169, 173, 179nn26, 29
Artigas, José Gervasio, 159–60
Association of Descendants of the Charrúa Nation. *See* ADENCH
astronomers, 1, 79, 111
Asunción. *See* Paraguay
Avilés, Gabriel de, 121
Azara, Félix de, 89, 103, 104, 110, 112, 122, 158
Azores and Canary islands, settlers from, 44, 116

Bandeira, Rafael Pinto, 107, 123–24, 130
bandeirantes, 42–43, 52, 183n40, 188nn12, 13
baptisms, 40, 61, 147, 148, 149, 150, 162, 183n38
baqueanos. See guides
Bartolomeo, 107–8, 130, 202n75
Batoví, 27, 75, 82, 107, 109, 114, 116, 122, 129, 152
Battle of the Yí, 17–18, 35, 182n21.
Batú da Gama, 71–72
Belén, 109, 116, 159, 201n48
Blasco, Miguel Angelo de, 97, 98
blockades: 19–20, 139; Colônia and, 34–34, 51; Montevideo and, 12, 26, 37, 60, 159

Bohán Indians, 15, 17, 36, 69; baptisms and, 147; Colônia and, 31, 35; captives of the Spanish, 140–42; ethnic categories and, 25, 32, 57, 131; Guaraní missions and, 4, 18–19; Guaraní War and, 84–86; identity as Spanish vassals, 39–40; mobility of, 15, 92, 124, 165–66; *reducciones* and, 62–64, 68, 119; trade and, 50. *See also* Indigenous women; tolderías
Bonifacio Redruello, José, 160
borderlands: definitions of, 177nn17, 18, 177–78n20; Indigenous authority and, 3, 82, 89, 129–30, 135, 153; imperial mapmaking and, 52, 54, 80, 105, 170; interethnic relations and, 5, 170; interimperial disputes and, 8, 72, 123; myth of tripartite borderland, 9, 14,
borderland settlements, 48, 112, 115–16, 136; Guaraní War and, 88; land grants, 6, 95, 112, 115–16, 126; *uti possidetis*, 43–44, 48, 52, 58, 65–67, 152. *See also* Batoví; Belén; Cayastá; Cerro Largo; Minas; Montegrande; Patagonia; Rio Pardo; Rio Piratiní; San Martín; São Gonçalo; São Miguel; Santa Tecla; Santa Teresa
borderlands studies, 5–7, 167
Borja, Francisco de, 12–13, 26, 37
Bourbon and Pombaline reforms, 112
Brazil: ethnic geographies and, 102, 166, 168–69, 173; interimperial borders and, 1–3, 52–53, 55, 57, 77, 89, 119, 158, 161, 163; captaincies and, 47–48, 112–13; settlements and, 21, 34, 37; relations with Indigenous Americans, 104, 122; relocation of capitals, 112; Santa Catarina, 88. *See also* Colônia; Brazil Island
Brazil Island (*Ilha Brasil*), 43, 45, 49, 188n15